Nā Kuaʻāina

The publication of this book was made possible through
sponsorship of the Native Hawaiian Center of Excellence,
John A. Burns School of Medicine, University of Hawaiʻi at Mānoa.
Partial funding for this publication was provided by the
Department of Health and Human Services, Health Resources Services
Administration, Bureau of Health Professions, Division of Health Careers,
Diversity and Development.

NĀ KUA'ĀINA

LIVING HAWAIIAN CULTURE

Davianna Pōmaika'i McGregor

University of Hawai'i Press

HONOLULU

Library of Congress Cataloging-in-Publications Data
McGregor, Davianna.
Nā Kuaʻāina : living Hawaiian culture /
Davianna Pōmaikaʻi McGregor.
p. cm.
Includes bibliographical references and index.
ISBN-13: 978-0-8248-2946-9 (cloth : alk. paper)
ISBN-13: 978-0-8248-3212-4 (pbk : alk. paper)
1. Hawaiians—History. 2. Hawaiians—Social life and customs.
3. Hawaiians—Interviews. 4. Oral history.
5. Hawaii—Social life and customs.
6. Subsistence economy—Hawaii—History.
7. Natural resources—Social aspects—Hawaii—History.
8. Social change—Hawaii—History. 9. Hawaii—Rural conditions.
10. Hawaii—History, Local. I. Title.
DU624.65.M39 2006
996.9—dc22
2006006901

Designed by Leslie Fitch
Printed by Sheridan Press

For My parents
Daniel Pāmawaho and
Anita Branco McGregor
. . . my roots

My love,
Noa Emmett Aluli
. . . my inspiration

My daughter,
Rosanna 'Anolani Alegado
. . . my life . . . my future

❧ CONTENTS ❧

❧ ACKNOWLEDGMENTS ❧

Nā kuaʻāina of Hāna, Molokaʻi, Puna, Waipiʻo, and Kahoʻolawe are at the heart of this book—their lives, knowledge, and spirit of resilience.

Our ancestral spirits and deities, ʻaumākua and akua of the ʻāina—from the ocean depths and reefs to streams and lush valleys, volcanic rainforests and sacred mountain peaks, and up into the sky with its many named winds, clouds, and rains—are the soul of this book.

My family and loved ones lifted me to connect to ancestors, ancestral lands, and lively times that have passed, by sharing their vivid memories in comfortable homes with fine wine and family dinners:

My parents, Daniel Pāmawaho and Anita Branco McGregor; their parents, Daniel Pāmawaho and Louise Aoe McGregor, and David William and Anna Meyer Branco.

My sisters, Danita ʻImaikalani Aiu and Myrna Anne Pualehua Kai, and hānai Claire Pruet.

My daughter, Rosanna ʻAnolani Alegado; her husband, Raymond Edward ʻAwa Kong, Jr.; and his parents, Leona and Alvin Abe.

My nieces and nephews, Puaalaokalani, Piʻimauna, Holly, Mohala, ʻImaikalani, Kapuaonālanii Kēhau o Waiʻaleʻale, Kamanaʻopono, and Kanoe Aiu, and Lehua Kai.

My uncles and aunts, Jackson and Rita Branco, Robert "Skippy" and Verna Mae Kawaiʻula Branco, and the late Marion LeeLoy.

My cousins, especially Pilialoha, Marylyn, and Samuel Lee Loy; Marion Louise and Gordon Machado; Wilmar, Lurline, and Momi McGregor; and Jackie, Billy, Gregory, Marvalee, Robert, Verna, Lola, Anna, Charlotte, Michael, and James Branco.

My love, Dr. Noa Emmett Aluli, and his ʻohana, Mokihana Cockett Aluli and Nick Teves, and Kalai, Pia, Hayden, Webster, and Noa Aluli.

Community leaders shared their vision and insights, experience and knowledge and inspired me to write about the lives of Nā Kuaʻāina:

Of the Protect Kahoʻolawe ʻOhana founders and their families, George Helm, Aunty Mae, and the Helm ʻohana; Uncle Harry Kūnihi Mitchell and his son Kimo Mitchell; Uncle Leslie Kuloloio and his mother, Aunty Alice, and son Manny; Noa Emmett Aluli; and nā kua ʻohana members, past and present.

Of the Edith Kanakaʻole Foundation, Pualani Kanakaʻole and Edward Kanahele; Ulunui Kanakaʻole Garmon; Parley Kanakaʻole; Nalani Kanakaʻole; Kekuhi, Huihui, Ahiʻena, Sig, Tangaro, and Kalā.

Of Hui Ala Loa, Judy Napoleon; Colette Machado, Joyce Kainoa, Wren Wescoatt, and John Sabas.

Of the Pele Defense Fund and Ka ʻOhana o KaLae, Palikapu and Lori Dedman, Margaret McGuire, and Mark Lunning.

The attorneys who supported all of these efforts, Alan Murakami, Nahoa Lucas, Melody Mackenzie, and Mahealani Kamauʻu of the Native Hawaiian Legal Corporation; Steve Moore of the Native American Rights Fund; Yuklin Aluli; and Tom Luebben.

Over the past 12 years I have worked on many joint projects with Jon Matsuoka, dean of the University of Hawaiʻi at Mānoa School of Social Work, and Luciano Minerbi, professor of the University of Hawaiʻi at Mānoa Urban and Regional Planning Department. As a team, calling ourselves "3-M" (Matsuoka, McGregor, and Minerbi), we journeyed to Molokaʻi, Hāna, and Puna. In the course of meeting with community leaders and their attorneys and organizing focus groups, resource mapping, interviews, and surveys with ʻohana from these cultural kīpuka, our team has developed a methodology to systematically gather and document subsistence and cultural customs and practices, inventory cultural and natural resources, and support the community in protecting all of these. The chapters on Molokaʻi, Hāna, and Puna are in part drawn from the larger studies and reports that we conducted as "3-M."

My patient colleagues of long standing in the Ethnic Studies Department of the University of Hawaiʻi at Mānoa have consistently given me support, time, space, and resources to pursue my research and community service and to progress professionally: Dean Alegado, Ibrahim Auode, Sandy Chock, Marion Kelly, and Noel Kent. Newer faculty are also supportive with their interaction and fresh insights: Monisha Das Gupta, Ulla Hasager, Jonathan Okamura, Ty Kawika Tengan, and Elissa Joy White. The dean of the College of Social Sciences, Richard Dubanoski, has encouraged my ongoing work and provided me with special recognition. Karl Kim, Kem Lowry, and Karen Umemoto of the Urban and Regional Planning Department have been special colleagues, as they also engage in parallel community research and service.

My oldest and dearest mentor and colleague, Franklin Odo, was a member of my dissertation committee and helped to critique the material in this book from that document. As the chairperson of the Ethnic Studies Department, he encouraged and supported my ongoing research and community service. As a director of the Asian Pacific American Program of the Smithsonian Institution, he allowed me to extend my research to Washington, D.C., as a scholar-in-residence. We also worked together with Elizabeth Tatar and Dave Kemble of the Bishop Museum, the Kahoʻolawe Island Reserve Commission, Barbara Pope, and Rowland Reeve to feature Kahoʻolawe and the Native Hawaiian movement in a national exhibit in the Smithsonian Arts and Industries Building called "Kahoʻolawe: Rebirth of a Sacred Hawaiian Island." Information gathered for that exhibit is part of the chapter on Kahoʻolawe.

I also want to acknowledge my colleagues in the Asian Pacific American History Collective and the Association for Asian American Studies, who impressed upon me the importance of publishing new books for a national audience that will give voice to a variety of Native Hawaiians and Pacific Islanders and enrich the appreciation of the Native Hawaiian culture. These colleagues include Franklin Odo; Henry Yu of the University of California, Los Angeles; Gayle Nomura and Steve Sumida of the University of Washington; Dana Takagi of the University of California, Santa Cruz; Gary Okihiro of Columbia University; Amy Kuʻulei Stillman and Vince Diaz of the University of Michigan; John Tsuchida of California State University, Long Beach; John Rosa of Arizona State University; and Dorothy and Tom Fujita-Rony of the University of California, Riverside, and California State University, Fullerton.

My students and especially my lab leaders continue to infuse me with new insights and perspectives. They daily demonstrate to me the importance of documenting the lives and culture and knowledge of our kūpuna and of our kuaʻāina so that Hawaiʻi will continue to be Hawaiian.

A special mahalo to my college freshman world civilizations history professor, Gavan Daws, whose own exciting work brings historical heroes, heroines, and villains to life, for kindly reading my manuscript, giving me advice, and speaking truth.

For her belief in me and assistance in preparing this manuscript for press, I thank Masako Ikeda. Mahalo to Barbara Dunn and Karen Sinn of the Hawaiian Historical Society in my search for photos. To Dr. Ben Young and the Native Hawaiian Center for Excellence at the University of Hawaiʻi at Mānoa Medical School, mahalo nui loa for their contributions to making this book more accessible.

mahalo . . . mahalo nui loa

❧ ONE ❧

Nā Kuaʻāina and Cultural *Kīpuka*

R AIN PELTED the decks and the howling wind and twenty-foot ocean swells madly rocked our boat as we made our way in dawn's first light from the port of Lahaina to the island of Kahoʻolawe. We struggled for a foothold, while grasping for trash bags to relieve ourselves of the queasy welling up of fluids deep in our guts. Uncle Harry Mitchell called out to us, "You had enough? And now, are you ready to turn back?" Everyone begged to turn around. Before the captain could steer the boat around to head back most of my students boldly jumped into the wild surf off of Olowalu and swam to shore rather than suffer the pangs of seasickness all the way back down the coast to Lahaina.

Uncle Harry sat me down. "You are a college professor, eh?" Yes. "And you saw the storm that has been gathering for the past few days?" No. "It was windy when you left Oʻahu?" Yes. "And you felt the storm?" No. "You know that we go across the channel to Kahoʻolawe on a small boat?" Yes. "Did you know that there were small-craft warnings before you left Oʻahu?" No. "What were you thinking about?"

I had been totally oblivious to the major elements of a huge storm swirling together for the past few days. I was the typical single-minded urban Hawaiian academic, bent on getting where I wanted to go, but completely out of balance with the natural forces around me. Uncle Harry explained, "If I had told you that you couldn't make it over to Kahoʻolawe this morning you would have disagreed, argued, and insisted on going. So I took you out in the boat, not too far off the coast, not even in the channel, until you had had enough and were begging me to turn around."

Through my bitter disappointment at not making it to Kahoʻolawe I learned one of the most important lessons of my life from kupuna Mitchell. Always be conscious and respectful of the natural elements around me. As

Uncle Harry would always say, "Watch . . . look at the moon, the stars, the clouds, they talk to you . . . listen . . . watch!"

"Aloha ʻāina, aloha ke akua, aloha kekāhi i kekāhi" (love and respect the land, love and honor God, love and look after one another, these are the three important things our kūpuna always ask us to remember): this was another mantra of Uncle Harry. From him I learned that one who understands and lives by these precepts embraces the world of Native Hawaiians. This Native Hawaiian worldview is called lōkāhi, or unity, harmony, balance. It refers to the unity, harmony, and balance in the universe between humans, nature, and deities or spiritual life forces. For personal well-being, we need to be in balance with the people around us, and with the natural and spiritual forces of life.

So, there I was, spring break 1980, out of balance and stuck with twenty college students, coolers full of food for a week, grounded by a wild late-March storm that I never saw coming. Uncle Harry took pity on us. He loaded us into vans, a truck, and a car and took us home with him to Keʻanae-Wailuanui, Maui. The community of taro farmers and fishermen graciously allowed us to camp in their church hall. For the next few days Uncle Harry threw us into the taro patches to earn our lodging and he taught us the moʻolelo of Keʻanae-Wailuanui, and of the valleys, streams, and gulches from Keʻanae through Hāna and out to Oheʻo. We immersed ourselves in the way of life of the kuaʻāina of Keʻanae-Wailuanui. I awoke to a worldview and lifestyle that I would devote my academic endeavors to helping perpetuate. This is the life ways of the kuaʻāina.

I do not write of ruling chiefs, but of those who made the chiefs rulers. I write of those who first held the lands of Hawaiʻi in trust for the Gods of our nature and whose descendants have a vested responsibility and right to hold these lands in trust today. I write of the kuaʻāina, the keepers of Hawaiʻi's sacred lands who are living Hawaiian culture. This is a moʻolelo, a history, or, in the Hawaiian sense, a succession of knowledge passed on orally from one generation to the next of kuaʻāina, who shared this knowledge with someone, such as Mary Kawena Pukui in the 1960s or me in the 1980s and 1990s, as oral history interviews. They are the source of the knowledge of which I write, and the shortcomings herein are my own.[1]

I can remember a time when it was demeaning to be called kuaʻāina, for it meant that one was an awkward and rough country person.[2] In Hawaiian, kua means back and ʻāina means land, so kuaʻāina is translated literally in the Hawaiian Dictionary as "back land." However, in the context of the Native

Figure 1 Uncle Harry Kūnihi Mitchell of Wailuanui, Maui, playing his guitar near Hakioawa, Kahoʻolawe. Uncle, sparkle in his eye, knee-deep in his loʻi, introduced me to the lives of the kuaʻāina and their role in the cultural regeneration of Kahoʻolawe. 1979. Franco Salmoiraghi.

Figure 2 The rural communities where kuaʻāina have remained are cultural kīpuka that have been bypassed by major historic forces of economic, political, and social change in Hawaiʻi. Uncle Harry Mitchell's Wailuanui is a cultural kīpuka from which Native Hawaiian culture was regenerated and revitalized on Kahoʻolawe and a new generation of taro farmers and traditional healers was trained. 1936. Bishop Museum.

Hawaiian cultural renaissance of the late twentieth century, the word kuaʻāina gained a new and fascinating significance. A kuaʻāina came to be looked upon as someone who embodied the backbone of the land.[3] Indeed, kuaʻāina are the Native Hawaiians who remained in the rural communities of our islands, took care of the *kūpuna* or elders, continued to speak Hawaiian, bent their backs and worked and sweated in the taro patches and sweet potato fields, and held that which is precious and sacred in the culture in their care.[4] The kuaʻāina are those who withdrew from the mainstream of economic, political, and social change in the Islands. They did not enjoy modern amenities and lived a very simple life. This moʻolelo recounts how the life ways of the kuaʻāina enabled the Native Hawaiian people to endure as a unique, distinct, dignified people even after over a century of American control of the Islands.

4

"Ke haʻawi nei au iā ʻoe. Mālama ʻoe i kēia mau mea. ʻAʻohe Mālama, pau ka pono o ka Hawaiʻi" (I pass on to you. Take care of these things. If you don't take care, the well-being of the Hawaiian people will end):[5] these words were used by kūpuna to pass on knowledge and stewardship of their lands to a chosen successor of the next generation. Gifted with this stewardship responsibility, the successors held their ancestral lands and knowledge sacred in their memories and passed it on in custom and practice from generation to generation up through the twenty-first century.

Daniel Pahupu was a kuaʻāina and a kupuna whom Mary Kawena Pukui interviewed on the island of Molokaʻi in 1961 as part of a project to gather ancestral knowledge about the sacred and significant places in the Hawaiian Islands, referred to in Hawaiian as *wahi pana*. In 1961 Mary Kawena Pukui traveled from island to island interviewing kuaʻāina, as the keepers of the wahi pana, in order to document and thereby perpetuate their unique and profound knowledge for future generations. Conducting the interviews in Hawaiian, the kuaʻāina shared knowledge with Pukui that had been passed on from one generation to the next about the lands where their ancestors lived, worked, and sustained a spiritual connection to the life forces of the universe.[6] The land and nature, like members of the *ʻohana* or extended family, were loved. The placenames they were given reflected their particular character and nature and contain traditional knowledge accumulated by Hawaiian ancestors in utilizing the natural resources of these areas, providing kuaʻāina with information they need to understand and adapt to the qualities and character of the land in which they live, such as soil conditions, local flora or fauna, and seasonal fluctuations. Native Hawaiian ancestors also named the various types of rain and wind of particular districts. The names of places and natural elements not only provide a profound sense of identity with the ʻāina or land and natural resources, they also convey a sense of responsibility to provide stewardship of the area where they live.

In his introduction to *Ancient Sites of Oʻahu*, Edward Kanahele explained the significance of wahi pana in the perpetuation of Native Hawaiian cultural knowledge. He also explained how the understanding of a place, its names, and the reason for its designation as a wahi pana is essential to understanding the area's function and significance in Native Hawaiian society:

> As a Native Hawaiian, a place tells me who I am and who my extended
> family is. A place gives me my history, the history of my clan, and the history of my people. I am able to look at a place and tie in human events that

affect me and my loved ones. A place gives me a feeling of stability and of belonging to my family, those living and dead. A place gives me a sense of well-being and of acceptance of all who have experienced that place.

The concept of wahi pana merges the importance of place with that of the spiritual. My culture accepts the spiritual as a dominant factor in life; this value links me to my past and to my future, and is physically located at my wahi pana.

Where once the entire Native Hawaiian society paid homage to numerous wahi pana, now we may give wahi pana hardly a cursory glance. Only when a Native Hawaiian gains spiritual wisdom is the ancestral and spiritual sense of place reactivated. Spiritual knowledge and the wahi pana are ancestrally related, thus spiritual strength connects to the ancestral guardians, or *'aumakua.* My *'aumakua* knew that the great gods created the land and generated life. The gods infused the earth with their spiritual force or *mana.* The gravity of this concept was keenly grasped by my ancestors: they knew that the earth's spiritual essence was focused through the wahi pana. (James, in E. Kanahele, 1991)

Kua'āina live in rural communities throughout the Hawaiian islands. In these areas, Native Hawaiians have maintained a close relationship to and knowledge of their wahi pana. These rural communities are special strongholds for the perpetuation of Hawaiian culture as a whole. An analogy which conveys a sense of the significance of these areas can be found in the natural phenomenon of the volcanic rainforest. From the island of Hawai'i come the *oli* or chants of Pele and her creative force. The *oli hulihia,* in particular, meaning overturned, overthrown, and upheaval, speak of volcanic events, such as in the following chant.

Kua Loloa Kea'au I Ka Nāhelehele/Kea'au Is a Long Ridge of Forest

Kua loloa Kea'au i ka Nāhelehele	Kea'au is a long ridge of forest
Hala kua hulu Pana'ewa i ka lā'au	The hala ridges of Pana'ewa are the trees
Ino ka maha o ka'ōhi'a	Numerous are the severed *'ōhi'a*
Kū kepakepa kamaha o ka lehua,	Zigzag are the severed *lehua*
Po'ohina i ka wela a ke Akua	The grayish mist is the Goddess's hot revenge
Uahi Puna i ka oloka'a pōhaku	Puna is smoky with hot rolling stones
Nā pe'a 'ia e ka Wahine	Persecuted by the Goddess

Nānahu ahi ka ka papa o Oluea	The plain of Oluea is bitten with fire
Momoku ahi Puna, hala i ʻāpua	Puna is cut off by fire, even to ʻApua
A ihu e, a ihu la,	The flow is heading this way and that.
A hulihia la i kai,	Turning upside down toward the sea,
A ihu e, a ihu la	The flow is heading this way and that,
A hulihi la i uka,	An upheaval toward the uplands,
A ua wāʻawaʻa	It is so desolate, uninhabitable,
A ua noho haʻahaʻa	Made low by the Goddess
A ua hele heleleʻiheleleʻi	Falling, falling, nothing but ashes.[7]

Even as Pele claims and reconstructs the forest landscape, she leaves intact whole sections of the forest, with tall old-growth *ʻōhiʻa* trees, tree ferns, creeping vines, and mosses. These oases are called *kīpuka*. The beauty of these natural kīpuka is not only their ability to resist and withstand destructive forces

Figure 3 The volcanic rainforest in Puna, Hawaiʻi, features numerous beautiful natural kīpuka of old-growth forest from which fresh fields of lava are eventually revegetated. Thus the Puna rainforest is a mosaic of old-growth forest and new-growth forest.

of change, but also their ability to regenerate life on the barren lava that surrounds them. For from these kīpuka come the seeds and spores carried by birds and blown by the wind to sprout upon and regenerate the forest on the new lava, sparking a dynamic new cycle of coming into and passing out of life.

The rural communities where kuaʻāina have remained are cultural kīpuka that have been bypassed by major historic forces of economic, political, and social change in Hawaiʻi. Like the dynamic life forces in a natural kīpuka, cultural kīpuka are communities from which Native Hawaiian culture can be regenerated and revitalized in the setting of contemporary Hawaiʻi. Moreover, from the examination of the lives of kuaʻāina in Hawaiian cultural kīpuka emerges a profile of the strongest and most resilient aspects of the Native Hawaiian culture and way of life. Such an examination provides insight into how the Native Hawaiian culture survived dynamic forces of political and economic change throughout the twentieth century.

Features of Cultural Kīpuka

Originally, cultural kīpuka were traditional centers of spiritual power. In traditional Hawaiian chants and mythology, major *akua* or Gods and Hawaiian deities were associated with these wahi pana. These districts were isolated and difficult to access over land and by sea. Owing to the lack of good anchorage and harbors, early traders often bypassed these districts in favor of more accessible areas. The missionaries entered these areas and established permanent stations during a later period than in other parts of Hawaiʻi. Thus, traditional Native Hawaiian spiritual beliefs and practices persisted there, without competition, for a longer period of time. When Christian influences entered these areas, they had to coexist with traditional beliefs and practices.

The geography of these districts discouraged the widespread or long-term development of sugar plantations. In the arid areas, the lack of water resources made development of sugar plantations unfeasible. In the areas with sufficient rainfall, the terrain was too steep or rugged for plantation agriculture. Where plantation agriculture failed, such as in Molokaʻi and the Hāna district, ranches were able to succeed. The ranches employed Native Hawaiian men as cowboys and allowed them to live with their families in these isolated districts and pursue traditional fishing, gathering, and hunting activities to supplement their wages. In some areas small stores provided kuaʻāina access to some basic Western commodities such as kerosene, lanterns, tools, flour, crackers, and sugar. However, for the most part kuaʻāina were not consumer oriented.

Money to purchase these basic provisions came from selling taro or fish or an occasional day's labor for a local entrepreneur or the government road crew.

Where neither plantations nor ranches were established, traditional subsistence activities continued to be pursued, undisturbed by modern economic development. In the wetland areas taro continued to be farmed, often in conjunction with rice. In the arid areas, sweet potatoes, dryland taro, and other traditional and introduced crops suited to the dry soil and climate were cultivated. Thus, the natural features and resources of these districts that rendered them unsuitable for plantation agriculture and ranching played a role in the survival, and eventual revitalization, of Native Hawaiian cultural, spiritual, and subsistence customs and practices. Concurrently, the quality and abundance of the natural resources of these rural communities can be attributed to the persistence of Native Hawaiian cultural and spiritual values and practices in the conduct of subsistence activities.

Very few *haole* or Caucasians settled in these districts, and kua'āina had very little interaction with the outside community. Chinese who completed their contracts on the plantation and did not return home or move to the mainland leased or rented lands from the kua'āina. Some served as middlemen, marketing whatever taro and fish kua'āina desired to sell in the towns and bringing back consumer goods for sale or barter in the rural communities. Where there was a small rural store in these districts, it was invariably owned by a Chinese, who in some cases was married to a Native Hawaiian woman.

By 1930 there were still seventeen rural districts where Native Hawaiians were predominant. Andrew Lind wrote of the significance of these areas for the continuity of Hawaiian culture:

> These racial havens—small population islands still relatively secure from
> the strong currents which have swept the archipelago as a whole into the
> world-complex of trade—are strikingly similar to those which appear in
> the census of 1853. The dry and rocky portions of Kau, Puna and the
> Kona coast, the deep valley of Waipio, the wild sections of Hana, Maui,
> portions of lonely Lanai and Molokai where industrial methods of agriculture have not succeeded, the leper settlement, and Niihau, the island of
> mystery—these are the places of refuge for some 4,400 or nearly one-fifth,
> of the native Polynesians . . .
>
> The old fish and poi company, with its accompaniment of tutelary
> deities, taboos, religion, and magic, still persists in modified form within
> many of these isolated communities. A small plot of taro and access to the

sea and the mountains are apparently all that is required for the satisfaction of their material wants. The wage from an occasional day's work on the government road enables them to purchase the necessary supplies which the old economy cannot now provide . . . The natives themselves have found these rural havens where the economy of life to which they are best adapted can survive.[8]

The seventeen districts where Native Hawaiians comprised a majority in 1930 were small isolated valleys and districts on the fringes of Hawai'i's economic and social life. The overall population in these districts averaged 341, and the number of Native Hawaiians in them averaged 248. The largest district, Pala'au-Ho'olehua on Moloka'i, had 1,031 inhabitants, of whom 826 were Hawaiian; and the smallest, Keōmuku on Lāna'i, had 54 inhabitants, of whom 33 were Hawaiian.

On Hawai'i Island, these districts included Kalapana (88 percent Hawaiian); Waipi'o and Waimanu (66 percent Hawaiian); Keaukaha, an area opened for Hawaiian homesteading in 1925 (83 percent Hawaiian); the Pu'uanahulu, Pu'uwa'awa'a, and Kīholo district (79 percent Hawaiian); the Kohanaiki, Kalaoa, Hu'ehu'e, and Honokōhau district (52 percent Hawaiian); 'Ala'ē, Pāhoehoe, Honokua, 'Opihihale, and 'Ōlelo-Moana district (82 percent Hawaiian); and Ho'ōpūloa, Papa, Alika, Kaunāmano, Kapua, and Miloli'i district (64 percent Hawaiian).

On Maui, the districts with a predominance of Hawaiians included Ke'anae to Nāhiku (78 percent Hawaiian); Nāhiku to Hāna (55 percent Hawaiian); Kīpahulu (80 percent Hawaiian); and Kaupō to Kahikinui (86 percent Hawaiian). On Moloka'i the districts with a majority of Hawaiians included Kawela to Ualapue (62 percent Hawaiian); Kalawao (66 percent Hawaiian); and the Hawaiian homestead lands at Pala'au-Ho'olehua (80 percent Hawaiian). The small district of Keōmuku on the island of Lāna'i was 61 percent Hawaiian. The island of Ni'ihau was 93 percent Hawaiian. On O'ahu, only the district that included the Kalihi Receiving Station and the hospital for Hansen's disease patients had a majority of Hawaiians; 61 percent of the patients were of Hawaiian ancestry. The statistics are summarized in table 1.

Except for the homestead districts of Pala'au-Ho'olehua, and Keaukaha, the Hansen's disease receiving station at Kalihi, and the settlement at Kalawao, the ethnic concentrations of Hawaiians were not induced or encouraged by governmental policy. Among the remaining districts, certain qualities and patterns of change and continuity can be observed as common to them.[9]

TABLE I RURAL DISTRICTS WITH POPULATION OVER 50% HAWAIIAN, 1930

DISTRICT	TOTAL	HAWAIIAN	% HAWAIIAN
Hawai'i			
Kalapana	235	207	88
Waipi'o, Waimanu	271	178	66
Keaukaha	754	625	83
Pu'uanahulu, Pu'uwa'wā'a, Kīholo	149	117	79
Kohanaiki, Kalaoa, Hu'ehu'e,			
Honokōhau	422	221	52
'Ala'ē, Pāhoehoe, Honokua,			
'Opihihale, 'Ōlelo-Moana	239	197	82
Ho'ōpūloa, Papa, Alika, Kaunāmano,			
Kapua, Miloli'i	146	94	64
Maui			
Ke'anae/Hāna	337	262	78
Nāhiku/Hāna	182	101	55
Kīpahulu	147	118	80
Kaupō	185	160	86
Moloka'i			
Kawela, Ualapue	789	487	62
Kalawao	605	400	66
Pala'au-Ho'olehua	1,031	826	80
Lāna'i			
Kahue to Kamaiki (Keōmuku, Lāna'i)	54	33	61
O'ahu			
Kalihi Receiving Station/hospital	114	70	61
Ni'ihau	136	126	93
Total	5,796	4,222	72

Statistics based on U.S. Bureau of the Census, 1931, pp. 70, 72, table 22.
The district boundaries were found in Governors' Proclamations, 1926–1930,
pp. 6–21, 128–47; and Map no. 301, O'ahu, State of Hawai'i Archives.

In the 1930s two anthropologists from the Bernice Pauahi Bishop Museum, E. S. Craighill Handy and Elizabeth Green Handy, in collaboration with Mary Kawena Pukui, traveled through all of the major districts of the Hawaiian Islands to assess the original native horticulture of the islands prior to the introduction of Euro-American plants. Their findings were published in *The Hawaiian Planter*, vol. 1, and in *Native Planters in Old Hawai'i: Their Life, Lore, and Environment*. These volumes provide a snapshot of the lives of the kua-'āina in the rural districts during the 1930s. In the foreword to *Native Planters in Old Hawai'i* Craighill Handy wrote:

> It was shown that the older generation of country natives still had an
> extraordinarily intimate and thorough knowledge of the many varieties of
> taro, sweet potato, sugar cane, and banana still cultivated . . . The Hawai-
> ians, more than any of the other Polynesians, were a people whose means
> of livelihood, whose work and interests, were centered in the cultivation of
> the soil. The planter and his life furnish us with the key to his culture.[10]

Only a handful of cultural kīpuka survived the onslaught of development after Hawai'i became a state in 1959. These included the islands of Moloka'i and Ni'ihau; on Maui, the districts of Hāna (from Ke'anae to Kahikinui) and Kahakuloa; on Hawai'i, the districts of Ka'ū, Puna, and Waipi'o Valley, and the small fishing communities of Kohala and Kona, excluding Kailua. On O'ahu, the Windward Valleys of Kahana, Waiāhole, Waikāne, Hau'ula, and Lā'ie and sections of the Wai'anae Coast, and on Kaua'i, Waipā, Kekaha, and Anahola retained features of cultural kīpuka, although the population of Native Hawaiians has fluctuated.

Cultural Kīpuka and Lōkāhi

Rural Native Hawaiians today descend from kua'āina who were content to remain in the isolated districts, though many others moved out during the twentieth century. For those who stayed behind, life was filled with interest-ing natural phenomena and forces that challenged them as they sought out their subsistence needs. The kua'āina way of life is a model of the Hawaiian belief, custom, and practice of *lōkāhi*. Kua'āina were intimately conscious of their 'āina—the lands and natural resources where they live. They built their economic activities around the life cycles of the various fish, animals, and plants they depended upon for food. Thus, from month to month, as the sea-sons shifted from wet to dry, their food sources changed in accordance with the type of fish, fruits, and plants that were in season. This knowledge of the environment and natural life forces was often passed on and remembered as Native Hawaiian traditions and beliefs. Native Hawaiians often chose to personify the forces of nature as spiritual entities or akua and ʻaumakua, Gods and ancestral spirits. They created legends and myths to describe and remember the dynamic patterns of change that they observed.

The Kumulipo, genealogy chant of the family of King Kalākaua and Queen Liliʻuokalani, exemplifies the Native Hawaiian belief in lōkāhi. It traces the origin of humans through a process of evolution in nature, beginning with day arising from the black primordial night. It continues with coral polyps as the first life form, which evolves into various forms of marine life and then into plants and animals on the land, through ancestral deities, and down to several generations of chiefly ancestors of the Native Hawaiian people. This chant, therefore, establishes that Native Hawaiians are descended from, and thus inextricably related to, natural life forms and the spiritual life forces personified as deities.[11]

We also learn of lōkāhi in the Hāloa tradition. In this moʻolelo the first-born offspring of Wākea, Sky Father, and his daughter Hoʻohokukalani, maker of the stars in the heavens, Hāloa Naka, is stillborn. When buried, Hāloa Naka grows into the first kalo plant. Their second-born child, Hāloa, is a progenitor of the Native Hawaiian people. This tradition, again, establishes that Native Hawaiians are the young siblings of the kalo plant and that both descended from the deities Wākea and Hoʻohokukalani. This relationship is eloquently described in *Native Planters in Old Hawaii*:

> When, therefore, the learned men in early times, all of them taro planters, compounded this myth as a part of their heritage of ancient lore, which describes the birth of nature and man as the consequence of the impregnation of Mother Earth by Father Sky, they sealed into their people's unwritten literature this idea, that the taro plant, being the first-born, was genealogically superior to and more kapu (sacred) than man himself, for man was the descendant of the second-born son of Sky and Earth. The taro belonged, then, in the native parlance of family status, to the kai kuaʻana (elder or senior) branch of cosmic lineage, man himself to the kai kaina or junior.[12]

In the "Oli Kūhohunu o Kahoʻolawe Mai Nā Kūpuna Mai" (Deep Chant of Kahoʻolawe from Our Ancestors), way-finding voyagers are elated at the sight of the island of Kahoʻolawe. They dedicate the island to Kanaloa, Hawaiian God of the ocean, out of gratitude for his guidance of their double-hulled canoe across the vast Pacific. In this example of lōkāhi, the Hawaiian way-finders who composed this chant bestow upon the island of Kahoʻolawe the distinction of being honored as a body form of the God Kanaloa. Subsequently, the voyagers develop Kahoʻolawe into a center to train navigators in celestial way-finding, which in its essence involves the acquisition of intimate knowledge of the natural forces of the ocean, winds, and stars collectively personified as Kanoloa.[13]

In tracing unbroken lineal descent from the original Native Hawaiians who had settled the districts, kuaʻāina also claim ancestry not only with the ʻaumakua, but also with the ʻuhane or spirits of the land and resources where they live. Kuaʻāina continue to acknowledge the presence of their spiritual ancestors in the surrounding land by maintaining respectful practices in the use of the land, streams, ponds, and ocean. These lands are treated with love and respect like a kūpuna of the ʻohana. They regularly visit the various areas in the course of subsistence gathering. While traveling to the various ʻili or sections of the traditional cultural practices region, through dirt roads and trails, along spring-fed streams, and the shoreline, practitioners continuously stay alert to the condition of the resources. If a resource is declining they will observe a kapu or restriction on its use until it recovers. They may even replant sparse areas. They are acutely aware of changes due to seasonal and life cycle transformations in the plants and animals. Plants and animals in their reproductive stage are not gathered. As kuaʻāina gather in their traditional area, they also renew their understanding of the landscape, the place-names, names of the winds and the rains, traditional legends, wahi pana, historical cultural sites, and the location of various native plants and animals. An inherent aspect of these practices is conservation to ensure availability of natural resources for present and future generations.

Many kuaʻāina have also continued to cultivate fish in ponds and the open ocean by regularly feeding the fish in conjunction with making offerings at the kūʻula shrines that mark their ocean fishing grounds. Taro and other domestic crops are planted according to the moon's phases to assure excellent growth. Kuaʻāina take advantage of seasonal fruits and marine life for their regular diet. Native plants are utilized for healing of illness by traditional methods that involve both physical and spiritual cleansing and dedication. Cultural knowledge attached to the traditional names of places, winds, and rains of their districts inform kuaʻāina about the effect of the dynamic forces of nature upon the ocean and the land in their area, and activities are planned accordingly.

Legends and chants inform them about how their ancestors coped with such elements. Thus, in the cultural kīpuka, traditional Native Hawaiian custom, belief, and practice continue to be a practical part of everyday life, not only for the old people, but also for the middle-aged and the young.

The undeveloped natural resources in these areas still provide an abundance of foods for the kua'āina who live in these districts. Forested lands provide fruits to eat. Vines, plants, and wood are used to make household implements and tools or as herbs of healing. The forest provides a natural habitat for animals that are hunted for meat. Aquatic life flourishes in the streams. The ocean provides an abundance of food. Subsistence activities continue to be the primary source of sustenance for the kua'āina. Production in these districts is heavily oriented toward home consumption.

Kua'āina also look after one another through maintaining relationships of 'ohana or large extended-family networks. *Hānai*, or the adoptive raising of children of relatives, continues to be commonly practiced. Ties with family members who move to another island, especially O'ahu, are maintained. If some of the children move away to the city, one or two remain behind to care for parents and the family *kuleana* or ancestral lands. Often those who move away send children home to be raised by the extended family during breaks from school and holidays. Families often visit each other between islands and exchange food gathered or raised through subsistence activities.

It should be noted that the methods and techniques of accessing, acquiring, or utilizing traditional natural resources may have changed over time. However, this does not detract from the fact that the purpose of the activities is to provide for Native Hawaiian 'ohana and their community and that the activities are guided by traditional Native Hawaiian kapu or restrictions and guidelines associated with customary subsistence, cultural, and religious practices. For example, Hawaiian fishermen may use motorboats rather than canoes to get to their ancestral fishing grounds. They may use a nylon net rather than one woven from native plant materials to surround fish or to entangle them in the overnight fluctuating tides. In most cases they are still utilizing ancestral knowledge of ocean tides, currents, and reefs to locate and catch the fish. Their catch is used to honor family 'aumakua and to feed their extended families and neighbors. Hawaiian hunters may drive a truck on a dirt road rather than walk along a trail to reach the area of forest where pigs roam. They may use a gun rather than a spear or knife. Since agriculture and residential development have destroyed the lowland forest areas where the pigs used to be plentiful and easily reached on foot trails, Hawaiians must go deeper into the same forests or higher up the same mountain hunted by their ancestors. The meat is shared with their large extended families as well as with neighbors who no longer have the stamina to go out and hunt.

Hawaiian custom and practice are distinguished not only by the honor and respect for traditional ʻohana cultural values and customs to guide subsistence harvesting of natural resources, but also by the uses made of the resources. Thus, when I speak of subsistence in this moʻolelo I do not mean that the kuaʻāina acquire all that they need to live from cultivation, gathering, fishing, and hunting. As the market economy evolved in Hawaiʻi, creating a demand for manufactured goods, and when taxes were imposed by the government, Native Hawaiians had to earn cash and interact with the market system. Instead, the definition of subsistence used in this moʻolelo is that developed by the Governor's Task Force on Molokaʻi Fishpond Restoration in 1993: "Subsistence is the customary and traditional uses . . . of wild and cultivated renewable resources for direct personal or family consumption as food, shelter, fuel, clothing, tools, transportation, culture, religion, and medicine for barter, or sharing, for personal or family consumption and for customary trade."

In addition, ʻohana values and customs that guide subsistence activities are models of the practice of lōkahi in modern Hawaiʻi. The first rule with regard to the land, ocean, and natural resources is to only take what is needed. Wasting natural resources is strongly condemned. It is also important to protect the ability of living resources to reproduce. Thus, kuaʻāina gather according to the life cycle of the resource and fish only during the particular species' non-spawning seasons: different fish are caught during different seasons of the year to allow the animals to reproduce. In addition, kuaʻāina alternate the areas where they gather, fish, and hunt in order to allow the resources to replenish themselves. If an area is observed to have stressed or declining resources due to drought, storm damage, or harvesting, a kapu on harvesting in the area is observed. Resources are replanted if appropriate.

Resources are always abundant and accessible to those who possess knowledge about their location and have the skill to obtain them. There is no need to overuse a more accessible area. More accessible resources are left for the kūpuna to harvest. Young men and women are expected to venture farther afield to acquire what they need. The knowledge and skill that has been passed down intergenerationally is respected and protected. It is kept within the family and not carelessly given away to outsiders. This knowledge includes an understanding of the areas which are kapu or reserved for various members of the community. Kuaʻāina usually fish, hunt, and gather in the areas traditionally used by their ancestors. If they go into an area outside of their own for some specific purpose, they usually ask permission and go with people from that area.

Kuaʻāina never speak openly about plans for going out to subsistence hunt, gather, or fish. When actually venturing out on an expedition, they keep focused on the purpose and goal for which they set out to fish, hunt, or gather. If they gather additional resources along the way, they do so when they are coming out of the area, never when they are headed for their destination. They are certain to stay aware of the natural elements and alert to natural signs. They respect the resources and the spirits of the land, forest, and ocean and do not act loud and boisterous. This enables them to better observe *hoʻailona* or natural signs important for their sense of direction, safety, and well-being. For example, the sound of falling boulders signals flash flooding in a stream. Sea birds flying inland before day's end signal that a storm is moving in from the ocean.

The resources acquired through subsistence enterprises are shared with members of the broader ʻohana, neighbors, and friends. In particular, the young kuaʻāina take care of the kūpuna who passed on their knowledge and experience to them and are now too old to go out on their own. They also take care of the widows and women who are single heads of households, who don't have men to provide for their subsistence needs. Finally, resources sacred to ʻaumakua of their ʻohana are respected as sacred to them and never gathered.

Thus, kuaʻāina living in cultural kīpuka are successful in acquiring the basic necessities for their families through subsistence activities by employing traditional cultural and spiritual knowledge and practices passed down to them from their kūpuna.

Benefits of Subsistence

Subsistence activities have added benefits related to family cohesion, health, and community well-being. A subsistence economy emphasizes sharing and redistribution of resources, which creates a social environment that cultivates community and kinship ties, emotional interdependency and support, prescribed roles for youth, and care for the elderly. Emphasis is placed on social stability rather than on individual efforts aimed at income-generating activities.[14]

Through subsistence, families attain essential resources to compensate for low incomes. They can also obtain food items, especially seafood, that might be prohibitively expensive in a strict cash economy. If families on fixed incomes were required to purchase these items, they would probably opt for cheaper, less healthy foods that would predispose them to health problems. In this respect, subsistence not only provides food, but also ensures a healthy diet.

Subsistence generally requires a great amount of physical exertion (e.g., fishing, diving, hunting), which is a valuable form of exercise and stress reduction and contributes to good physical and mental health. It is also a form of recreation that the whole family can share in. Family members of all ages contribute to different phases of subsistence, be it active hunting, fishing, gathering, or cleaning and preparing the food for eating. Older family members teach younger ones how to engage in subsistence and prepare the food, thus passing on ancestral knowledge, experience, and skill.

Another benefit of subsistence is sharing and gift giving within the community. Families and neighbors exchange resources when they are abundant and available, and the elderly are often the beneficiaries of resources shared by younger, more able-bodied practitioners. Most kua'āina believe that generosity is rewarded with better luck in the future.

Resources obtained through subsistence are also used for a variety of special life cycle occasions that bond families and communities. Resources such as fish, *limu 'opihi*, wild venison, and so on are foods served at *lū'au* for baby birthdays, graduations, weddings, and funerals. 'Ohana and community residents participate in these gatherings, which cultivate and reinforce a sense of family and community identity. If 'ohana members had to purchase such resources rather than acquire them through subsistence, the cost would be prohibitive, and the number of 'ohana gatherings would decrease. Subsistence activities therefore enable 'ohana to gather frequently and reinforce important relationships and support networks.

The time spent engaged in subsistence in the natural environment also cultivates a strong sense of environmental kinship that is the foundation of Hawaiian spirituality. Kua'āina reinforce their knowledge about the landscape, place-names and meanings, ancient sites, and areas where rare and endangered species of flora and fauna exist. This knowledge is critical to the preservation of natural and cultural landscapes because they provide a critical link between the past and the present. For example, wahi pana that are referred to in ancient chants and legends can be lost amidst changes due to modernization. However, visiting such places and sites while engaged in subsistence provides a continuity that is critical to the survival and perpetuation of the knowledge of these cultural places.

Moʻolelo

I write this moʻolelo, or succession of oral traditions, to acknowledge the role of the kuaʻāina in the various cultural kīpuka of the Hawaiian Islands in perpetuating traditional and customary Native Hawaiian belief, custom, and practice. I hope to show that protection of natural resources and of the subsistence livelihoods of the kuaʻāina in the cultural kīpuka is essential to the perpetuation of Native Hawaiian culture, as a whole, for future generations. What is at stake in planning for the future of these cultural kīpuka is the perpetuation not just of a rural lifestyle, but of the Native Hawaiian way of life itself. In order for those of us who live in Hawaiʻi to attain lōkāhi and live in balance

Figure 4 Representative of two distinct generations and ʻohana of Molokaʻi subsistence fishermen, "Mac" Kelsey Poepoe and Kanohowailuku Helm walk the old fishing trail to Mokio Point near the northwest corner of Molokaʻi, monitoring the subsistence fishing grounds for Native Hawaiian homesteaders. 2005. Richard A. Cooke III.

with our fragile island environment, we need to protect our cultural kīpuka. This may be a way to offset and perhaps begin to reverse the dramatic transformations of the natural and cultural landscapes of places such as Honolulu, Oʻahu; Kailua-Kona; and Lahaina, Maui.

Intrigued by Andrew Lind's account of cultural kīpuka in the 1930s, I decided to select an island, a *moku* or district, and an *ahupuaʻa* or basic geographic subdistrict usually coinciding with a valley from his list of remote areas to research as case studies. This would allow me to study the life ways of the kuaʻāina within the distinct traditional land use regimes from the level of an ahupuaʻa through that of a district to that of an island. I selected Molokaʻi as the island; Hāna on Maui, from Keʻanae to Kaupō, as the district; and Waipiʻo on Hawaiʻi as the ahupuaʻa.

As for the island, Molokaʻi was the larger in size and population and had more diverse and abundant resources than Lānaʻi and Niʻihau, the other two islands mentioned by Lind. On Molokaʻi, Hawaiians comprised a majority of the population through 1930. Among the small islands, Molokaʻi had the largest number of kuleana holders in 1930, despite the large concentrations of land under Molokaʻi Ranch, Puʻu o Hoku Ranch, the Bishop Estate, and the Territorial Government. Kahoʻolawe, as lands of the Kingdom of Hawaiʻi that were ceded by the Republic of Hawaiʻi to the U.S. government, was entirely under the control of the Territorial Government. It was leased out to Angus MacPhee for ranching in 1930. Ninety-eight percent of Lānaʻi was owned by the Dole Corporation in 1930. The entire island of Niʻihau was owned by the Niʻihau Ranch Company.

In modern Hawaiʻi, the people of Molokaʻi continue to proudly proclaim their island as the "Last Hawaiian Island." In addition, the kuaʻāina of Molokaʻi led the movement to reclaim Kahoʻolawe as sacred Hawaiian land and to revitalize the Hawaiian cultural practices of *aloha ʻāina* or love and respect for the land on every island. This connection between the kuaʻāina of Molokaʻi and the cultural renaissance that developed around the Kahoʻolawe movement clearly illustrated the regenerative quality of the cultural kīpuka.

I selected Hāna, on Maui, as the district because of its distinctive landscape and its pristine and diverse native natural resources, and because the kuʻaʻāina from that district had also played an important role in the Kahoʻolawe movement and the Hawaiian cultural renaissance. In addition, as discussed at the beginning of this chapter, I was first introduced into the world of the kuaʻāina through Uncle Harry Mitchell in the Keʻanae-Wailuanui community of the Hāna district.

I selected Waipiʻo as an ahupuaʻa in order to develop a case study on the island of Hawaiʻi and because it played a critical role in the survival of taro cultivation in the islands as a whole. My research revealed that the island of Molokaʻi, the Hāna Coast, and Waipiʻo Valley were highly valued by Native Hawaiian chiefs as areas over which to maintain control. These areas comprised lands that were extremely well suited for the cultivation of taro and useful native plants, had streams abundant with edible aquatic resources, and were close to abundant ocean resources.

These case studies were initially developed for sections of my dissertation,[15] which documented the life of Native Hawaiians during the first thirty-two years of direct American rule, 1898 through 1930. Subsequently, I had the opportunity to conduct additional oral history interviews and historical research and studies on the island of Molokaʻi and the Keʻanae-Wailuanui ahupuaʻa of the Hāna district. In addition, I conducted ethnographic research in the district of Puna, on Hawaiʻi, and the ahupuaʻa of Waiāhole, Waikāne, and Hakipuʻu, on Oʻahu, in separate studies.

In preparing this manuscript I decided to include the additional material gathered for Molokaʻi and Keʻanae-Wailuanui and to include a chapter on the district of Puna. Puna enriches the case studies because it is the home of Pele and her family of deities. Its landscape and resources are constantly transformed by seismic episodes and volcanic flows. The Puna families sustain a dynamic relationship to Pele as ʻaumakua.[16]

These case studies are not exhaustive histories of the kuaʻāina and the cultural kīpuka selected. They are designed to provide an essential history of each area, to share the insights and perspectives of the kuaʻāina who live there, and to convey the importance of protecting the resources and cultural practices of these and other cultural kīpuka. They also provide insight into the importance of continuing to document both the oral and the written histories of Hawaiʻi's kuaʻāina and the cultural kīpuka.

The case studies emphasize the experiences of the kuaʻāina in the early twentieth century up through World War II. The war and the 1946 tidal wave, which struck right after the end of the war, served as the major turning point in the social and economic development of the islands, even in the cultural kīpuka. Moreover, the collections of oral histories of kūpuna for Waipiʻo, Hāna, Puna, and Molokaʻi focus on their experiences growing up and living in these communities in the prewar period.

Through my research of these areas and interaction with the kuaʻāina who live there, I have come to the realization that the mainstream history of

Hawai'i focuses too narrowly on the history of change and of cultural impact upon Hawaiian society, concentrating on O'ahu and the ruling elite. A broader and more inclusive history of the Hawaiian islands would document not only the changes, but also continuity of Native Hawaiian culture. It would develop a history of the experiences of Native Hawaiian women as well as of men who raised their extended families by farming and fishing throughout the various islands of Hawai'i, including the rural communities I call cultural kīpuka. This work contributes to a much broader history of the Native Hawaiian people and the Hawaiian Islands. Because time and space limited my ability to conduct ethnographic research on all the cultural kīpuka on all our islands, it is my hope that this work can inspire and inform new research to be conducted on the cultural kīpuka not selected and contribute to the development of a more comprehensive history, one that includes the rural districts on all the major Hawaiian Islands.

Each case study begins by examining the traditional cultural significance of the district. The 'ōlelo no'eau or descriptive proverbs and poetic sayings for which the area is famous are interpreted, and a descriptive chant for the area is translated and interpreted. These provide valuable insights into the cultural resources and features for which the area was known and thus the role of this area overall in the cultural practices and customs of Native Hawaiians. This is followed by a discussion of the history of the landscape and its settlement, the deities who dwelt there, and the ruling chiefs who controlled the area. Next the case studies review how developments in the nineteenth century affected the life of the kua'āina in the area. Each case study then provides elaborate descriptions of the natural cultural resources available to the kua'āina for their subsistence and livelihoods and of the beliefs, customs, and practices which guided their lives. Finally, an overview of the social and economic changes in each area through the end of the twentieth century as well as a discussion of the elements of continuity still evident in the lives of the kua'āina in these communities is provided.

There is a final chapter on Kaho'olawe, which is not a cultural kīpuka. Instead, it is included to demonstrate how the kua'āina from the cultural kīpuka studied were instrumental in restoring the natural and cultural resources of Kaho'olawe and reviving Native Hawaiian beliefs, customs, and practices on the island. Kaho'olawe demonstrates the regenerative function of the kua'āina from the cultural kīpuka examined in the earlier chapters of the book.

Establishment of the Indigenous Hawaiian Nation

Research by archaeologists, anthropologists, and ethnographers over the past thirty years suggests that the history of settlement, before continuous contact with Europeans in 1778, may be looked at in four distinct *wā kahiko* or historic eras: the Colonization Period (1–600 CE), the Developmental Period (600–1100), the Expansion Period (1100–1650), and the Proto-Historic Period (1650–1795).[17]

Ongoing subsurface archaeology continues to uncover evidence that suggests the date of first settlement is close to the time of Christ.[18] Archaeological evidence suggests that the initial population was small, consisting of a few canoe loads of families and numbering at most around a hundred. They probably originated from the Marquesas or Tahiti and came fully prepared to permanently settle outside of their home islands, bringing with them food plants and domestic animals. Hawaiian legends, myths, and chants record, in story form, the experiences of the original Native Hawaiians. They describe the primal natural elements encountered by the original Native Hawaiians and how they adjusted to and coped with them. Often these original ancestors are personified as akua, kūpua, and ʻaumakua. To them is ascribed the bestowal upon the islands of special features and resources, including springs, streams, fishponds, mountain formations, caves, offshore islets, craters, cinder cones, and the varied rains and winds.

These deities or original ancestors made it possible for the Native Hawaiian people to adjust to the natural environment and resources of the islands and to live and flourish as a society. For example, in *Tales and Traditions of the People of Old: Nā Moʻolelo a ka Poʻe Kahiko*, Samuel Kamakau describes how Kāne and Kanaloa were honored as Gods who opened springs of fresh water for the people:

> According to the moʻolelo of Kane and Kanaloa, they were perhaps the
> first who kept gods (ʻo laua paha Na kahu akua mua) to come to Hawaiʻi
> nei, and because of their mana they were called gods. Kahoʻolawe was first
> named Kanaloa for his having first come there by way of Ke-ala-i-kahiki.
> From Kahoʻolawe the two went to Kahikinui, Maui, where they opened up
> the fishpond of Kanaloa at Lua-laʻi-lua, and from them came the water of
> Kou at Kaupo . . . They broke open rocks so that water would gush forth—
> sweet, flowing water—at Wai-hee and at Kahakuloa on Maui, on Lānaʻi,
> at Waiakane in Punakou on Molokaʻi, and at Kawaihoa on Oʻahu.[19]

The landscape was also made livable by the feats of Maui, who, according to tradition, fished the islands up from the ocean with the magic fishhook the constellation Manaiakalani. He is also said to have lifted the heavens high above the earth so that humans could walk upright. He ensnared the sun in order to lengthen the day. He also forced the ʻalae or mud hen to share the secret of making fire so that humans could cook their food and have warmth at night: "There may be seen the things left by Maui-akalana and other famous things: the tapa-beating cave of Hina, the fishhook called Manai-a-ka-lani, the snare for catching the sun, and the places where Maui's adzes were made and where he did his deeds." [20]

During the Developmental Period (600 to 1100) distinctively indigenous Hawaiian cultural patterns and implements emerge. Throughout this period, the inhabitants of Hawaiʻi shared ancestry and heritage and developed an indigenous culture and language uniquely adapted to the islands of Hawaiʻi and distinct from that of other Polynesian peoples. These indigenous Hawaiians developed a highly organized, self-sufficient subsistence social system and extended sovereign control over the Hawaiian archipelago.

The social system was communal and organized around subsistence production to sustain ʻohana, the large extended multigenerational families. Hawaiian spiritual beliefs, customs, and practices focused on maintaining harmonious and nurturing relationships with the various life forces, elements, and beings of nature as ancestral spirits who were honored as deities. Land and natural resources were not privately owned. Instead, the Hawaiian people maintained a communal stewardship over the land, the ocean, and all the natural resources of the islands.

The kūpuna provided leadership and guidance to the mākua or adults who performed most of the daily productive work of fishing, cultivation, and gathering. Between the islands of Hawaiʻi there was some variation of dialect and names for plants, animals, rains, and winds. There were also variations in physical structures and cultural and art forms. Origin myths varied according to the particular migration and genealogical line from which the families descended. The prominence of akua and kūpua also varied by island—for example, Pele and her family of deities for Hawaiʻi, Maui on the island which bears his name, and various moʻo or mythical dragonlike lizards on Molokaʻi. However, qualitatively, the language, culture, social system, and spiritual beliefs, customs, and practices were shared among the inhabitants of the islands, and the origin of the indigenous Hawaiian people's sovereign nation can be traced to this era.

Dated to this period are basalt adzes and fishhooks that are distinctively

Hawaiian in form, as well as unique Hawaiian articles such as the ʻulu maika or stone bowling disc and the lei niho palaoa or tongue-shaped neck ornament. By the end of this period, leeward areas of the islands were settled, indicating an expanding population.

The Expansion period, between 1100 and 1650, includes a period of long voyages between Hawaiʻi and Tahiti up through approximately 1400. These 550 years are distinguished by geometric growth of the population, technological innovation, intensification of production, and the emergence of a stratified social system. Remnant structures and artifacts dating to this time suggest that the leeward areas were extensively settled and cultivated during this period. The chants, myths, and legends record the transpacific voyages of great Polynesian chiefs and priests, such as the high priest Paʻao, the aliʻi nui or high chiefs Moʻikeha and Moʻikeha's sons Kiha and Laʻamaikahiki. The high priest Paʻao introduced a new religious system that used human sacrifice, feathered images, and walled-in heiau or temples. Traditional chants and myths describe how Paʻao introduced a system of ruling chiefs who appropriated rule over the land through intermarriage, battles, and ritual sacrifice.

The ruling chiefs organized great public works projects that are still evident today. For example, ʻUmialīloa constructed taro terraces, irrigation networks, and heiau throughout Hawaiʻi Island, including Ahu a ʻUmi on Hualalai. Kihaapiʻilani oversaw the construction of the Ala Nui or trail around the entire island of Maui and the Ke Ala a ka Pūpū, a whiteshell pathway, on Molokaʻi after he became ruler over all of the districts on these islands. The construction of major fishponds, irrigation networks, and field cultivation systems resulted in surpluses that sustained the stratification of Hawaiian society into three basic classes—aliʻi (chiefs), kahuna (priests), and makaʻāinana (commoners).

Despite these advances and the provision of food, barkcloth, and household implements by the common people for the households of the chiefs, Hawaiian society was predominantly a subsistence agricultural economy. There is no evidence of a monetary system or commodity production, although a system of barter in essential goods between fishermen, mountain dwellers, and taro cultivators existed within the framework of the ʻohana. Such exchange within the ʻohana functioned as a sharing of what had been produced upon the ʻili that the ʻohana held and worked upon in common:

> Between households within the ohana there was constant sharing and
> exchange of foods and of utilitarian articles and also of services, not in

barter but as voluntary (though decidedly obligatory) giving. ʻOhana living inland (ko kula uka), raising taro, bananas, wauke (for tapa, or barkcloth, making) and olona (for its fibre), and needing gourds, coconuts and marine foods, would take a gift to some ʻohana living near the shore (ko kula kai) and in return would receive fish or whatever was needed. The fisherman needing poi or awa would take fish, squid or lobster upland to a household known to have taro, and would return with his kalo (taro) or paiai (hard poi, the steamed and pounded taro corm) . . . In other words, it was the ʻohana that constituted the community within which the economic life moved.[21]

Under the ruling chiefs, land was not privately owned. The chiefly class provided stewardship over the land and divided and redivided control over the districts of the islands among themselves through war and succession. A single chief controlled a major section of an island or a whole island on the basis of his military power. Up until the time of Kamehameha I, however, no one chief was ever paramount over all of the islands.[22]

The high chief divided his landholdings among lower-ranked chiefs called *konohiki.* They functioned for the chief as supervisors over the people who lived on the lands and cultivated them. The konohiki's tenure on the land was dependent upon their benefactor, the chief. Konohiki were often related to the chief and were allocated land in recognition of loyal or outstanding service to him. However, unlike elsewhere in Polynesia, the konohiki were rarely related to the makaʻāinana on the land under his supervision.[23] Thus, the konohiki represented the collective interest of the aliʻi class over the makaʻāinana as well as the individual interest of his patron chief over the ahupuaʻa.

The lands allocated to the konohiki were called ahupuaʻa. Ahupuaʻa boundaries coincided with the geographic features of a valley. They ran from the mountain to the ocean, were watered by a stream, and included landscape features such as mountain ridges or *puʻu* and cinder hills.[24]

The ahupuaʻa of the konohiki were further divided into strips of land called ʻili, allocated by either the chief or the konohiki to the ʻohana. These ʻili either extended continuously from the mountain to the ocean or were made up of separate plots of land located in each of the distinct resource zones of the ahupuaʻa. The ʻohana was afforded access to all the resources within the ahupuaʻa necessary for survival—vines, timber, thatch, and medicinal plants from forested mountain areas; sloping land for sweet potatoes and crops that require higher altitudes; low-lying lands irrigated by stream waters for taro and fresh water; and shoreline, reef, and ocean areas for fish, limpids, crustaceans, and seaweed, the principal sources of protein for Hawaiians.[25]

Ahupuaʻa boundaries reflected the pattern of land use that had evolved as the most efficient and beneficial to the ʻohana throughout previous centuries. The boundaries were adopted and instituted by the aliʻi and konohiki to delineate units for the collection of tribute. These boundaries did not restrict access by the ʻohana to those natural resources needed for survival that were unavailable within their own ahupuaʻa. For example, the adze is an essential tool for the ʻohana, yet the basalt used to hew adzes was not available within every ahupuaʻa. ʻOhana could access the adze quarries even if they were located outside the ʻohana's ahupuaʻa. On the island of Molokaʻi, members of ʻohana living in the ahupuaʻa of the windward valleys would annually reside for part of the summer months in the ahupuaʻa of Kaluakoʻi to make adzes and to gather and salt fish. The salted fish would sustain them during the winter months when the ocean off their ahupuaʻa was too rough for fishing. Evidence suggests that the island of Kahoʻolawe was also a place of temporary residence for Maui ʻohana to gather fish and to acquire the basalt needed for making adzes.

The tenure of the ʻohana on the land was stable, unlike that of the aliʻi and the konohiki. Two Hawaiian sayings illustrated this principle. The first was "Ko luna pōhaku no ke kaʻa i lalo, ʻaʻole hiki i ko lalo pōhaku ke kaʻa" (A stone that is high up can roll down, but a stone that is down cannot roll).[26] This means that the chief and his retainers, including the konohiki, who were over the people could be overthrown and lose their positions of influence. A chief could be defeated in war and lose his lands. When a chief died and a new chief succeeded him, the lands were redistributed, and the previous chief's konohiki could be displaced. However, the common people who lived on the land from the days of their ancestors were stable on the land. They were not displaced when the chief or konohiki over them changed. They continued to live on and cultivate the land of their ʻili from one chief's rule to the next.

The second saying was "I ʻāina no ka ʻāina i ke aliʻi, ai waiwai no ka ʻāina i ke kanaka" (The land remains the land because of the chiefs, and prosperity comes to the land because of the common people).[27] In other words, the chiefs held the land, but the common people worked the land and made it valuable.

Though the tenure of the makaʻāinana was stable, they were not tied to the land and did have the option to move away if they chose to. There is little evidence, however, that moving off of the land of one's birth was ever a common practice.

The makaʻāinana produced all the necessities of life for their extended families from the ʻili that was allotted to them. In addition to cultivating their own plots for the subsistence of their ʻohana, the makaʻāinana were obligated to cultivate plots of land set aside for the konohiki and chiefs. These were called *haku one* and *kōʻele*, respectively. The common people were also required to provide the chiefs and konohiki with an annual *hoʻokupu* or tribute that included food and all types of household needs, from tapa cloth and woven mats to stone and wooden containers and implements, as well as feathers to make the cloaks and helmets that were symbols of the aliʻi rank. In addition, the makaʻāinana were obligated to provide labor service and products from the land upon the request of the chief or konohiki. The aliʻi enjoyed full appropriation rights over all that was produced upon his land grants; however, it was the labor of the makaʻāinana that supported the entire society.

Makaʻāinana worked cooperatively and shared the fruits of the labor or *laulima*. Most of this labor was done within the context of the ʻohana as the primary unit of production. The ʻohana lived in dispersed clusters of households called *kauhale* on the ʻili land granted to them. Within the ʻohana there was also cooperative enterprise and reciprocal exchange of labor service called *kōkua*. This was practiced in the undertaking of major projects such as the chopping down, hewing out, and hauling of a log for a canoe or the construction and thatching of a house structure. These types of projects required the labor of more people than made up one single ʻohana. In addition, all the ʻohana within an ahupuaʻa could be organized to do massive public works projects under the supervision of the konohiki. This included construction and maintenance of the irrigation systems and fishponds.

Although the chiefs and their konohiki had full appropriation rights over the land and the people, in the main this was a system of mutual obligation and benefit between the chiefs and the people. The chiefs controlled the land and distributed it among the makaʻāinana. The chief was required to manage and oversee the production on the land. He regulated the use of scarce resources and apportioned these resources among the people according to principles of fair use. Of these resources, water was the most valued, and the chief assured that the irrigation system was properly maintained. He conserved the resources of the land through restriction and replacement policies. Of great spiritual significance, the chief was responsible for conducting the proper rituals for the Gods who controlled nature. In return, the makaʻāinana were obliged to provide labor service and products of the land to the chiefs and konohiki.

Although Hawaiian tradition records cases of arbitrary, irresponsible, and self-serving chiefs who abused the people, they were clearly exceptional cases and were quickly replaced with responsible chiefs who cared for the well-being of the people.[28] The Hawaiian proverb "I ali'i no ali'i no Nā kanaka" (A chief is a chief because of the people) reflects the Hawaiian attitude that the greatness of a chief was judged according to the welfare of the people under him.[29] According to the Hawaiian historian David Malo, "In former times, before Kamehameha, the chiefs took great care of their people. That was their appropriate business, to seek the comfort and welfare of the people, for a chief was called great in proportion to the number of his people."[30]

From 1650 to 1795, the time of the Proto-Historic period, just prior to the arrival and settlement of Europeans, Hawaiian society was highly stratified under ruling chiefs who controlled whole islands and groups of islands and vied for control as a paramount chief. Individual high chiefs continuously competed to extend their control over more and more districts and islands through marriage alliances, religious ritual, and military conquest. The archaeologist Patrick V. Kirch provides an incisive description of this period:

> With the development of highly sophisticated and intensive agricultural and aquacultural production, an elaborate political hierarchy and land tenure system, a religious ideology and ritual practice that included war and fertility cults performed on massive stone temple platforms, and a highly stratified social structure, the Proto-Historic Hawaiian culture can be closely compared with other emergent forms of "state-level" societies elsewhere in the world (for example, the Olmec culture of Mesoamerica, the Pre-Dynastic Period of Egypt, or the Mississippian culture of North America).[31]

To the extent that Hawaiian society had evolved into a socially and economically stratified system by the eighteenth century, the responses of the Hawaiian people to contact and change after 1778 were divergent and largely influenced by the social and economic role the individual played in society. The acceptance or rejection of Western culture was largely the prerogative of the ruling class of ali'i. The common people did not play a major role in determining the political and economic future of Hawai'i. They let the ali'i take the lead, while they struggled to survive the burden of contact—war, disease, famine, and the tragic widespread loss of beloved family, neighbors and friends.

As discussed above, the political, economic, and social development that came with contact, trade, and a plantation system were experienced unequally in the various districts of each of the islands. The case studies presented relate the experience of the Native Hawaiians in the selected districts as these broader developments unfolded. Below is an overview of the key developments that affected the lives of the Native Hawaiian people from contact through the end of the twentieth century.

Contact and Monarchy

In 1778, the year the English explorer Captain James Cook arrived in Hawai'i, the Native Hawaiian population was estimated at 400,000 to 800,000 inhabitants.[32] Beginning in 1785 Hawai'i became a regular stopover in the fur trade between America, Europe, and China. By 1810 Hawai'i was an integral part of the China trade route as a source of sandalwood. Gradually Hawai'i was pulled into the economic web of the worldwide market economy, causing far-reaching and irreversible changes that devastated the Native Hawaiian people. Periodically, the common people suffered famines that gripped the land as the chiefs gave priority to meeting the needs of the fur and sandalwood traders. According to Handy and Pukui, "As the desires of the chiefs and the pressure of the trading captains grew, more and more people were put to the task, fewer and fewer were left for the normal duties of everyday living; in many areas planting and fishing virtually ceased, and for a season thereafter there would be little harvested beyond the needs of the ali'i and their konohiki (supervisors). It was the people who went hungry."[33]

Exposure to Western continental diseases such as gonorrhea, syphilis, colds, flu, dysentery, whooping cough, measles, and influenza killed thousands of Hawaiians. David Malo recorded that in 1804 alone half of the Islands' population died of *ma'i oku'u*, a disease that was either cholera or bubonic plague.[34]

Kamehameha began a series of military campaigns to conquer all of the Hawaiian Islands upon the death of his uncle, the chief Kalaniopu'u, in 1782. In 1790 Kamehameha acquired the Western ship *Fair American* and the services of two Englishmen, John Young and Isaac Davis, to train his warriors in the use of Western military technology. In 1795, after a four-year period of peace during which Kamehameha trained his army, built his canoes, and planted acres of food to feed his army of warriors, he launched his military campaigns, which led to the conquest of Maui, Moloka'i, Lāna'i, Kaho'olawe, and O'ahu. In 1810 Kaua'i also came under Kamehameha's central authority when the chief Kaumuali'i agreed to become a tribute chief of Kamehameha rather than try to fight off an invading force of Kamehameha's war canoes.[35] Thus, by 1810 King Kamehameha I, for the first time in the history of the Hawaiian Islands, established a central absolute monarchy with sovereign rule over all the islands.

Upon the death of King Kamehameha I in 1819, those chiefs who were closely allied to him feared a rebellion from rival traditional chiefs. As a means of undermining their rivals, the Council of Chiefs, under the leadership of Mōʻī Kamehameha II, Kuhina Nui Kaʻahumanu, and High Chief Kalanimoku, instituted the ʻAi Noa or abolition of the state religion.[36] By abolishing the traditional chiefly religion under which rivals could claim rank, prestige, and position, the Kamehameha chiefs consolidated political power under the control of their monarchy.

Although Native Hawaiian religion ceased to have the official sanction of the royal government, Hawaiian spiritual beliefs and customs continued to be honored and practiced in most of the rural communities and settlements of the kingdom. Families continued to honor their ʻaumakua. Traditional *kahuna lāʻau lapaʻau* or herbal healers continued their healing practices using native Hawaiian plants and spiritual healing arts. Family burial caves and lava tubes continued to be cared for. The hula and chants continued to be taught, in distinctly private ways. Among the deities who continued to be actively honored, worshipped, thought of, and respected, even to the present, were Pele and her family of deities. Every eruption reinforced and validated her existence to her descendants and new generations of followers.[37]

In 1820, the year following the ʻAi Noa, American missionaries began to settle Hawaiʻi and convert Hawaiians to Christianity. In the same year commercial whaling began to attract increasing numbers of foreign settlers, who demanded rights of citizenship and private ownership of land.[38] In 1839, nineteen years after King Kamehameha had established absolute rule over all of the islands, his son, Kauikeaouli, King Kamehameha III, initiated a serious of steps to set up a constitutional monarchy wherein the rights of the makaʻāinana, distinct from those of the chiefs and of the king, were recognized. The rights of foreigners who became naturalized citizens were also distinguished.

Native Hawaiian Responsibilities and Rights Are Vested in the Land

The first step in this process was the signing of the 1839 Bill of Rights. Up to this point, foreigners were unable to become naturalized citizens. Thus, when the law refers to "Nā Kanaka a pau," or all of the people, it refers only to the native people of the Hawaiian Islands, the Native Hawaiians. It does not refer to foreigners residing in Hawai'i. The Bill of Rights recognized a division of rights, the king being sovereign and distinct from the chiefs and the common people. It guaranteed the protection of the rights of the people, the Native Hawaiians, together with their lands, their building lots, and all their property. The 1839 Bill of Rights states in part:

> 5. Ua hoomalu ia ke kino *o Na Kanaka a pau*, a me ko lakou aina, a me
> ko lakou mau pa hale, a me ko lakou waiwai a pau; ke Malama lakou i
> Na kanawai o ke aupuni, aole hoi e lawe ia kekahi mea, ke olelo ole ia kela
> mea ma ke kanawai. O ke ali'i e Hana i kekahi mea kue i keia Kumukana-
> wai, e pau kona noho alii ana ma keia pae aina o Hawaii nei, ke hoomau
> ia ma laila, pela Na kiaaina, a me Na luna a me Na konohiki a pau
> [emphasis added].

> 5. Protection is hereby secured to the persons *of all the people*, together
> with their lands, their building lots and all their property, while they con-
> form to the laws of the kingdom, and nothing whatever shall be taken from
> any individual except by express provision of the laws. Whatever chief shall
> act perseveringly in violation of this Constitution, shall no longer remain a
> chief of the Hawaiian archipelago, and the same shall be true of the gov-
> ernors, officers and all land agents [emphasis added].[39]

The second step was the enactment of the 1840 constitution and the compilation of laws for the Hawaiian kingdom. Under the constitution, executive, legislative and judiciary branches of government were set up. The constitution included the same statement regarding protection of the people, their lands, their building lots, and all of their property. In addition, the constitution clearly stated that although the lands from Hawai'i to Ni'ihau belonged to the king, he did not own them as private property. Instead, the constitution states that the king held the lands of the islands of Hawai'i in common with the chiefs and the people. Under this constitution, the responsibilities and rights of the king, the chiefs, and the people were vested together, in common, in the land, at a time when Native Hawaiians were the only citizens of the islands. Foreigners were not allowed to own land in Hawai'i until a special law was passed in 1850. The 1840 constitution states in part:

> Eia ke ano o ka noho ana o Na alii a me ka hooponopono ana i ka aina.
> O Kamehameha I, o ia ke poo o keia aupuni, a nona no Na aina a pau mai
> Hawaii a Niihau, aole Na e nona ponoi, no Na kanaka no, a ma Na alii, a o

Kamehameha no ko lakou poo nana e olelo i ka aina. No laila, aohe mea pono ma mua, aohe hoi mea pono i keia manawa ke hoolilo aku i kekahi lihi iki o keia mau aina me ka ae ole o ka mea ia ia ka olelo o ke aupuni.

The origin of the present government, and system of polity, is as follows. Kamehameha I, was the founder of the kingdom, and to him belonged the land from Hawai'i to Ni'ihau, though it was not his own private property. It belonged to the people, and the chiefs in common, of whom Kamehameha I was the head, and had the management of the landed property. Wherefore, there was not formerly, and is not now any person who could or can convey away the smallest portion of land without the consent of the one who had, or has the direction of the kingdom.[40]

In 1846 Kamehameha III, the heir of Kamehameha I and ruling monarch of the Hawaiian Islands, initiated a process to establish private property in the Hawaiian Islands in response to the irrepressible demands of European and American settlers and their respective governments. The king and the legislature adopted "An Act to Organize the Executive Departments of the Hawaiian Islands," which established a Board of Commissioners to Quiet Land Titles. This act also included the "Principles Adopted by the Board of Commissioners to Quiet Land Titles in Their Adjudication of Claims Presented to Them." These principles served to guide the establishment of a system of private property in Hawai'i.

The introduction to the principles reaffirmed the joint responsibilities, rights, and interests of the king, the chiefs, and the 'ohana in the lands of the Islands. From the time of High Chief Kamehameha Paiea and up until the creation of a system of private property, the king and the chiefs held all land as a sacred trust, and the indigenous 'ohana continued their stewardship responsibility and tenure over the lands of their ancestors. Under the new law, members of the 'ohana were now called *hoa'āina*, or tenants of the land (literally translated, the term means "friend of the land"). The principles stated in part:

> O Na pono a pau i pili i ke Alii maluna o Na konohiki nui, a me Na mea malalo o lakou, oia Na pono o Na konohiki nui maluna o Na hoaaina o lakou, a me Na lopa a pau i noho i ko lakou aina. Nolaila, me he poe hui la lakou, a ua pili ka aina ia lakou a pau . . .
>
> Nolaila, he mea kupono maoli, a he mea pololei no hoi i ka haawi ana o ke Alii i ke kuleana alodio, ke haawi i ke konohiki maluna, oia hoi ka

mea i loaa mua ka aina Na ke Alii mai, no ka mea, i ka Hana Na pela, aole
i Hana ino ia Na konohiki, a me Na hoaaina malalo ona; ua hoomaluia
lakou e ke kanawai, e like ma ka wa mamua. He mea akaka loa hoi ka hiki
ole i ke Alii ka haawi aku i ke kuleana alodio ia hai, no ka mea, ina pela, ua
nele ke konohiki mua. Aka, ina loaa i ke konohiki mua kona aina ma ke ano
alodio, ma ke kuai, a ma ka haawi wale o ke Alii, ua mau no ke kuleana o
Na hoaaina, a me Na lopa, no ka mea aole nele kekahi mea e ae no ka
hoolilo ana o ka Moi i kona iho. Nolaila, o ke konohik i kuai me ke Alii a
loaa kona aina ma ke ano alodio, ua hiki ole ia ia ke pai i ka poe malalo
ona, e like ma ka hiki ole i ke Alii i keia manawa ke pai i ke konohiki.

The same rights which the King possessed over the superior landlords
and all under them the several grades of landlords possessed over their
inferiors, so that there was a joint ownership of the land; the King really
owning the allodium, and the person in whose hands he placed the land,
holding it in trust . . .

    It seems natural then, and obviously just, that the King, in disposing
of the allodium, should offer it first to the superior lord, that is to the person who originally received the land in trust from the King; since by doing
so, no injury is inflicted on any of the inferior lords or tenants, they being
protected by law in their rights as before; and most obviously the King
could not dispose of the allodium to any other person without infringing
on the rights of the superior lord. But even when such lord shall have
received an allodial title from the King by purchase or otherwise, the rights
of the tenants and sub-tenants must still remain unaffected, for no purchase,
even from the sovereign himself, can vitiate the rights of third parties. The
lord, therefore, who purchases the allodium, can no more seize upon the
rights of the tenants and dispossess them.[41]

    In a later section, the principles clearly state that there are three classes of
persons who have vested rights in the lands of Hawai'i—the government, the
landlord, and the tenant:

Ua akaka loa hoi, ekolu wale no mea kuleana ma ka aina hookahi. 1. O ke
Aupuni. 2. O Na konohiki. 3. O Na hoaaiana, a nolaila he mea nui ka
hoakaka i ka nui o ko kekahi kuleana, a me ko kekahi.

    It being therefore fully established, that there are but three classes
of person sharing vested rights in the land,—1st, the government, 2nd, the
landlord, and 3rd, the tenant, it next becomes necessary to ascertain the
proportional rights of each.[42]

These principles, looked at together with the declaration in the constitution of 1840, actually describe how any one section of land in the Hawaiian Islands is vested with multiple layers of responsibilities and rights. Native Hawaiian 'ohana, referred to as hoa'āina in the principles, who had cultivated their gardens and taro pond fields for generations and had gathered resources from *mauka* to *makai*, from the mountain to the ocean, in their resident ahupua'a had one layer of vested interest, responsibilities, and rights in the lands of the ahupua'a. Over them, the landlord chief or konohiki responsible for the overall management of the ahupua'a and the well-being of the 'ohana and hoa'āina who resided there also had a layer of vested interest, responsibilities, and rights in each of gardens and taro pond fields that made up the ahupua'a and in the ahupua'a as a whole.

Finally, King Kamehameha III was descended from King Kamehameha I, who had conquered all of the chiefs and wrested control over each island. Therefore, King Kamehameha III, ultimately, had inherited a vested layer of interest, responsibilities, and rights over the individual gardens and taro pond

Figure 5 Kua'āina have inherited the rights of the hoa'āina. A Hawaiian taro farmer in Waipi'o Valley embodies the image of the kua'āina featured in this book, who, like the ho'āina, bent their backs and worked and sweated in the taro patches and sweet potato fields and held that which is precious and sacred in the culture in their care. 1974. Franco Salmoiraghi.

fields in each of the ahupua'a, as well as over each of the ahupua'a in each of the districts on each of the islands. The principles provided the following example of how the multiple interests in any one tract of land might be divided out:

> Ina hookoia kela manao, e hiki no, ina he aina i ka lima o ke konohiki, a e noho ana Na hoaaina, a ina like wale no ka aina a pau, hiki no ke mahele maoli, i ekolu Apana like, a e haawi i ke konohiki i palapala alodio no kona Apana, a pela no ko ka hoaaina, a koe hoi kekahi hapakolu i ke Alii i waiwai no ke Aupuni.
>
> According to this principle, a tract of land now in the hands of a landlord and occupied by tenants, if all parts of it were equally valuable, might be divided into three equal parts, and an allodial title to one then be given to the lord, and the same title be given to the tenants of one-third, and the other one-third would remain in the hands of the Kings, as his proportional right.[43]

Therefore, the establishment of a private property system in Hawai'i was a process of dividing out the multiple layers of interest in each piece of land, each ahupua'a, and each island. The first step in this process of dividing out multiple interests in the land was for the king and the landlords, or the chiefs and konohiki, to distinguish their respective claims. The second step was for the king and the chiefs to commute a portion of their respective claim to the government of the Kingdom of Hawai'i. The third step was for the commoners who lived on the lands to file for their portion of the lands claimed by the king and the landlords or chiefs and konohiki.

Each of the *māhele* or divisions was in essence a series of quitclaim arrangements between the king, on one hand, and a particular chief or konohiki, on the other, relating to lands in which both had previously claimed an interest. The summary is as follows:

1 That the King should retain all of his private lands as his personal and individual property, subject only to the rights of tenants.

2 That one-third of the remaining lands be allocated to the Hawaiian government; one-third to the chiefs or konohikis; and the remaining one-third to the tenants or common people.

3 That the division between the chiefs or konohikis and the tenants might be effected whenever either party required such a division, subject to confirmation by the King and Privy Council.

4   That the tenants on the King's private lands were entitled to one-third of the lands actually possessed and cultivated by them, and that such division should be made whenever either the King or the tenant required it.

5   That the divisions provided for in rules 2, 3, and 4 should be made without any prejudice to any fee simple grant theretofore made by any of the Hawaiian Kings.

6   That the chiefs or konohikis might satisfy the commutation due by them, by the payment to the government of a sum equal to one-third of the unimproved value of the lands awarded to them, or by conveying to the government a one-third part of such lands.

7   That the lands allocated to Kamehameha III were to be recorded in the same place and manner as all other allodial titles but that all lands allocated to the Hawaiian government were to be recorded in a separate book.[44]

The results of this Māhele were as follows:

Crown lands reserved for the monarchy	984,000 acres (23.8%)
Lands granted to 245 chiefs	1,619,000 acres (39.2%)
Government lands, distinct from Crown	1,523,000 acres (37%)
	4,126,000 acres (100%)[45]

All of these lands granted by the Board of Commissioners to the Crown, the government, and the chiefs continued to be subject to the rights of the hoaʻāina. The phrase "koe wale no ke kuleana o Na kanaka e noho ana ma ua mau aina la," which the government translated as "subject or reserved only to the rights of the tenants," is at the end of the declaration by the board establishing the Crown and government lands and appears on the grants of land issued by the board.[46]

The establishment of a private property system in Hawaiʻi transformed the relationships and mutual responsibilities between the aliʻi and the ʻohana, who remained as hoaʻāina or tenants under the aliʻi. The rights and claims of the aliʻi were addressed through Ka Māhele, under which 245 aliʻi were granted a combined total of 1.6 million acres.[47]

The rights of the hoaʻāina were twofold. First, through February 14, 1848, they had the right to file a claim against the lands apportioned to the chiefs and konohiki for those lands which they cultivated and upon which they lived. When the final land grants were made under the Kuleana Act of 1850, 8,205 hoaʻāina received 28,600 acres, or 0.8 percent of all of the lands of Hawaiʻi. All of the land granted to the hoaʻāina could have fit into the island of Kahoʻolawe, which has 28,800 acres. Although all of the 29,221 adult males in Hawaiʻi in 1850 were eligible to make land claims, only 29 percent received land; 71 percent remained landless.[48]

Several factors may have contributed to the low number of applications and awards. Overall, the concept of private ownership of land was a totally foreign notion. The Hawaiian language does not even have a word for private property ownership of land. The word *kuleana*, which was used to translate the law, refers to personal possessions such as clothing. Thus, many Hawaiians did not appreciate or understand the importance of filing a land claim within the given two-year period in order to continue living upon their ʻili. And although the law was published and posted in key locations, it was vaguely worded, using foreign concepts that were not understood by the common people. Another reason may have been that those who lived in out-of-the-way places did not hear about the law or heard of it too late to file a claim. Furthermore, some of the makaʻāinana were intimidated by the chiefs not to make land claims against them. And finally, most of the makaʻāinana lived as farm tenants of the chiefs and functioned outside the nexus of a cash economy. Therefore, the fee for surveying the land, between $6 and $12, was beyond the reach of a majority of the makaʻāinana.

In the campaign to set aside the Crown lands for Native Hawaiians to homestead in 1921, Prince Jonah Kūhiō Kalanianaʻole focused on these lands as the principal trust held by the Hawaiian monarchy for the Native Hawaiian people. According to Kūhiō, King Kamehameha III and the Council of Chiefs had recognized that the common people had one-third interest in the lands of Hawaiʻi at the time of the Māhele. When the common people only received 0.8 percent of the land on an individual fee simple basis, the remaining portion of the one-third interest of the common people in the of the lands were held in trust by the monarchy as the Crown lands. Prince Kūhiō explained this point in an article he wrote for *Mid-Pacific Magazine* in February 1921:

> The act creating the executive department contained a statute establishing a board of royal commissioners to quiet land titles . . . This board decided that there were but three classes of vested or original rights in land, which were in the King or Government, the chiefs, and the common people, and these three classes of interest were about equal in extent . . . The common people, being left out in the division after being recognized as owners of a third interest in the kingdom, believing that new methods had to be

adopted to place them in possession, assumed that these lands were being held in trust by the crown for their benefit. However, the lands were not reconveyed to the common people, and it [*sic*] was so held by each monarch from the time of the division in 1848 to the time of the dethronement of Queen Liliʻuokalani in 1893.[49]

What remains clear is that the king and government of the Kingdom of Hawaiʻi recognized that the Native Hawaiian landlords and common people had vested interests, responsibilities, and rights in the land. The vested rights of 245 chiefs and konohiki or landlords were transformed into fee-simple ownership of a combined total of 1.6 million acres through the process of the Māhele. The vested rights of more than three-fourths of the common people were never transformed into fee-simple ownership. Kūhiō, who was also Hawaiʻi's delegate to the U.S. Congress, presented a compelling argument that the people believed the land in which they held a vested interest continued to be held in trust by the monarchy for their benefit.

The second right of the hoaʻāina was provided by the king and the legislature in section 7 of the Kuleana Act, which granted to them their traditional gathering rights, rights to drinking water and running water, and the right of way, provided that permission was obtained from the landlords. Thereafter, in 1851, the legislature amended section 7 of the Kuleana Act and deleted the requirement that the hoaʻāina obtain the permission of the landlords in order to exercise their traditional rights. Since 1851, the law has read as it now does in Chapter 7, section 1, of the Hawaiʻi Revised Statutes (HRS):

> Where the landlords have obtained, or may hereafter obtain, allodial titles to their lands, the people on each of their lands shall not be deprived of the right to take firewood, house-timber, aho cord, thatch, or ki leaf, from the land on which they live, for their own private use, but they shall not have a right to take such articles to sell for profit. The people shall also have a right to drinking water, and running water, and the right of way. The springs of water, running water, and roads shall be free to all, on all lands granted in fee simple; provided that this shall not be applicable to wells and watercourses, which individuals have made for their own use.[50]

In 1850, over the protests of Native Hawaiians, foreigners were given the right to own land. From that point on foreigners, primarily Americans, continued to expand their interests, eventually controlling most of the land, sugar plantations, banks, shipping, and commerce of the islands.[51]

In the same year, new taxes were imposed upon the common Hawaiians: a kuleana land tax, a $2 school tax for males, a 50-cent horse tax, a 25-cent mule tax, and a $1 dog tax. Changes in the traditional land system and newly imposed taxes forced greater numbers of Hawaiians to enter the work force as wage laborers. They labored in the plantations as well as on ranches and in small enterprises such as the gathering of *pulu* (tree fern fiber used to stuff pillows and mattresses) and *pepeiao akua* (tree fungus), coffee growing, and production of salt for export.[52]

Though the foundation for wage labor to develop into the dominant form of labor was laid by the 1850s, it was the emergence of sugar as the primary commodity around which the Hawaiian economy would be organized that provided the impetus for the complete transformation of the Hawaiian social system. The ʻohana began to gradually change from the primary unit of work and the context within which to make a livelihood to having no direct relationship to the organization of work and production. Instead, the ʻohana began to serve as a source of refuge, comfort, and support to Hawaiian laborers who felt overworked and socially alienated from their ʻohana and family homesteads when they labored on the plantations and in port towns. An 1873 article in the *Ka Nūhou* newspaper described the ʻohana in just these terms:

> The kanaka [Native Hawaiian] has no need to be very constant, and does not suffer if he has neglected accumulation and aprovision [*sic*] for old age. The bounty of the whole race affords a sure refuge to any bankrupt, cripple, or pauper among their number. A kanaka can never become dead broke and dread the poor house, because he will always be welcome to fish and poi in any native hut that he enters. And so it is hard to get plantation hands out of such easy going, spending, mutually helping people.[53]

Though coffee, rice, tobacco, cotton, livestock, and silk were experimentally developed for large-scale commodity production and export, ultimately sugar proved to be the most viable and profitable to produce on a large-scale plantation basis.

Reciprocity, Overthrow, and Annexation

The critical turning point in the establishment of sugar as Hawaiʻi's principal trade commodity was the U.S. Civil War. However, when the Civil War ended and the United States imposed tariffs upon sugar imported from Hawaiʻi, a Reciprocity Treaty between Hawaiʻi and the United States was negotiated, which became effective in 1876. The reciprocity treaty stimulated the unprecedented growth of the sugar industry and Hawaiʻi's economy. Immense amounts of capital were invested in land, labor, and technological developments. The profits derived from it were reinvested in further expansion of sugar production. The phenomenal expansion of the sugar industry was under the direction and for the benefit of the American and European factor-planter-missionary elite. Native Hawaiian elite lacked the capital to invest and benefit from the sugar industry, and common Native Hawaiians were displaced from their traditional lands as the cultivation of sugar expanded. In 1893 U.S. Commissioner James Blount described the treaty in his report on the conditions that led up to the illegal overthrow of the Hawaiian monarchy: "From it there came to the islands an intoxicating increase of wealth, a new labor system, an Asiatic population, and alienation between the native and white race, and impoverishment of the former and enrichment of the latter, and the many so-called revolutions, which are the foundation for the opinion that stable government cannot be maintained."[54]

The Reciprocity Treaty effectively resulted in Hawaiʻi's becoming an economic colony of the United States. When it expired in 1886, King Kalākaua

Figure 6 In the 1890s Hawaiians still fished for subsistence off of Waikīkī, but this changed at the turn of the century when tourism developed along its shores. 1890s. J. A. Gonsalves, Hawaiian Historical Society.

was reluctant to renew it. Not to be deprived of their economic wealth, American planter interests organized a coup d'état against King David Kalākaua, forcing him to sign the Bayonet Constitution, which took away his sovereign powers as king and restricted the civil rights of Native Hawaiians. The cabinet installed by the coup renewed the Reciprocity Treaty, and the king was compelled to approve it. In 1889 eight men were killed, twelve wounded, and seventy arrested in the Wilcox Rebellion, which attempted to restore the Hawaiian constitution. By 1890 non-Hawaiians controlled 96 percent of the sugar industry, and Hawaiians were reduced to only 45 percent of the population owing to the importation of Chinese, Japanese, and Portuguese immigrant laborers by the sugar planters.

In 1893 the United States Minister assigned to the Kingdom of Hawai'i, John L. Stevens, conspired with a small group of non-Hawaiian residents of the kingdom, including citizens of the United States, to overthrow the indigenous and lawful government of Hawai'i.[55] On January 16, 1893, U.S. military forces invaded Hawai'i, and the next day a provisional government was declared. It was immediately recognized by the U.S. minister plenipotentiary to Hawai'i.

In 1898 the United States annexed Hawai'i through the Newlands Joint Resolution of Annexation without the consent of or any compensation to the indigenous Hawaiian people or their sovereign government. Hawaiians were thereby denied the mechanism for expression of their inherent sovereignty through self-government and self-determination. They also lost control over their national lands and ocean resources.[56]

Through the Newlands Joint Resolution of Annexation and the 1900 Organic Act, the Republic of Hawai'i ceded to the United States government 1.8 million acres of land owned by the Crown and government of the original Kingdom of Hawai'i. The U.S. Congress exempted these lands from the existing public land laws of the United States by mandating that the revenue and proceeds from these lands be "used solely for the benefit of the inhabitants of the Hawaiian Islands for education and other public purposes." This established a special trust relationship between the United States and the inhabitants of Hawai'i.[57]

Territorial Period

From 1900 through 1959 Hawai'i was governed as a territory of the United States. The official U.S. policy was to Americanize the multiethnic society of the Hawaiian Islands, beginning with educating Hawaiian children through the American public school system. Hawaiian and other non-English languages were banned as a medium of instruction; English was made the only official language. An elite group of Americans who were the owners and managers of what was called the Big Five factors had monopoly control over every facet of Hawaiʻi's economy.[58] They controlled the sugar plantations, shipping, banking, and commerce.

In 1900 plantations harvested 289,544 tons of sugar from 66,773 acres of Hawaiian land. By 1920 the plantations harvested 556,871 tons of sugar from 114,100 acres of Hawaiian land. This increased in 1930 to 930,627 tons of sugar from 136,136 acres of land. The security of a stable American market for Hawaiian sugar after annexation led the sugar planters to expand the number of acres planted in sugar and to invest in an infrastructure to accomplish that. Of critical importance to the expansion of the industry was the development of vast irrigation systems that carried millions of gallons of fresh water from the wet windward sides of the islands to the dry leeward plains. On Oʻahu, the planters constructed the Waiāhole tunnel and ditch system from 1913 to 1916; ultimately, stream waters from Waiheʻe to Kahana on windward Oʻahu were diverted for the production of sugar on the dry ʻEwa plains. On Maui, additional ditch systems were constructed from 1903 to 1920 to carry the waters of the Koʻolau streams from Nāhiku through Haʻikū over into Puʻunene. On Hawaiʻi, the upper and lower Hāmākua ditch systems were constructed in 1906 and 1910, respectively, and the Kohala ditch from 1905 to 1906.

The impact of these irrigation systems upon rural Hawaiian taro farmers reverberated throughout the twentieth century. Cut off from the free flow of stream waters into their *loʻi kalo* or taro pond fields, many kuaʻāina gave up taro farming and moved into the city to find new livelihoods. Some of these families stopped paying taxes on their rural lands when they moved into the city and as a result eventually lost ownership of their ancestral lands through adverse possession by plantations and ranches. In other areas, the long-term impacts led to lowering of the water table, reduction of aquatic stream life and nearshore marine life dependent on the infusion of fresh water into nearby bays, and neglect of traditional irrigation networks.

The military was another force in the Americanization of the islands. In 1908 the United States began to develop Puʻuloa into Pearl Harbor—dredging the channel and constructing a dry dock, barracks, warehouses, an ammunition depot, a submarine base, a radio center, and a hospital. By 1930 the harbor was a major industrial base for the servicing of the U.S. Pacific Fleet. At the same time, the army established bases on Hawaiian national lands under its control at Lēʻahi (Diamond Head) for Fort Ruger; at Waikiki for Fort DeRussy; at Kalihi for Fort Shafter; and in Wahiawa and the Waiʻanae mountains for Schofield Barracks. By 1941 the American naval presence at Pearl Harbor was so massive that the Japanese attacked Hawaiʻi, convinced that this would cripple the American fleet in the Pacific. The military had become the largest single source of income and employment in the Islands, thereby guaranteeing the support of a major part of Hawaiʻi's local population.

By 1900 the pure Native Hawaiian population had declined to 29,800, with another 7,800 Hawaiians of mixed ancestry. Immigrant plantation workers and their descendants made up the majority of the population, but under U.S. law first-generation Asians were excluded from becoming naturalized citizens. Thus, in the realm of politics, Native Hawaiians held the plurality of votes and controlled the legislature and the delegate to U.S. Congress up through World War II. It was not until after World War II that second-generation Asian descendants matured to voting age and became a major political force in the islands. Hawaiian leaders allied with the Big Five under the banner of the Republican Party during the Territorial years. Thanks to political patronage, Hawaiians held a majority of the government jobs and dominated certain private-sector jobs such as cowboys on ranches, longshoremen on the docks, and in the electric and telephone companies. In 1927 Hawaiians held 46 percent of executive-appointed government positions, 55 percent of clerical and other government jobs, and over half of the judgeships and elective offices. Through 1935 Hawaiians held almost one-third of the public service jobs and dominated law enforcement, although they made up only 15 percent of the population of the islands.[59]

Despite these obvious advantages, close to half the Hawaiian population failed or refused to assimilate and mainstream into the developing economy. Instead they remained in remote valleys and isolated rural pockets, providing for their large extended families through subsistence farming and fishing. During this period a major distinction internal to the Hawaiian community evolved between the urban Hawaiians who assimilated and accommodated to the socioeconomic system dominated by the American elite and the rural Hawaiians or kuaʻāina who remained in the backcountry areas and maintained a traditional Hawaiian way of life.

During the Territorial period a "local" culture combining Native Hawaiian culture with the cultures of the various immigrant groups who settled in Hawaiʻi began to evolve. Most of the immigrants who were imported to work on Hawaiʻi's plantations had been peasant farmers in their countries of origin. They shared with the majority of Hawaiians, who were planters and fishermen, a reliance upon the land and its resources and a strong respect for extended family relationships. Loyalty, respect, and caring for family elders and the overall well-being of all family members were important values that came to characterize "local" people. In rural plantation communities, the immigrant workers shared the common experience of oppressive working conditions, living in plantation camp housing, and being in constant debt to the plantation store. Children of immigrant workers and Native Hawaiians alike attended Hawaiʻi's public schools. There they were socialized by the American school system. The children learned together, ate and shared meals together, and communicated across cultural barriers in pidgin. They learned to hunt for pigs and gather fruits in the forest. They caught fish or gathered marine or aquatic life from common fishing grounds. The rate of intermarriage between Hawaiians and immigrant groups, particularly the second and third generations, was very high.

World War II ushered in major changes in the social, economic, and political life of the islands. Many Hawaiians left their rural enclaves to join the service or to work in high-paying military jobs in Honolulu. The military were also stationed in rural areas throughout the islands. The war experience broadened the social horizons and raised the expectations and aspirations of all Hawaiʻi's people for a higher standard of living. Raising the age for compulsory education to eighteen also forced rural families out of the most remote areas in order to comply with the law and send their children to intermediate and high school. There was also a large exodus of people in search of better job opportunities from Hawaiʻi to the U.S. mainland.

The tidal wave of April 1, 1946, hit many rural coastal communities with a force they were never able to recover from. The tidal wave took lives, smashed houses, tore up roads, inundated taro fields and farms, destroyed fishpond walls and breakwater walls, and scared many families into permanently moving out of their isolated low-lying rural peninsulas and valleys to live on higher ground. Many coastal communities never rebuilt. A few coastal communities became sparsely repopulated over the long course of the twentieth century.

Labor unions successfully organized workers and gained collective bargaining contracts on the docks and plantations, at utility companies, and in trans-

Figure 7 The tsunami of April 1, 1946, hit coastal cultural kīpuka with a force from which few recovered and contributed to the exodus of 'ohana to urban centers. Downtown Hilo, April 2, 1946. U.S. Army Signal Corps, Bishop Museum.

portation, hotels, restaurants, and the public sector. Leaders of the Japanese community joined ranks with labor to reorganize the Democratic Party. The Democratic Party defeated the Republican Party in 1954. Gradually Hawaiians were replaced in government jobs by Japanese. The Democratic Party led the movement to gain statehood for Hawai'i.

Statehood

Statehood stimulated unprecedented economic expansion in Hawai'i. The number of hotel rooms more than tripled, and the number of tourists increased fivefold within the first ten years. Pineapple and sugar agribusiness operations were phased out and moved to cheaper labor markets in Southeast Asia. The prime agricultural lands that remained were developed into profitable subdivision, condominium, and resort developments. Left jobless, former plantation and cannery workers had few employment options. They obtained lower-paying and less stable jobs in the expanding tourist industry. An excerpt from a social impact statement concerning the effects of a proposed freeway connecting rural Oʻahu to urban Honolulu offered an insight into the frustrations and social pressures that Hawaiian and local people began to associate with development:

> Some long-time residents have the feeling that they are being dispossessed of their traditional access to the beauties and bounties of nature around them. Anxieties arise as open space is filled up by newcomers and the taxes on land keep going up. Frustration is felt as the future character of their shrinking world is being decided by landowners and developers, government planners and elected officials in offices and meeting rooms far away. And there is a problem of the carry over of these insecurities to the younger generation. There are indications of social breakdown as reflected in the rate of unemployment, the growing incidence of family separations, the heavier welfare loads and the increase in juvenile delinquency and adult crimes.[60]

Changes to the rural and agricultural areas concerned all of Hawaiʻi's local people, but especially the Hawaiian community, because of its traditional con-

Figure 8 This photo poignantly shows the tides of change that swept through the islands when Hawaiʻi became a territory of the United States and tourists began to visit the islands, a trend that exploded after statehood. 1930s. Hawaiian Historical Society.

centration in the rural pockets. American progress seemed to be overdeveloping the islands and replacing the Native Hawaiian and local way of life. However, beginning in the 1970s, through an extraordinary convergence of events, the island of Kahoʻolawe became the focal point of a major political movement challenging American control of Hawaiʻi. This movement became a catalyst for a widespread Native Hawaiian cultural renaissance, which ultimately galvanized into a movement for Native Hawaiian recognition and sovereignty. Kahoʻolawe and the cultural renaissance that it spawned will be discussed in a later chapter of this work, as an example of the role of the kuaʻāina from the cultural kīpuka in the regeneration of Native Hawaiian culture in the late twentieth century. Moreover, the cultural renaissance highlighted the importance of the cultural kīpuka and helped reinforce the efforts of the kuaʻāina to protect their way of life from the assaults of proposed tourist and industrialization projects in their communities.

Haʻina Ia Mai Ana Kapuana: Tell the Story

Here is my moʻolelo of the Native Hawaiian kuaʻāina. May their simple lives in cultural kīpuka of the Hawaiian islands live on—not just in memory but in determined efforts to protect and perpetuate their way of life and to have the people of Hawaiʻi attain and live lōkāhi.

❦ TWO ❧

Waipiʻo Mano Wai:
Waipiʻo, Source of Water and Life

During a spell of great drought, when a great famine was experienced all
over the lands from Hawaii to Kauai all the wet lands were parched and the
crops dried up on account of the drought, so nothing remained even in the
mountains. Waipio was the only land where the water had not dried up, and
it was the only land where food was in abundance; and the people from all
parts of Hawaii and as far as Maui came to this place for food.

—ABRAHAM FORNANDER, *Fornander Collection of Hawaiian Antiquities*, vol. 4

WAIPIʻO MANO WAI (Waipiʻo, source of water and life) is a popular
saying about Waipiʻo because of its ability to sustain the people
of Hawaiʻi and Maui during an early thirteenth-century drought
and enable them to survive. Located on the Hāmākua Coast of the island of
Hawaiʻi, the remote, lush, and peaceful Hawaiian valley of Waipiʻo is rich in
natural resources, of which water is the most significant and abundant. For 650
years, from the time of ʻUmialīloa, around 1450 CE, through to the twenty-
first century, Waipiʻo has been renowned as one of the premier wetland taro
valleys of the Hawaiian Islands.

Picturesque Waipiʻo Valley lies across nine square miles, or 6,100 acres. At
the river's mouth, along the ocean shore, Waipiʻo is a little more than three-
fourths of a mile wide, and its floor continues broad and nearly flat for about
three and a half miles inland. There the valley narrows to 600 feet wide and
then extends into a deep gorge for another five miles.[1] At the mouth of the
valley, the walls of Waipiʻo are 1,000 to 1,300 feet high. Two miles inland
they are 2,000 to 2,300 feet high, and six miles inland the valley walls rise to
3,000 feet. Five tributary streams form *ʻili* or smaller valleys that make up the
greater Waipiʻo Valley—Hiʻilawe, Waimā, Kuiawa, Alakahi, and Kawainui.
These streams cascade down the sheer Waipiʻo cliffs in long, silvery, majestic
waterfalls. Hiʻilawe, the largest and most prominent of these waterfalls, is

Figure 9 *Waipi'o mano wai,* source of water and life—past, present, and future. 1974. Franco Salmoiraghi.

widely celebrated in two famous songs about Waipi'o—"Hi'ilawe" and "Waipi'o."[2] Two large streams and several small ones traverse the valley floor, depositing the fertile alluvial soil that makes the land ideal for the planting of taro. The streams converge into one large river about half a mile inland before emptying into the ocean. The primary natural hazards in the valley are high winds, floods, and tsunamis.

Historically, water for all of the taro land was plentiful. It ran through *'auwai* or irrigation ditches and flumes into the taro pond fields. Frequent rains kept the streams and 'auwai running steadily. Only wetland taro was raised in Waipi'o. Numerous great old trees grow along the stream and at the base of the hillsides. Overall, the valley is wet and cool.

A Traditional Center of Spiritual Power

The natural beauty and abundant natural resources of Waipi'o are celebrated in legend and oral tradition in accounts of the many spiritual deities who are believed to have lived in the valley during their time on the earth. These spiritual forces are honored as ancestors of great, powerful, and prominent Hawaiian chiefs. The productive kua'āina of Waipi'o cultivated and sustained the valley's rich resources and enabled their chiefs to prevail against and ultimately dominate the chiefs and people of the entire island of Hawai'i.

Wākea, God of the sky, mated with Papa, Goddess of the earth, and she gave birth to the islands of Hawai'i. In his old age, Wākea is said to have retired to Waipi'o to live out the rest of his days.[3] The godly Milu succeeded Wākea as chief in Waipi'o. The brother Gods Kāne and Kanaloa, who traveled throughout the islands opening up freshwater springs to mix with their *'awa*, dwelt at Alakahi in Waipi'o in company with lesser Gods.[4] Maui, the demigod associated with fishing throughout the islands, lifting the sky, slowing the pace of the sun across the sky, and stealing the secret of fire making from the Gods, obtained the Ipumakaniakamaumau (gourd of constant winds) from the kahuna Kaleiiolu in Waipi'o Valley in order to fly his kite. Maui also fought with Kāne and Kanaloa at Waipi'o. According to legend, they killed Maui in Waipi'o when he tried to steal their bananas.[5]

Puapualenalena, a *kupua* or spirit in the form of a dog, lived in Waipi'o. He was a great thief who was caught stealing the sacred and restricted 'awa of the chief. In order to earn his pardon, Puapualenalena had to steal the magic conch shell, Kihapū, from the spirits who lived above Waipi'o and who constantly disturbed the people of the valley by blowing on it at all hours of the night.[6] The spirit dog returned Kihapū to the Waipi'o chiefs. In the twentieth century, the major landowner in Waipi'o, the Bernice Pauahi Bishop Museum, exhibited the Kihapū as part of its permanent Hawaiian artifact display.

Nanaue was a shark-man born in Waipi'o Valley. He frequented the pool at the base of Waipi'o Falls and preyed upon his neighbors when they went swimming or fishing in the ocean. When discovered as the shark who attacked and ate the people of Waipi'o, he escaped to Hāna and then went on to Moloka'i, where he was finally killed at a place thenceforth named Pu'u Mano or Shark Hill.[7]

Lonoikamakahiki first met his beautiful wife, Kaikilani, in Waipi'o Valley beside the falls of Hi'ilawe, where she dwelled in a breadfruit grove. Waipi'o became the resting place of the *ka'ai* or woven sennit casket that held his sacred remains.[8]

Migratory Chiefs

In the mo'olelo of Waipi'o, the migratory chief Olopana settled in the valley and married Lu'ukia. There they lived with Olopana's brother, Mo'ikeha, and their sister, Hainakolo. When the valley was devastated by a flood, Olopana and Lu'ukia set out for Kahiki. In some accounts, Olopana was accompanied by his brother, the chief Moʻikeha; in others, Moʻikeha was already living in Kahiki.

Moʻikeha later returned to Hawaiʻi but settled at Kapaʻa, Kauaʻi, where he became the ruling chief of that island. Upon his death, his son Kila became the ruling chief of Kauaʻi. His brothers, jealous of Kila's status, enticed him away to Waipiʻo and abandoned him there. In Waipiʻo, Kila lived as a commoner until his rank was discovered by a priest of the Pakaʻalana heiau. He was adopted by Kunaka, then chief of Waipiʻo, who made him a *konohiki* or land agent. As land agent he is credited with introducing the system under which the common people were obliged to work a set number of days for the chief. Later the evil deed of his brothers was exposed and punished. Kila, however, remained in Waipiʻo, leaving only to journey to Tahiti with Laʻamaikahiki in order to deposit the bones of his father, Moʻikeha.[9]

Pilikaeaea, the chief who, according to oral tradition, was brought by Paʻao from Tahiti to rule Hawaiʻi in the year 1090, first established his reign in Waipiʻo Valley.[10] Through intermarriage with descendants of the Nanaulu or Ulu line of indigenous rulers he established the Pili line of rulers of Waipiʻo, from whom Kamehameha I ultimately descended.

The Ruling Chiefs

In 1240 the ruling chief of Waipiʻo, Kahaʻimoelea, built up the royal residence in Waipiʻo.[11] He was succeeded in 1270 by his son Kalaunuiohua, who is famous for having waged successful wars of conquest against the chiefs of Maui, Molokaʻi, and Oʻahu. He might have been the first ruling chief to unite all of the islands under his control if he had not been defeated by the high chief of Kauaʻi.[12] About 1390 Kihanuilulumoku, grandfather of ʻUmialīloa, ruled Waipiʻo.

ʻUmialīloa is estimated to have ruled over Waipiʻo around 1450.[13] At that time, with the extensive taro lands of Waipiʻo as a resource base, ʻUmialīloa conquered the entire island of Hawaiʻi and ruled it as one chiefdom. He then moved the capital of the island chiefdom away from Waipiʻo to Kailua-Kona. ʻUmialīloa constructed a system of heiau associated with astronomical observation and the maintenance of a lunar and solar calendar. ʻUmialīloa was one of the greatest ruling chiefs of Hawaiʻi, noted not only for his conquest of Hawaiʻi but also for his contributions to the social and economic development of the island, especially in farming and fishing. He is credited with developing the systematic cultivation of taro in Waipiʻo, using terraces and irrigation ditches and the expansion of paved roads linking Kona and Ka'ū up across the mountains.[14] The Hawaiian historian Samuel Kamakau described his contributions:

> During 'Umi-a-Līloa's reign he selected workers and set them in various positions in the kingdom. He separated those of the chiefly class (papa ali'i), of the priestly class, of the readers of omens (papakilo), those skilled in the affairs of the land (po'e akamai o ka 'āina), farmers, fishermen, canoe builders, warriors, and other skilled artisans (po'e pale 'ike) in the work they were best suited for; and each one applied himself to his own task.
>
> 'Umi-a-Liloa did two things with his own hands, farming and fishing. He built some large wet taro patches in Waipi'o, and farming was done on all the lands. Much of this was done in Kona. He was noted for his skill in fishing and was called Pu'ipu'i a ka lawai'a (a stalwart fisherman).[15]

In more recent history, Kamehameha I was raised in the districts of Kohala and Waipi'o from infancy to boyhood.

Associated with these high-ranking and sacred chiefs were the most sacred heiau on the Hawai'i island—Paka'alana, Hale o Līloa, Honua'ula, Hokuwelo-welo, Moa'ula, and Kuahailo (Kuwahailo). Of these, the most revered was Paka'alana, and it was built before the time of Kila. At the time of Kila and Kunaka it functioned as both a *luakini heiau* or sacrificial temple and a *pu'u-honua* or place of refuge. Līloa built the luakini heiau Honua'ula and dedicated it to Ka'ili. When Līloa died, his son Hakau built the Hale o Līloa or mausoleum for his father's ka'ai, which held the *'iwi* or sacred remains of Līloa.[16] Moa'ula Heiau was built by Hakau but dedicated by his half brother 'Umialīloa, who sacrificed Hakau as the first offering. Hokuwelowelo Heiau is in the Lālākea 'ili of Waipi'o. It is said to have been built by the Gods and was where the magic conch shell, Kihapū, was guarded until it was stolen by the mischievous spirits and later returned by Puapualenalena. In the Ka'au 'ili of Waipi'o is the Kuahailo Heiau or Kuwahailo Heiau, which, according to oral tradition, was built by Kuwahailo, one of the ancient Gods of Hawai'i, who named it after himself. He is believed to have lived in a cave in a small side valley near the top of the south cliff.[17]

Wars of Kamehameha

Indicative of the continued prominence of Waipi'o at the time of High Chief Kamehameha are two fierce attacks upon Waipi'o, as a central base of support for Kamehameha. In 1790 High Chief Kamehameha launched a war against High Chief Kahekili of Maui with the assistance of canoes provided by High Chief Keawemaʻuhili of Hilo. While Kamehameha was at war on Maui, High Chief Keouakūahuʻula of Kaʻu decided to make war on Keawemaʻuhili and to ravage the lands of Kamehameha, including Waipiʻo. According to Samuel Kamakau, Keouakūahuʻula killed Keawemaʻuhili at Alae in Hilopalikū and then carried the war to Hāmākua. Kamakau provides an account of the ruthless attack on Waipiʻo by Keouakūahuʻula: "He descended into Waipiʻo and broke down the fishponds, drying up Lālākea, Muliwai, and all the other ponds. He pulled up the taro of Waipiʻo, broke down the banks of the taro patches, and robbed the people from Waipiʻo to Waimea." [18]

Learning of the attacks upon his people, High Chief Kamehameha suspended his war against High Chief Kahekili and returned to Hawaiʻi to retaliate against High Chief Keouakūahuʻula and protect his people. High Chief Kamehameha was able to rout Keouakūahuʻula from Kohala, Waimea, and Hāmākua. He then ordered his people from these districts to farm the land and restore it to prosperity. Kamehameha was able to retain his rule over Hāmākua, Kohala, and Kona, while Keouakūahuʻula succeeded in expanding his control beyond Kaʻu to the districts of Hilo, and Puna, lands previously ruled over by High Chief Keawemauhili, whom Keouakūahuʻula had slain. [19]

The second major attack upon Waipiʻo was a year later, in 1791. High Chief Kaʻeokulani of Kauaʻi, in league with High Chief Kahekili of Maui, invaded Waipiʻo from Hana. According to Samuel Kamakau, High Chief Kaʻeokulani rallied his men from Kauaʻi, saying, "O you of Kauai! chiefs, soldiers, warriors, and dear little ones, be strong, be brave! Drink the water of Waipiʻo and eat the taro of Kunaka!" Upon landing at Waipiʻo, Kaʻeokulani viciously plundered the valley:

> They landed at Waipiʻo. There Kaʻeokulani carried out his vow. He
> wantonly destroyed everything in Waipiʻo. He overthrew the sacred
> places and the tabu threshold of Līloa; he set fire to Kahoukapu's sacred
> threshold of nioi wood and utterly destroyed all the places held sacred for
> years by the people of Hawaiʻi. No one before him, not even Keoua who
> had passed through there the year before and destroyed the land and the
> food had made such wanton destruction. [20]

In retaliation, Kamehameha engaged the forces of Kaʻeokulani and Kahekili in the ocean off of the cliffs of Waimanu in what is called the Battle of Kepūwahaʻula the Red-Mouthed Cannon. The battle was named for Kamehameha's Western cannons, which were manned by his British advisors Isaac Davis and John Young.

> It was because of the sound of the cannons (pū kuni ahi), the firing of the muskets, and the flame flashing from these weapons that this battle was called the Battle of the Red-Mouthed Cannon . . . After a hot battle between the two sides, it was seen that most of the damage was done to Ka'eokulani and his companion, Kahekili. The greater part of his fleet was sunk, and some of the men of those canoes swam to other canoes so that Ka'eokulani and Kahekili began to seek means of escaping being taken prisoner by Kamehameha . . . Kamehameha's forces had also received damage. Some of his canoes had sunk, having been struck by cannon balls from the other side.[21]

Warriors and canoes on both sides were lost. The battle ended indecisively, and Ka'eokulani and Kahekili managed to escape back to Hāna.

Passing of the Sacred

Upon the death of King Kamehameha I, successor chiefs abolished the sacred kapu or religious distinctions of the chiefs and the sanctity of their places of worship. However, the sacred sites of Waipi'o continued to function as centers of religious worship. William Ellis's 1823 description of the valley estimated that there were 1,325 kua'āina who lived in 265 houses in the valley and farmed and fished for their livelihoods. There was no developed trail into the valley. Entry required sliding down the sides of the cliff and clinging to trees and bushes on the way down. Ellis's journal reveals a valley heavily cultivated by the kua'āina of Waipi'o, who also continued to honor the sacred bones of their ancestral chiefs.

> The bottom of the valley was one continuous garden, cultivated with taro, bananas, sugar cane, and other productions of the islands, all growing luxuriantly. Several large ponds were also seen in different directions, well stocked with excellent fish. A number of small villages, containing from twenty to fifty houses each stood along the foot of the mountains, at unequal distances on each side, and extended up the valley till projecting cliffs obstructed the view.[22]

According to Ellis, the Hale o Līloa, where the 'iwi of Līloa were enshrined, stood intact within an enclosure of the Paka'alana heiau under a wide-spreading *hala* tree. In light of its status as an active and sacred place of worship, the man in charge of the heiau did not allow Ellis to enter the Hale o Līloa:

> We tried, but could not gain admittance to the pahu tabu, or sacred enclosure. We also endeavoured to obtain a sight of the bones of Riroa, but the man who had charge of the house told us we must offer a hog before we could be admitted; that Tamehameha, whenever he entered, had always sent offerings; that Rihoriho, since he had become king, had done the same, and that no one could be admitted on other conditions.[23]

Six years later, in 1829, High Chiefess Kaʻahumanu, who had converted to Christianity and was the regent for King Kamehameha III, made a special trip to this heiau on a personal mission to end the persistent idolatrous worship of the sacred chiefs of Waipiʻo.[24] She removed 6 chiefly kaʻai of deified Waipiʻo chiefs that Native Hawaiians had continued to actively honor and worship. Among these were kaʻai that contained the iwi of the high chiefs Līloa, Lono-ikamakahiki, Kauhola, and Lole.[25] Subsequently, High Chiefess Kaʻahumanu also journeyed to Honaunau to remove the kaʻai of twenty-three deified chiefs from the Hale o Keawe. The kaʻai from Waipiʻo and Honaunau were taken to the cave of Hoʻaiku in the great cliff at Kaʻawaloa and concealed.[26]

On the eve of the Māhele in 1847 the missionary Hiram Bingham wrote of Waipiʻo's "numerous garden-like plantations of bananas, sugar cane, potatoes, the cloth plant and the kalo, in different stages of advancement." He estimated the population at 1,200 to 1,500 Hawaiians.[27]

Despite the numerous kuaʻāina living in Waipiʻo, only 102 land awards totaling 374 acres were made under the 1848 Māhele and 1850 Kuleana Act in Waipiʻo Valley. The bulk of the land, 5,800 acres, was claimed by and awarded to Queen Hakaleleponi Kapakuhaili (Hazalaleponi) Kalama, wife of Kaui-keaouli, King Kamehameha III.[28] Most of the area of Waikoloa in Waipiʻo, listed as an ahupuaʻa with unspecified acreage, was awarded to William Pitt Leleiohoku. Until her death on December 30, 1836, Leleiohoku was married to High Chiefess Nahiʻenaʻena, daughter of Kamehameha I with Keʻōpūo-lani, and sister of Kamehameha II and Kamehameha III. At the time of the māhele, Leleiohoku was married to Princess Ruth Keʻelikolani, a half sister of Alexander Liholiho, Kamehameha IV, and Lot Kamehameha, Kamehameha V. Princess Ruth inherited Leleiohoku's lands upon his death in 1850. Ultimately these lands became part of the Bernice Pauahi Bishop Estate. An unspecified number of acres were granted to Mary Kaoanaeha as an ʻiliʻāina in the area within Waipiʻo called Kalaokui. Kaoanaeha was the daughter of the

English officer John Young, who had played a critical role in the victory of
Kamehameha in the Battle of Kepūwahaʻula. Her mother, also named Kaoanaeha, was the daughter of Keliʻimaikaʻi, a brother of King Kamehameha I.[29]
The 374 acres awarded to the kuaʻāina of Waipiʻo ranged in size from half an
acre to fifteen acres, with an average size of three and half acres per award.

The forces of change that transformed the Hawaiian Islands as a whole also
penetrated the rural isolation that otherwise buffered Waipiʻo. The flu epidemic of 1850 had a devastating impact on the Hawaiian families in the val-

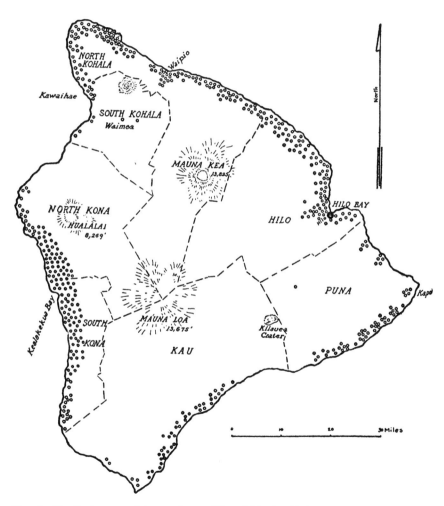

Map 1   The Coulter map of the population of Hawaiʻi Island in 1853 indicates a population of
750 in Waipiʻo Valley. The Puna section indicates a population of 2,850 persons in 1853.
○ = 50 persons. *Source:* Coulter, *Population and Utilization of Land and Sea,* p. 28.

ley. Though the number of persons who succumbed to the flu is not recorded, the impact can be measured by the food shortages that resulted from the debilitating effects of the epidemic upon the kua'āina of Waipi'o. The Waimea district, which depended upon Waipi'o for food, experienced shortages because regular deliveries of taro from Waipi'o were interrupted.[30] As shown in map 1, John W. Coulter estimated that the population in Waipi'o had declined to 750 in 1853.

Six years later, in 1859, the congregational church was completed in Waipi'o. However, no mission station was ever established in the valley itself. The ministers who served the people of the valley were based in Waimea and in Kohala and made periodic visits to Waipi'o. The lack of a permanent mission station in Waipi'o meant Christianity presented less of a direct threat to the traditional Native Hawaiian spiritual beliefs and practices that persisted among the kua'āina who were born and raised in the valley.[31]

The kua'āina of Waipi'o continued to actively raise taro for markets through Hawai'i Island. The *Pacific Commercial Advertiser* of May 5, 1866, reported that *pa'i'ai* or hard, pounded, undiluted taro would be shipped rather than transported overland to Kawaihae, Kona, Ka'u, and Hilo by the farmers of Waipi'o. According to the article, the people of Waipi'o had formed an association and declared that they would not take their poi to the market but would instead have the market come to them via supply ships. The writer observed that Waipi'o "probably furnishes more of the Hawaiian staff of life than any equal area of land on the islands."[32]

In 1867 Father Bond visited Waipi'o and commented on the trade that had developed between Waipi'o and the surrounding districts. He was singularly impressed with the enterprising qualities of the 640 Waipi'o Hawaiians whom he estimated to reside in the valley.

> The rich bottom of Waipio Valley affords inexhaustible quantities of food for Hilo and South Kohala, as well as for Hāmākua markets; and the people, accordingly, have a thrifty, well-to-do appearance; and what was particularly gratifying to my own mind, was the open wide-awake countenances which met our gaze in the congregation; and not less the spirit and bearing of independence, which made the people seem to me more like our own than had any previous gathering with whom we have met.[33]

In 1880 George Bowser observed only thirty to forty houses in Waipi'o Valley and estimated the population to be reduced to 150. As a result, he noted, only half of the valley floor was under cultivation in both taro and rice. The following year Charles Reed Bishop bought land in the ahupuaʻa of Waipiʻo from Hazaleleponi Kalama at a public auction. Fifteen years later, in 1896, Bishop donated these lands to the Bernice Pauahi Bishop Museum.[34]

Despite the social changes affecting the island of Hawaiʻi, when Isabella Bird stood at the overlook at the top of the *pali* (cliff) and looked down into Waipiʻo in 1886, she observed a productive and thriving Native Hawaiian community of farmers and fishermen.

> I should think the valley is not more than three miles long, and it is walled in by high inaccessible mountains. It is in fact, a gulch on a vastly enlarged scale. The prospect below us was very charming, a fertile region perfectly level, protected from the sea by sandhills, watered by a winding stream, and bright with fishponds, meadow lands, kalo patches, orange and coffee groves, figs, breadfruit and [coconut] palms. There were a number of grass-houses, and a native church with a spire, and another up the valley.[35]

Chinese Influence and the Turn of the Twentieth Century

Between 1880 and 1920 the valley's Native Hawaiian population was augmented by the influx of Chinese whose contracts with the neighboring plantations at Honokaʻa and Kukuihaele had expired. Many intermarried with the daughters of the kuaʻāina living in the valley. They subleased Bishop Museum lands in order to cultivate rice on a commercial basis—first from Samuel Parker and later from the Hawaii Ditch Company (later called the Hawaiian Irrigation Company). Through 1901 the Bishop Museum lands were leased to Parker for $7,500 a year. He grazed cattle in the upper valley and subleased portions of the lower valley to rice and taro farmers.[36] The population is estimated to have grown from 150 to over 1,000 during this period. Though the increase was largely due to new Chinese residents, because of intermarriage there were always more full and part Hawaiians than full-blooded Chinese in Waipiʻo Valley.[37]

On January 1, 1901, a new twenty-one-year lease was negotiated with Parker that contained a clause requiring that outside offers be made for surplus water and water power from the lands. Parker was given sixty days to meet the offer or otherwise lose the lease. In 1904 the Hawaii Ditch Company made an offer to the Bishop Museum for Waipiʻo's water that Parker did not care to meet. By mutual agreement, the lease was transferred to the Hawaii Ditch

Company for the remainder of its term at an annual rent of $3,000. The Hawaii Ditch Company was primarily interested in the upper valley, where it developed an extensive irrigation system.

In 1907 the Hāmākua Ditch Company constructed the Upper Hāmākua Ditch, which diverted water from the Kawainui, Alakahi, and Koʻiawe streams above Waipiʻo. Upon its completion, the upper ditch was able to deliver 15 million gallons per day to various sugar mills along the Hāmākua coast. Soon thereafter, the Hawaiian Irrigation Company began to construct the twenty-five-mile Lower Hāmākua Ditch to supply water for cane fluming, mill operations, and domestic water systems along the Hāmākua Coast outside of Waipiʻo Valley. When it was completed in 1910 it was able to carry 30 million gallons of water a day from three of the five streams that feed Waipiʻo itself —Kawainui, Alakahi, Koʻiawe.

The company continued to lease out the lower valley for taro and rice cultivation and the grazing of cattle. In 1915, for example, it had 151 acres subleased for taro and rice at $25 per acre per year, from which it grossed $3,775.[38]

By 1906 there was one store in Waipiʻo Valley, and it was owned by a Chinese family. There were two churches, a Congregational and a Catholic church, in the valley.[39] Seven Chinese rice growers grew large quantities of rice in the valley with twelve to thirty helpers apiece. At harvest time, tin cans were strung out over all the paddies on long cords attached to a central tower. When the cords were pulled, the tin cans banged throughout the valley and scared the birds away.[40]

Hawaiians never grew rice. They continued to cultivate taro for both home consumption and outside markets throughout this period in the upper part of the valley, where the streams flowed swift and cold. In the lower valley, where the streams meandered and slowed in their flow, the water was warmer. These lands were marginal for growing taro and were therefore leased to Chinese for rice cultivation.[41]

David Makaoi, who was born in 1904 and lived in Waipiʻo Valley from the age of two until he was fifteen, provides a description of how the valley looked in the early twentieth century:

> Well, it was beautiful in my time. We had rice patches near the ocean. And then, taro patches further up in the valley. Hardly any trees on the floor. Course there were guava groves along the edges of the stream, you know. Especially rice patches at a certain time of the year when they were just

young, nice and green. You see green patches down there along near the beach. And then, before harvest time they were all yellow. So, it was one color one time, and another the next time . . . further up were the taro patches . . . taro farms . . . most were operated by the Chinese—for the Chinese poi factories. They had their own taro farms, to grind their poi. But once in awhile, if they were short of taro, they came to buy some from Hawaiians.[42]

In 1917, near the end of World War I, the price of rice soared, and Waipi'o rice farmers prospered. However, disaster struck in the form of floods in April and December 1918. The April flood damaged 25 percent of the rice crop. The December flood destroyed 50 percent of the rice crop.[43] After 1918 the cost of labor increased, and the prices for taro and rice began to decline. One by one the Chinese gave up their rice fields, and the growers and their helpers moved out of the cottages they had built upon their leased lands. As more and more of the land was abandoned, the Hawaiian Irrigation Company steadily lost its income from the subleases.[44]

The last grass houses built in Waipi'o were dedicated by Native Hawaiian families in 1920 in accordance with traditional Native Hawaiian rituals. Once the framework was completed, the 'ohana baked a pig together with taro and lauloa in an *imu* or underground oven in the center of the house. When the food was cooked and the imu opened, the owner and everyone who was to live in the house sat down and ate the pig and vegetables. They saved the bones and threw them into the stream for their 'aumakua. After this ceremony, the house would be thatched, and the door opening would be made by the kahuna.[45]

In 1922 the Bishop Museum signed a new thirty-two-year lease with the Hawaiian Irrigation Company for an annual rent of $3,000 or, at the museum's discretion, at the rate of 5 percent of the market value of products obtained from the land. The president and manager of Hawaiian Irrigation claimed to be losing money on the lease because of low lease rents that, combined, totaled only $150 per annum. The cost of re-leasing and collecting rents from their Chinese tenants, paying the land tax, and keeping up roads, fences, and buildings was higher that the amount of money collected from the lease rents.[46]

The last rice crop raised in Waipi'o Valley was harvested in 1927. Rice produced in Waipi'o was simply too expensive compared to that imported from California. In 1928 it cost $4.50 to produce a 100-pound bag of rice in Waipi'o, while a 100-pound bag of rice grown in California could be purchased in Hilo for $2.98.[47] With the phasing out of rice production in Waipiʻo, families moved out of the valley, and the population decreased to 271 in 1930. Of this number, 178 people, or 66 percent, were Hawaiian. Of the remaining 34 percent, 63 persons were Chinese, 9 were Japanese, 2 were Korean, and 19 were Filipino, according to the 1930 census.[48]

Waipiʻo Valley, circa 1931

Circa 1931 Waipiʻo typified the remote and secluded cultural kīpuka described by Andrew Lind and studied by E. S. Craighill Handy, Elizabeth Handy, and Mary Kawena Pukui. The small community was predominantly Native Hawaiian, and the pace of life was slower than that of people exposed to the social and economic changes that were transforming the rest of the island.

In 1931 the anthropologist Stella Jones conducted fieldwork in Waipiʻo Valley. The unedited and unpublished transcription of her interviews with the Native Hawaiian residents provide a unique snapshot image of the life of the kuaʻāina in Waipiʻo Valley in 1931. This account is augmented by oral history interviews conducted in 1978 by the Ethnic Studies Oral History Project of people who grew up in Waipiʻo Valley around 1931. Together, these shared memories provide insight into the lives of the kuaʻāina of Waipiʻo and are representative of the lives of kuaʻāina in other similarly situated cultural kīpuka throughout the islands of Hawaiʻi at that point in time. For this reason, I will explore the life of the kuaʻāina in Waipiʻo in 1931 through the shared moʻolelo of those who directly experienced it.

Community

According to Jones, only 200 people lived in Waipiʻo Valley in 1931. Of this number, there were twenty children who were under school age, fifty-four children who were enrolled in one of the six grades of the one-room elementary school in the valley, and ten children who walked up the pali to the intermediate school at Kukuihaele. A number of children had been hānai or informally adopted into Hawaiian families upon the death of one of their parents.

Most of the young adults went to intermediate school in Kukuihaele. Those who pursued high school had to live in Hilo, returning home only during school breaks. However, once they completed their schooling, the majority of high school graduates sought jobs outside the valley and did not return to live and to raise their families. Usually, one of the children remained behind to care for the kuleana and to look after the old folks. In one Hawaiian family with three boys, the oldest boy worked as a draftsman in Honolulu; the second boy worked as a machinist in Honolulu; and the third boy remained in the valley and farmed with his parents.

The Waipi‘o school had six grades in two rooms, three grades per room. David Makaoi described the classes: "The teacher cannot talk to all at once. So, what he would do is to talk to one class in one subject and then go on down the line. Each time he takes the next class, the previous class would have to do their written assignment in class . . . Of course if you finish your homework before time, your classwork, you can tune in on what they're saying."[49] The teachers were very strict. For any little offense the teacher would whack the students with a yardstick. Some teachers would hit the students' heads against the blackboard for making a mistake.

School started at eight o'clock in the morning. The children would get up at seven o'clock and eat a simple breakfast of taro, or maybe nothing at all. Recess was short, and lunch, was just a half hour. Lunches were not served, so the children were expected to bring their meal to school. Some of the Hawaiian children would take fish and poi; others just took a couple of crackers; many simply skipped the meal. If they were fortunate to earn some money by picking lū‘au leaves for the poi factory, serenading at Christmas or New Year's time, or selling frogs or fish, the children would buy something from the store, usually bread with butter and jelly. Half a loaf of bread with jelly sold for only five cents. Sometimes wild beans similar to lima beans were boiled, pounded into a paste, and wrapped up for lunch. The Chinese children usually had money to buy their meal. Often the children would exchange lunches.[50]

Subjects taught in the school in Waipi‘o ranged from English, history, and geography to math and hygiene. They did not teach physical education. The children did work in the school garden, however, once a week. Each child could choose his or her own little patch to raise something such as peanuts or beans.

After school, the children had chores to perform. They would have to haul fresh water in buckets for the family and also gather and chop wood for cooking. Sometimes they could earn anywhere from two to five cents by hauling water and carrying wood for the Chinese. The children also fed any animals the family raised, such as pigs and chickens. Some of the children also performed chores in the morning before school started. They might have to mix the poi for the family's breakfast or lunch and make the coffee. Those with cows would milk them in the morning and cut grass for them in the afternoon.[51]

When their chores were done on weekends and during the summer vacation, the children swam and fished in the streams and mountain pools and played marbles, hide and seek, bean bag, and other such games. Sometimes they challenged each other to see who could catch the most fish. They also constructed their own toys: they would make a ball by stuffing rags inside a larger bag and sewing it up or make cars and trucks out of wood, spools, and soda-water corks.[52]

David Makaoi provided a vivid description of his childhood days in Waipi'o:

> Once in awhile they had maybe a baseball game between some Waipio boys and somebody from Kukuihaele. Not every time though, but just once in a rare while. So, the rest of the time, you just had to find your own recreation. Fishing, swimming, things like that. Just on your own . . . I went fishing. I had so many places to fish, too . . . We had to work most of the time so if we had a free time—of course, we went to swim at Nenewe Falls, or even in the streams. And of course when holidays came I enjoyed playing music.[53]

With the exception of the ten kuleana, most homes were built upon land leased from the Bishop Museum. Most of the Hawaiians' homes were small and very old; the larger homes were owned by Chinese. The Hawaiian dwellings usually included a *lanai* or extended porch that was thatched with braided coconut leaves. For a typical family there was one bedroom for the parents; a living room, where the children slept; and a small lanai. The parents had a *koa* wood bed, but the children simply put a sheet or mat on the floor and slept with a blanket and a pillow.[54]

Only one thatched house remained in the valley in 1931. It was thatched with sugarcane and occupied only intermittently by a Japanese fisherman who lived there while watching over the mullet pond.

Most of the Hawaiian households raised a few pigs, which were penned near the homesites. They also raised a few chickens on taro peelings from the poi factory. The chickens were usually killed for a feast at Christmas, and a pig was usually cooked in an imu for a New Year's lū'au. Pigs were also cooked for lū'au on other special occasions, especially for a baby lū'au, held on a child's first birthday.

The few Chinese had garden plots around their homes where they grew peanuts, lettuce, cabbage, onions, parsley, bitter melons, and tomatoes. They also raised Muscovy ducks and pigeons for home consumption.

Land Tenure

In 1931 there were ten Native Hawaiian–owned kuleana, estimated to total 100 acres. The rest of the taro land in the valley was primarily owned by one major landowner, the Bishop Museum and leased to the Hāmākua Ditch Company. The Honoka'a Sugar Company managed the land for the ditch company. The annual rental for taro land ran from $20 a patch to $50 an acre per year, which the Hawaiians considered to be inconsistent. For example, a Mr. Kanekoa rented two acres for $52 a year, while a Mr. Kaohemoku paid $40 for only three-quarters of an acre.[55] About 100 acres of land in the valley were not planted in taro. Waipi'o residents felt that this deliberate practice enabled the landowner to maintain a high price for the cultivated taro lands.[56]

At one time the Hāmākua Ditch Company let the uncultivated land be used for pasturage at a cost of 50 cents a head per month. However, by 1931 the company had subleased all of the pasture land to one Chinese immigrant, Mock Chew, who charged $1 a head per month for all cattle, horses, mules, and donkeys over six months old that were not penned up.[57] Most of the horses and mules were owned by Chinese and kept fenced in upon pasture land that they leased directly from the Hāmākua Ditch Company. Several Native Hawaiian families owned approximately 200 head of free-roaming cattle, which sometimes wandered outside of the pasture area and damaged the taro. They did not have enough grass to produce good milk. Most of the Hawaiians in the valley felt that Mock Chew should not have been allowed the privilege of charging a fee for pasturage on these cattle when he made no effort to cultivate good pasture land or to provide fences.

Livelihoods

Most of the kua'āina worked for themselves. They lived primarily on poi and freshwater fish, occasionally eating meat or seafood. They cultivated and harvested their own taro, which was cooked and pounded for home consumption. They also made their own fishing nets and caught the fish themselves.

Twice a week, the Hawaiian taro farmers would take boiled taro to the Chinese poi factory owner to sell. When the Hawaiians wanted to earn cash, they would work for the Chinese in the taro patches, at the factory, or by hauling taro out of the valley. A few of the residents in 1931, such as Sam

Kaaekuahiwi, principal of Waipiʻo School, John Thomas, and Mr. Wilson, were educators in the Waipiʻo school and at Kukuihaele. There were no professional fishermen in the valley. Sometimes, when the Chinese wanted to earn extra money, they would fish out in the ocean and sell their catch outside the valley. Native Hawaiians who fished the deep sea did so only for home consumption.

Taro Production: The Major Livelihood in Waipiʻo

From cleaning the land to scraping freshly steamed corms, taro was the mainstay of the Hawaiians of Waipiʻo. Most of the Hawaiians did not plant taro for sale. Instead, they usually planted only enough taro for home consumption.[58] The men maintained the loʻi kalo—cleaning the banks, planting, weeding, and harvesting. The families would cook enough taro for the week. The women and children in the family peeled the taro with coconut shells. Then the men would pound the poi on a board, using a stone to mash the cooked taro with water. Some families used a big board about five feet long, and the men would sit at either end and pound the poi. The taro was usually mashed into *paʻiʻai*, wrapped in *ti* leaves, and placed in a wooden barrel. At each meal,

Figure 10 The Mock Chew family, descendants of Hawaiian and Chinese farmers in Waipiʻo Valley, sit on the front steps that, before the 1946 tsunami, led into their family home. 1974. Franco Salmoiraghi.

66

the amount of pa'i'ai needed would be taken out of the barrel and mixed with water to eat as poi.[59]

Sam Kaaekuahiwi described the steps involved in cultivating taro.[60] First, the land was cleared of weeds and grass. Then the soil was plowed and left dry for one week. After one week, water was let in and the lo'i lay flooded for three weeks. At that point, the farmers harrowed the land using a horse, a mule, or an ox. When the land had been properly prepared, the taro shoots were planted in twos in alternate rows, two feet apart. The lo'i was kept wet the entire time for the first three to four months, the water regulated so that it just covered the roots and so the correct amount of cool running water flowed through the patch. The patch was also weeded periodically. Fertilizer was not used at this time.[61] One man could take care of about 6 acres of taro alone. With one worker he could usually farm ten acres.

Different varieties of taro matured at different rates. The *api'i taro*, called the short taro, matured in 8 or 9 months. It included the *'apu wai* and *lehua* varieties of taros. The *uaua* taro, called long taro, took eighteen months to mature. It included the *uaua elele, uaua piko*, and *uaua molino* varieties. These taros could even be left in the field up to two or two and a half years until a market for it could be found, provided the water was properly regulated at the right temperature. The land for these types of long taro did not have to lie fallow between crops as it did for the short taro.

When pulling taro for sale, the farmer usually broke off the tops with his hands, threw the tubers into gunnysacks, and loaded the sacks onto a mule. Some farmers, however, tied the plat ends together and threw them across the mule's back. The best tops were retained for seeding. A bag of taro averaged 100 pounds. The average yield was 200 to 300 bags to the acre. Good taro lost little weight in being made into poi. The water added usually made up for the weight lost by peeling the tuber. Poor taro, however, did lose weight.

The mules carried the taro to one of two poi factories in Waipi'o, both owned by Chinese—Akioka and Chang. At the factory the taro was washed by flumed water and placed in the steamer, where it was steamed for three hours. After it was cooked, the taro was placed in a tub and hosed down. Then the tubers were scraped by women, one by one. They sat around the tub on wooden boxes and used coconut shells to scrape the taro clean. One woman could clean six tubers in a minute. The women earned 50 cents a day and worked from 6:00 A.M. to 10:30 or 11:00 A.M.

The troughs used to receive poi at the two poi factories were immense old poi boards formerly used by two men sitting on either end. Before the intro-

Figure 11 Uncle Joe Kala working in his loʻi in Waipiʻo, where taro cultivation has been a way of life for generations. 1974. Franco Salmoiraghi.

duction of engines to grind the poi, around 1911, the Chinese employed old Hawaiians to pound poi for them. At that time there were three factories, and the elderly Hawaiians were paid $1.50 a day for pounding.

In 1931 the poi factory that had the big engine made $80 worth of poi on Tuesdays and $120 worth of poi on Thursdays. The little engine made about $80 worth of poi once a week.

Farmers also sent 100-pound bags of taro out of the valley to other parts of the island. One farmer sent a thousand 100-pound bags out of the valley, every month. Another farmer sent eighty 100-pound bags to Kona every month. Others sent around two hundred 100-pound bags. When the bags left Waipi'o they usually weighed 105 pounds, to allow for 5 pounds' water loss by evaporation during transport before it reached its final destination.

Hilo controlled the market for taro and poi on the island. During World War I, there was a shortage of taro. The price of taro soared, and the poi factories bought up all the taro produced in Waipi'o and sent it to Hilo and Kamuela. The Hawaiians even sold the taro that they normally consumed at home because they could make so much money, eating breadfruit and buying flour to make up for the lack of taro. During this time, the Hawaiians had a lot of money. One year after the war ended, though, prices went back down to their normal level.[62]

In 1925 taro sold for $2.50 a bag in Hilo. At one point it had sold for as much as $3.75 a bag. However, after 1925 Maui farmers started to ship their taro to Hilo via steamship. They undersold the Waipi'o farmers by selling at $1.25 a bag. To compete, Waipi'o taro sold for as low as 50 cents a bag in the field or 75 cents a bag pulled.

Subsistence Resources

Waipi'o Valley provided its people with an abundance of natural resources for their day-to-day sustenance. They did not have to seek high-wage jobs or venture outside of the valley for their subsistence. Taro was the staple food of the Hawaiians. It was boiled or fried and eaten whole or else pounded into poi. Poi was pounded on an ongoing basis in the valley with pounders that had been fashioned by their fathers and grandfathers out of beach stones. Breadfruit, which was available on a seasonal basis, was usually cooked in the imu and pounded into poi. It was eaten by itself or mixed together with taro poi.

The leaves of the taro, especially the young lū'au or taro shoots, were cut up and boiled for greens with pork, chicken, or jerked beef.[63] They were also gathered along the streams and in common land areas. The aquatic life of the mountain streams was the main protein source for the Hawaiians of Waipiʻo in 1931. *ʻOʻopu* fish and *ʻōpae* or shrimp were caught in the streams and taken home, cleaned, and either salted for later consumption or cooked right away by boiling or frying with salt or *shoyu*. Sometimes the ʻoʻopu were baked in ti leaves. Freshwater shrimp were sometimes eaten raw. David Makaoi provided a graphic description of the preparation of fish for eating: "I didn't tire of eating ʻoʻopu. That's one thing I found out. Could cook it and maybe roast it sometimes, or boil it. The gravy tastes nice, it's fat. It's tasty. And fry. And sometimes cook in the ti leaf too over the fire. Gives a different flavor. So, you can cook it in many ways. So, you never get tired of eating fish. So we had fish most of the time."[64]

The people of Waipiʻo made fish traps with the *ʻieʻie* vine to catch oʻopu and shrimp. The trap would be placed in the stream, facing a rock, and the ʻoʻopu and shrimp would be scared into the trap. During floods, the ʻoʻopu washed downstream and could be easily caught with traps placed at strategic points in the stream. In the ocean, the ʻoʻopu spawned and hatched their young, called *hinana*. The Hawaiians would go to the mouth of the river and scoop hinana up with the nets. Many escaped and swam upstream, where they lived in the pools deep in the back of the valley and in the stream along the muddy banks. In dry weather, the ʻoʻopu could be caught in the upper pools of the valley. Slapping the water would scare them into holes in the sides of the pool. Then one could stick a hand into the hole and gently grab the fish by the head.[65]

Mullet found in the lower valley were usually cooked in ti leaves and fried or boiled. *Pūpū* and escargot-like shellfish were raised in the taro patches. They were usually left to stand for three days in a kerosene tin and then cleaned, after which they could be heated on a stone until they cracked and were either removed with a needle or sucked out. Sometimes they were boiled with garlic, black beans, and salt and then served.

Freshwater fish were plentiful in Waipiʻo. George Farm described how he once took the father of a friend to Waipiʻo Valley during the depression of 1929–30. He drove by car to the top of the valley and then rode by horse down into the valley. He was very impressed with the abundance of fish:

> Lot of fish, Waipio. You don't have to go hunt for it. The fish in the taro patches, fish in the ditches, fish in the streams, all over the place. And then one night when we slept there, the first night, they had big storm down there. Lot of rain. And the streams got flooded over, eh? and in the morn-

ing, about 7 o'clock, I see young children with the bucket. They running in the bushes, they pick up fish. Fill up the buckets, going home, empty and bring it back again. Filling up fish whole morning, you know. So I stopped them one time. I say, "say, where you get that fish from? Where you buy that fish?" "No, no. No buy. Plenty in the bushes." You see, that much fish in Waipio Valley.[66]

Limu or seaweed was a very important source of vitamins and minerals to the Hawaiians. They would gather it from the ocean, clean it, salt it, and eat it raw with poi. It was never cooked. The ocean provided *limu kohu*, *limu huluhuluwaina*, *'ele'ele*, *lipu'upu'u*, *mane'one'o*, and *lipahe'e* varieties of seaweed. Limu kohu, the hardest to get, also lasted the longest, two to three months, while the others usually lasted a week. Salt was not made in Waipi'o but was obtained from Kawaihae, Hawai'i, or directly from Honolulu by the Chinese store-keeper.

The valley was also rich in fruits, trees, and plants for eating and healing. It had *'ōhi'a'ai* or mountain apple, papaya, banana, avocado, breadfruit, guava, and mango trees. Coffee also grew wild in the valley. It was gathered, dried, and roasted in a skillet for home use. There were also lemon trees, orange trees, coconuts, *hau* trees, *noni* fruit, *'awa*, and chili peppers. *Kukui* trees were plentiful, and its nuts were used for garnishing food, for medicine, and to make small torches. *Wauke* and *olonā*, traditionally important for making tapa and cordage, also grew wild in the valley, although they were not actively used in 1931. Pandanus trees grew in the valley; its leaves were gathered for weaving. Even as late as 1931 women wove mats, hats, purses, handbags, and headbands from the pandanus leaves.[67]

Wild goats in the mountains were sometimes shot for food. Both Hawaiians and Chinese owned 200 head of cattle which grazed in the valley. They were periodically slaughtered for home consumption by families in the valley. Every two months or more someone would plan to slaughter a cow and go throughout the valley to all the families to let them know. He would butcher it in the pasture, and the meat would be placed in piles on fern or water lily leaves. Everyone who wanted to buy meat would come to the site and select the piles, which sold for $1, $2, or $5, that they wanted to buy. The bones, which were used for soup, were given away free. They did not use a scale. People brought their own bags to take home their meat. The meat was usually salted, dried, and kept in crocks or barrels until it was ready to be eaten, because there were no iceboxes or freezers.[68]

Aside from these occasions, meat was rarely eaten in the valley, and the nearest butcher was at the town of Honoka'a. One would have to make an order ahead of time, and he would arrange for the meat to be delivered to Kukuihaele on the specified day. David Makaoi explained why meat was not often eaten:

> Hardly any meat. 'Cause only once in awhile, when somebody kills a cow for the whole valley. Then they get to buy beef, so many pounds to take home. And salt it most of the time. And that's *pipikaula* [smoked beef]. That's the only way to preserve it and still be nice for eating. So that's why I enjoy pipikaula, nowdays, here, because it has a good flavor.[69]

Interaction with the Market Economy

Despite the abundance of natural resources for food, certain items—sugar, flour, salt, shoyu, rice, canned salmon, canned sardines, salt salmon, cod fish, dried shrimp, corned beef, cooking oil, matches, kerosene oil, soap, beer, wine, sake, and clothing—were purchased in stores in Waipi'o, Kukuihaele, and Honoka'a.[70] The store in Waipi'o also sold baked goods, such as bread with butter and jelly, doughnuts, and cakes, which were popular with the school children.

In general, the people of Waipi'o only purchased the bare necessities. According to David Makaoi:

> We didn't buy too much, though, because for the rest of the things we were self-supporting. We just say, "Why spend money? Get up and make our own." We were independent. We didn't need much cash for things in the store. So, that's why they said, "Why live in town? You have to buy everything with cash." (Laughs) In the country, you don't need much cash.[71]

Those Hawaiians who sold taro to the store could purchase goods on credit. Those who sold the taro to another broker or who did not sell taro had to purchase goods on a cash basis.[72]

Transportation

At one time, there was an entrance to Waipi'o from Waimea and Kawaihae by means of a trail in the rear of the valley. There was also a lower road beneath the pali. The narrow trail connecting the valley with the outside world was eventually widened into a horse path to facilitate the transport of taro and rice by land.

In 1904 residents from Waipi'o and Waimanu wrote a letter to Governor George R. Carter asking the territorial government to spend money appropriated by the 1903 legislature for a new road down the Waipi'o pali. They also asked for government lands between Waipi'o and Waimanu to be turned into homesteads for poor American citizens of the valley.[73] The road was never constructed, and in 1931 there was still only a horse-and-mule trail leading into and out of the valley.

To send taro to Hilo, the farmers and poi factories paid 25 cents per 250-pound bag for it to be transported by mule to Kukuihaele. They then paid 30 cents a bag to transport the taro by truck to Pa'auilo, where it was loaded onto a train for Hilo. In 1931 the Chinese owned ninety-five mules, and the Hawaiians owned about ten mules or horses.

By 1930 public opinion in Waipi'o had turned against the construction of a road. They feared that it would bring others into the valley to plant and would lower the price of taro and increase the rent on the land. They also did not like the prospect of having prison labor in the district while the road was being constructed.

Everything that went in and out of the valley by land traveled on a horse, a mule, or humans. Sometimes two men would haul produce on a pole slung between their shoulders.[74] About half a dozen outrigger canoes were owned by Hawaiians in the lower valley. However, they were primarily used for fishing, not transportation.

Lifestyle, Beliefs, Customs, and Practices

Fannie Hauanio Duldulao, who was born in Waipi'o in 1911 into a Hawaiian family that raised taro in Waipi'o, probably expressed the feelings of everyone who was born and raised there:

> Well, I love the place because I was born and raised there until I grew up
> —a great-grandmother today. And then the feelings of the place is actually
> really warm feelings . . . it's a valley of aloha and then full of love. And
> when I was born and raised there, I had everything that I can think of
> without spending money. Everything was really from the land, what we
> raised. The valley. Like taro and everything.[75]

There were no major crimes reported in Waipi'o prior to World War II. It was a valley that modern developments had bypassed. Occasionally a politician would go into the valley at election time and make a speech on the veranda of the store. But for the most part, it was too difficult to access the valley. And the residents preferred it that way. A road would mean the end of the abundance of resources that made life in a valley as isolated as Waipi'o not only possible, but also desirable.[76]

In 1931 there were three churches with active memberships—a Protestant church, a Mormon church, and a Chinese temple. There were two cemeteries—a Hawaiian one and a Chinese one. A Catholic church had been built and established at one time but was no longer in use by 1931.[77]

The Christians held one joint service in a church built by the missionary Titus Coan. In general, twenty-five adults who were Mormon, Christian Scientist, and Catholic participated in the services. However, there were only seven members who contributed to the support of the church, including the salary of a part-time minister.

The Mormon church had the strongest following. According to Sam Kaaekuahiwi, many of the members had joined the church because the Mormons were reputed to be good at healing. Several had joined after apparently being cured of a sickness by prayers offered by the Mormon congregation for their recovery. The ex-sheriff was Mormon. He had two wives and two families.

Figure 12 Fannie Duldulao and Romualdo Duldulao at their Waipi'o kuleana. 1978. Franco Salmoiraghi.

Although the Waipi'o Hawaiians participated in Christian services, they still maintained their traditional beliefs and practices. In particular, most of the families in Waipi'o acknowledged and retained a respect for their 'aumakua, their family guardians. One of the residents in 1931 shared an experience she had with her family's 'aumakua, the shark:

> One of my 'aumakuas was a God-damn fool. He caused the sickness in my ankles. I went to kahuna after kahuna, but always the sickness came back. For two years I was unable to stand on my feet. Then a kahuna told me what to do. He made me go at 12 o'clock at night to the water, and he dipped me 5 times in the water to please one 'aumakua so that he would help me (against the malevolent 'aumakua), and when I came back, dogs mustn't pass, chickens mustn't pass, man mustn't pass or get in my way. After that I went back and dipped again 5 times and took awa root as a gift to the 'aumakuas in the sea, the shark 'aumakuas.[78]

Many of the families in Waipi'o traced their ancestry to a shark 'aumakua who frequented the offshore waters in the form of a big shark. They were told not to look at that shark if they saw it in the ocean, or they would be blinded. They were not to treat the shark badly. The 'aumakua of others was black with a red mouth. If they saw that shark when they went out fishing, it was considered a good sign, and they would proceed with confidence that help was available if needed.[79]

Other families traced their ancestry to turtles. If a family member related to the turtle was in trouble out on the ocean, a huge turtle, large enough for a human to ride on, would appear to rescue that person. Fannie Hauanio Duldulao related how her mother believed in the turtle 'aumakua and told the children, "They know if the family need help. It's a surprise, you can see the turtle float."[80] A few of the families were related to the *mo'o* or lizard 'aumakua. They were careful not to treat lizards roughly.[81]

The residents who served as informants to Stella Jones in 1931 remembered when each house had an 'aumakua shrine. They could recall how people used to pray to the 'aumakua. Their parents had shared stories with them about how *kahuna 'anā'anā* or sorcery could be used to break someone's back, and about how a boy who was in love with a girl who did not reciprocate could go to a kahuna or sorcerer who could employ *manulele* or love sorcery to make the girl care for the boy.

With regard to fishing, Sam Kaaekuahiwi remembered how the old people had practiced the kū'ula rituals. He explained the kū'ula ritual as he understood it: "Maybe it is an idol placed on the shore at a certain spot. They would bury the image there . . . Sometimes they would have a wooden god of kauwila wood, it was in the form of a tapa beater. They would tie a cord to it and drop it in the water, praying to the akua and leaving it overnight. When fishing the next morning they would be successful."[82]

In addition, one man was designated as the *kilo*, or observer of fish. He would go along the path and look for the fish, then tell the fisherman what kind of fish he saw and where they were. The fisherman, following his directions, would take his net, cast it, and surround the fish.

Hawaiian taro farmers in Waipi'o planted according to the moon phase. They carefully observed the moon and could predict when the full moon or *mahealani* phase would occur. Taro and most other Hawaiian plants grew best if planted on the night of the full moon.[83]

Hawaiian rituals and practices were also important in healing. *Honohono* grass was pounded and used for healing cuts and sores. *Laukahi* leaves were also pounded and used to cure sores. The pistil of the laukahi was boiled into a tea and drunk to heal cancer. *Pōpolo* berries and leaves were used to cure colds. Fannie Hauanio Duldulao described the use of pōpolo:

> Well, they call that popolo. You know those leafy things, eh? They have
> that small little purple seed. And then, they just pound that and then
> squeeze it. And then you drink the juice. Even the shoots, that's how they
> pick up. Like this, you just pick 'em up, you know, so much, one handful.
> And then you go home, put in the cheesecloth or whatever, as long it's
> clean. Then you pound that. But some, they put in the ti leaf then they
> heat 'em up. But mom said it's better to have fresh from the plant. And
> that is good for cold, too; especially when babies start to cough.[84]

The bark of the mountain lehua could also be boiled into a tea and drunk to heal colds. Burns and boils could be healed with the application of certain leafy native Hawaiian plants. Hawaiian herbs could even be used to cure broken, sprained, or dislocated bones.[85]

Waipi'o: "'Āina Aloha"

Waipi'o, secluded abode of akua and legendary chiefs, persisted into the middle of the twentieth century as a heartland of traditional Hawaiian culture and lifestyle. While living in distinct households and cultivating individual patches of taro for their own families, Waipi'o Hawaiians shared in the abundance of natural resources in the valley. Together, they respected and cared for the streams and irrigation system that fed their individual loʻi kalo. Together, they respected the balance of natural resources, taking only what was necessary for their family's daily sustenance and respecting the reproductive cycles of the aquatic and plant life in the valley. Their children played together, attended school together, and matured to adulthood together. The people in the valley occasionally joined together to celebrate life's great events—a baby lūʻau, a birthday, a wedding. They also celebrated Christmas and New Year's together.

David Makaoi described a memorable Chinese New Year's when he was in the eighth grade:

> On New Year's Eve and on Chinese New Year's Eve, several musicians would serenade the Hawaiian and Chinese homes, respectively. I was one of them, beginning with the sixth grade, until my high school years. I welcomed that opportunity to earn some good money. We usually serenaded in groups of two or more musicians. On one occasion, however, on Chinese New Year's, I performed all alone with my adopted uncle, Kamaka,

Figure 13 Waipiʻo Hawaiians shared in the abundance of natural resources in the valley. 1978. Franco Salmoiraghi.

77

as chaperone and lamp holder. This happened during my eighth grade year.
I netted $5, though I had to split 50/50 with my adopted Hawaiian uncle.
In those days, $1 a day was the average laborer's daily wage. The next day
was a school day. Without any sleep I went to Kukuihaele School the next
morning. With nickels and dimes jingling in my pockets, I did not fall
asleep in school . . . I was walking on "cloud nine."[86]

One New Year's Eve, David Makaoi joined Sam Li'a, the famous song-
writer and musician from Kukuihaele, in serenading the Hawaiian families in
Waipi'o Valley. Sam played the violin, David played the ukulele, a third man
played the banjo, and the last played the guitar. At the end of the night, the
group split the proceeds for the night evenly.[87] They composed songs that
told of their love for Waipi'o and committed to memory their exploits and
experiences.

During Prohibition, a number of families made okolehao from ti root
cooked in an imu. They would make about ten gallons at a time, which would
last about three months. It was not sold, but made solely for home consumption and shared with visitors and friends.[88]

The Hawaiian way of life continued to thrive among the households and
taro patches nestled at the foot of the towering cliffs of Waipi'o Valley. All
along the rest of the Hāmākua Coast, though, the sugar plantation economy
dynamically transformed the landscape and social life of Hawaiian communities and villages. Throughout 1931 Waipi'o remained an enclave of Hawaiian
people and a Hawaiian way of life, despite the influx of Chinese rice planters
and their wage workers. The lifestyle of the Waipi'o Hawaiians starkly con-
trasted with the lifestyle of urban Hawaiians. The persistence of Hawaiians in
Waipi'o Valley provided an important continuity for Native Hawaiians to
their heritage. The Waipi'o Hawaiians demonstrated well into the twentieth
century the knowledge, skills, and resourcefulness of their people, who maintained harmonious and respectful relations to the land and with each other.

Forces of Change

Waipi'o Valley continued to be a Native Hawaiian enclave through the end of
World War II. In 1941 a flood ravaged the kua'āina of the valley. Throughout World War II, young men were attracted out of Waipi'o into the military
and the more lucrative military jobs in Honolulu, especially at Pearl Harbor.
In 1945 the Waipi'o Valley Grammar School closed. Finally, a second natu-

ral disaster dramatically altered the lives of the Waipiʻo kuaʻāina. The 1946 tidal wave, which reached a height of fifty-five feet, inundated the valley and destroyed most of the homes and taro patches. Many of the dislocated families left Waipiʻo, never to return. Only fifteen to twenty kuaʻāina continued to live in the valley.[89]

The 1946 tidal wave devastated the valley. As a result, many kuaʻāina moved to nearby outside rural towns along the Hāmākua coast. Nevertheless, two years later *Paradise of the Pacific* magazine characterized Waipiʻo as a remote valley where old Hawaiians spent their days catching fish, growing taro, and pounding it into poi, and their nights retelling stories of the past.[90]

By 1954 the resident population in the valley increased to between thirty and forty people. There were three Hawaiians living in the valley, and the rest were Filipinos living in makeshift shanties. At the same time, there were 170 kuleana owners, whose land holdings amounted to 309.4 acres. Bishop Museum owned another 534.6 acres, and the government controlled 66 acres.[91] Not all of the kuaʻāina who had land or who farmed in Waipiʻo lived in the valley. Most lived nearby in surrounding rural communities above the valley, especially in Kukuihaele. Combined, the kuaʻāina still cultivated 300 acres of taro, 2–3 acres of lotus, less than 2 acres of water chestnuts, 11 acres of macadamia nuts, and 15 acres of coffee in the valley.

A 1958 flood again destroyed the taro crops in the valley. A 1960 Land Study Bureau report completed only two years later estimated that 100 acres were still cultivated in taro, along with 11 acres of macadamia nut trees, 5 acres of lotus root, and 2 acres of coffee. According to the report, the permanent resident population was virtually nonexistent; most of the farmers lived outside the valley and commuted in order to work on their taro patches.[92]

The launching of a full-scale tourist industry on Hawaiʻi included widening, realigning, and improving the Hawaiʻi Island belt highway. As part of this construction, the Honokaʻa-Kukuihaele extension was completed in 1962, opening the Waipiʻo Valley Lookout to thousands of visitors. Meanwhile, the county constructed a mile-long road accessible by four-wheel-drive vehicles into the valley. It descends 800 feet to the valley floor at a 20 percent grade, with as much as a 45 percent grade at some points. The road dramatically increased the number of visitors to the valley and created the potential for tourist businesses to operate there.[93] The farmers replaced their mule teams with four-wheel-drive trucks to market their crops outside the valley.

These developments coincided with the stationing of Peace Corps trainees in the back of Waipiʻo Valley, near Hiʻilawe Falls. They built their own thatch huts, farmed, and fished in preparation for volunteer work in the Pacific and Asia. They also practiced how to construct a bridge.[94]

The first actual threat of tourist development in the valley itself came in 1966 in the form of a proposal to build a restaurant and rest stop in the valley, to be called the Waipiʻo Ti House. Because the rest stop was to be built on land zoned for conservation, the developers needed a conditional use permit from the State Board of Land and Natural Resources. The board approved construction of the rest stop but not the restaurant.[95] The Waipiʻo Ti House was built and dedicated in February 1971 as a rest stop for hikers, with a restroom and facilities where lūʻau or parties could be held. In April 1972 a public outcry was raised over the installation of an unauthorized power line from the pali down to the Ti House because it was considered to be a precursor to development of a restaurant. By November 1972 1,900 people had signed a petition opposing a restaurant in Waipiʻo Valley. The State Board of Land and Natural Resources denied the permit for a restaurant license in January 1973. At that point, the developer gave up and donated the 5.5-acre property on which the Ti House sat to the Bernice Pauahi Bishop Museum.[96]

The Continuing Significance of Waipiʻo

Water and taro production remain the key determinants in the future of the Waipiʻo and the kuaʻāina with ancestral ties to the valley. Flooding continues to limit the capacity of the kuaʻāina of Waipiʻo to live there and the viability of cultivating commercial crops. Flooding has also limited tourist development.

In the 1960s a fourth Waipiʻo stream, Waimā, was diverted into the Lower Hāmākua Ditch system. Combined, the water ditches diverted half of the water that would naturally flow through Waipiʻo Valley.[97] In 1963 heavy flooding in Waipiʻo wiped out nearly half of the taro crop and farmers lost between $200 and $1,500 worth of crops. The upper valley had six and a half inches of rain in 24 hours, washing out the roads as the water rose up to five feet in some areas.[98] The last major flood, in 1979, destroyed many taro farms.

The maintenance of the Lower Hāmākua Ditch is a factor in sustaining the healthy flow of the Waipiʻo streams. In 1989 the Lower Hāmākua Ditch tunnel, which runs behind Hakalaoa Falls, collapsed. A temporary flume was constructed around the collapsed tunnel, which ultimately involved the diversion of Hakalaoa Stream. This reduced the twin falls of Hiʻilawe to a single waterfall. In 1993 the Hāmākua Sugar Company shut down and abandoned the

Lower Hāmākua Ditch System. In 1995 the State Department of Agriculture stepped in to operate and maintain the ditch system. By that point, one of the four intakes was blocked by rubble, and twenty wooden flumes showed signs of saturation, rot, and leaking. It was estimated that the system lost 4 million gallons of water a day.[99] In 1999 the U.S. Department of Agriculture's Natural Resources Conservation Service completed a Watershed Plan to repair the Lower Hāmākua Ditch to provide water to individual farmers along the Hāmākua Coast and allocating water for Waipi'o Valley itself. The Hāmākua Ditch system remains a major factor in the availability of water and the control of flooding in the valley. The ability of the farmers of Waipi'o to work in coordination with various agencies and the farmers of the Hāmākua Coast to harness and balance the flow of the waters of Waipi'o is of critical significance.

Taro continues to be the primary crop cultivated in Waipi'o. Waipi'o is upheld as a model for traditional ahupua'a management organized around taro production. Commitment to taro production and farming by the kuleana owners and Bishop Museum has been crucial to protection of this unique cultural

Figure 14 Taro cultivation is pursued as both a commercial enterprise and a cultural and educational learning opportunity by contemporary generations in Waipi'o Valley. 1974. Franco Salmoiraghi.

and natural resource from the ravages of tourist development. Conservation zoning has provided protection to the valley's natural and cultural resources. Taro production within the framework of traditional Native Hawaiian ahupua'a management also makes Waipi'o an ideal place for ecotourist operations as well as Native Hawaiian cultural and educational programs. Taro is pursued as both a commercial enterprise and a cultural and educational learning opportunity. The development of cultural learning activities centered on the historical cultural sites and on Waipi'o's taro irrigation and cultivation network complexes will help sustain Waipi'o as a traditional center of taro farming. These educational centers also train a new generation of taro farmers steeped in the traditions of Waipi'o and in protocol related to the cultivation of taro and the cultural resources of the valley. The Edith Kanaka'ole Foundation and the Kanu O Ka 'āina Charter School have been pioneers in initiating such activities. Students learn about the complexity of cultivating and irrigating taro and about the cultural protocols and chants traditional Hawaiian farmers used to invoke their Gods to make their crop healthy and abundant. Students also practice the values of shared and cooperative enterprise and of respect and care for the land as they work together to grow and harvest taro.

As Waipi'o moves into the twenty-first century, it remains a cultural kīpuka, a center of traditional and customary Hawaiian cultural, subsistence, and religious activities. For the most part, the "kua'āina" who participate in these activities in the valley do not reside in the valley itself, as did the kua'āina prior to World War II, but in neighboring rural communities that bridge into the modern society and the market economy. Just over 100 people actually reside in the valley itself. Waipi'o continues to be a center for training new generations in taro cultivation, related cultural practices, and the kua'āina values and practices of lōkāhi. Recognized also as a traditional cultural and spiritual center, Waipi'o Valley and its new generation of kua'āina are contributing to the regeneration and perpetuation of Native Hawaiian cultural beliefs, customs, and practices as a whole. *Waipi'o mano wai*—source of water and life.

THREE

Hāna, mai Koʻolau a Kaupō:
Hāna, from Koʻolau to Kaupō

Nā Koʻolau

ʻIke ʻia i ka nani o nā pali uliuli	I see the beauty of the deep green cliffs
Aloha kuʻu home o nā Koʻolau	love my home in Koʻolau
E huli māua i Waiʻānapanapa	Two of us travel to Waiʻānapanapa
He wai lukini ʻānapanapa mai nei	The fragrant glistening waters ripple in the wind
Kū mai ka puʻu o Kaʻuiki	Kaʻuiki Hill stands upright
ʻO Hāna ʻiuʻiu pōhai ke aloha	And Hāna lives in peace with my love
Kau mai ke ʻānuenue i Kaupō	A rainbow is placed over Kaupō
Pā mai ka makani kāʻili aloha	The gentle wind caresses me and I take the feeling of love.

—HARRY KŪNIHI MITCHELL

HĀNA, ONE OF the largest districts of Maui, is celebrated in the song printed here as the epigraph as a place of natural beauty and romance. The traditional *ʻōlelo noeʻau* or saying *Hāna, mai Koʻolau a Kaupō* (from Koʻolau to Kaupō) provides us with the traditional boundaries of Hāna, starting in the *moku* or district (also called *kalana* or *ʻokana*) of Koʻolau and extending through the moku of Hāna and Kīpahulu to the *kona* or leeward moku of Kaupō.[1] The Hāna district consists of almost one-third of the island of Maui. On Maui, the ahupuaʻa are marked from stream to stream, rather than from ridge to ridge. On the northwest, Oʻopuloa Gulch marks the Hāna district's boundary with the Hāmākua district. On the southeast side, Waiʻōpai Gulch marks the boundary of the Hāna district with Kahikinui.

The land surveyor Curtis J. Lyons, writing in 1875 about the principles of Hawaiian land divisions, described the system used in East Maui:

On East Maui, the division [of land] in its general principles was much the same as on Hawaii, save that the radial system was better adhered to. In fact there is pointed out, to this day, on the sharp spur projecting into the east side of Haleakalā crater, a rock called the "Pohaku oki aina"—land-dividing rock, to which the larger lands came as a centre. How many lands actually came up to this is not yet known.[2]

Within the districts of Hāna are located smaller land divisions, or ahupua'a. These sub-district land divisions in general extend from the sea to the uplands. Some extend inland only as far as the forest, while others sweep up to the top of the mountain. A few go into the crater to meet ahupua'a from other districts at the *piko* (umbilical) stone, Pōhaku Pālaha, on the northern rim of Haleakalā crater.

Before 1927, settlements along the Hāna Coast were accessible only by ocean or along rugged horse and mule trails. The Hāna district is a prime example of an isolated rural district where the pace of economic, social, and cultural change proceeded more slowly than on other parts of the island. Hāna

Figure 15 The road connecting "Hāna, from Ko'olau to Kaupō," opened in 1927 and afforded intermittent work for Hāna Hawaiians on road maintenance crews. 1927. Tai Sing Loo, Hawaiian Historical Society.

remained an area of continuity of Hawaiian culture and lifestyle through the end of the twentieth century. The Hawaiian families and communities that remained in Hāna from generation to generation, pursuing subsistence livelihoods and employing traditional methods of fishing and planting, provided all Hawaiians with a connection to a unique Hawaiian way of life.[3]

Carving the Landscape

Wind and rain carved the dramatic landscape of the Hāna district and shaped the lives of the residents. Set patterns of the wind and the rain as they moved across the land and ocean were named for their qualities and effect upon nature and the kuaʻāina. In 1922, when Thomas Maunupau and Kenneth Emory journeyed to Kaupō, they met sixty-year-old Joshua Ahulii, who had been born and raised in the district. He shared with them the names of the famous winds of Kaupō and the neighboring ahupuaʻa of Hāna:

Kualau or Kuakualau—is the strong wind and the rain out in the ocean. In Kona this wind brings in the ohua like fish along the beaches. It is customary for it to blow in the evening and in the morning but sometimes blow at other times—. Where are you, O Kualau, Your rain goes about at sea.

Moaʻe—this is a customary wind. It blows strongly but pleasantly from the sea and sometimes from the land. It is sung about, thus: "Where are you, O moaʻe wind/you're taking my love with you."

Moaʻe-ku—this is a customary wind like the Moaʻe but much stronger. This wind was said to have been born in Hāna, grew up in Kīpahulu, attained maturity in Kaupō, became aged in Kahikinui, grew feeble at Kanaio, rested and let its burden down at Honuaʻula. Here is a song for this wind: "Where are you. O Moaʻe-ku/You make much work on a stormy day."

Malualua—This is the companion of the white, misty rain of Hāna. This is a famous wind of this land. It blows strongly and pleasantly from the ocean and blows the rain back to the mountain. This is the song of this wind, The misty white rain of Hāna, Companion of the Malualua.

Kulepe—This wind comes with rain. It is strong and blows out to sea from the land.

Kaomi—It was a strong, blustering wind whose strength does not last long but blew like a gentle pressure. It is sung of thus: "The wind blows in a gale, Then it gently presses."

Naulu—This wind goes with the Naulu clouds. The Naulu is the wind, It bears the Naulu clouds along.

Kiu—It is a wind that flies along and seems to sneak by to the mountain of Haleakalā. It is called the Kiu of Haleakalā. Here is a song of this wind: "The Kiu is the wind that lives on the mountain."

Hoolua—It is a strong wind from the sea, making the billows rise and the white caps come on the ocean. This is a song sung by fishermen: If the Hoolua is the wind, The skill of a canoesman is seen.

Mumuku—It is a strong wind blowing from the land and it is as though it was being blown out by another wind.

Koholalele—It is a strong wind blown over the dry area of Kohala to this place and on up to the mountain.

Koholaleleku—Is a wind like the Koholalele but stronger.

Makani kaʻili aloha o Kīpahulu. The love-snatching-wind-of-Kīpahulu is the usual Kīpahulu wind. It blows down from the mountain and goes out to sea.[4]

Upon being asked, Ahulii also shared the names of the rains of the district:

Noenoe uakea o Hāna—is a misty rain and white. It comes in the morning and ends as the morning waxes . . . the song of the rain, Misty and white is the rain of Hāna, Companion of the Malualua wind.

Hāna ua lani haahaa (Hāna of the low rains from heaven)—is described thus: A low hanging cloud comes from the ocean and then the rain falls. That is why it was so named. The names of the rains of this very famous place are pretty and I do not think there are rains anywhere else to compare with these. No wonder it is said that Maui is the best.

Awa rain—It is a dark cloudy rain that falls all day in the mountains.

Koko rain—It spreads over the surface of the sea with a rainbow. It is a sign of trouble of some importance when seen.

Naulu rain—It is a rain that moves over the mountain on a clear day with a Naulu cloud.

Noe rain—It is a light shower and mist that remain in kula lands.

Haleuole rain—This is a naughty rain. When one wants to relieve nature that is the time it comes with such suddenness and clears up just as suddenly and then falls again. That is why it was so called (wipeless). [Maunupau noted that he thinks this was not an ancient name.]

Lilinoe rain of Haleakalā—A famous rain belonging to that mountain.

Ukiu rain of Makawao—It is a fine rain with wind that blows down from the mountains.

Peepapohaku (Hide-behind-rocks) rain—is an annoying rain something like the Haeuole in falling and clearing away suddenly, thus sending people to hide behind the rock walls. That's how it got its name. [Maunupau noted that he does not believe that the ancients named it.]

The winds and rains identified by the kūpuna of Kaupō grace the entire Ko'olau district as they blow in from the east across the 'Alenuihāhā Channel and encounter the lush, steep, magnificent slopes of Haleakalā.

Godly Inhabitants of Hāna

Maui, the Hawaiian demigod credited with feats that made the earth livable for humans, performed many of his famous deeds in the Hāna district. He snared the sun at the Ko'olau Gap on the rim of Haleakalā and forced it to slow down during the summer months.[5] He hooked the islands of Hawai'i and pulled them up from the ocean when he went fishing with his brothers in the fishing ground called Po'o, directly off Kīpahulu and in line with the hill Kaiwiopele.[6] He also lifted the sky so that humans could walk upright while standing on Ka'uiki in Hāna. Thus, while the clouds may hang around Haleakalā, they still do not touch Ka'uiki.[7]

The gods Kāne and Kanaloa are credited with going about all the islands to establish springs of fresh water, including east Maui. It is said that they landed at Pu'uokanaloa (hill of Kanaloa), a small hill just north of Keone'ō'io when they first came from Kahiki. They dug a water hole by the beach and found the water brackish. So they went about 200 yards inland, dug another hole, and created the spring called Kawaiakala'o. These gods also opened the Kanaloa fishpond at Luala'iluakai, providing the brackish water needed for fish to spawn.[8] From here, they went on to Nu'u, where they dug another spring.[9] They also opened the Kāne and Kanaloa springs at Ke'anae near the 'ōhi'a gulch.[10]

A hairy type of wauke plant, useful for the beating out of bark cloth, is said to have first sprouted in Kaupō out of the body of Maikoha, the youngest son of Konikonia and Hina'aikamālama.[11]

Mo'o and sharks are the two prominent 'aumakua associated with Hawaiian families from Hāna. Stories about men being held hostage by female mo'o in legendary times abound. For example, the chief Puna'aikoa'e was kidnapped from Kaua'i by the mo'o woman Kalamainu'u and held captive as her husband in a cave in Hāna.[12]

The Hāna people believed that mo'o lived in certain ponds and springs. Fish that lived in mo'o ponds were forms of the mo'o and not to be eaten. If one were caught and opened up, they were usually found to be soft and bitter. If these ponds were used by someone for washing dirty clothing or were polluted in some other way, the person responsible was usually punished with an illness or some other form of misfortune.[13]

Even as late as the 1960s kūpuna informants spoke of an old blind woman, Tutu Pale, who claimed kinship to a mo'o who lived in a nearby pond. She often walked to the pond in the moonlight to fish and talked as she went along. She explained that she was talking with her cousin, the mo'o, who frequently accompanied her to the pond. After ten years, she regained her eyesight. Her son eventually put her in a nursing home, but his legs swelled up and would not heal until he asked forgiveness for placing his mother in the home rather than taking care of her.[14]

Sharks were also honored as 'aumakua in Hāna. The shark 'aumakua lived and bred in the waters off Kīpahulu. According to Josephine Marciel, a resident of the district:

> This land was famous for sharks. Because it was full of sharks. People with bad mouths, if [they] went swimming would be taken by sharks. Those who defy sharks would be taken. This land is famous with tales of sharks before. When the wiliwili blooms watch out for the sharks. The sharks bite. It's mating season. That's the time when the sharks chase the females. When the wiliwili blooms, the sharks become fierce. At Nu'u, the wiliwili is plentiful.[15]

The shark-man, Nanaue, a being with a human body and a great shark mouth on his back, was driven out of Waipi'o when he was exposed as the predator who killed the people of the valley. He settled for a while at Kīpahulu until he was forced out to flee to Moloka'i, where he was finally killed.[16]

According to kūpuna informants, Hāna was also famous for the apparition of Kānehunamoku, the floating island of Kāne. Mary Waiwaiole claimed to see it floating on the water by Ka'uiki Hill on certain mornings when she rode by truck to work on the plantation. Once, members of the Waikaloa family saw the island and then actually packed their things and went down to the shore to wait for the island to return so that they could go away on it. However, the island never floated back for them.[17]

Laka, the male god of forest growth and patron of the hula dance, is named as the son of Kumuhonua (Earth firmament) and Lalohonua (Earth underground) thirty-six generations before Papa and Wākea, the first parents of human progenitors.[18] Laka was born at Kīpahulu and brought up at ʻAlae Nui ("the great mudhen"), a land division in the Kīpahulu valley.[19]

Kūʻula, Hina, and Aʻiaʻi

The first fishpond in Hawaiʻi is said to have been built by the fish god himself, Kūʻulakai, where he lived with his wife, Hina, and their son, Aʻiaʻi, at Leho-ʻula, ʻAleamai, in Hāna, near Kaiwiopele. He was the head fisherman for the ruling chief of Hāna. His marvelous fishpond attracted a lot of attention especially because the pond, through his power, was always full of fish. At Wailau on Molokaʻi was a chief who had the power, as a kupua or demigod, to turn into a gigantic eel, 300 feet long. In his eel form he was attracted to the fishpond and slipped into the inlet. However, after he had fed well he could not get out without breaking down the wall. He hid in a deep hole beyond ʻĀlau island called "hole of the ulua," and Kūʻulakai baited the famous hook, Manai-akalani, with roasted coconut meat to lure him out of hiding. When hooked, the eel was dragged ashore by two ropes held by men who stood on opposite sides of the bay while Kūʻulakai stoned the eel to death. The body of the eel turned to stone and can still be seen today. A follower of the dead chief/eel moved from Wailau to Hāna determined to avenge the death. He managed to be appointed as a messenger of the chief to the fishpond. One day, upon returning from the fishpond, he conveyed instructions that he said Kūʻulakai had given him about how to prepare the fish for cooking as instructions for killing the chief. He said that Kūʻulakai told him that the chief's head should be cut off and the body sliced, salted and baked in an imu. The angered chief ordered the death of Kūʻulakai, Hina, and Aʻiaʻi by burning them in their house at night while they were asleep. Kūʻulakai knew of the order and decided that he and Hina should return to the ocean. They left Aʻiaʻi behind with objects to use in attracting fish and instructions on how to construct koʻa or altars to mark fishing grounds and to honor Kūʻulakai and Hina as patrons of fishing. Beckwith provided a description of the fishing koʻa that Aʻiaʻi established in the Hāna district:

> The first fishing ground marked out by Aiai is that of the Hole-of-the-ulua where the great eel hid. A second lies between Hamoa and Haneoo in Hana, where fish are caught by letting down baskets into the sea. The

third is Koa-uli in the deep sea. A fourth is the famous akule fishing ground at Wana-ula . . . At Honomaele he places three pebbles and they form a ridge where aweoweo fish gather. At Waiohue he sets up on a rocky islet the stone Paka to attract fish. From the cliff of Puhi-ai he directs the luring of the great octopus from its hole off Wailua-nui by means of the magic cowry shell and the monster is still to be seen turned to stone with one arm missing, broken off in the struggle. Leaving Hana, he establishes fishing stations and altars along the coast all around the island as far as Kipahulu. At the famous fishing ground (Koʻa-nui) in the sea of Maulili he meets the fisherman Kane-makua and presents him with the fish he has just caught and gives him charge of the grounds, bidding him establish the custom of giving the first fish caught to any stranger passing by canoe. Another famous station and altar is at Kahiki-ula.[20]

Aʻiaʻi taught people how to make nets and lines and showed them how to lure octopus with the cowry shell. Aʻiaʻi eventually left Maui and established fishing koʻa from Kahoʻolawe to Lānaʻi and Molokaʻi, Oʻahu, Kauaʻi, Niʻihau, and finally Hawaiʻi.[21]

Kaiwiopele

Pelehonuamea also shaped the landscape of the Hāna Coast. The goddess dwelt at Haleakalā and built it up to its present size until her mortal enemy—her sister, Nāmakaokahaʻi, an ocean deity who could assume the form of a dragon—discovered where she lived. Nāmakaokahaʻi arrived at Haleakalā with another sea dragon, Haui, and together they viciously attacked Pelehonuamea and dismembered her body. Parts of the body landed in Hāna near Kauʻiki and formed the hill called Kaiwiopele (the bones of Pele). Nāmakaokahaʻi believed that she had finally destroyed her enemy. However, the spirit of Pelehonuamea lived beyond her body form and transformed into a more powerful force as a goddess. The goddess Pelehonuamea fled to the island of Hawaiʻi, where she found a permanent home at Halemaʻumaʻu, Kīlauea, Hawaiʻi.[22]

Settlement and Development of Koʻolau, Hāna, Maui

Menehune are believed to be among the original settlers of the earliest sites in the Koʻolau district, such as the Hale o Kāne, Lonaea, and Loʻaloʻa heiau of Kaupō.[23]

Throughout the Koʻolau district, Native Hawaiians settled in valleys watered by streams with proximity to the ocean. Here they planted along the streams and up the sides of gulches. Gradually, they terraced the gulches in a network of interconnected loʻi kalo or taro pond fields. Native Hawaiians also settled on the slopes and flatlands above and between the valleys, regions that were favored with lots of rain and also had access to the ocean. Here, they cultivated dryland taro as well as sweet potatoes, yams, and bananas for food, wauke for bark cloth, olonā for cordage, ʻawa for a relaxant drink, and other edible and useful native plants. Native Hawaiians also developed settlements along coastal areas of the drier sections where springs percolated up through the rocky shore or in shallow waters of the bays. From the streams and near-shore ocean they harvested fish, shellfish, and seaweed.

Moving along the coast, north to south, from ʻOʻopuloa Gulch and eastward to Nāhiku, Native Hawaiian families settled and cultivated gardens in the narrow valleys fed by small streams—ʻOʻopuloa, Waikamoi, Puohokamoa, and Haipuaʻena.[24] Next, in the broad, deep valley of Honomanū, which has a large stream and a broad beach for fishing canoes and net fishing, a large Native Hawaiian population constructed terraces deep into the valley for taro cultivation. The Nuaʻailua Valley and the adjacent slopes and flatlands were also settled and cultivated in taro terraces. At Keaʻane, the early Hawaiians first settled in the uplands above the peninsula and cultivated dryland taro up into the forested areas. Under the direction of a Keʻanae chief, the people also carried soil from the uplands onto the lava peninsula and, in a unique feat of engineering, diverted water using an old canoe as a wooden flume in order to develop an extensive network of taro pond fields.[25] A large population of Native Hawaiians also settled in and developed irrigated taro terraces in the adjacent valley and broad lands of Wailuanui. Going east from Wailuanui, Native Hawaiian families lived in the gulches of East Wailuaiki, West Wailuaiki, Kapiliʻula, Waohue, Paʻakea, Kapaʻula, and Makapipi and cultivated taro and other useful crops.[26]

There are no large streams or gulches from east of Nāhiku out to Hāmoa, but the area receives a lot of rain. The soil is made up of decomposed lava with humus. At ʻUlaʻino , Honomaele, Honokalani, Helani, Olopawa, Hāna, and Hāmoa, Native Hawaiian families built homes and cultivated dryland taro on the slopes and flatlands. They also cultivated yams, sweet potatoes, bananas, wauke, olonā, and ʻawa. Upland from Hāmoa, the Native Hawaiians cultivated their food crops in a valley named ʻŌpaekuʻi during the dry season. The valley is fifteen miles long and an offshoot of the marshy upland called Waihoʻi. While working in their upland gardens, Hawaiian planters subsisted on mashed shrimps *(ʻōpae kuʻi)*, which they took with them in calabashes, and poi pounded from the starchy core of the hapuʻu fern, which was cooked in imu ovens of stone in the earth. The planters also gathered wild *uhi* and *hoi* (types of yams) in the forest of this area.

South of Hāmoa, several streams carved out gulches into the landscape, and Native Hawaiians settled along the streams and developed taro terraces at Makaʻalae, Waiohonu, Puʻuiki, Pōhue, Pukuilua, Hāʻōʻū, Hulihana, Mūʻolea, and Koali. Beyond Koali, the deep little valley of Wailua was extensively settled and cultivated at four distinct levels, moving in from the sea up the valley toward the mountain. Past Wailua, the land is steep and high and unsuited to fishing or planting.

In Kīpahulu, Native Hawaiians settled and cultivated wet taro at Kukuiʻula, Lolokea, Hanawī, ʻAlele, Kalepa, and Nuanualoa. Dryland taro was cultivated in the low forest that fringed the area.

Kaupō is a dry area. Dryland taro was planted in the lower forest belt. However, sweet potato was the staple food of the families who settled here. Even their poi was made from sweet potatoes. There were some settlements in Waiha and Punaluʻu where a few taro terraces were developed. Water came from springs such as Punahoe and Waiū and in the Manawainui Valley.

Figure 16 Waikauikalāʻau, or "the suspended water," a wooden flume made of an old canoe, carried water from the Palauhulu Stream into the Keʻanae Peninsula in the nineteenth century. 1883. C. J. Hedemann, W. T. Brigham Collection, Bishop Museum.

Hawaiian *mauka-makai* (mountain-ocean) use of the ahupuaʻa in southeast Maui was linked to the planting cycle, which was dependent upon the variations in rainfall according to elevation and seasons. In the uplands, where it usually rained daily, planting could be done year round. In the lowlands, planting was usually done in conjunction with the rainy season. When the rains moved on to the lowlands, each family lived at temporary habitation sites along the coast where they cultivated small plots of sweet potatoes and gourds. This important seasonal habitation cycle is documented in the interviews with Sam Po, a native of Kanaio. According to him, even up through the latter half of the nineteenth century the kuaʻāina in the district continued to live seasonally mauka and makai and plant in accordance with the annual rains.[27]

The ocean along the entire Koʻolau District provided Hawaiians with various sources of food, including numerous varieties of fish, crab, shellfish, and seaweed. Fishing, such as diving, was an individual enterprise. Deep-sea fishing in canoes was conducted by the men in the ʻohana, while *hukilau* or large-net fishing was a community enterprise.

Fishing and ocean gathering were carried out according to the moon phases and the stars. When the stars were numerous and bright, that was the time to go and look for the shellfish such as *kūpeʻe (Nerita polita)*, which usually hide during the day. This gathering was done in the utmost silence, lest the shellfish drop and burrow to hide themselves.[28]

Figure 17 All members of the Hāmoa community of Hāna would gather to pull in the great hukilau fishing nets. 1936. Harold T. Stearns, Bishop Museum.

Salt for the Hāna district was gathered at Nuʻu, where there were *kaheka* (natural hollows) in the rocks in which salt *(paʻakai)* accumulated when the shallow ponds that formed during rough seas dried up in the sun. People from throughout the Hāna district would travel to Nuʻu in the summertime to gather salt. Nuʻualoʻa, in Kaupō, had several veins of *ʻalae*, a red earthy mineral that gets its color from its high iron content. The Hawaiians commonly ground their salt together with ʻalae to enrich it with iron.[29] Families would gather an entire year's supply during the summer, dry it, and store it in caves. Summer was also the spawning time for the *manini*, the *humuhumunukunukuapuaʻa*, the mullet, and the *āholehole* fishes. These would be caught and salted to provide food throughout the year.

At the end of the development period on Maui, during the time of Kakaalaneo, the division of lands on Maui was carried out under the priest Kahuna Kalaihaʻohiʻa ("hew the bark of the ʻōhiʻa tree"). This marked the beginning of the rule of chiefs over islands, with landlords over large divisions under them and agents appointed by the landlords overseeing districts and small divisions. At about this time on Oʻahu, Mailikūkahi marked out the boundaries for the land divisions and initiated measures to strengthen the rule of a chief over an expanding population.[30]

The Migratory and the Ruling Chiefs of Hāna

Nuʻu and his wife Nuʻumea or Nuʻumealani, or "the female who propagates from heaven," arrived at Nuʻu on Maui with their canoe, called the canoe of Kāne. Nuʻu was a great kahuna, associated with the era of overturning and the time of the great flood. In the genealogy of Kumuhonua, Luanuʻu, son of Nuʻu, also called Kānehoalani, was the ancestor of the Mū and the Menehune people. Nuʻu came after the first Hawaiian from a foreign place, and after him came Hawaiʻi Nui or Hawaiʻiloa.[31]

The moʻolelo of Hāna provides at least two different accounts of the origin of the ruling chiefs of Maui. In both versions, Hāna was ruled separately from West Maui. According to one source, the ancestors of the *mōʻī* (kings) of Maui were Paumakua, a southerner voyager, possibly a Tahitian (975 or 1200), and Haho (1000 or 1225). However, the districts of Koʻolau, Hāna, Kīpahulu, and Kaupō were often under different mōʻī not closely connected with the rulers of western Maui.[32]

A second source states that Maui was divided into two separate kingdoms, where the Nanaʻulu line governed the Hāna Coast and the ʻUlu line controlled the remainder of the island. At the time that High Chief ʻUmialīloa ruled Hawaiʻi, High Chief Piʻilani, from the ʻUlu line of western Maui conquered the Hāna coast and united the island under his rule.[33] At the time of his conquest, Piʻilani may have dedicated the great temple, Piʻilanihale, believed to be the largest heiau in the Hawaiian Islands, at Honomaʻele.[34] To consolidate an alliance with the Maui chiefs, ʻUmialīloa arranged to marry Piʻikea, the daughter of High Chief Piʻilani.

The history of the Hāna district in East and South Maui also involves many chiefs from Hawaiʻi. Given Hāna's proximity to Hawaiʻi, it periodically served as a residence and sanctuary for chiefs of both islands. The distance between East Maui and ʻUpolu Point on Hawaiʻi could be crossed in either direction in a couple of hours. It was an ideal location for ruling aliʻi of either island. Hāna had an abundance of the type of wood used for making scaffolds and ladders to scale fortresses, and it had the best smooth, round stones for warriors to use in slingshots. Fish and taro were plentiful. The surfing was fine. The Hawaiian historian Samuel Kamakau described the features that made Hāna so attractive:

> Hāna was in those days a noted place famous for the fortified hill Kaʻuiki, the surf at Puhele, the fresh-water bathing pool of Kumaka, the diving at Waiohinu, the flying spray of Kama, the changing color of the fronds of the amaʻu fern, the yellow-leafed ʻawa of Lanakila, the delicious poi of Kuakahi, the fat shell fish (ʻopihi) of Kawapapa, the fat soft uhu fish of Haneoʻo, and the juicy pork and tender dog meat dear to the memory of chiefs of that land, moistened by the ʻapuakea rain that rattles on the hala trees from Wakiu to Honokalani.[35]

Altogether, it was then, as it remains today, a pleasant, bountiful, and beautiful place to live.[36] The fortress of Kaʻuiki also made Hāna one of the most attractive places for the Native Hawaiian chiefs to live.

Kaʻuiki and the Ruling Chiefs

The ʻolelo noʻeau "O Wananalua ia ʻāina; o Punahoa ka wai; o Kaʻuiki ka puʻu" (Wananalua is the land; Punahoa is the pool; Kaʻuiki is the hill) identifies famous wahi pana of Hāna.[37]

Of these, Kaʻuiki hill is the most famous and culturally significant. It figured prominently in the myths and history about Hāna. Martha Beckwith wrote about the hill's mythical origins and significance in *Hawaiian Mythology:*

Some say that it sprang from the navel of Hāmoa. Others that it was born to the parents of Pele, or to the hill Kai-hua-kala by his wife Kahaule. Others relate how Ka-lala-walu (The eight-branched) brought the hill from Kahiki as an adopted child, but grew tired of its nibbling at her breasts and tried to leave it along the way, first at Kaloa, then at Kaena, then at the Ka-wai-papa stream. Others tell of the wanderings and death of Puʻuhele, little sister of Pele . . . men say that formerly Kāne and Kana-loa planted a garden below the hill, and they point out two rocks below the hill on the inaccessible sea side which are called "the coconuts of Kāne and Kanaloa" and the "root-stock" (kumu) of Kauiki . . . Here lived Hina-hana-ia-ka-malama, she who worked at tapa making in the moon, and her husband, father of Puna and Hema on the Ulu line of chiefs.[38]

During the epoch of Hawaiʻi's ruling chiefs, Hāna was reputed to be a favorite and beloved district because of the fortress of Kaʻuiki and the ease of living in that district.[39] A chant for Kaʻuiki recalls, "Healoha no Kaʻuiki / Au i ke kai me he manu la" (Kaʻuiki is beloved / Afloat on the sea like a bird).[40]

Kaʻuiki was famous for its strength as a refuge in times of danger. Its summit was approached by a ladder made of ʻōhiʻa wood from Kealakomo and fastened with the ʻieʻie vine from Paiolopawa. The summit was covered with kana-wao plants from Kawaipaka, furnishing a natural bedding for those defending the fortress. The fishponds of Kihahale provided an abundance of fish. The big ʻawa roots of Kualakila delighted the nostrils of the first-born chiefs with their aroma. Below the fortified walls of Kaʻuiki was the excellent battlefield of Wānanalua. A lookout was stationed at Mokuhana to warn those in the fortress where to strike against their enemies.[41]

Numerous chiefs of Maui and Hawaiʻi settled with their families and entourages at and around Kaʻuiki. These included Hua, son of Pohukaina, descendant of the Ulu line of chiefs; Kanaloa and Kalahumoku, sons of Hualani (the wife of Kanipahu) and half brothers to Kalapana, who ruled Hawaiʻi; Eleio; Kalaehaeha; Lei; Kamohoaliʻi; Kalaehina; and Hoʻolaemakua.

Kaʻuiki featured prominently in the rivalry between the sons and heirs, Lonoapiʻilani and Kihaapiʻilani, of the ruler of Maui, High Chief Piʻilani. Lonoapiʻilani, as ruler of Maui, felt threatened by his younger brother Kiha-apiʻilani and sought to kill him.[42] Kihaapiʻilani escaped and then conspired to overthrow Lonoapiʻilani. Kihaapiʻilani married the daughter of the chief Hoʻolaemakua, who controlled Kaʻuiki, in order to recruit his support for the rebellion against Lonoapiʻilani. Hoʻolaemakua remained loyal to Lonoapiʻilani, and Kihaapiʻilani was forced to seek the support of his brother-in-law, ʻUmialīloa of Waipiʻo. Kihaapiʻilani and ʻUmialīloa spent a year preparing for the invasion of Maui by building canoes and making clubs and other implements for battle. When the fleet of canoes reached Hāna, Hoʻolaemakua commanded the battle from Kaʻuiki. The Hawaiʻi warriors were unable to land at Hāna. Kihaapiʻilani directed the Hawaiʻi canoes to land on the shores of Wailuaiki and Wailuanui, where they were dismantled and set upright so that all of the great fleet could beach. The Hawaiʻi warriors marched over land to Hāna. Hoʻolaemakua fought against the Hawaiʻi warriors for days, until the warrior Piʻimaiwaʻa discovered that at night, the fortress was guarded only by a wooden image cunningly set up to look like a huge armed warrior. The Hawaiʻi warriors finally defeated the forces of Hoʻolaemakua and killed him at Kapipiwai, near Nāhiku. Piʻimaiwaʻa assumed the chieftainship of Kaʻuiki.

The war fleet of Kihaapiʻilani and ʻUmialīloa proceeded to attack Lonoapiʻilani at Wailuku. Hearing of their approach and fearing defeat, torture, and death, Lonoapiʻilani is said to have trembled with fear and died. Kihaapiʻilani became one of the greatest rulers of Maui. He oversaw the construction of the Alaloa road: 138 miles long and paved with water-worn stones laid out four to six feet wide between curbstones, it completely encircled the island of Maui.[43]

Kaleikini, who also dwelt at Kaʻuiki, is remembered for sending canoes to Lanaʻi to gather logs of kauila wood to seal the many blowholes along the Hāna coast, which had previously sprayed salt water on the good agricultural lands and natural vegetation of Hāna. At Honokalani, remnants of those logs can still be seen.[44]

In Kamehameha's time, Kaʻahumanu, the most influential and powerful wife of Kamehameha I and *kuhina nui* or prime minister for Kamehameha II and Kamehameha III was born at Kaʻuiki in 1768. Her parents, Keʻeaumoku and his wife, had sought refuge there from Kahekili. Keʻeaumoku and the Hāna chiefs played a major role in Kamehameha's rise to power and in his central government.[45] On the eve of European contact, Hāna continued to be fought over by the ruling chiefs of Hawaiʻi and Maui.

High Chief Kekaulike resided at Kaupō and in 1700 built the great heiau of Puʻumakaʻa at Kumuni and Kanemalohemo (Keakalaʻauae) at Popoiwi near Mokulau in Kaupō. High Chief Kekaulike also rededicated the Loʻaloʻa heiau in Kaupō around 1730. He left his youngest son, Kamehamehanui, as ruler when he died in 1736 at Lelekea, near Kaupō.[46]

Later, Alapaʻinui, king of Hawaiʻi, landed a large force at Mokulau near

Kaupō to raid Maui. However, in 1736, when he discovered that his own nephew, Kamehamehanui, was the new mōʻī of Maui, he negotiated a peace agreement.[47]

In 1754 Kalaniopuʻu became the ruling chief over Hawaiʻi.[48] In 1759 High Chief Kalaniopuʻu went to war against High Chief Kamehamehanui to win control of Hāna and Kīpahulu. Kalaniopuʻu won control of the marvelous fortress of Kaʻuiki. Kamehamehanui, with the support of chiefs from Moloka'i and Lānaʻi, sought to regain Kaʻuiki, Hāna, and Kīpahulu in the battle known as Kapalipilo. The battle extended from Akiala to Honomaele, but Kalaniopuʻu and the Hawaiʻi warriors were victorious, and Hāna and Kīpahulu remained under the control of Hawaiʻi. When Kalaniopuʻu returned to Hawaiʻi, he left the chief Puna in control of Kaʻuiki. Mahihelelima, independent chief of Hāna, Kīpahulu, and Kaupō deceived Puna and thus managed to replace him as head of the fortress of Kaʻuiki. Nevertheless, Kalaniopuʻu retained control over Hāna and Kīpahulu.

In 1765 High Chief Kamehamehanui died. He was succeeded as the ruler of Maui by High Chief Kahekili. From 1775 to 1779 Kalaniopuʻu continuously waged battles against High Chief Kahekili of Maui from his stronghold in Hāna and Kīpahulu.[49] In the battle of Kalaehohoa ("the forehead beaten with clubs"), Kalaniopuʻu sent his warriors from Hāna to raid Kaupō and take control of the district. The Hawaiʻi warriors abused the local people and beat them over the head with clubs. Kahekili sent his warriors, led by Kāneʻolaelae, to Kaupō to retaliate against Kalaniopuʻu and restore his control over that district. Kamehameha distinguished himself as a strong warrior in this battle, known as Kalaeokaʻilio where it was fought. He rescued the warrior Kekuhaupiʻo, his instructor in the fighting arts, from death. However, as described by Stephen Desha, the Hawaiʻi warriors were defeated: "The Hawaii warriors fled but many were slaughtered by the Maui people at that battle at Kaupō which was named the Battle of Kalaeokaʻilio. It was a battle in which the bodies of the Hawaiʻi warriors were heaped like kukui branches before Maui's exceptional warriors."[50]

Contact and the Rise of Kamehameha over Hāna and Maui

When Captain James Cook returned to Hawaiʻi in November 1778, he first anchored at Haʻaluea, below Wailuaiki on Maui.[51] At the time, Kalaniopuʻu and his forces were in the Koʻolau district of Maui fighting Kahekili. The young Kohala chief, Kamehameha, and his mentor, Kekuhaupiʻo, boarded Cook's ship and sailed with Cook toward Hawaiʻi Island until a canoe sent by Kalaniopuʻu caught up with the ship and summoned it to return to Maui.[52] In 1781 Kahekili made war on the Hawaiʻi chiefs and their Maui allies in Hāna. Mahihelelima joined forces with Kalaniopuʻu against Kahekili. The fortress of Kaʻuiki was impenetrable and held out against Kahekili's warriors for one year until Kahekili was able to cut off the water supply to Kaʻuiki. Thus, he finally wrested control of Hāna and Kīpahulu away from Kalaniopuʻu and his allies.[53]

In 1785 Kahekili vanquished Kahahana as chief of Oʻahu and went to Oʻahu to consolidate his rule over that island, leaving his son, High Chief Kalanikupule, to rule Maui. At that time, Kamehameha sent his brother Kalanimalokulokuikepoʻolani to retake control over Hāna and Kīpahulu for the Hawaiʻi chiefs.[54] He met with no resistance and instituted a policy of benevolent rule over the people, gaining the name Keliʻimaikaʻi or "good-hearted aliʻi," which he kept until his death. When Kalanikupule learned that Hāna and Kīpahulu were under the rule of the Hawaiʻi chiefs, he dispatched a great army of warriors that defeated and ousted the Hawaiʻi warriors. Keliʻimaikaʻi escaped back to Hawaiʻi.

In 1790 Kamehameha invaded Hāna and defeated the Maui warriors in a battle called Kaua o Kawaʻanui (Battle of Great Canoes). Moving on from Hāna, he slaughtered the Maui chiefs at Iao Valley in a battle called Kaua i Kepaniwai o Iao (Battle at the Dammed Water of ʻIao; the name referred to the damming of the ʻIao stream with bodies of slain warriors). Despite these victories, as discussed in chapter 2, Kamehameha had to return to Hawaiʻi to protect his lands and people from the assaults of his rival, Keouakūahuʻula of Kaʻū. At that point, Kahekili formed an alliance with High Chief Kaʻeokulani of Kauaʻi and returned to Maui. Together, Kahekili and Kaʻeokulani retook control of Hāna and launched an attack upon Kamehameha and his forces on Hawaiʻi. Landing at Waipiʻo, Kaʻeokulani viciously attacked the people of Waipiʻo and desecrated the sacred heiau of the Hawaiʻi chiefs, as described in chapter 2. When Kahekili joined Kaʻeokulani, their forces were defeated by Kamehameha off of Waimanu in the naval battle Kaua o Kepuwahaʻulaʻula, (Battle of Red-Mouthed Cannon).[55] Kahekili retreated back to Maui in defeat, having fought his last battle. He died on Oʻahu in 1793. Kamehameha finally assumed the rule over all of Maui, including Hāna, through his victory over High Chief Kahekili's successor, High Chief Kalanikupule, in the Battle of Nuʻuanu on Oʻahu in 1795.

Hāna in the Nineteenth Century

In the early 1800s missionaries made an estimate of the population in the various districts of Maui in order to determine the number of missionaries to assign. The missionary Jonathan S. Green concluded that Hāna, Kaupō, and Kīpahulu were well-populated districts in need of missionaries, as he wrote in December 1835:

- Kaupō district: similar in appearance to the Kīpahulu district, but larger and more populous. Small vessels frequently anchor here. Missionaries are needed here.
- Kīpahulu district: rough country, fertile, and populous. In need of two missionary families and a missionary station.
- Hāna district: large populous densely inhabited in need of four missionaries.[56]

In 1837, seventeen years after the settlement of missionaries in Hawai'i, a permanent mission station was established in Hāna. Prior to that date, missionary presence and influence in the district were weak because the missionaries ventured to the Hāna Coast only once or twice a year. However, mission schools were established in the Hāna district by 1850.[57] Churches in the area were built in the 1850s and 1860s with beach rocks that were washed up to shore by extraordinary storms.[58] Even after the churches were established, mission duty in the Hāna district was considered to be among the most difficult because of its isolation.[59] Thus, Hawaiian spiritual beliefs and practices persisted without competition from Christian beliefs longer in Hāna than in other parts of Maui.

Continental diseases killed much of the Native Hawaiian population in east Maui. Samuel Kamakau described how a measles epidemic in 1848 wiped out a third of the population of the Islands. About the impact in east Maui he wrote: "I know personally of two families in Kipahulu, those of 'Ili-mai-healani and Kuku-'ula, in which only three persons were left out of fourteen. In Ka-pule's home at Papauluna [Kipahulu] nine died out of thirteen. At this rate more must have died than survived."[60]

Samuel Kamakau also described the impact of the smallpox epidemic that swept through the Hāna district in 1853: "The whole population was wiped out from Wakiu, the uplands of Kawaipapa, Palemo, and mauka of Waika'akihi in the Hana district, and so for ipahulu and Kaupo."[61]

The Māhele in 1848 and the Kuleana Act in 1850 established a system of private property ownership of all the lands on Maui and the Hawaiian Islands. In the entire Hāna district a total of 1,690.718 acres were awarded to 324 makaʻāinana. The awards ranged in size from 0.03 acres to 211 acres; the average size was 5.218 acres. Table 2 shows the number of Land Commission awards granted in each subdistrict.

Hāna Māhele Awards to Aliʻi

Ten awards of ahupuaʻa or large sections of ahupuaʻa were also made to aliʻi and konohiki in the Hāna district.[62] In Koʻolau, the ahupuaʻa of ʻUlaʻino was awarded to James Young Kanehoa, son of Kamehameha's British military adviser, John Olohana Young, and his first wife, Namokuelua. He accompanied King Liholiho and Queen Kamāmalu to England as an interpreter. From 1846 to 1847 he served on the Board of Commissioners to Quiet Land Titles.

In Hāna, Julia Alapai Kauwa, the wife of Kanehoa's brother, Keoni Ana (John Young, Jr.), was awarded 873.89 acres of the ahupuaʻa of Haneoʻo. The ahupuaʻa of ʻAleamai, with 1,093.5 acres, was awarded to Enoka Kuakamauna for his wife, Henrietta Kaleimakaliʻi. According to the claim in the Native Register, ʻAleamai was his wife's share from the mōʻī. Kaleimakaliʻi was a descendant of Keawekuikekaai, son of Keakealanikane and Kaleimakaliʻi I. Her mother was a niece and namesake of John Papa Ii's mother, Wanaoa Kalaikane. The konohiki Kahanu was awarded half of the ahupuaʻa of Honomaele—990 acres. He relinquished his share in the other half of the ahupuaʻa to the government.

The ahupuaʻa of Mūʻolea was awarded to Keohokalole, the mother of King Kalākaua and Queen Liliʻuokalani.

In Kīpahulu, the two ahupuaʻa ʻAlaenui and Wailamoa were awarded to Kekauonohi, who was married to Aarona Kealiʻiahonui, governor of Kauaʻi and hānai son of the kuhina nui Kaʻahumanu. She married Levi Haʻalelea in 1850, a year after Kealiʻiahonui's death. Kekauonohi was an heir of her uncle

TABLE 2 LAND COMMISSION AWARDS IN HĀNA

DISTRICT	NO. OF AWARDS	NO. OF ACRES	AVERAGE SIZE
Koʻolau	131 awards	361.573 acres	2.76 acres
Hāna	111 awards	785.418 acres	7.075 acres
Kīpahulu	56 awards	354.53 acres	6.33 acres
Kaupō	26 awards	189.197 acres	7.276 acres

Kalanimoku as well as of her mother's husband, Kaukuna Kahekili. She also received awards of Māalo, Puʻulani, Popoʻōʻio, and Kahuai in Kaupō. The ahupuaʻa of Kaʻapahu was awarded to William Charles Lunalilo, who later became king. The ahupuaʻa of Maulili was awarded to J. A. Kuakini.

In Kaupō, 12,140 acres in the ahupuaʻa of Nuʻu was awarded to Kalaimoku. He was a cousin of Kuhina Nui Kaʻahumanu and descended from Kamanawa I. His wife was the sister of Kamakahonu.

Five awards were also made to foreigners in the Hāna district. In Koʻolau, 471 acres were awarded to Stephen Grant, Pakea, and Poakea. In Hāna, the American Board of Commissioners for Foreign missions acquired 27.64 acres in Wananalua. John Richardson and Company was awarded 211 acres in Olewa. In Kaupō, 1.5 acres were awarded to a Dr. Baldwin in Pualaea, Kalianu, and 145 acres were awarded to William Harbottle in Kumunui 1.

The first sugar mill was established in Hāna in 1849 by George Wilfong, a haole sea captain who invested his profits from whaling activities in sixty acres of land at Kaʻuiki.[63] In 1852 the first Chinese laborers arrived in Hāna on five-year contracts, but Wilfong's mill burned down soon thereafter. In

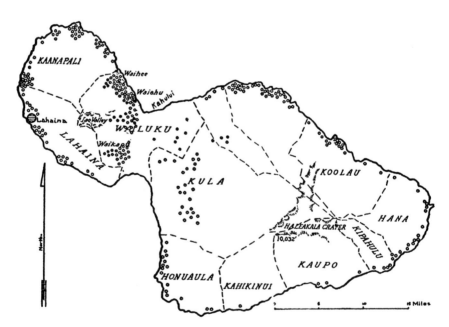

Map 2 The Coulter 1853 population map of Maui shows a population of 2,000 for the Koʻolau, Hāna, Kīpahulu, and Kaupō districts. ○ = 50 persons. *Source:* Coulter, *Population and Utilization of Land and Sea*, p. 22.

1864 two Danish brothers, August and Oscar Unna, raised $47,000 to start the Hāna plantation. Beginning in 1868 they imported Japanese laborers through the Hawaiian Labor and Supply Company.[64] By 1883 there were six separate sugar plantations on the Hāna Coast—the Hāna Sugar, Kaʻelekū Sugar, and Reciprocity Sugar Companies, and the Hāmoa Agricultural, Kawaipapa Agricultural, and Haneoʻo Agricultural Companies.[65]

As the Chinese immigrant laborers who had been brought in to work on the Hāna Coast plantations either completed or broke their contracts in the late 1800s, they looked for a place to settle. Along the Hāna Coast, Keʻanae provided an excellent location, given its isolation and the traditional terracing and irrigation of the land for taro. The Chinese were able to cultivate rice wherever taro farmers were interested in earning cash by renting out their traditional taro growing land.[66]

Throughout the nineteenth century and until the Hāna road was built in 1927, the Koʻolau district of Maui, between Keʻanae and Hāna, was practically inaccessible by land. Travelers entering the district from Wailuku, usually rode on horseback to Keʻanae, and then journeyed by canoe to Hāna, generally taking two days. However, if one traveled entirely by canoe from Wailuku, the trip took only five and a half hours.[67] Through the 1860s, when the Hāna sugar plantation was established, Hāna maintained a reputation of being one of the most isolated places in all of Hawaiʻi.[68]

At Nuʻu, in the 1800s, the king's ship used to come from Lahaina to obtain fish. The kuaʻāina would catch mullet for the king in the fishpond. Originally, the pond had an outlet to the ocean, but it was later blocked off. At Nuʻu landing, fishermen who perished when their canoes overturned in the rough surf as the men were trying to land were buried in a small graveyard.[69]

The District during the Territorial Period

In 1900 the average pay for the plantation workers was $15 a month for twenty-six days of work, ten hours a day in the field or twelve in the mill. This was less than 5 cents an hour. They were also provided with camp housing, schooling, some medical care, and recreation programs. Many of the workers supplemented their meager incomes by fishing, hunting, and gardening, learning from the Hawaiians of the district how to best utilize the natural resources available along the Hāna Coast.[70] By 1905 both Hāmoa Agricultural Company and the Haneoo Agricultural Company had been absorbed into the Kaeleku Company, a subsidiary of C. Brewer.

The principal limitation to the modernization of the Hāna Coast was the difficulty encountered in traveling over land to Hāna for trucks and cars in 1927. The people of the Hāna Coast overcame the obstacles to transportation and communication by maintaining contact with the outside world through the inter-island steamers that called at the district at least once a month. Hāna, the safest harbor for these steamers, developed as the major center of commerce for the Koʻolau district.[71]

Although Hāna was regularly serviced by steamers, because of the difficulty of the voyage, visitors to the district were rare, and the manner of life among the Hawaiians was quaint by comparison to that of urban Honolulu, Oʻahu, or even Wailuku, Maui. In 1910 H. M. Ayres, a reporter for the *Pacific Commercial Advertiser*, wrote a series of articles about an excursion through the Hāna Coast. He described the arrival of passengers from the SS *Claudine* at Hāna:

> While the landing is all right for freight, it is mightily inconvenient for passengers and when the swell is heavy it must be dangerous to life and limb. Passengers leaving here have to jump into the arms of the boat boys, and on occasion have to be grabbed and thrown from the boat to the wharf.
>
> The visitor to Hāna put up at the comfortable club maintained by L. Y. Aiona, a Chinese gentleman of parts who runs the club rather as an accommodation for visitors than as a money-making proposition. A man at the house of whom every visitor to Hāna calls is W. P. Haia, the Bismarck of the Maui County Board of Supervisors.[72]

Mr. Ayers was still able to observe a traditional *lauhala* thatched house in the Hāna area. Nearby, men were making fishhooks out of wire and women cooked papayas in ti leaves.[73]

Even though Keʻanae had a landing, Harry Kūhini Mitchell, a Keʻanae taro farmer born in 1919 in Keʻanae of Hawaiian and Chinese ancestry, recalled that if the ocean was too rough for loading and unloading there, freight would be dropped off at Hāna, and the people of Keʻanae would have to go to Hāna by horseback to pick up their goods. He also remembered how the Chinese owner of a poi factory in Keʻanae, Ah Lum, had a twelve-mule wagon train that he used to deliver poi between Keʻanae and Hāna. When he reached Hāna he would go down to the pier to look for freight for the Keʻanae people. He would then take the freight back to Keʻanae for a small fee. According to Mitchell:

Hāna was the major place. The same boat come Keʻanae. Too rough . . . they cannot land . . . so they come Hāna, unload our goods. And we got a horse trail eh. And we come all the way Hāna, pick up our freight, come home.

And the Chinese, Ah Lum, he had the poi factory . . . He pound his own poi. Deliver the poi. Come Hāna . . . pick up, he go down the pier. Look for freight for the Keʻanae people. You know, then he charge you so much, so much, for bringing the freight, eh.

The Keʻanae landing—too small, eh. And, uh, where they land, you know, the whaler come in. The big boat then come outside. Then the rowboat come inside. The whaler deliver passengers, deliver freight, we get donkey engine. The old way only up and down. Then, uh, gotta get one man with the rope, one on each side, yeah. Then pull ʻem. Come on land then they—only can go up and down. And steep.[74]

Sugar freighters also made port calls to transport the sugar produced in the district to mainland markets.

The population of the Hāna district in 1930 was 2,436, of which 1,177 people were Hawaiians, accounting for 48 percent of the population. In Kaupō and Kahikinui the total population was 185, of which 160 people were Hawaiian, accounting for a percentage of 86 percent.[75]

A few Native Hawaiians worked for the sugar mill, and some worked as cowboys for the Kaupō Ranch, but the majority of Hawaiians were subsistence farmers and fishers, occasionally selling or exchanging their labor, agricultural products, or fish for money, cloth, or tools. They farmed, hunted, and fished to provide their families with food and basic necessities. When money was needed, the men would usually work for a day's wage shoeing horses, pouring cement, clearing land, harvesting rice, mending fences, catching wild cattle, or hauling goods overland.[76]

TABLE 3 POPULATION OF HĀNA DISTRICT IN 1930

DISTRICT	TOTAL POPULATION	NO. HAWAIIAN	% HAWAIIAN
Hāna Town	1,585	536	34
Kīpahulu	147	118	80
Kaupō-Kahikinui	185	160	86
Total	2,436	1,177	48

Source: U.S. Bureau of the Census, *Fifteenth Census of the United States: 1930, Occupation Statistics Hawaii* (Washington: Government Printing Office, 1931), p. 72, table 22. The precincts were identified in "Governors' Proclamations," 1926–30, pp. 6–21.

The ʻOhana of Hāna

Native Hawaiian households of the Hāna coast tended to be larger in size than those of the urban Native Hawaiian families on Oʻahu. They were usually multigenerational, that is, they consisted of grandparents, parents, and grandchildren. Married children were encouraged to live at home. The tradition of hānai was actively and extensively practiced among the Hāna Coast Hawaiians.[77]

The homes of the Hāna Hawaiians were generally small two- or at most three-room wooden structures with outhouses. The large families usually crowded together on the floor to sleep. Cooking was usually done outside over open wood fires.

Along the Hāna coast, the extended family or ʻohana was still a viable social and economic unit. Food was constantly shared and exchanged within the ʻohana. Relatives were always ready to share whatever they had with relatives and to take in destitute relatives and friends.

Douglas Yamamura, who became a professor of sociology and chancellor of the University of Hawaiʻi at Mānoa, was born and raised on the Hāna plantation. In 1939 he conducted interviews with families from Hāna, Kīpahulu, and Kaupō for his master's thesis in sociology at the University of Hawaiʻi. Yamamura made a number of observations about the Native Hawaiian ʻohana of the Hāna Coast on the eve of World War II, in 1939–41:

> The Hawaiian household is still a closely knit group. The bilateral kin or
> family group functions today as a cooperative and jointly responsible unit
> in the household organization. This is a survival of the old Hawaiian
> culture in which the "large family" or ʻohana, a kin group—the bilateral
> kinship grouping of all those related by blood, marriage, or adoption, and
> including a number of households—functioned as a unit in economic and
> social affairs of the community.
>
> The average Hawaiian depends largely on relatives and friends for
> support when he is destitute. Relatives are always ready to share what they
> have or to take others into the household, even though there are no visible
> means of supporting the enlarged group.[78]

Nearly 75 percent of the households along the Hāna Coast had horses or mules for transport between the communities of the coast and for traveling outside the district. However, most people just traveled on foot within their community and ahupuaʻa or between ahupuaʻa. The churches, one-room schoolhouses, and general stores, which were commonly located at the center of each of these communities, were all readily accessible on foot. Whatever jobs were available were also within walking distance. The communities were loosely organized units composed of households scattered over a wide area. The churches and schools served as unifying forces for the community. The churches brought the community together for the Sunday service, and the schoolhouse brought the children together for daily classes.[79]

Family obligations often put a heavy strain on ethnically mixed marriages. It also made it almost impossible for a Hawaiian to survive in any storekeeping business, because the Hawaiian owner was expected to automatically extend unlimited credit to his family and friends.[80]

Yamamura took note of Hawaiian attitudes toward money and work in his study of factors affecting the success of Hāna Hawaiian children in school:

> Under the old culture and economy of Hawaii, there was no need for the individual to accumulate wealth, for the land was always present and provided all the necessities of life. Thus periods of hard work were followed by long periods of relaxation. These values of the ancient culture to some extent still condition the life of the average Hawaiian in the Hāna district. To have an adequate amount of leisure the Hawaiians may be contented with earnings that put them on a subsistence level.[81]

The Hawaiian children of Hāna were required to attend school through the eighth grade, as were children throughout Hawaiʻi between 1900 and 1930. However, Hawaiian children tended to be indifferent to Western education. The culture of the classroom did not match the culture of the family. The conflict between the Hawaiian values the children lived day by day and the Western values the schools taught them tended to alienate Hawaiian children from achieving in the school. One manifestation of Hawaiian children's poor adjustment to school was their high rate of absenteeism.

Yamamura observed this problem and attributed it to the conflict between Western values and Hawaiian values. He even suggested that Hawaiians' absenteeism from school may have been one form of resistance to a culture that submerged native culture. He believed that the indifference of Hawaiian parents to the school system was a form of rejecting domination by Western values:

> The economic status of the Hawaiian families, their passive resistance to the ideals of the west, and the conception of responsibility of older for younger children sponsored by the solidarity of the kin group are important causes for the frequent absences of the child from school.

Even before the child comes to school, he has acquired, to a certain extent, an immunity to the teachings of the western culture. Therefore, much of the school work is passed off as inconsequential. Such patterns of action make possible the continuance of ideals and values of the native culture, hindering the complete assimilation of the Hawaiians into the American culture.[82]

Harry Mitchell explained the conflict he experienced between what was taught in school and what was practiced at home. He also described the punishment he received for speaking Hawaiian in the school.

> You go school, learn. You come home, you try apply. They [grandparents] scold you. You gotta live their lifestyle. Not the one they teach you from the school. The school, junk eh. We only play in the damn school. No study. Play hookey, eh. Go fishing. Forget it. Go hunting. They punish you. You pull weeds they catch you speaking Hawaiian. They make you stand in the corner on one leg till you fall asleep. No way, eh.[83]

The conflicts the Hawaiians in the Hāna district experienced between Western and Hawaiian values were mitigated in different ways. According to the oral accounts of kūpuna who were interviewed, some family members left Hāna to assimilate into urban living in Wailuku or Honolulu, while others chose to stay in Hāna as their parents had before them and to maintain their Hawaiian way of life.

Yamamura also reported that the Hāna Hawaiians, lacking access to Western medicine, continued to rely upon lā'au lapa'au, or traditional Hawaiian healing practices, for their health care. One of his informants described how her father had fallen off a small cliff and smashed his face. Thought to be dead, he was nonetheless taken to a kahuna lā'au lapa'au, or Hawaiian herbal healer, who pounded medicine from native Hawaiian mountain plants to heal the woman's father. A second informant related the experience of a man whose foot was smashed by a rock. A kahuna lā'au lapa'au was engaged to nurse the man back to good health. The sister of a third informant fell from the rock near the Hāna lighthouse and broke her hip. The kahuna lā'au lapa'au prayed for her to get well without suffering too much pain. The young woman recovered and suffered very little pain while recuperating.[84]

These traditional approaches to healing were commonplace in Hāna and a natural part of the people's lives. Yamamura's informants also provided accounts about akua lele, large balls of fire with tails, which were regarded as omens of misfortune; and *lapu*, the wandering spirits of the dead, who usually bother persons traveling at night with food such as pork or fish.[85] The informants also believed in menehune, guardian spirit ʻaumakua, and night marchers on Po Kāne. They also shared a list of dos and don'ts to avoid misfortune, from not whistling at night to not picking a *lehua* flower to not eating bananas when one goes fishing.[86]

Subsistence Resources of Hāna

Overall, life in the district of Hāna, thanks to the abundance of natural resources available to the Hawaiian people who lived there, was pleasant and healthy. Several of the kūpuna interviewed by Mary Kawena Pukui confirmed this observation. For example, Mrs. Kapeka Kaʻauamo concluded: "Maikaʻi, maikaʻi kēia ʻāina, maikaʻi kēia. Hoʻopiha mau i ka ʻōpū, ʻaʻale pilikia ka ʻōpū" (Excellent, excellent this land, this place is fine. The stomach is always filled, the stomach is not troubled).[87]

The numerous streams that flowed down from Haleakalā to the ocean along the rugged Hāna Coast not only provide the Hāna Hawaiians with an abundant supply of fresh water, they also serve as a habitat for native Hawaiian aquatic life, which was an important source of food for the Hāna Hawaiians. Kūpuna from the Koʻolau sections of the district all described to Pukui the importance of *ʻoʻopu* (gobbi fish), *ʻōpae* (shrimp), *hīhīwai* (limpet), and *wī* (limpet) to their regular diets.

There were many types of ʻoʻopu in the streams of Hāna. Harry Mitchell named five that he was familiar with catching and eating—*nākea, nāpili, ʻowau, hiʻukole,* and *ʻalamoʻo.*[88] Kūpuna Josephine Medeiros named two additional types, the *ʻakupa* and the *ʻapohā.* The nākea type was either fried or salted and then baked with ti leaves for a dish called *lāwalu.* The ʻowau was usually good in soup. The small ʻoʻopu nāpili was usually dried and then eaten.[89]

The streams were filled with ʻoʻopu between 1900 and 1930. Harry Mitchell recalled catching two or three 30-gallon buckets full of ʻoʻopu overnight when flood waters washed them downstream to the ocean. The first heavy rains usually arrived in August or September, carrying the ʻoʻopu to the ocean where they spawned. Once she laid her eggs, the mother ʻoʻopu died. The baby ʻoʻopu, called *hinano*, would hatch and develop in the salt water from August or September through November. The salt water made them strong enough to swim upstream, where they would mature. About November, the hinano began to make their way upstream to the large freshwater pools in the mountains. Their migration upstream coincided with the arrival of the migratory birds from the north, which fed upon the hinano as they made their perilous journey to the uplands.[90]

Being intimately knowledgeable about the life cycle and habitats of the 'o'opu and other aquatic animals enabled the Hāna kua'āina to plan out what types of food sources to gather at different times of the year. Mrs. Pū, of Pa'uwela, recalled how Wailua was full of 'ōpae, or black mountain shrimp. They used to eat it with a mountain fern that the Maui people called *pohole* but that is more widely known as *hō'i'o*. Mrs. Ka'auamo also recalled the abundance of *'ōpae kuahiwi* or mountain shrimp in the Ke'anae and Wailua area.[91] "Mullet also spawned in the Wailuaiki district. They would usually go where the stream met the ocean to spawn, around December. At that time, millions of baby mullet could be seen swimming around. *Hīhīwai* and *wī* were also plentiful in certain streams at the points where they flowed into the ocean."[92]

While the aquatic life that thrived in the Hāna streams was an important source of protein to the Hāna kua'āina, the stream waters also made possible the widespread cultivation of the Hawaiian "staff of life," or *kalo*. Mrs. Ka'auamo of Wailua expressed the importance of taro to the Hawaiians of Hāna: "Taro is perhaps most important here. If it wasn't for taro perhaps all the people here would soon perish."[93]

Aside from taro, the patches also sustained important aquatic life, which the Hāna kua'āina relished. These included the *pūpū pake*, or snails, which resemble escargots, and the *'ula'ula* goldfish.

In the drier areas of Kaupō, Hawaiians planted sweet potatoes, pumpkins, and dry land taro for home consumption. Patch after patch of sweet potato was planted. Just as taro was the staple food for the people of Ke'anae and Wailua, the sweet potato was the staple food for the Kaupō families. The plantings did especially well during the rainy season. As their ancestors had taught them, they followed the annual cycle of the rain. About one month before the rainy season began, they would carry dirt down from the mountains to the coast in lauhala baskets and fill holes in the lava in preparation for planting. Children also helped to carry some dirt in lauhala bags. While on the coast, the Hawaiians would subsist on fishing and various gourd plants such as Hawaiian watermelon, *ipu oloolo*, *ipu nūhoulani*, pumpkin, and *pohā* or *ipu 'ala*, which were cultivated in the pockets of lava and nurtured by the rain. When the vegetables matured they were consumed. After a period of about six months, just when the climate became dry, the families would make the return journey to their upland habitation sites.[94]

If there was a drought, the families of Kaupō visited their relatives in Kīpahulu to gather and get food. Most of the families in the two districts were related to each other, and exchange and sharing were common and expected.[95] A Hawaiian riddle for Kaupō and Kīpahulu linked the two districts and noted the importance of sweet potato cultivation as a staple food for the people of the districts: "Pō nā maka, a i ka pahulu ke ola" (The eyes become dim with hunger, the hunger is appeased by old food patches). The saying originated when a famine developed during a drought and the starving people of the districts became hollow-eyed. They were able to survive by eating broken pieces of sprouting potatoes left in the mounds by sweet potato harvesters to grow to maturity.[96]

Pigs and goats thrived in the forested uplands throughout the Koʻolau district, and the Hāna kuaʻāina would hunt them from time to time and salt, dry, and smoke the meat. Many families also raised a few pigs, cows, and chickens for home consumption.[97]

As with their ancestors, the ocean along the entire district, from Koʻolau to Kaupō, continued to provide the Hāna kuaʻāina with fish, crab, shellfish, and seaweed. They would gather shellfish and limu along the shore; go deep-sea fishing in canoes; lay nets, including large hukilau nets in the bays; dive; pole fish; and even cultivate fish in ponds or by feeding the fish at designated

Figure 18 About 2,000 fish each averaging 8 inches in length were harvested by the Hāmoa community hukilau in Hāna. 1936. Harold T. Stearns, Bishop Museum.

koʻa or traditional fishing grounds. Salt for the district continued to be annually gathered at Nuʻu.[98]

Throughout the 1930s Hawaiian women continued the practice of weaving hats and mats out of lauhala—both the light and dark varieties. Kūpuna informants also identified many other plants used for weaving, including the *ʻekaha* or bird nest fern; the pāmoho fern; the red ti plant known as "Kaupō Beauty"; the *hāpapa pueo kalo,* a white taro top; banana bark, especially the *ʻeleʻele* or black variety; stems of pili grass; large leaves of the *ʻulu* or breadfruit tree; the *nānaku* sedge; the *ʻiwaʻiwa* fern; and the ʻieʻie vine.[99]

Keʻanae and Wailuanui in the Territorial Period

The ahupuaʻa of Keʻanae and Wailuanui are the first of the Hāna districts to be reached on the road to Hāna by travelers setting out from Haʻikū. The famous and picturesque taro patches of Keʻanae have been continuously cultivated by the families who lived there from the time that their ancestors created them by carrying soil to cover the barren lava penninsula.[100]

Wailuanui was favored with more fertile and extensive agricultural lands. Three streams provided the water for the patches—Wailuaiki, Waiohue, and Hanawī.

In 1910 H. M. Ayres, a reporter with the *Pacific Commercial Advertiser,* hiked through Keʻanae to Hāna along the East Maui Irrigation Company's Koʻolau ditch trail. He reported what he observed in the feature section of the *Advertiser* on September 4, 1910. The beauty of Keʻanae's lush forests and the waterfalls cascading through ravines down to the magnificent ocean below impressed Ayres, and he was also interested in the lifestyle of the Hawaiian and Chinese families who had homesteads in the district:

> At the house of Halemano we were made very welcome, supper being ordered by our host at a Chinese restaurant nearby. He naively remarked that poi and fish were not good for haoles. Halemano, who is postmaster and political boss of the precinct, is a dignified old native. His house is on the campaign circuit and when election time rolls round there are stirring times at his residence. His daughter, Annie, is easily the belle of the district.
>
> Keanae is a sugarless settlement, rice being the main industry of the place. The natives live contentedly in their homesteads and are unusually well informed on matters of the world, for dwellers in such an out-of-the-world place. It is one of the prettiest settlements on Maui. Across from

Keanae is Wailuanui, a place well worth a trip over the ricefields, if one has the time. Back of Halemano's house is a natural bathing pool formed by a cascade and large and deep enough to allow of a really good swim.

Many of the Keanae girls have Chinese husbands and appear to be quite happy with them. They are better providers than the Hawaiians and this probably accounts for the phenomena.

Before leaving Keanae we offered to buy a squid stone from Halemano but the old man refused to part with the relic, declaring that it was his wife's and that he didn't need the money.[101]

Harry Mitchell observed that when he was young the Hawaiians usually leased out the lowlands downstream, where the water tended to be too warm for the taro to grow well and the taro often spoiled. The Hawaiians continued to cultivate taro in the cool uplands for home consumption and for sale. Many of the Chinese men who moved to Keʻanae intermarried with Hawaiian families of the district and helped to cultivate the Hawaiian lands.[102] Keʻanae became a center for rice cultivation through 1927, when, as in Waipiʻo, low prices for California rice drove the Keʻanae rice growers out of the business. At that point Keʻanae farmers shifted back to the cultivation of taro for market.[103]

The Keʻanae kuaʻāina developed a system of exchanging labor for tools and materials with the Chinese rice farmers. The enterprising Chinese imported lumber, pots, shovels, sickles, muslin, and other tools and materials for use in the production of rice. Occasionally, Hawaiians would perform work for the Chinese, such as plowing and hauling bags of rice in exchange for tools and materials rather than for money. According to Mitchell, his grandfather and others worked for the Chinese in order to get lumber and metal pots:

> Chinese bought lumber, eh, and they got a big pot. Yeah, you know for cook their rice. And the Hawaiians like for cook taro . . . So now you gotta work, eh, maybe three, four months before they give you one pot, eh. Maybe every month they give you one lumber, eh. You know 1 x 12 x 8 feet long . . . And those Hawaiians, they tough, they work for the Chinese because they look, see, that pot—so everybody start getting pot.[104]

Prior to using pots, the Hawaiians cooked their taro in the imu. The taro came out dry and hard and had to be pounded while it was still hot. Boiled taro was moist and could be easily pounded even when cool.

The Hawaiians also exchanged work for clothing and canvas. If they worked two days they could earn a pair of pants or a raincoat. The Chinese would coat canvas with linseed oil to make waterproof raincoats.[105] Work was also exchanged for shovels, picks, and saws. In addition to exchanging work for materials, with the Chinese, work was also exchanged between households or ʻohana, as in traditional times. The families would help one another in the taro patches and exchange labor and food:

> Every weekend, lūʻau someplace. You know why? They laulima. This
> family go help the other family clean taro patch. Then if I go clean your
> taro patch, you kill the pig. Next week maybe me. Keep on going like that,
> huh. We go on the horse—go this house, they singing and everything. Play
> mandolin, they get guitar, ukulele. My uncle, he play the clarinet. He was
> good too, wow.

The Keʻanae kuaʻāina also had a system of barter and exchanged with Kona and Molokaʻi. Taro in the form of paʻiʻai would be exchanged for ʻōpelu or akule from Kona and squid from Molokaʻi:

> Most time they exchange. You know, then they get boats. They put paʻiʻai
> in the box—maybe four or five hundred pounds—put ʻem on the boat.
> They go Molokaʻi. That same crate come home full with dry squid. Or
> they go Kona, eh—that same crate come home full with dry ʻōpelu. And
> they distribute. How many paʻi ʻai you get four? Five? Well here—one
> pound ʻōpelu, all dry, you know—one kauna—forty. You get more? Then
> two kauna. That's how you know—divide. That's how they do—trade.[106]

Subsistence work and exchange for goods was the dominant form of work in Keʻanae until the Hāna road was constructed by prison labor based at the Keʻanae Prison Camp. From 1890 till 1920 Keʻanae's commercial directory listed most of the Hawaiians in the district as taro planters. In 1920 the directory listed three Hawaiians as laborers. However, in the 1930 directory, Hawaiian taro planters and homesteaders were listed as laborers and truck drivers employed by the East Maui Irrigation Company, the road department, and Keʻanae Prison Camp.[107]

In 1934, when the anthropologist E. S. Craighill Handy conducted a survey of the natural resources of the Hāna Coast, he observed that the Keʻanae Valley mauka of the road was a water reserve with no inhabitants. The wetland taro patches for which Keʻanae is famous were entirely located on its broad, flat peninsula of lava, which extended about a mile out into the sea from the base of the cliffs. Polaukulu Stream provided the water for the patches, which were still under active cultivation in 1934. However, at Wailuanui, only half of the taro terraces originally developed by Hawaiians of the district were still being cultivated by Hawaiians in the 1930s.[108]

Josephine Kauakeaohana Roback Medeiros described the livelihood of the people of Keʻanae:

> Keʻanae people there make a living by fishing, gathering oysters, sea shells, catching shrimps from the mountain streams, clams, catfish, water shells and planting their own sweet potatoes and taro which they used for starch and vegetable. Also they hunt for wild pigs, fowl, etc. Very few of them work for the county as road clearing gang, and only work for 15 days out of a month at a time, even only 8 days a month sometimes—so they depend a lot by the ocean and mountain for their livelihood. They also market some of their catch and harvesting.[109]

A prison camp was built at Keʻanae in 1926 to house the prisoners who would construct the road, including several bridges from Kailua to Hāna. As described above, when the road was completed in 1927, men from Keʻanae to Hāna town were hired to maintain the road, especially during the rainy season. In 1934 the prison camp was converted into quarters for the Civilian Conservation Corps. This federal program, created by President Franklin D. Roosevelt to provide jobs to get the United States through the depression, brought in men from other parts of Maui and other islands to plant thousands of eucalyptus and other introduced trees throughout the Hāna coast. Eventually, in 1949, the camp was acquired by the YMCA. Part of the land area continued to be used as a base yard for the Maui County public works projects.[110]

Nāhiku to Hāna Town, Under the Territory

Nāhiku, like Wailua, was a fertile ahupuaʻa where Hawaiians had cleared and terraced the lands for irrigated taro cultivation. The land to the east of Nāhiku sloped gently down to the ocean. There were no large streams or gulches. Along the shore was a hala forest that extended from ʻUlaʻino to Hāna. Hawaiians living in this part of the Hāna district also raised dry-land taro around their homes, together with other food plants.[111]

Other agricultural ventures were attempted along the Hāna Coast. In 1899 the Nāhiku Rubber Company planted thousands of rubber trees makai of the road. After some initial experimentation in producing rubber, the company incorporated in 1905. The American and Koʻolau Rubber Companies also established rubber plantations in the district. At one point there were more than 25,000 rubber trees of different varieties growing in and around Nāhiku. By 1912 the rubber companies had begun to phase out their operations. A former field worker recalled that a ten-hour day with a thirty-minute lunch break netted him only 50 cents. At that rate for labor, the quality and quantity of rubber produced on the wet Hāna Coast was too low to make a profit.[112]

At the height of rubber production, Nāhiku had a Chinese grocery and post office; a plantation general store; Protestant, Mormon, and Catholic churches; and a schoolhouse attended by twenty children. As shown above, there were only 182 people living in Nāhiku in 1930. By 1941 only fifteen Hawaiian families and two non-Hawaiian families lived in Nāhiku, clustered around a one-room school and the churches.[113] After the rubber plantations closed, the residents planted bananas as a cash crop and subsequently planted roselle for jelly. Eventually, when these economic ventures failed, the population shifted out of Nāhiku.[114]

In 1910, when Ayres hiked through Nāhiku, the community bustled with activity related to the production of rubber. Although planted in rubber trees, the surrounding tropical forest was still impressive to the visitor:

> Every place has its peculiarities and characteristics; so with Nāhiku. It is rubber, first, last and all the time there. And while the population of the place tend the trees, the owners work and dream of what the future holds in store, for they are handling a new thing and it may yield them fabulous profits or only a pittance.
>
> There is a very good class of Hawaiians at Nāhiku, industrious and contented. The rubber affords them more or less constant employ and fish are very plentiful off the shore. The natives working for Mr. Austin regard him as a friend. He speaks their language fluently and both he and his mother have, by their helpful attitude, endeared themselves in the hearts of the Hawaiians of Nāhiku.[115]

As the rubber companies phased out their operations in 1912, some of the residents moved out of Nāhiku. Those who remained resumed the cultivation of native crops—bananas and taro. Some of the terraces below the settlement were still under cultivation in 1934. In addition, each of the Hawaiian families also cultivated dry-land taro patches around their homes.[116]

Hāna Town during the Territorial Years

Despite its isolation, Hāna was a bustling little town in the 1920s and 1930s. Beginning in 1919 there were two movie theaters, one at Kaʻelekū and the other in Hāna town, where there were two showings each night in addition to a Saturday matinee. There were also fifteen different stores, three barber-shops, a pool hall, and a choice of several restaurants. The small general stores in Hāna emerged as centers for commercial and social exchange.[117] The Haiku Fruit and Packing Company planted pineapple in Mūʻolea in the Kīpahulu district in 1922 and built a cannery in Hāna town in 1924. However, by 1927 the pineapple cannery had closed.[118]

In 1927 the Hāna road, constructed by prison labor, linked the Hāna Coast to the "outside" world. After completion, it was maintained by Hāna kuaʻāina hired by the territorial government. During the rainy winter season, mud-slides, downed trees, and flooding streams frequently made the road impass-able. County road work enabled many Hawaiian families to earn cash to sup-plement their subsistence lifestyles.[119] Eventually, trucks replaced trains as the method of transporting the harvested cane to the mills, and road work declined.

In 1930 Hāna, as the center of commerce and plantation operations, had 65 percent of the population of the Koʻolau district, the majority of which were non-Hawaiian. Most of the Hawaiian families enumerated as living in Hāna in the 1930 census lived in the small self-sufficient communities outside the town, from Keʻanae through Waiʻānapanapa and from Hāmoa to Wailua, and outside the control and organization of the plantation camps. The Hāna planters had to import Chinese and later Japanese and Filipino laborers to produce sugar in the district.

In 1934 E. S. Craighill Handy observed that in north Hāna, above the sea cliffs and lava caves of Waiʻānapanapa, was the native settlement of Hono-kalani. Here and on the forest land called Helani, Hawaiians raised dry-land taro primarily for home consumption. Given the lack of streams at Hāna and Hāmoa, wetland taro was not cultivated. Hawaiians who lived there raised dry-land taro on forested lowlands about two miles inland. In south Hāna, past Hāmoa, streams begin to cut across the landscape again. Hawaiian home-steads at Makaʻalae, Waiohonu, Puʻuiki, Pohue, Pukuilua, Hāʻōʻū, Hulihana, Mūolea, and Koali had extensive wet taro patches, many of which had been originally constructed by the ancient Hawaiians.[120]

Kīpahulu, Territory of Hawai'i

Traveling southeast from Hāna, Wailua was the first valley outside of Hāna. It had extensive wetland taro terraces at four different levels sustained by water from three streams that converged at Kaumakani. The Kahalawe Stream waters provided water for patches on the steep slopes of Paehala. Most of the patches in the valley and along the slopes were still being cultivated in the early 1930s. Dry taro was also planted in unirrigated terraces where the steepness of the slope allowed sufficient aeration of the soil without running water.[121]

Historically, Kīpahulu was a district with rich and diverse agricultural resources scattered throughout its vast valley. The moku of Kīpahulu included many smaller ahupua'a or valleys fed by streams. Historically, these little valleys were terraced and planted in taro. A sugar plantation and mill were established approximately ten miles from Hāna at the turn of the century and operated through the 1920s.

In 1922 Thomas Maunupau and Kenneth P. Emory of the Bishop Museum

Figure 19 Joe Kahaleuahi, shown here with his granddaughter, is a kua'āina fisherman and farmer of Kīpahulu, Maui. 1971. Franco Salmoiraghi.

traveled through Hāna and Kīpahulu on their way to Kaupō. Their trip was chronicled in the *Nūpepa Kūʻokoʻa* of June 1, 1922:

> We arrived at Kīpahulu and saw the plantation on the upper side of the road and the homes of the laborers. I saw the laborers cutting cane and the cane cars bearing them to the mill. Now and then we passed a Hawaiian house. Some people were farming, some pounding poi and some of the Hawaiian mothers were plaiting mats. Our car continued and came to a place called Kukuiʻula.[122]

Kukuiʻula Stream is where the ridge-and-valley trail to Kaupō began. Twelve years before Emory and Maunupau made the trek to Kaupō, a staff correspondent with the *Hawaiian Gazette* hiked the trail between Kukuiʻula and Kaupō. His observations about the district were published in the *Gazette* on September 6, 1910. His descriptions of the scattered Hawaiian households and the sights, sounds, and flavors of the resources of the area provide an excellent picture of life in the district.

> The road was good till the first gulch was arrived at. The down-go wasn't so bad, but going up again was a caution. I rested a good quarter of an hour in the shade of a lauhala tree half-way up.
>
> On the Kīpahulu side of this gulch is a grass house, the occupants of which, judging by the number of bamboos about the place, do a good deal of fishing. This house is very picturesquely situated. For a way the trail led by the sea, and by its side I passed an ancient canoe, a sad reminder of other days, when the stone fences enclosed prosperous kuleanas, and when the natives were thick upon the countryside . . .
>
> The third gulch is waterless, but in the fourth, close to the house of Inaiana, is a pool of fresh water, supplied by the stream above.
>
> Passing up the far side of the fourth gulch, the smell of orange blossoms was borne to me, and I soon located several trees full of excellent fruit, to several of which I did ample justice. The guavas on this hill, by the way, are very sweet and finely flavored.[123]

In 1922 the Haiku Fruit and Packing Company planted pineapple in Mūʻolea in the Kīpahulu.[124]

In 1934 Handy found the sugar plantation closed and replaced by a cattle ranch. Native Hawaiians lived in homes in the lower *kula* lands above the sea and raised dry-land taro around their homes for consumption by their own households. Several small groups of taro terraces were still cultivated by the Hawaiians who lived in the district. The Lolokea and Kalepa Valleys were not in active cultivation in 1934. Hanawī Valley was watered by the ʻAlelele Stream, and some of the terraces there were being replanted in wet taro in 1934. Nuanualoa, the last valley before Kaupō, had a handful of Hawaiian households in 1934. They cultivated wet taro in the traditional terraces.[125]

Kaupō, Territory of Hawaiʻi

Five miles down the coast from Kīpahulu is Kaupō. The district is arid along the seacoast but receives a moderate amount of rainfall three to four miles inland at an elevation of 2,000 feet, where the land ascends to Haleakalā Crater. Manawainui is the large stream that drains the higher slopes east of the Kaupō Gap, an access point into Haleakalā Crater. The valley of the stream is canyonlike. The Hawaiians of Kaupō got their water from numerous springs in the area, such as Punahoa and Waiū. In Manawainui Valley, there were several large springs until landslides caused by heavy rains and earthquakes covered the springs over and broke the pipelines that had carried the water to households.[126]

At one point in the early 1900s attempts were made to cultivate wheat at Kaupō.[127] A reporter with the *Hawaiian Gazette* who traveled to Kaupō in 1910 described life in the area:

> At Kaupō are to be found Hawaiians living industriously and contentedly, as they do in the few places on the Islands which one has to go off the beaten track to reach. Sweet potatoes are largely grown and they have to take the place of poi, of which there is none here. There are plenty of fish, however, and some of the finest ʻopihis procurable anywhere. There are several grass houses here and the garden of every house is overrun with geraniums, carnations and beautiful roses. A fine new schoolhouse is being built here to provide for the large number of children in the district. This evening a single party, gaily decorated with leis, is going from house to house serenading.[128]

The reporter also sent his story to the *Pacific Commercial Advertiser*, which ran the report as a series of articles on September 5 and 9, 1910. The September 9 article carried a description of the living conditions of Hawaiians who lived between the new schoolhouse and the Kaupō Gap. It described the traditional houses that the reporter observed along the way as well as the types of foods cultivated and animals raised by the native Hawaiians of the district. Problems that the kuaʻāina had with marketing the fruit were also identified:

> It is nearly two miles from the schoolhouse to Marciel's house, the trail running past several pohaku houses, grass thatched, and all-grass houses. The occupants raise pigs and sweet potatoes and working a little and resting a great deal, appear to drift in from day to day happily enough.
>
> All take a turn at fishing at times and the toothsome aweoweo is so abundant hereabouts that it helps out the commissary problem materially during the moonlight season.
>
> Excellent oranges and limes are grown at Kaupo, the former being sweet and finely flavored. The Kaupoans could earn many a dollar by shipping their fruit to Honolulu, could they rely on a regular steamer. As it is impossible to tell when a steamer is going to call. The steamer Claudine used to call here regularly once a month but the service was discontinued last July, the steamer now going direct from Hana to Hawaii and return.
>
> Several shipments of limes and oranges from here have rotted on the wharf waiting for a steamer to call. The Kaupō people suffer in another way by lack of a regular steamer service. Many of them order their household supplies from Honolulu and are often reduced to famine rations as far as some of the necessities of life are concerned.[129]

In 1922 Maunupau and Emory took note of the majesty of Kaupō: "Kaupō is indeed a green land and so is Hāna. They look so open and pleasant to live in because the wind is always blowing. The coast is good to look at and fine for inshore fishing. The whole of Kaupō faces West Hawaii. Looking upward one sees the majestic Haleakalā mountain, the Kaupō Gap and many small waterfalls."[130] Nuʻu is an ahupuaʻa within Kaupō. In 1922 Maunupau and Emory observed five Hawaiian households in the area: "When we came to level land, that was Nuu proper. It is a seaport and cattle is [sic] shipped from here. This was a landing place for fishermen in the olden days and even down to the present. There are about five houses at Nuu and the inhabitants are all Hawaiians."[131]

In the 1930s the federal Works Progress Administration financed the construction of a motor road from Kīpahulu to Kaupō. In 1934 Handy observed that almost the entire area of Kaupō was ranch land, although Hawaiians who worked for the ranch still raised sweet potatoes for home consumption.[132]

Working as a ranch cowboy was the type of job Hawaiians enjoyed. It involved intense periods of strenuous activity followed by periods of relaxation. One such intense period was when cattle were shipped out to be slaughtered and marketed from the landing at Nuʻu. Mrs. Marciel, an informant for Mary Kawena Pukui in the 1960s, was born and raised in Kaupō, near Nuʻu. The Marciel family once owned Kaupō Ranch, but during a great drought, they sold it to the Baldwin Estate. Marciel described what was involved in shipping the cattle from the landing:

> The boat used to come over there. We had a shipping pen. Where we shipped our cattle before. The boat came outside and we shipped the pipi out to the boat—swim, swim out. Then they swing them up into the boat. You have to get good horses to take the pipi out. Huki me ka lio—hoʻau i ka pipi (tug with the horse—make the cattle swim).[133]

Marciel explained that her family planted sweet potatoes there during the rainy season when the earth was soft. They used the planting enclosures left behind by the ancient Hawaiians. They planted the *piko* variety, which bore potatoes in four, five, or six months; and the *mōhihi* potato which took several months to bear but could be stored for several months after harvesting. Her family also planted the *ipu ʻawaʻawa* calabash gourds and pumpkins at Nuʻu.

Figure 20 Kaupō Ranch hired Hawaiian men living in the district to work as cowboys. 1923. Kenneth P. Emory, Bishop Museum.

The sweet potato, gourd, and pumpkin plants bear well in dry land and flourished at Nuʻu. The people of the district also wove hats using nānaku sedge as well as ʻiwa stalks for material.[134]

Marciel described an active Hawaiian community at Nuʻu and Kaupō that was involved in fishing, making salt, and planting; some worked on the ranch. According to Marciel, there were five boat houses and two canoe houses at Nuʻu prior to the 1946 tidal wave. There was a medicine house, right where Kaupō Landing is, in a small *hale* (house). *Lapaʻau*, or medicinal plants, are everywhere in the area; they were tied in bundles and kept in the building. This was also the salt house. Great schools of *akule* frequented the bay, and the salt was used to dry the akule. Right against the pali, where the landing and the medicine house was, was a canoe house that had Hawaiian canoes in it.

Figure 21 Kaupō Ranch shipped out cattle from Nuʻu. May 1922. Bishop Museum.

At Nu'u, all the stones with small hollows were put on the edge of the pond, and people would put ocean water in them. The sun would evaporate the water, leaving the salt. They used wooden spoons to scoop out small amounts of salt. Nu'u Bay had a nice pond, behind, which is now all overgrown. People used to keep it clear of hau trees. The Navy used *kaili hau* for rope on an almost daily basis, and this kept the hau in check.

Nu'u Bay has a black stone beach. The Hawaiians used the stones for weighting their nets with *palu*, or bait. The stone bait consisted of a flat weight with two ears; they tied it and put the sweet potato peelings inside, covered the bag, rolled and twisted it, and laid it in the net. They also used pumpkin, squash, ipu, and sweet potato as bait. When they made sour potato mash, which looked like a big pudding, they kept the liquid part, fermented it, and drank it as liquor. There was a cave with a water well in front if it and also a Hawaiian house. Beach equipment was stored there as well. Photos record that Hawaiians in *malo* or loincloths launched canoes in the bay. The fishing houses consisted of Japanese-style skiffs, with miles of net. People that lived there were part of a *hui* or organized group. They fixed nets, made floaters, and made salt. Nu'u was also famous for *holoholo he'e*, a very big squid with short tentacles and a large body. The *uhu*, a fish that Hawaiians like to eat fresh, would come in schools, turning the sea red beyond the bay. As many as thirty people would gather, start a fire, make coffee, and go out fishing, one group at a time. Even before the fishing was over, they would start loading these fish up on donkeys and try to get mauka and give it away. This was the ancient Hawaiian way of life: when there was something to be had, everybody shared. Hukilau nets were used more often in those times.

Changes during and after World War II

The forces of change for the Hāna coast included World War II, the phasing out of sugar plantations, and the 1946 tsunami.

The war came to Hāna in January 1942, when a Japanese submarine torpedoed the transport ship *General Royal T. Frank* in the 'Alenuihāhā Channel. Twenty-nine persons were killed, but thirty-three survivors were taken to Hāna and cared for at the Hāna School gymnasium.[135]

In December 1942 Governor Ingram Stainback tried to assist the war effort by sending forty inmates from O'ahu Prison to the Ke'anae Prison Camp to revive the old Nāhiku rubber plantation in the hope of yielding 20,000 to 50,000 pounds of crude rubber annually.[136] The venture was not successful.

Residents in Keʻanae and Wailuanui reported that they cached explosives in two caves at Nuaʻailua to use to blow up the Hāna Road in the event of a Japanese invasion.[137] By far the biggest impact of the war was the induction into military service of the Hāna Coast's young men, some attracted to high-paying jobs at Pearl Harbor. Many never returned to their subsistence livelihoods on the Hāna Coast when the war ended.

The San Francisco entrepreneur Paul I. Fagan acquired the Hāna Sugar Company from the Unna brothers in the 1930s. In 1944 he closed the Hāna sugar plantation and began to transform the former plantation lands into a cattle ranch. After the war, sugar workers organized under the International Longshoremen and Warehousemen's Union (I.L.W.U.), increasing the cost of producing sugar, and C. Brewer closed Kaelekū Plantation.[138] In 1946 Fagan opened the Hotel Hāna-Maui; from then on he focused his marketing efforts on wealthy travelers who could afford to spend luxury time in a world-class resort.

A huge tidal wave hit the islands on April 1, 1946. Of the fourteen persons who died on Maui, twelve died along the Hāna Coast. In the Keʻanae Peninsula, several buildings were damaged, and two persons died.[139] Residents whose homes on the peninsula were destroyed resettled along the Hāna highway.

During the 1950s the population of Hāna dropped to 500, the low point for the twentieth century. In 1956 Fagan built the Hāna Ranch Center, which included a post office, a bank, a barber shop, and a lunch room. He also built a center at the harbor, which he named Helene Hall in honor of his wife, and donated it to the county for the community. With the money from Helene Irwin Fagan's estate, the Fagans established a trust fund for the nonprofit Hāna Community Association to oversee the recreational needs of Hāna's children.

The paving of the fifty-five-mile Hāna highway in 1962 opened the coast to tourists who usually drove in and out for the day. However, the curves and one-lane bridges saved the Hāna coast from the full-scale development seen in other parts of Maui such as Lahaina, Kaʻanapali, and Kīhei.

Over the years, some of the clients of the Hotel Hāna-Maui bought land along the Hāna Coast for retirement or vacationing. These wealthy new residents of the Hāna Coast have included Sam Pryor, a vice president of Pan American Airways; the aviator Charles Lindbergh; the actors Jim Nabors and Kris Kristofferson; and the singers George Harrison and Willie Nelson.

When Paul Fagan died in 1970, the community erected an impressive lava rock cross upon a grassy knoll overlooking Hāna Town as a memorial.

Hotel Hāna-Maui and Hāna Ranch were sold to the Rosewood Corporation of Dallas, Texas, in 1984. In 1989 Rosewood sold the hotel and ranch to Keola Hāna-Maui, an international investment group made up of Japanese, British, and Hawaiian investors.[140]

By the end of the twentieth century there were 2,000 residents along the Hāna coast.

Changes to Kīpahulu developed with the acquisition of Kīpahulu Valley by the U.S. Department of the Interior for inclusion within Haleakalā National Park. The pristine upper valley was incorporated into the park in 1951. The lower valley and coastline, including the pools of ʻOheʻo, were added in January 1969. Haleakalā National Park is recognized by the United Nations as an international biosphere reserve. Park policy now limits development in Kīpahulu to park facilities and shapes the lives of the kuaʻāina of Kīpahulu. The Kīpahulu section of the park attracts 500,000 visitors annually.[141] In 1974 the world-famous aviator Charles Lindbergh decided to spend his last days in Kīpahulu, where he died and is buried. His grave in the Palapala Hoʻomau Church cemetery has become an attraction for tourists who venture to drive along the winding Hāna highway. The road built by the Works Progress Administration during the depression is usable, but subject to periodic closures after storms and landslides. Sections of the road have been paved and some of the one-lane bridges replaced with modern two-lane bridges. Kīpahulu was also designated an International Biosphere Reserve in 1980 in recognition of its unique and diverse ecosystem. The area from Kīpahulu to Kaupō is rural. Commercial horseback riding stables and local farming are the primary business in the district.

Kaupō is largely enjoyed by the local people of Maui as a pristine and unspoiled refuge. The Kaupō General Store at the center of the district is the only private commercial store between Hāna and ʻUlupalakua. It serves the small pool of local residents, tourists who pass by in rental cars, and hikers coming out of Haleakalā Crater through the Kaupō Gap. Kaupō Ranch is the main employer for a handful of residents in the district.

The panoramic view of the southern slopes of Haleakalā Crater, the island of Kahoʻolawe, and Hawaiʻi Island is unobstructed, uncluttered even by utility lines and poles. The primary impact upon the traditional cultural landscape comes from cattle and goats. The small pond behind Nuʻu Bay was fenced by the U.S. Fish and Wildlife Service in 1997 to keep the cattle out, and it has become a reserve for native birds such as the *koloa* (native duck) and Hawaiian stilts and coots. Huakini Bay and Nuʻu Landing are regularly frequented by weekend campers. During the summer, families camp there for weeks at a time; the setting engenders a feeling of self-reliance and independence. Here, Maui residents can feel in contact with nature, physically and spiritually. Native Hawaiian campers and fishermen feel a connection to their cultural roots.

Keʻanae-Wailuanui in the Late Twentieth Century

As late in the twentieth century as 1994, the State of Hawaʻi Department of Land and Natural Resources recognized the Keʻanae-Wailuanui ahupuaʻa as an Historic Cultural Landscape with unbroken continuity to the original pre-contact uses of its lands for Native Hawaiian subsistence and cultural activities. This led to a study titled *Kalo Kanu O Ka ʻaina: A Cultural Landscape Study of Keʻanae and Wailuanui, Island of Maui,* in which I was privileged to participate as historian. The study documented the importance of protecting Keʻanae and Wailuanui because of the persistence of Native Hawaiian cultural practices in relation to taro cultivation and subsistence activities. I will close this chapter about the Hāna district with the moʻolelo shared with me by the descendants of the earliest Native Hawaiian inhabitants of the Hāna Coast, who, as modern kuaʻāina, continued to rely upon their ancestral knowledge to provide for their ʻohana. These experiences verify that key elements of Native Hawaiian culture centered around subsistence activities have persisted in Keʻanae-Wailuanui. In fact, Keʻanae-Wailuanui exemplifies the perpetuation of Native Hawaiian culture into the twenty-first century within the Hāna district as a whole.

In 1990 the area known as Keanae-Wailuanui had a population of 241 people living in sixty-seven households.[142] In the 1994–95 school year, the Keʻanae Elementary School had eleven students in kindergarten to third grade. Adult education programs were held at the school in the evening. During the day, the community organized senior citizen programs at the school so the kūpuna could interact with the children.[143]

According to the kuaʻāina who were interviewed, the original region which continued to be used and cared for by generations of Native Hawaiian kuaʻāina of Keanae-Wailuanui, extended from Makapipi in the East to Honomanū in the West, and all the way mauka to Pohaku Palaha on the northern rim of the Haleakalā Crater.[144] The Makapipi stream and forest access road forms the boundary between Keanae-Wailuanui and Nāhiku on the east. The Kaumahina ridge above the Honomanū stream forms the Keanae-Wailuanui boundary on the West.

Although the traditional ocean boundary for an ahupua'a is the reef, or one mile out where there is no reef, most of the Keanae-Wailuanui residents who regularly fished went out as far as the offshore buoy, seven miles out to sea: that is how far they consider their traditional access area in the ocean to extend. The Ke'anae-Wailuanui kua'āina fished and gathered 'opihi or limpets by boat along the coast from Kailua in the west and over as far as the Hāna airport, to a place called Honomae'ele in the east (also popularly called Pine Trees). The entire shoreline and nearshore waters have abundant marine resources.

Along the mauka section of the ahupua'a, the common practice was to follow the ditch trail looking for signs of pigs and then to follow the tracks into the forest. The 2,000-foot elevation was usually as high as most hunters and gatherers needed to venture to get pigs. Nevertheless, those who hunted and gathered could go as high as 3,000 feet, into the Waiakamoi area and up to Olinda. Some (Moki Day, Doug Chong, Paul Sinenci, Harry Pahukoa, and Keola Hueu) have hiked up the mauka trail all the way into Haleakalā Crater through the Ko'olau Gap.

The families who live in Ke'anae-Wailuanui are part of 'ohana from Kailua, Nāhiku, Hāna, and Kaupō. They also have continued to exercise their access and gathering rights in those ahupua'a. For example, Awapuhi Carmichael, a kua'āina of Ke'anae, said, "All I know is that my mom said that because they came from Kaupō all the way back, we use from Kaupō to Punalu'u, that's near Kailua. And we have always practiced our gathering rights that way, from Kaupō all the way to Punalu'u, by Kailua."

The area included within the boundaries described, therefore, constitutes the true traditional Keanae-Wailuanui cultural landscape, as established through custom, use, and practice for cultural, religious, and subsistence purposes by the people of Keanae-Wailuanui. The resources used for traditional customs and practices in the Ke'anae-Wailuanui area are located at all elevations, from the ocean to sea level and up to over 10,000 feet at the summit of Haleakalā. Rainfall in the area varies from 40 inches a year to over 300 inches a year in the wet rainforests. The forests above Ke'anae-Wailuanui are part of the east Maui watershed, which is the largest single source of surface water in the state, with an average harvested flow of 60 billion gallons a year. In addition, artesian water is harvested from wells within the watershed.

The area mauka of the Hāna highway is dominated by the state-owned Koʻolau Forest Reserve and Hanawī Natural Area Reserve. Vegetation varies according to elevation. The upper elevations have grass and shrublands. The forest begins at approximately 7,200 feet and extends down to the coastline. It is dominated by ʻōhiʻa but includes native koa and introduced trees such as eucalyptus, strawberry guava, common guava, paper bark, rose apple, and java plum. Some of the most intact and extensive native forests occur here and support the state's greatest concentration of endangered forest birds. The forests are home to twelve species of native Hawaiian birds, native insects, snails, and other invertebrates. The native species and ecosystems provide a stable and beautiful watershed which would be nearly impossible to replace if destroyed. Clearly, Native Hawaiian subsistence practices have resulted in a sustainable use of the natural resources of these ahupuaʻa.

Traditional Practices and Way of Life

What is special about the way of life in Keʻanae-Wailuanui? Here is what the modern-day kuaʻāina of Keʻanae-Wailuanui have observed:

> Life is easier here than the outside world. Here, can hunt, can fish, can farm. (Charmain Day, 30s)

> Over here, I got free things to eat . . . That's how we live over here, ʻōpae, oʻopu, hīhīwai, ʻopihi. The sea clear, we go get ʻopihi, fish. (Enos Akina, 94)

> We're lucky. This is the place. We're blessed, we took such good care of everything we had. Awapuhi said, and til today I remember the word she used is "selfish." The word selfish is for the people over here, to protect the area. Selfish doesn't mean that we going to make money, selfish is because the area, we don't want it to get spoiled. This is the difference between selfish and stingy. We have to be selfish. (Kaipo Kimokeo, 50s)

> Wailuanui they have everything. They have the taro patch, they have the fishing ground, they have the ʻōpae, they have the oʻopu, they have the shell in the patch, you know, they have everything what you want. It's that, you have to do it yourself, you see . . . you got to work hard for everything that you want. (Mary Kaʻauamo, 82)[145]

The ability to make a living from taro cultivation, fishing, gathering, and hunting is the highlight of life in Keʻanae-Wailuanui.

Family members of all ages engaged in some level of gathering activity in the Keʻanae-Wailuanui district in the 1990s. Kūpuna such as eighty-three-year-old Helen Nakanelua still went out and gathered ʻōpae with her home-made ʻaʻaniu net in the ʻauwai that ran through her property at Lakini. Waio-kamilo Stream still has ʻōpae that is accessible to the kūpuna. The Kaʻauamo family is best known for its gathering activities. Awapuhi Kaʻauamo Car-michael, in her fifties, still went to gather ʻōpae, hīhīwai, and ʻopihi from Kai-lua and over through Kūhiwa. Paul Sinenci, an ʻōpio or young member of the Kaʻauamo family in his twenties, did extensive gathering with friends of his age. He had access to a broader area because he worked for the East Maui Irrigation Company (EMI). Awapuhi Carmichael identified some of the areas they regularly accessed for gathering of ʻōpae, hīhīwai, and oʻopu:

> We have our own names. Kapaʻula, gather ʻōpae. We use Puaakaʻa, we call it
> Kaunoa. Above the road, the ditch above the road, we use that stream, and
> then it branches off. Even Makapipi, we use Makapipi stream. We use all
> the way to the tunnel. We use it. Kūhiwa gulch is used by our family.
> Kūhiwa gulch we use also. Makapipi is just mauka. Kūhiwa is mauka.[146]

Gathering from a variety of places is important in order to conserve resources. The choice of place to gather is determined by the weather and other natural signs. Awapuhi Carmichael described the factors that affected her decision as to where to gather on a particular expedition:

> It depends on what we're getting, and how we feel, the ocean. We never go
> to the same place. You know how the Hawaiians used to do, they don't go
> back to the same place, so can restore. It depends on the weather, and then
> we go by the moon, the stars. If use one place, then go to another place,
> depends on the moon and the stars. We go up far. Especially for hunting
> too, we go all the way up. We all go to the same places, although each of us
> have our favorite hole, places, where we go for ʻōpae, you know. All mauka
> for ʻōpae. And then below have the ʻoʻopu and the prawns, they introduced
> the prawns, and hīhīwai. Above the road is more the ʻōpae. Above the road
> is where all the ʻōpae are. Above the main highway. And then below the
> road has hīhīwai, ʻoʻopu, you know.[147]

Within the traditional cultural landscape area for Keʻanae-Wailuanui, unoccupied areas with pristine flowing streams and forested areas are integral to the livelihoods of the families in the district. For example, nobody lives in the area from Wailuaiki to Kopiliʻula and over to Hanawī, and there are many gulches and streams flourishing with hīhīwai and ʻoʻopu that are routinely harvested by the Keʻanae-Wailuaiki kuaʻāina.

ʻŌpae, Oʻopu, and Hīhīwai

Keʻanae-Wailuanui is one of the few remaining areas in the Hawaiian Islands where ʻōpae could be gathered. Virtually every stream had ʻōpae at some time during the year. However, it was easier to gather in large amounts in the tunnels of the EMI ditch system. The irrigation ditch itself was an excellent breeding area for the ʻōpae because it had flowing water year round. Some streams below the ditch, however, did not have enough flowing water to sustain the ʻōpae year round when water was diverted into the ditch system.

Commercial sale of ʻōpae was prohibited under a state law that went into effect in 1993. Prior to that, certain families gathered ʻōpae for sale in Honolulu. The kūpuna explained that when they were growing up, the gathering of ʻōpae for sale was an important source of income for their parents and grandparents who did not hold full-time jobs. Helen Nakanelua, for example, would accompany her grandmother to gather and dry ʻōpelu for sale to the Asahi market in Honolulu:

> And I used to go along with my grandma, with a five gallon can, you know those tall ones, and I pack some wood, and I pack salt, so that whenever my grandma goes with the ʻupena net, do you have an idea what the ʻupena net looks like and they have a little bag there? Some of the bags are small, but she used to have these long bags. And then she cleans that where I am, she takes that out, we clean it and we cook it in this can. Salt it and cook it there, with the wood that I take we cook it. And after it's cooked, I begin spreading it on an oil tablecloth and a mat I used to pack along and then she leaves me there. I attend that ʻōpae while it's drying. By the time she comes back here, it's partly dried, I gather that ʻōpae again, and separate it in another bag, because that's partly dried, and we continue on, she gets another bag to do the same thing, cook, so that by the time she ends up her day, most of the ʻōpae, except the last one she has is partly half dried already. Do you know how the ʻupena look like? I show you, cause I have made some for me, because I use it.[148]

Although ʻōpae cannot be gathered for commercial sale, it is still a popular delicacy among the families in the district. They also gather ʻōpae to share with family and friends outside and on different islands. ʻŌpae, the ʻaʻaniu net used to gather it, and the methods of preparing it continue to be a distinctive aspect of the cultural lifestyle for which Keʻanae-Wailuanui is known and distinguished.

Oʻopu and hīhīwai, which require pristine and flowing stream waters, are becoming increasingly scarce in the Hawaiian Islands. Certain species of oʻopu are endangered, and others are rare. Keʻanae-Wailuanui is one of the few areas where they still thrive in sufficient size and abundance to be occasionally caught for subsistence food.

The gathering of hīhīwai is also carefully managed. The location of the hīhīwai is knowledge that has been passed down from one generation to the next for protection and proper management. It is not made available to the general public.

Plants and Trees

Traditionally, the mountain area above Keʻanae, Wailuanui, and Kopiliʻula is forested with native trees and plants such as koa and ʻōhiʻa lehua. There is also sandalwood at Nāhiku. The plateau looking from Keʻanae and over toward Honomanū has grasses, pia, and ʻōlena. Beginning in 1934, the federal Civilian Conservation Corps planted the non-native trees that became dominant in the lowland forests.

Most Native Hawaiian plants have some medicinal property. Native plants throughout the district are still used for medicinal purposes, such as the maile hohono, ʻieʻie, lauaʻe, koali, noni, ʻuhaloa, pōpolo, and even watercress.

James Hueu, the eighty-year-old caretaker of the Keʻanae YMCA camp, recounted how he had been recruited by two kūpuna, his father and brother, when he was just eleven years old to climb the small islet called Keōpuka to collect an Hawaiian herb called mokou:

> But way back in 1931, two old men from Honolulu, they came up and they wanted this medicine. One of the old patients he used to live here, his name was Kalilimoku. So he knew, when he left here he was a young boy, he knew where the medicine was. My dad was living yet, my brother was supposed to climb that moku. You see that moku down there [points toward Hāna side, in the ocean]? We call that Keōpuka, but it's Puahakumoa Bay, but we call it Keōpuka. When we went down there, I was young, I was only about 11 years old. So my brother was to climb, so I told my brother I think I better climb because you have a family and I'm a single boy. So I

did climb and I brought that herb. And til today I ask all these lapaʻau people. They don't know the name. The medicine they told me was mokou. So I told Larry about it and then he made a song about it. It was about me going up on that moku. About that mokou and that island. The herb is something like a dahlia, it grows like a dahlia plant. It grows something like a taro or a lily, and then certain times of the year, it dies. Then, certain times of the year, it grows. So when I went it just was growing, that's why I knew, but I didn't know what kind of herb that was, but my grandfather said that's the one. Anyway I tried, I taste, oh boy, it burn in my chest. So what for, I don't know. They came to collect that for a doctor by the name of Kaonohi. He was the first Hawaiian herbalist, from down Kāneʻohe or somewhere. That's what they came for. It grows only on that kind of moku. This thing is like a dahlia. A dahlia grows something like a lily. The color is green. I never seen the flower. But the leaves are similar to taro. And in the bottom has a potato. I got the whole thing. The potato, but I don't know what part he used. That grows just like the ʻōlena, certain time of the year it dies.[149]

A Native Hawaiian black banana, as well as ʻieʻie and the Hawaiian bamboo, was at one time used for weaving mats and hats of natural fiber by weavers in Keʻanae-Wailuanui. Pohole, a native fern, was popular for eating as a salad. One type of pohole is native to Keʻanae-Wailuanui. Another type of pohole was introduced in the district from the Big Island by Mrs. Kanoa, but the older people preferred the taste of the native variety. They only gathered it in the morning.

Fishing

The entire shoreline, reef, and nearshore area have abundant marine resources. Those who have boats dive, fish, and gather marine life from Kailua to Hāna, going out as far as the buoy, seven miles offshore. They gather ʻopihi, crab, and other shellfish from the rocks; dive for squid, lobster, and reef fish; bottom-fish for ono and uku; and troll for aku, ʻahi, and mahimahi. They occasionally surround akule in the bays such as at Honomanū. It is possible to use the hukilau method of surrounding and catching fish in any of the bays, but the practice has been discontinued because it depletes marine resources. Launching points for fishing are Keʻanae Point, Honomanū Bay, Wailuanui Bay, and Hāna Harbor.

The bays, where fresh water mixes with ocean water, are important spawning grounds for fish. Moki Day, in his fifties, described how the bays are important breeding grounds that deserve protection:

> You can consider all the shoreline area between here and Kaupō as breeding grounds for all these shoreline species of fish. They come into our rivers here because we have the fresh water, and they come in here and breed here and lay their eggs here. You go around here in certain seasons or certain times of the year and you see them, they come out in schools. I remember when we were small, before we even started grade school we used to go out with my grandfather and set net, and do all this fishing, you know, pole fishing, we used to hook moi. We seen fifty-pound moi already. They look like sharks in the water. But the only difference is that you see them as a school, a great big school, and there are these big huge monsters in there, and they're all in the waves, and I seen them. My brother and I have been fortunate to see them. And that's what I'd like to see again. And the only way to do that is to do this. And so I'd like to see the fishponds open up so we can restock the moi, and clamp down on fishing, block it up for a couple of years. They're hooking babies.[150]

The men and young boys could fish in any number of areas, all along the shoreline. For this reason, fishing down at Keʻanae, Honomanū, and Wailua-nui was reserved for the kūpuna. It was easy for them to access these two areas. Unfortunately, outsiders who are unfamiliar with the variety of fishing and gathering spots also went to these easy areas, and made it more difficult for the kūpuna to get a good catch. Moki Day explained how the easily accessible areas were reserved for the kūpuna:

> It seems like everyone here has their spot, where they go and harvest. Like Wailua Bay to Wailuaiki, this is an area that we keep for our kupunas because it's easy to go to. If you are an ʻōpio or mākua, well you have to hoof it. You haven't reached that age or to be honored in such a manner. That's why we have problems with the outside people because they come here and this is where they go. Because they see the opihi. Little do they know that it's for our kūpuna.[151]

There is interest among the members of the community in restoring the fishpond down near Pauwalu Point. On the map it is identified as Puʻuolu fishpond; however, James Hueu said that the fishpond is called Poʻulu fishpond. It has brackish water and is swampy, and the wild ducks used to go there every year. The fishermen believe that it would be worth restoring.

Hunting, Swimming, and Trails

The area above the highway is accessed for the hunting of wild pigs. On the Wailuku side, hunters usually go as far as Honomanū. However, the access road is through Nuaʻailua and up to Piʻinaʻau. From above Keʻanae, the access road starts above Ching's Pond and goes up to the forest reserve and to the ditch road. It is easy to go along the ditch road and look for pig tracks and then go deeper up into the forest once the tracks are sighted. Hunters go to Wahinepeʻe and up as far as Waiakamoi. Kupaʻu is a popular hunting spot. However, above Wailuanui, the gulches get deeper and hunting grows more difficult. The hunters go as far as Makapipi, then accessed along the four-wheel-drive road at Makapipi and go up mauka as far as Kūhiwa. There used to be a cabin above Kūhiwa for hunters to use for overnight stays. A hunting license is required. Pigs are tracked using hunting dogs, which pin the pig down so it can be killed by the hunter using a knife.

Freshwater ponds are popular swimming areas. Probably the most popular is Ching's Pond, originally known as Pāhoa Pond. As the stream continues down to the ocean, there are pools and additional swimming places. Throughout the district there are waterfalls that cascade into great swimming ponds.

Along the shoreline, Wailuanui Bay and the Keʻanae landing are popular swimming areas. Nuaʻailua is a beach for both swimming and surfing.

The Piʻilani Highway Trail is the primary shoreline access route for gathering and fishing all around the island of Maui. In the Keʻanae-Wailuanui district it is still used, particularly from Wailuanui over to Wailua Iki and to Kaliaʻe and over to Kopiliʻula.

There are several makai-to-mauka access trails and four-wheel-drive roads between the highway and the shoreline. Access to these trails and roads is vigilantly maintained by the community. Once, the use of a trail at Kaliaʻe running makai from the highway was blocked by a new landowner from outside the community. He put up a fence, bulldozed his land, and tried to cut off access. The community insisted on maintaining their access and retained the services of the Native Hawaiian Legal Corporation to assert their Native Hawaiian access rights.

Awapuhi Carmichael described some of the trails used by her family:

We go all over here. From the road, we go down, on the ridge, not the
gulch, (makai), right down to Waiohue, right down in the bay. And then
there's the island there, and from here you go to Kopili'ula too. All over
here is the King's Highway, you can walk all along the shoreline. We have
gathering rights all over here, along the stream. You can go either way. But
for our family, we walk 'em. We walk, we walk from the main highway
down and along the coast. We used to walk with my mom up until 1988
we walked this whole area, from the main highway down to the beach and
to the rivers. And we used to take like a caravan. My brothers were in high
school and they would carry the provisions and the 'opihi. And on the way
back to the highway we would stop for 'ōpae. And my dad, he used to cut
all the trails. Like he used to say, oh I think we should go to this part, like
to Kopili'ula. So then a day before he would go down and cut the trail.
And then, you know, he had a four wheel jeep and we would go just up
to Kalia'e and then walk from there to Kopili'ula.[152]

Four-wheel-drive roads were the primary access routes from the highway
to mauka hunting and gathering areas. One of the main four-wheel-drive
roads from the highway to the ditch trail began at Pahoa by Ching's Pond.
Until the original bridge fell down in 1958–59, this access road used to start
by the arboretum. Helen Nakanelua described how she and her grandmother
accessed the streams mauka of the highway using this route:

You know where the arboretum is? There used to be a bridge there. But
because the bridge was broken, the county did not want to build another
bridge. So they brought the bridge to where the swimming pool is. So
that's the road you go up to Pi'ina'au they call it. So looking from the
school, you can see that trail that goes up on that mountain there. That's
were we used to go on horseback until we get to Kopili'ula, Wailuaiki,
Wailuanui. Way up Pi'ina'au on the mountain, that's where they had a
camp for all the irrigation company to live, and across there, you cross that
kahawai, and there is that trail there to go. If you go by the school and you
look, you can see it. Pi'ina'au is toward the mountain, you take the road to
this way, you go to Wailuaiki, Wailuanui and all that, that the trail you
take. To Pa'akeke from Pi'ina'au, but I went with my grandma, Wailuaiki,
Kopili'ula, that's where the end of the trail, when people go to Hāna, we
go there and we stay there in a cave to get a car to go to Hāna. Now we
would climb up that river, to get 'ōpae, every week we were doing that my

grandma and I because my brothers and sisters, they didn't want to go to that kind of place.[153]

The East Maui Irrigation (EMI) ditch road was the popular route for access in the mauka area for hunting and gathering. Before the main Hāna road was constructed, the ditch road was used to travel from Keʻanae-Wailuanui to Hāna or to Wailuku. According to the ninety-four-year-old kūpuna Enos Akina, "If you go Hāna, telephone to the one who get car to go Kopiliʻula, wait for you. Go with horse along ditch trail to Kopiliʻula, leave horse, go on car. You like go outside, you go on the horse until Kailua. From Kailua on, you get car to go Wailuku. Come back, get the horse, come back. Bumbye they open this road, get car. Like go outside, go outside."[154]

The EMI ditch road is referred to as the old road since it was regularly used for travel between Kopiliʻula and Kailua by the residents' parents and grandparents. Residents are therefore accustomed to using it for their hunting and gathering activities.

Water

Keʻanae-Wailuanui is part of the east Maui watershed, where forty-eight streams originate. Of these, thirty-five are perennial (they flow to the sea year round) and thirteen are intermittent (they flow year round at higher elevations and intermittently at lower elevations). East Maui Irrigation (EMI) collects, stores, and transports water from over 50,000 acres of the east Maui watershed, including from the Keʻanae-Wailuanui cultural landscape. The system, owned and built by EMI, consists of approximately 400 intakes (stream diversions), seven reservoirs, seventy-five miles of aqueduct (fifty miles of tunnel and twenty-five miles of open ditches), sixty miles of four-wheel-drive roads, and many miles of trails. The system provides irrigation water for agricultural plains in central Maui, county water to upcountry Maui residents and farmers, and domestic water for Kula, Pukalani, Makawao, Haliʻimaile, Haʻikū, and Peahi.

Fresh water is an integral part of the cultural landscape for taro cultivation, the gathering of aquatic and marine resources, recreation, and domestic use. Awapuhi Carmichael explained the importance of the streams: "All of our streams need to be protected for recreational and gathering purposes, because if we don't, then they'll divert all of the water, and then the streams will be empty. Fishes need water too. Certain fishes need water to spawn. That's why we're lucky, we have enough water for the fishes."[155]

Water flows throughout the Keʻanae-Wailuanui landscape from both streams and springs. The taro patches of Keʻanae and Wailuanui are primarily fed by spring waters. Some of both the stream and spring waters have been diverted into the EMI system. Awapuhi Carmichael, the genealogist for the Kaʻauamo family, discovered a letter written in 1881 to two commissioners, A. P. Carter and J. S. Walker, by her ancestors opposing the turning over of the water rights in Honomanū to Claus Spreckels for construction of the irrigation ditch now controlled by EMI. The letter reads in part:

> Keanae, Koolau
> September 12, 1881
> Hon. A. P. Carter a me Hon. J. S. Walker
> Na Komisina (Commissioners)
>
> ʻO makou o na komimike, ke nonoi aku nei i ko olua ʻaʻole lilo ke kahi pono wai o na aina lei aliʻi o Honomanu, Keanae, Wailua i na ona miliona.
>
> J. W. Kehuhu (Kahuhukaunihiakami Halemano), K. Makaena J. K. Hueu (John Kalawaianui Hueu), S. Kamakahiki, K. E. Maiailua, D. W. Napihaa, M. Kaleba, B. B. Kalilimoku, Kamanele, J. S. Lono, J. Kuluhiawa, Keliʻi (Keliʻiaukai), J. B. Kaakuamoku
>
> [We are the committee members, we request of the two of you not to turn over the water rights of the crown lands of Honomanu, Keanae, Wailua to the millionaire (Claus Spreckels).]
>
> [Signed] J. W. Kehuhu (Kahuhukaunihiakami Halemano), K. Makaena J. K. Hueu (John Kalawaianui Hueu), S. Kamakahiki, K. E. Maiailua, D. W. Napihaa, M. Kaleba, B. B. Kalilimoku, Kamanele, J. S. Lono, J. Kuluhiawa, Keliʻi (Keliʻiaukai), J. B. Kaakuamoku]

There is continuing concern about the impact of water diversion upon marine life and taro cultivation. Without spring water, Keʻanae and Wailuanui would have be cut off from free-flowing water when the streams were diverted into the EMI system. The water for Wailuanui originates way up at Plunket Spring and flows down to Wailuanui through Lakini. At Lakini, an ʻauwai carries the spring water together with water drawn in from the Waiokamilo Stream down into Wailuanui. In Wailuanui, the water is distributed through three separate channels to different sections of taro land.

The water for the taro patches in Keʻanae comes from the Palahulu stream and the Waikuna spring above Ching's Pond. Another ʻauwai carries water into Keʻanae from a creek named Waihaoawa. James Hueu told the story of how J. A. Chamberlain dug the ʻauwai for his taro patch in Keʻanae:

> The guy dug an ʻauwai from there, irrigated his taro patch down Keʻanae and has his name under, J. A. Chamberlain. The name of that creek is Waihaowa. Waihaowa iki is the one above, so there must be a Waihaowa nui. Waihaowa means the separating water. So it was separated up there and then they met again up there. So this man, he dug a ditch to use in his taro patch and he named the ditch, the ditch name is ʻauwai hoʻomanawa-nui, and he put his name under, J. A. Chamberlain.[156]

The ʻōhiʻa spring is in one of the ʻili between Keʻanae and Wailuanui. James Hueu provided a description of the spring waters that feed this ʻili:

> Where the watercress is, that's the ʻōhiʻa spring. That's Waikāne and Kana-loa. Well they call it ʻōhiʻa spring. Waikāne and Kanaloa is right under the road. There's two holes where the water comes out, right when you make that turn. Right under there is where.
>
> That stream, the Palauhulu stream, on the east side, until the other way, they call that Pāhoa-Waianu. Waianu is at that spring, Waikāne-Kanaloa, and Pāhoa is that river.[157]

At the time the interviews were conducted, hau bushes were overrunning the streams and clogging up the water (during heavy rains, debris would get caught in the bushes and block the free flow of water), a problem that affected the EMI system, state lands, and the taro farmers. There was general interest in having the streams cleared through a cooperative effort between the state, EMI, and the taro farmers.

Taro

The Keʻanae-Wailuanui district is famous for its taro, and the community is proud of this legacy. The Keʻanae-Wailuanui kuaʻāina proudly shared traditional family accounts of how their district was never touched by the wars between the Maui and Hawaiʻi chiefs during the time of Kamehameha I. According to them, Keʻanae-Wailuanui was very important to the chiefs as a source of taro, poi, and water. To ravage the landscape would have been reckless and wasteful. Moki Day provided the following insights:

Thousands of canoes came in for water and for poi. But Keʻanae-Wailuanui
were never touched by war. The people took food to Hāna and to Nāhiku
by the Piʻilanihale heiau where the war was. They carried the food to
Nāhiku and came back to mahiʻai (farm).

This is the bread basket of Maui, this area here all the way to Kīpahulu.
There are more taro patches here than anywhere else on our island. So
there's any valley that you can go in here and see taro patches, loʻi formations. These things are still here.[158]

As noted above, some of the historic taro patches in the district were converted to rice paddies between the 1880s and the 1920s. During that period,
taro was primarily grown for home consumption rather than for commercial
sale. James Hueu shared his insights on the origins of some of the taro patches
in the district:

They say, the Chinese make the taro patch. I say not. The taro patches
were there before the Chinese ever came to Hawaiʻi. But because the Chinese came, they planted rice in the taro patches and they marry into the
Hawaiian women. But they never did the taro patches. The taro patches
were there long before that. I have two taro patches down here [at the
YMCA camp]. It wasn't made by the old Hawaiians, I made 'em. I made
that on the dry land. But over here, when we started the CCC camp, I saw
terraces over here. So I think they had taro patches, long time ago. There's
one taro patch over here on that land, Chamberlain's land, now it's Keppler's, it's a small taro patch. If you don't go around that taro patch, you
didn't see Keʻanae. The name of that taro patch is Keʻanae. And they have
some taro patches named Kalihi, they have Makaʻiwa. The taro patches had
a name. Even me I don't know some of the names. But for Keʻanae, I knew
that from way back. In the back of the Keppler house, that area is called
Keʻanae. My son takes care of the patches. I told him, you take care of that
patch, even if you not even get half a bag of taro, but that patch has history,
so don't let it get filled up with grass.[159]

At the time that the 999-year homesteads were established at the beginning of the twentieth century, each house lot also had a taro patch assigned
to it. According to Moki Day, "Everyone who chose a homestead got two acre
lots, a house lot and taro land."[160] Each house lot continued to have a taro
patch. Taro began to be produced for commercial sale to Hāna and to Wailuku beginning in the 1920s. However, the families of many of the kuaʻāina

who are now producing taro for commercial sale mainly began to sell taro for poi after World War II. Before that, most of the taro in the district was grown for home consumption. Many of the families continued to sell taro to supplement their salaries from employment with the Maui county road crew, EMI, or jobs outside in Kahului or Wailuku. However, there were a few families whose sole source of income was from taro production.

Many of the current owners of the house lots still cultivate their own taro patches; however, some of the patches have been passed on to family members living in Keʻanae or outside. In some cases, the taro patch was being leased to other residents in the community. Many of those cultivating taro sold their taro to the Molokaʻi poi mill.

Taro was also raised in the Keʻanae arboretum by the State Department of Land and Natural Resources. At one point the taro collection included seventy varieties, but disease reduced the collection to ten. The taro was grown in restored taro terraces and patches.

Throughout the district, old taro terraces could be found with wild taro in the valleys along streams. Some families went out to gather lūʻau leaves from the wild taro because they had good flavor, distinct from that of the cultivated varieties. Some of the areas where wild lūʻau was gathered included Piʻinaʻau, Nuaʻailua, Kupaʻu, Waipiʻo, Awiowio, Pohole, and Pāhoa.

The growing demand for poi made the production of taro a profitable venture, and there was a lot of interest in taro production. Taro was farmed by kūpuna, mākua, and ʻōpio. As the kūpuna grew old, their children and grandchildren carried on the work. As the mākua generation reached retirement age, they returned to their family lands to maintain and open up ancestral taro patches. In addition, being able to cultivate the taro lands of their ancestors provided cultural and personal satisfaction to the kuaʻāina of Keʻanae-Wailuanui. Kaipo Kimokeo described the spiritual connection he felt to his ancestors when he worked with the taro:

> Anyway, I got this job at the arboretum, we started to open the taro patch, spiritually, I can see my family around me, because, that was the main food . . . So now, spiritually, I'm involved . . . spiritually motivated this way [to grow taro], because what I can see tells me. All these valleys. We supplied an army. We had all our taro patches. We supplied Kamehameha when he came here. Aunty Mary Kaʻauamo told me, I was asking her about the ʻapowai taro. She told me that water is spiritual water, it doesn't touch the ground. That water, it can be used for medicine and things like that.[161]

Persistence of Lifestyle

Keʻanae-Wailuanui has persisted into the twenty-first century as a center of traditional Hawaiian culture and lifestyle. Although they live in distinct households and cultivate individual patches of taro for their own families and for commercial sale, the residents also share in the abundance of natural resources from Honomanū to Makapipi. Together, they respect and care for the springs and streams that feed their individual loʻi kalo and sustain an abundance of resources. Together, they continue to balance the conservation of natural resources with their own needs, taking only what is necessary for their family's daily sustenance and respecting the reproductive cycles of the animal and plant life in the valleys along the Koʻolau coast of Maui. Their children play together, attend school together, and mature to adulthood, sometimes intermarrying.

The Native Hawaiian way of life continues to thrive among the households and taro patches of Keʻanae-Wailuanui, despite the influx of retired Chinese plantation workers who farmed at the turn of the twentieth century and the post-statehood settlement of outsiders seeking a quiet lifestyle in rural Maui. The persistence of the Native Hawaiian lifestyle in Keʻanae-Wailuanui provides an important source of continuity and connection for all Native Hawaiians, not just those living there, to their rich heritage. We will more fully appreciate the role of Keʻanae-Wailuanui and the Hāna district as a cultural kīpuka in chapter 6, where I discuss the role of the kuaʻāina of Hāna in the revitalization, beginning in 1976, of the cultural and natural resources of Kahoʻolawe.

FOUR

Puna: A *Wahi Pana* Sacred to Pelehonuamea

Puna is the land section that inspires hula creation because of the natural movements of wave, wind and trees. Puna is the source of regenerative power. Some examples are the rising of the sun, volcanic creation of new land and the growth of new vegetation on this new formed land.

— PUALANI KANAKAʻOLE KANAHELE, *Ka Honua Ola: The Living Earth*, 1992

T HE INTERPLAY of many dynamic primal natural elements in Puna make it one of the most sacred areas in all of Hawaiʻi. The regenerative power inherent in the lands and atmosphere of Puna are also reflected in the role and contributions of the kuaʻāina of Puna to the perpetuation of Native Hawaiian culture through the twenty-first century. "Puna, mai ʻOkiʻokiaho a Māwae" (Puna from ʻOkiʻokiaho to Māwae): as this ʻōlelo noʻeau says, the Puna district spans from Māwae on the northern boundary with Hilo south to ʻOkiʻokiaho on the southern boundary with Kaʻū.[1] Comprising 311,754 acres, the island of Kauaʻi (354,112 acres) could almost fit within the district.

Puna is located in the easternmost part of the easternmost island of the Hawaiian chain, so all of Hawaiʻi's days begin there. The ʻōlelo noʻeau that reminds us of this daily phenomenon goes: "Mai ka hikina a ka lā i Kumukahi a ka welona a ka lā i Lehua" (From the rising of the sun at Kumukahi to the fading of the sunlight at Lehua).[2]

The northeast tradewinds, with their rain-infused cloud formations and rainfall, first reach Hawaiʻi in Puna. A Hawaiian proverb, "Ka makani hali ʻala o Puna" (The fragrance-bearing wind of Puna), speaks of how these winds grow fragrant as they travel over Puna, luxuriant with *maile, lehua,* and *hala*.[3]

The name Puna means wellspring and derives from observations by Native Hawaiian ancestors of how the forests of Puna attract the clouds to drench he district with its many rains, such as "ka ua moaniani lehua o Puna" (the rain that brings the fragrance of the lehua of Puna).[4] The rains refresh and enrich the Puna water table and sustain the life cycle of all living things in Puna and the entire island of Hawai'i.

The waters of Puna are believed to originate with Kāne, the Hawaiian God of freshwater sources. His domain is traditionally in the east, where the sun rises. Kāne is a guardian of the Pelehonuamea fire clan, the family of deities who migrated from the south to Hawai'i and are manifest in the Puna district's volcanic activity. Kāne protects the subsurface waters, the main source of the volcanic steam that forms the bloodstream of the volcano deity, Pelehonuamea.

The steam is believed to be the *mana*, the life force and energy of Pelehonuamea. When Pelehonuamea does not actively erupt, the steam is the main form in which she manifests herself. When there is steam in the forest, Pelehonuamea is thought to be there. That is her identity, her imagery, and her manifestation. Throughout the district of Puna, traditional chants tell of warm pools in caves and under ground, such as Kaukala and Punahakeone. These

Figure 22 Pelehonuamea is the dynamic creative energy that shapes the lives and livelihoods of the kua'āina of Puna. K. Maehara, Bishop Museum.

are the sacred bathing places of Pelehonuamea. Pelehonuamea practitioners believe that the waters of the Puna district are sacred to Kāne and that the steam generated by the heat of Pelehonuamea is sacred to her.

Puna is where new land is created and new growth and new life sprout. The new land is sacred, fresh, clean, and untouched. After vegetation begins again to grow upon it, it is ready for human use.[5] Puna is also the center of the ongoing creation of new land through volcanic activity. It is where new vegetation comes to life on the newly formed land, repeating a sequence of evolution that is millions of years old.

A chant translated by Pualani Kanahele describes the primal elements and features of Puna that Hawaiians celebrate and honor in legend, chant, and hula.[6]

Ke Ha'a La Puna I Ka Makani

Ke ha'a la Puna i ka makani	Puna is dancing in the breeze
Ha'a ka ulu hala i Kea'au	The hala groves at Kea'au dance
Ha'a Hā'ena me Hōpoe	Hā'ena and Hōpoe dance
Ha'a ka wahine	The woman dances
'Ami i kai o Nānāhuki	[She] dances at the sea of Nānāhuki
Hula le'a wale	Dancing is delightfully pleasing
I kai o Nānāhuki	At the sea of Nānāhuki
'O Puna kai kuwā i ka hala	The voice of Puna resounds
Pae i ka leo o ke kai	The voice of the sea is carried.
Ke lū la, i na pua lehua	While the lehua blossoms are being scattered.
Nānā I kai o Hōpoe	Look toward the sea of Hōpoe
Ka wahine 'ami i kai o Nānā huki	The dancing woman is below, toward Nānāhuki
Hula le'a wale	Dancing is delightfully pleasing
I kai o Nānāhuki	At the sea of Nānāhuki

Pualani Kanaka'ole Kanahele's elaborate and compelling interpretation of this chant in her manuscript "Ka Honua Ola: The Living Earth" reveals its true significance. According to Kanahele, "Ke Ha'a La Puna" is the first recorded hula in the Pele and Hi'iaka saga. Hi'iaka performed a hula to this *mele* or song to please her older sister, Pelehonuamea. The hula was performed at Ha'ena and represented the birth of the hula sacred to Pele. The chant refers to weather phenomena, movements of nature, and the natural imagery for which Puna is famous—the breeze, the hala groves, the sea, and the vol-

canic eruption. The rain together with the rising sun of Puna are the nurturing substances that induce the growth of vegetation on the new land.

Proceeding from the context of Puna for the chant, Kanahele interpreted
the meaning of the lines in the chant. In the first line, "Ke haʻa la Puna i ka
makani" (Puna is dancing in the breeze),

> Hiʻiaka, the youngest sister of Pele is asked by Pele to do a haʻa and a mele.
> She satisfies her older sister's request with "Ke haʻa la Puna i ka makani."
> The haʻa or dance which she exhibits is a creative exposition in praise of
> the environment around her and a celebration of the regenerative power
> of the coupling of land and flora. Hiʻiaka's own kinolau or body forms are
> the flora which readily grows on new lava flows. Therefore it is Hiʻiaka's
> place to celebrate this newly made land upon which her body forms are
> given life.

Kanahele goes on to elaborate that the line "Puna kai i ka hala" (The voice
of Puna resounds) refers to the beating of the sea on the cliffs of Puna.

> This sound is magnified through the groves of hala. The hala grove
> becomes the resonator. The sea movements of Puna as it heaves, rolls,
> dashes, splashes, sprays and vibrates, produces various distinct sounds and
> chords. The various sounds emanating from the hala grove are symbolic
> of the sounds reproduced by the hula implement which excites and provokes
> movement for the dancer.[7]

According to Kanahele, the chant explains the roles of the deities Pelehonuamea and Hiʻiaka in hula:

> Imitation of nature gives praise to those Deities responsible for different
> aspects of nature. Pele's energy, her explosive, dramatic creative tactics of
> land birth deserve praise. The dualistic nature of Hiʻiaka and her pro-
> creative powers of vegetable growth also deserve praise. The land and
> vegetable manifestation of these sisters provide initial movement and
> energy in creating hula. The hula associated with these deified sisters
> are pure original movement and pure sound.[8]

Having reviewed the major primal forces and deities associated with the
Puna district, as well as the singular importance of Puna as the birthplace of
the Pelehonuamea forms of hula, we will look at the patterns of change in the
landscape reflected in myth and legend.

Puna's Mythical Era

The myths and legends of Puna are dominated by Pelehonuamea, Hawaiian Goddess of the volcano, and the members of her fire clan, who migrated from their distant homeland through the northwest islands of Hawai'i until they settled in Puna, Hawai'i. The Hawaiian proverb "Ke one lau'ena a Kāne" (The rich, fertile land of Kāne) was interpreted by Mary Kawena Pukui as a reference to the idea that Puna was a beautiful and fertile land loved by the God Kāne. According to Pukui, Pelehonuamea changed it into a land of lava beds, cinder, and rock when she settled there from Kahiki.[9]

The legends, myths, and chants that describe the early development of the Puna district relate the dynamic tension between the deities of the Pelehonuamea fire clan and the deities honored by other Hawaiian families as their ancestors. Each of the deities represents a different elemental force in the natural landscape of the Puna district. Throughout all of the folklore for Puna, Pelehonuamea and her family of deities emerge as the natural primal elements that dominate and shape the lives of the chiefs and the people of Puna. Here are two traditional mo'olelo that reflect the conflict between Pelehonuamea or the volcanic fire and deities representing other natural elements in Puna, the mo'o or dragon lizards who dwelled in mountain pools and shoreline ponds before the Pelehonuamea clan came to Hawai'i, and the Pig God who dwelled in the old-growth forests. The volcanic deity conquers the mo'o but reaches a compromise with the Pig God.

Waka the Mo'o

Traditional mo'olelo describe Ka'ū and Puna as beautiful lands without lava beds. It is said that there was only earthen soil from one end to the other. The mo'olelo reveal the existence of a very long sandy stretch called Keonelaue-naakāne ("Kāne's great sand stretch") in the district of Puna. The lava covered the earth and sand and transformed Puna into a land of lava rock.

The mo'o, Wakakeakaikawai and Puna'aikoa'e, were destroyed by Pelehonuamea of the eternal fires. According to this legend, the fight between these mo'o and Pelehonuamea began in Punalu'u in Ka'ū, continued in Puna, and ended in Waiākea in Hilo. Through the course of the battle, a long stretch of sand extending from Waiākea, Hilo, to Pānau, in Puna, called Keonelau'ena-akāne, was covered with lava. Because Waka ran through Puna, with Pelehonuamea in pursuit, most of the land in Puna became covered with rough and smooth lava and remains so to this day. The famous stretch of sand disappeared. Only traces of it can be seen in small pockets, scattered here and there, from Waiākea to Puna.[10]

Pele and Kamapuaʻa

Legends also relate the dramatic struggles between Pelehonuamea and the forces of the storm and forest represented as Kamapuaʻa, the hog-man or Pig God. Kamapuaʻa goes to the crater of Halemaʻumaʻu and courts the Goddess in the form of a handsome man. Her sisters attract her attention to him. Not at all deceived, Pelehonuamea refuses him with insults, calling him "a pig and the son of a pig." His love songs change to taunts, and the two engage in a contest of invective. He attempts to approach her, but she sends her flames over him. Each deity summons its own God. Pelehonuamea's brothers encompass Kamapuaʻa "above and below" and would have smothered him had not the lovemaking God of Kamapuaʻa lured them away with a beautiful woman. Kamapuaʻa threatens to put out the fires of the pit with deluges of water, but Pelehonuamea's uncles and brothers and the fire tender Lonomakua keep them burning. The reigning chiefess of Makahanaloa sends fog and rain to support her brother against the fire Goddess. Hogs run all over the place. The pit fills with water. The lovemaking God sees that if Pelehonuamea is destroyed Kamapuaʻa will be the ultimate loser. The fires are all out; only the fire sticks remain. These the God decides to save. Pelehonuamea yields, and Kamapuaʻa has his way with her. They divide the districts between them, Pelehonuamea taking Puna, Kaʻū, and Kona (districts that are periodically overrun with lava flows) and Kamapuaʻa ruling Kohala, Hāmākua, and Hilo (the windward districts, always moist with rain).[11]

Settlement and Expansion

Archaeological excavations in Puna set the date for the earliest settlements in the district between 300 and 600 A.D.[12] Very little subsurface excavation has been conducted in the Puna district; as such studies are conducted, it is possible that the date for earliest settlement could be revised. Because of the lack of running streams in Puna, early settlers first lived along the shoreline, where they had access to the ocean, freshwater springs along the shoreline and in the ocean, and arable land.

Legends possibly set in this era document the trials of Puna chiefs and their followers with Pelehonuamea and her fiery temper. Chief Kanuha of Kona shared the legend of the Puna chief Keliikuku with the French explorer Jules Remy in the nineteenth century.[13] The event was believed by Kanuha to have occurred in the 1600s. The legend of how the young chief Kahawali and his hula students perish after rebuffing a challenge from Pelehonuamea to compete at hōlua or mountain sledding is also related in many sources and probably occurred around the same time.[14]

The Legend of Keliʻikuku

According to the chief Kanuha, up until the 1600s the district of Puna was renowned as magnificent country, with smooth, even roads and a sandy soil that was favorable to vegetation. Native Hawaiians at the time of Kanuha had grandparents who related stories of the great volcanic floods they had personally witnessed in Puna during their lifetime.

A certain high chief reigned in Puna. He journeyed to the island of Oʻahu where he met a prophet of Kauaʻi named Kāneakalau, who asked him who he was. "I am," replied the chief, "Keliʻikuku of Puna." The prophet then asked him what sort of country he possessed. The chief said: "My country is charming. Everything is found there in abundance. Everywhere are sandy plains which produce marvelously." "Alas!" replied the prophet, "Go. Return to your beautiful country. You will find it overthrown, abominable. Pelehonuamea has made of it a heap of ruins. The trees of the mountains have descended toward the sea. The ʻōhiʻa and pandanus are on the shore. Your country is no longer habitable." The chief made answer: "Prophet of evil, if what you now tell me is true, you shall live. But if, when I return to my country, I prove the falsity of your predictions, I will come back on purpose and you shall die by my hand."

Unable, in spite of his incredulity, to forget this terrible prophecy, Keliʻikuku set sail for Hawaii. He reached Hāmākua, landed, and traveled home by short stages. From the heights of Hilo at the village of Makahanaloa, he beheld in the distance his entire province overwhelmed in chaotic ruin, a prey to fire and smoke. In despair, the unfortunate chief hung himself on the very spot where he first discovered this sad spectacle.

This tradition of the mountain of Keliʻikuku and Kāneakalau continued to be told and retold among Hawaiian storytellers. It was even put to meter and sung by the ancients. According to the chief Kanuha, whether the prediction was made or not, the fact that Puna had been ravaged by volcanic action had come to pass.

Kahawali and Pelehonuamea

The handsome young chief Kahawali lived near Kapoho in the Puna district of Hawaii in the days of the chief Kahoukapu. He had a wife and two children named Paupoulu and Ka'ohe. His mother lived at Kūki'i, and he had a sister, Ko'ae who lived at Kula. His father and another sister named Kāne-wahinekeaho lived on O'ahu. Kahawali was an expert in the hula dance and in riding the hōlua. At the time of the Makahiki festival, when the hula pupils gathered for a public appearance, a sled race was arranged with his friend Ahua. Pelehonuamea in the guise of an old woman also offered to compete with Kahawali and he laughed at her impertinence. Angry at the chief's rebuff, Pelehonuamea pursued him down the hill in her fire form. Kahawali fled first to the hill Pu'ukea, then hastened to bid good-bye to his wife and children. He paused to say farewell to his favorite pig, Aloipua'a, and had just time to greet his sister at Kula before he escaped to the sea in a canoe his brother had opportunely brought to land. Upright lava rocks are said to mark the fate of members of Kahawali's family and of his favorite pig. The famous tree molds (Papalauahi) above Kapoho are identified as a group of hula pupils caught in the track of Pelehonuamea's wrath.[15]

Migration, Ruling Chiefs, and 'Ohana

For the period of the Tahitian migration to Hawai'i Island between 1100 and 1300, Puna is prominent in legends as the district where the high priest Pa'ao made his first landfall and built the Waha'ula heiau for his God. The Hawaiian historian Samuel Kamakau provides a brief account: "Puna on Hawai'i island was the land first reached by Pa'ao, and here in Puna he built his first heiau for his God Aha'ula and named it Aha'ula [Waha'ula]. It was a luakini. From Puna, Pa'ao went on to land in Kohala, at Pu'uepa. He built a heiau there, called Mo'okini, a luakini."[16]

Pa'ao, according to Hawaiian mo'olelo, was a powerful priest and prophet. According to Kamakau, he originated from Wawau and 'Upolu, lands in the mythical Polynesian homeland, Kahiki.[17] In Hawai'i he established a new order of religious priesthood and practices that included human sacrifices at the lua-

kini heiau whose form of construction he introduced in Hawai'i. The priesthood of Pa'ao served the ruling chiefs of Hawai'i until the time of Hewahewa,
high priest of Kings Kamehameha I and II who collaborated with Kamehameha II in the abolition of the traditional chiefly kapu in 1819.

Abraham Fornander gives a description of Waha'ula heiau:

> It was built in the quadrangular or parallelogram form which characterized
> all the Heiau built under and after the religious regime introduced by Paao,
> and in its enclosure was a sacred grove, said to have contained one or more
> specimens of every tree growing on the Hawaiian group, a considerable
> number of which, or perhaps their descendants, had survived when last the
> author visited the place in 1869.[18]

According to Kamakau, Hawai'i Island was without a chief when Pa'ao
arrived in Hawai'i. Evidently the chiefs of Hawai'i were considered ali'i maka-
'āinana or just commoners, maka'āinana, during that time.[19] Pa'ao sent back
to Tahiti for a new ruler for Hawai'i, thereby ushering in a new era of ruling
chiefs and kahuna in the Hawaiian archipelago. The new ruler was Pilika'aiea,
ancestor of the future King Kamehameha I. Kamakau, Fornander, and Thrum
place Pa'ao in the eleventh century, sixteen generations from Heleipawa. Cartwright places Pili, the chief brought to Hawai'i by Pa'ao, in the twenty-fifth
generation before 1900—that is, 1275 CE.[20]

In the legend of the migration of Mo'ikeha to Hawai'i, his party first
touched at the easternmost point of Hawai'i, Cape Kumukahi, and his younger
brothers Kumukahi and Ha'eha'e remained in Puna. Of the others in his family, the kahuna Mo'okini and Kaluawilinau made their home at Kohala; Honu-
aula landed in Hāna on Maui; and his sisters Makapu'u and Makaaoa landed
on O'ahu. The rest of the party went on to Kaua'i.[21]

In the Kumuhonua legend about the migration of Hawai'iloa, also known
as Kekowaihawai'i, he, his family, and his followers migrate to Hawai'i. He
alone takes his wife and children. They are credited with being the ancestors
of the Hawaiian people. Hawai'iloa named the island of Hawai'i after himself,
the other islands after his children, and various land divisions after the navigators who sailed with him. From time to time Hawai'iloa voyages south to bring
back mates for his children from the family of his brother Ki. He brings Ki's
oldest son, Tunuiaiateatua, as husband for his favorite daughter, O'ahu. Their
son, Tunuiatea, is born at Keauhou on Hawai'i. Hawai'iloa names the district
of Puna for the birthplace of his nephew Tunuiaiateatua, Punaauia, in Tahiti.[22]

Ruling Chiefs of Puna

"Hilina'i Puna, kālele iā Ka'ū" (Puna leans and reclines on Ka'ū) refers to the common origin of the people of Puna and Ka'ū. The ancestors of these two districts were originally of one extended family. The time came when the people of each district decided to have a name of their own, without breaking the link entirely. Those in Ka'ū referred to themselves as the Mākaha, meaning fierce, savage, ferocious. Those in Puna called themselves Kūmākaha, or standing fierce, savage, ferocious. Both names are related in chants of the chiefs of Puna and Ka'ū.[23] Again referring to the common origins of the Mākaha of Ka'ū and the Kūmākaha of Puna is the rallying cry "E ala e Ka'ū, Kahiko o Mākaha; e ala e Puna, Puna Kūmākaha; e ala e Hilo na'au kele!" (Arise, O Ka'ū of ancient fierce descent; arise, O Puna, stand fierce; arise, O Hilo of the water-soaked foundation).[24] The distinction between the families of Ka'ū and Puna may have occurred during this period.

Puna's political history throughout this period is bound up with the fortunes of the ruling families of Hilo or Ka'ū. No one single Puna family emerges upon whose support either the Hilo or Ka'ū chiefs seeking power could depend upon for success. Thus, the political control of Puna did not rest upon conquering Puna itself, but rather upon control of the neighboring districts of Ka'ū and Hilo.[25]

Nevertheless, there were two notable Puna chiefs in this era, Hua'a and 'Imaikalani, who were identified as enemies of High Chief 'Umialīloa and were killed by he and his warriors. During the time of High Chief Līloa, approximately 1475 CE, the chiefs of the six districts of Hawai'i, including Puna, were autonomous within their own districts, but they acknowledged Līloa as their paramount chief. Hakau, son of the sacred wife of Līloa, succeeded him. According to Kamakau, Hakau failed to look after the well-being of the people under him: "But in the later years of his rule he was lost in pleasure, mistreated the chiefs, beat those who were not guilty of any wrongdoing, and abused the priests of the heiaus of his God and the chiefs of his own government."[26]

The chiefs and priests conspired with 'Umialīloa, Hakau's half brother, and killed Hakau. Hakau's death left 'Umi in possession of Hāmākua. The chiefs of the remaining districts of Hawai'i declared their independence from 'Umi. 'Umi went to war, conquered those chiefs who resisted him, and reunited the districts of the entire island under his rule. According to Kamakau, Hua'a, the chief of Puna, was conquered by ʻUmialīloa: "Hua-ʻa was the chief of Puna, but Puna was seized by ʻUmi and his warrior adopted sons, Piʻi-mai-waʻa, ʻOmaʻo-kamau, and Koʻi. These were noted war leaders and counsellors during ʻUmi's reign over the kingdom of Hawaiʻi. Hua-ʻa was killed by Piʻi-mai-waʻa on the battlefield of Kuolo in Keaʻau, and Puna became ʻUmi-a-Liloa's."[27]

ʻImaikalani is the first chief of Kaʻū who is said to have control over parts of Puna. In the time of ʻUmialīloa, circa 1500 CE, he reconditioned the heiau of Wahaʻula. This is an indication that he held supreme authority over the ahupuaʻa of Pūlama in Puna. He was a chief of power and prestige and can be found in several chiefly genealogies, including that of Queen Emma. According to Barrere, ʻImaikalani may well have been one of the chiefly ancestors of the Mākaha and Kūmākaha lines of Kaʻū and Puna.[28]

Kamakau provided the following account of the conquest of chief ʻImaikalani by the ʻUmi warrior Piʻimaiwaʻa:

> ʻUmi-a-Līloa feared I-mai-ka-lani. Although he was blind and unable to see, his hearing was keen. He had pet ducks that told him in which direction a person approached, whether from in front, at the back, or on either side. All depended on the cries of the birds. In former days I-mai-ka-lani was not blind, and ʻUmi was never able to take Kaʻū. The war lasted a long time. ʻUmi went by way of the mountains to stir up a fight with I-mai-ka-lani and the chiefs of Kona . . . I-mai-ka-lani was never taken captive by ʻUmi, but Piʻi-mai-waʻa was crafty and studied the reason for his great strength and skill with the spear . . . All these men were destroyed by Piʻi-mai-waʻa, and the blind man was at a loss for the lack of helpers. Well could Piʻi-mai-waʻa say in a boast, "Death to him from Piʻi-mai-waʻa." After I-mai-ka-lani's death Kaʻū became ʻUmi-a-Līloa's.[29]

In the next generation, Kahalemilo, son of ʻImaikalani and Lililehua, and the son of Huaʻa were both killed by ʻUmi's son, Keawenuiaʻumi, when he gained control of Hawaiʻi. According to Barrere, this seems to have extinguished the lines of ʻImaikalani and Huaʻa as autonomous chiefs of Kaʻū and Puna. From the time of Keawenuiaʻumi, Kaʻū was ruled by the Kona chiefs descended from Keawenuiaʻumi. Puna is linked with Kaʻū until the time of Keaweikekāhialiʻiokamoku, when the ʻI family of Hilo controlled parts of Puna. While control over the other part of Puna is not specifically mentioned, it can be inferred that it continued to be linked with Kaʻū.[30]

Puna on the Eve of European Contact

On the eve of European contact, Puna seemed to have enjoyed a brief resurgence of semiautonomous rule. In the time of Kalani'opu'u, the chief 'Imakakoloa of Puna became powerful enough to attract the wrath of the ruling chief.

'Imakakoloa was probably a descendant of 'Imaikalani through the 'I family. Kalaniopu'u, having gained control of all Hawai'i, found his latter days troubled by a suspected rebellion in Puna and Ka'ū. Kamakau gives the following account:

> Meanwhile rebellion was brewing. It was I-maka-koloa, a chief of Puna,
> who rebelled, I-maka-koloa the choice young 'awa [favorite son] of Puna.
> He seized the valuable products of his district which consisted of hogs,
> gray tapa cloth ('eleuli), tapas made of mamaki bark, fine mats made of
> young pandanus blossoms ('ahu hinano), mats made of young pandanus
> leaves ('ahuao), and feathers of the 'o'o and mamo birds of Puna.
>
> Nu'u-anu-pa'ahu, chief of Ka-'u, was also in the plot to rebel, but he
> was at this time with Ka-lani-'opu'u, and Ka-lani-'opu'u feared Nu'u-anu-
> 'opu'u.[31]

Kalaniopu'u first disposed of Nu'uanupa'ahu by conspiring with his kahuna to have sharks devour him. Although Nu'uanupa'ahu successfully killed the attacking sharks, he died from the mortal wounds that he sustained in the struggle with them.[32] After disposing of Nu'uanupa'ahu, Kalani'opu'u hunted down 'Imakakoloa. Kamakau, again, offers an excellent account of this event:

> Ka-lani-'opu'u the chief set out for Hilo with his chiefs, warriors, and
> fighting men, some by land and some by canoe, to subdue the rebellion
> of I-maka-koloa, the rebel chief of Puna . . . The fight lasted a long time,
> but I-maka-koloa fled and for almost a year lay hidden by the people of
> Puna . . . Puhili went until he came to the boundary where Puna adjoins
> Ka-'u, to 'Oki'okiaho in 'Apua, and began to fire the villages. Great was
> the sorrow of the villagers over the loss of their property and their canoes
> by fires. When one district (ahupua'a) had been burnt out from upland to
> sea he moved on to the next . . . Thus it was that he found I-maka-koloa
> where he was being hidden by a woman kahu on a little islet of the sea . . .
> I-maka-koloa was taken to Ka-lani-'opu'u in Ka-'u to be placed on the altar
> as an offering to the god, and Kiwala'o was the one for whom the house of
> the god had been made ready that he might perform the offering . . . Before

he had ended offering the first sacrifices, Kamehameha grasped the body of I-maka-koloa and offered it up to the god, and the freeing of the tabu for the heiau was completed.[33]

The stage was therefore set for the usurpation of Kīwalaʻō as heir to his father, High Chief Kalaniʻopuʻu, by Kamehameha, in the period after European contact.

European Contact in Puna

The surgeon David Samwell and Lieutenant James King, British officers on the Cook voyage, provided the first written accounts of Puna. According to King: "On the southwest extremity of Opoona the hills rise abruptly from the sea side, leaving but a narrow border, and although the sides of the hills have a fine verdure, yet they do not seem cultivated."[34] Samwell observed: "Many people collected on the Beach to look at the Ship . . . many canoes came off to us . . . [with] a great number of beautiful young women."

Soon after Kalaniʻopuʻu died in 1782, Kīwalaʻō was killed by the forces of Kamehameha in the battle of Mokuʻohai. For the next ten years, Kamehameha fought the chiefs of Hawaiʻi for control of the island. The districts of Kona and Kohala and portions of Hāmākua acknowledged Kamehameha as their ruler. Hilo, the remaining portion of Hāmākua, and a part of Puna acknowledged Keawemaʻuhili as their ruling chief. The lower part of Puna and the district of Kaʻū supported their chief, Keouakūahuʻula. The battles among these three chiefs culminated in the triumph of Kamehameha.[35] "He moku ʻāleuleu" (district of ragamuffins) was a description the followers of Kamehameha I had for the people of Kaʻū and Puna. According to Hawaiian scholar Pukui, this was because the people of these two districts were hard-working farmers who dressed most of the time in old clothes.[36] The saying indicates that the people of Puna were not among those who prospered under the reign of King Kamehameha.

Puna in the Nineteenth Century

Table 4 shows the population of the Puna district throughout the nineteenth century. Descriptions of the Puna district in the nineteenth century paint an image of the living conditions of the Native Hawaiians of Puna.

The first missionary to journey through Puna was William Ellis in 1823. In his published journal he described the natural resources available to the residents of the district and some of their living conditions and subsistence and exchange practices. He estimated that there were approximately 725 inhabitants at Kaimu and another 2,000 Hawaiians in the immediate vicinity along the coast. At Kauaea, about three and a half miles from Kaimu, he reported, 300 people gathered to hear him preach.[37] The journal entries excerpted below describe the diversity of conditions he observed traveling through Puna, from Kīlauea through Kealakomo, toward Kalapana, over to Kapoho, and finally to Kea'au.

In the area between Kealakomo and Kamoamoa more people lived along the coast, close to where they could fish for subsistence, than inland. The resources of the land alone were not sufficient to allow the 'ohana to subsist:

> We saw several fowls and a few hogs here, but a tolerable number of dogs, and quantities of dried salt fish, principally albacores, and bonitos. This latter article, with their poe [poi] and sweet potatoes, constitutes nearly the entire support of the inhabitants, not only in this vicinity, but on the seacoasts of the north and south parts of the island.

TABLE 4 CENSUS OF THE PUNA DISTRICT

YEAR	POPULATION ESTIMATE	SOURCE
1823	142,050	Ellis, 1823, in *Journal of William Ellis*
1832	12,755	Jarves, *History of the Hawn Islands* (1872), p. 202 (North Hilo & South Hilo included)
1834	4,000	American Board of Commissioners for Foreign Missions
1835	4,807	Ke Kumu, April 13, 1836
1854	2,702	Lyman, letter to Armstrong, Jan. 14, 1854
1860	2,158	Anderson, *Hawaiian Islands*, p. 278
1866	1,932	Jarves, *History of the Hawn Islands* (1872), p. 202
1872	1,228	Thrum's, 1876
1878	1,043	Gen'l Supp. of the Census (G.S.P.), Dec. 27, 1878
1884	944	G.S.P., Dec. 27, 1884
1890	834	Bureau of Public Instruction, G.S.P., Census, 1890
1896	1,748	Department of Public Instruction, G.S.P., 1896

Source: Robert C. Schmitt, *The Missionary Census of Hawai'i,* Pacific Anthropological Records 20 (Honolulu: Bernice Pauahi Bishop Museum Press, 1973).

Besides what is reserved for their own subsistence, they cure large quantities as an article of commerce, which they exchange for the vegetable productions of Hiro [Hilo] and Mamakua [Hamakua], or the mamake and other tapas of Ora [Olaa] and the more fertile districts of Hawaii.

The area past Kamoamoa and toward Kaimu was verdant with gardens and groves of coconut and of kou trees. There were approximately 725 people living at Kaimu. The fine sandy beach afforded a safe landing for fishing canoes.

Leaving Kehena, the village of Kamaili, in a gently sloped valley, was cultivated and shaded by large coconut trees. The lava around Puala'a was picturesque. While some areas had soil, here only grass and trees ornamented the landscape. Between Puala'a and Kapoho the lava was barren and rugged until they reached Kapoho, which Ellis described as charming:

> We soon left this cheerful scenery, and entered a rugged tract of lava, over which we continued our way till about two p.m., when we reached Kapoho. A cluster, apparently of hills three or four miles round, and as many hundred feet high, with deep indented sides, overhung with trees, and clothed with herbage, standing in the midst of the barren plain of lava, attracted our attention . . . On reaching the summit, were agreeably surprised to behold a charming valley opening before us. It was circular, and open towards the sea. The outer boundary of this natural amphitheater was formed by an uneven ridge of rocks, covered with soil and vegetation. Within these there was a smaller circle of hills, equally verdant, and ornamented with trees. The sides of the valley, which gradually sloped from the foot of the hills, were almost entirely laid out in plantations, and enlivened by the cottages of their proprietors.

Kea'au was the last Puna village visited by Ellis. As the one ahupua'a with a stream, it was well populated and intensely cultivated, as Ellis noted: "It was extensive and populous, abounding with well-cultivated plantations of taro, sweet potatoes, and sugar-cane; and probably owes its fertility to a fine rapid stream of water, which, descending from the mountains, runs through it into the sea."[38]

It was not until 1836 that the next missionary, Titus Coan, traveled through Puna. He preached to villages throughout the district, creating a Christian revivalist atmosphere wherever he went. Following his visit, some of the Puna Hawaiians formed Christian congregations. In the 1840 Annual Station Report for Hilo it was noted that six new "meeting houses" had been built and that fifteen congregations were meeting in houses in the districts around Hilo. When Chester Lyman, another missionary, toured Puna with Coan in 1846, he described visiting a meeting house in Kamoamoa and a "church" in Kalapana.[39]

In 1840 a Catholic priest, Father Walsh, was assigned to the island of Hawai'i, and in 1841 he baptized Hawaiians in Puna and Ka'ū. Soon thereafter a resident priest was assigned to Ka'ū, and he made periodic visits to Puna. However, it was not until a Belgian priest, Father Damien de Veuster, was assigned to Puna in 1864 that more Hawaiians were baptized into the Catholic faith and regular services were held. During the year Father Damien spent there before being assigned to Moloka'i, the number of Catholics in Puna increased from 350 to 450. Damien built several thatched grass churches and began to build a mortar church with a thatched roof. Originally called St. Joseph's, it later came to be known "Father Damien's Church."

In 1841 Coan estimated the Hawaiian population of Puna at 4,371. He wrote that most of the inhabitants of Puna lived along the shore, although there were hundreds also scattered inland.[40] The same year Captain Charles Wilkes of the U.S. Exploring Expedition explored the Kīlauea volcano and the East Rift Zone in Puna. He observed agricultural activities in the Puna Forest Reserve in the vicinity of Kahauale'a: "We left Pānau after half-past eight o'clock, and passed on towards the east. After traveling about three miles, we came in sight of the ocean, five mile off. Our course now changed to the northeast, and before noon we reached an extensive upland taro-patch."[41]

In 1846 Lyman traveled through Puna with Coan and reported on agricultural activity in what was probably the interior of the Puna Forest Reserve near Kahauale'a:

> Our route from Kahauale'a [village] lay northerly, gradually rising. By half
> past 2 p.m. we had reached a plantation in an unsettled region where a good
> old man had been at work all day putting up a small neat house of ti leaves,
> in expectation that we would stop here for the night. Plantains, pawpaws,
> taro, etc. were growing around . . . We went on about 5 miles further, or
> 10 miles from Kahauale'a [village] over an exceeding rough and jagged path
> and through a dense miry thicket to a small grass shanty.[42]

Ka Māhele of Puna

Puna is distinguished as the district on Hawai'i with the smallest amount of private land awards under the 1848 Māhele and Kuleana Act. It is remarkable that in a district with 311,754 acres, only nineteen awards of private land were granted. Of these awards, sixteen grants of 50,876 acres, four ahupua'a, and two portions of a third 'ili were given to ten chiefs who lived outside of Puna. Three small parcels totaling 32.33 acres were granted to commoners, Baranaba, Hewahewa, and Haka. The bulk of the Puna lands were designated as public lands either to the monarchy, as Crown lands, or to the government of the Hawaiian kingdom.[43] This means that the interests of the majority of the Native Hawaiians in Puna were never separated out from the lands of Puna and remained vested in the lands held by the Crown and the government.

Among the chiefs who received lands in Puna was William Charles Lunalilo, who later reigned as king from 1873 to 1874. He received 26,000 acres in Kahauale'a, 5,562 acres in Keahialaka, and 64.275 acres in Kea'au. His father, Charles Kana'ina, received 4,060 acres in Kapoho. Victoria Kamāmalu, the daughter of High Chiefess Kaho'anoku Kina'u and Mataio Kekuanaoa, was the sister of Kamehameha IV and Kamehameha V. She received 1,568 acres in Kauaea, 1,822 acres in Kauwalehua, and 2,869 acres in Kahuwai. Keohokalole Ane, mother of King Kalākaua and Queen Lili'uokalani, received 4,919 acres in Puua and an ahupua'a in Puna. Miriam Kekauonohi received the ahupua'a of Pānau and Waiakahiula. Hakaleleponi (Hazaleleponi) Kalama, the wife of Kamehameha III, received 2,902 acres in Puna *(kula)*. Kale Davis, daughter of Isaac Davis, the second British military advisor (with John Young) to Kamehameha I, received an apana in Waikahekahe. Gina Lahilahi, daughter of John Young, received a portion of Waikahakahe. William Leleiohoku, whose first wife was Nahi'ena'ena and whose second wife was Princess Ruth Ke'elikolani, received 1,110 acres in Puala'a. Mary Kaoanaeha, wife of John Young and niece of Kamehameha I, received the ahupua'a of Kamoamoa.

Among the Puna residents, Barenaba was a school superintendent at the time of the Māhele. He was one of the first converts to Christianity and the first to teach the Hawaiian language to Titus Coan. Given his position, he was probably aware of the process and had the money needed to conduct the survey. He received 11.32 acres in Kalaihina. Hewahewa filed for a 13.64-acre coffee patch in Hapaiolaa, Kea'au, which he had received in 1842. Haka received six fields totaling 7.37 acres in the 'ili of Pakalua. He was possibly a former house servant of Coan's who kept a house for the minister at Ke'eke'e near Kehena.[44] In 1854, four years after the Kuleana awards were granted, the estimated population of Puna was 2,702. Why then, were only three of the inhabitants of Puna awarded land?

An examination of the possible reasons (aside from those discussed in chapter 1) that almost the entire population of Puna did not apply or receive a land award illustrates the plight of Native Hawaiian kuaʻāina who lived outside of the mainstream of Hawaiʻi's economic and social development. First, Puna was isolated from the mainstream of communication and transportation networks. It is very probable that the kuaʻāina of Puna were not aware of the process or did not realize the significance of the law proclaimed in February 1846 to "No Na Mea kuleana ʻāina a Pau Ma Ko Hawaiʻi Pae ʻāina" or "All Claimants of Lands in the Hawaiian Islands." Second, it is possible that the Puna Hawaiians did not have a way to raise the cash needed for the land surveys, which cost between $6 to $12. Wages at the time were normally between 12½ cents and 33 cents a day. There were few wage-earning jobs in Puna. Cash would have to be raised from selling extra fish or other products, which was difficult given the people's subsistence level of living. Third, continuing volcanic activity in Puna may have discouraged claimants from filing for a particular lot. It is also possible that some Native Hawaiian families believed that the lands of Puna were the domain of Pelehonuamea and her family of deities and could not be claimed for ownership by individuals. Fourth, at least some of the Puna Hawaiians filed their land claims after the deadline. In an 1851 petition to the legislature, several Puna residents asked to be issued land grants without penalty because they had filed their claims after February 14, 1848.[45]

Between 1852 and 1915, 526 land grants and patents were issued in Puna. Out of this number, 275 were issued for the ahupuaʻa of Olaʻa. Some of these grants represent kuleana claims that were not awarded. Eventually more public lands were opened for homesteading in Puna. However, large tracts remained in the public domain and continued to be openly accessed for hunting, gathering, and spiritual practices by Native Hawaiians with a long history of settlement in Puna.

The 1858 tax records for Puna shows how many men over twenty and how many men under twenty were living in each ahupuaʻa and paid taxes. There were a total of 894 males over the age of twenty who paid poll taxes in Puna in 1858. A hundred and thirty males under the age of twenty paid taxes. This would have been after the devastating measles epidemic of fall 1848 that, according to Samuel Kamakau, claimed the lives of one-third of the population, and also after the smallpox epidemic of 1853 and the epidemic of colds in 1857. Very definitely, in February 1848 there were substantially more than three Kanaka ʻōiwi who would have qualified as applicants for land.

With the break-up of the traditional land and labor system by the establishment of private property, Hawaiians were pushed into the market economy to earn cash to purchase, lease, or rent land and to pay taxes. In Puna the primary resources for commercial sale were the coastal fisheries, salt, pulu (the hairy fibers from the hapuʻu fern), ʻōhiʻa timber, and open land for cattle and goat grazing. Isaac Davis traveled around Hawaiʻi to conduct an assessment of the Crown lands. Of the Crown land in Puna he wrote:

> Kaimu ahupuaʻa in Puna, was the first land that I saw. Cocoanuts and pandanus are the only things growing, there is sand on the sea shore, and rocks are the most. Waiokolea, and Ili in Kaimu, is of the same quality, but there is a fish pond in Waiokolea, it is a good pond, and I have leased it for $909.00, and R. Keelikolani has it.
>
> Apua, Ahupuaa in Kau, I do not know the extent of this land, not at the sea shore, but, on making observation, there is a lot of stone on that land, Kapaakea's man told me that salt is the only product on this land, but it is very little. And I called the natives to lease it, but there was no one wanted it, and no one made a reply.[46]

Pulu processing became an industry in Puna in 1851. Pulu was used for mattresses, pillows, and upholstery. At its peak, in 1862, Hawaiʻi exported 738,000 pounds of pulu worldwide to San Francisco; Vancouver; Portland, Oregon; and Australia. It sold for 14 to 28 cents a pound.

In 1860 Abel and C. C. Harris and Frank Swain leased the ahupuaʻa of Pānau for the hapuʻu on the land. Kaina and Heleluhe requested government leases on Laeʻapuki and Panauiki. Kaina maintained two pulu picker camps, one near Makaopuhi Crater and the other near the present Keauhou Ranch headquarters. Pulu was collected, processed, and dried at these camps and then hauled down the pali to Keauhou Landing on mules.

In an article about pulu in 1929, Thomas Thrum suggested that the pulu industry broke up homes and dispersed the Hawaiians:

> The sad part of the story lies in the fact that the industry caused homes in various sections to be broken up, the people moving up into the forests to collect the pulu. In many cases whole families were employed, who provided themselves with rude shelter huts meanwhile, to live long periods at a time in damp, if not actually rainy quarters, without regular and proper food, that resulted in colds and illness.

As a survey report by H. L. Lyman in 1865 showed, much of the unsold government lands of Puna were covered by lava, barren of resources and unsuitable for agriculture:

Figure 23 Mules were popular for traveling on the unpaved roads and rugged country-side of Puna. 1894 or 1895. H. W. Henshaw, Bishop Museum.

1 Makuu to Kaohe, a large tract mauka, rocky land, worth little.

2 Kalapana, about 200 acres, mauka, rocky land.

3 Kaapahu, about 300 acres or 400, mauka, rocky land.

4 Laeapuki, about 200 acres, mauka, rocky land.[47]

A description of the Ola'a area at the end of the nineteenth century gives an insight into the changes in the way of life of the kua'āina of Puna during the nineteenth century:

Some fifty years ago about 1,000 natives were living on the margin of the virgin forest and Pahoe-hoe rock along the trail connecting Hilo town with the crater of Kilauea, island of Hawai'i, in a spot corresponding to the present 22-mile point of the Volcano road. Making of "kappa" [native bark] out of "mamake" bark [*Pipturus albidus*], of olona fiber for fishing nets out of Touchardia latifolia, and capturing "O-U" birds for the sake of the few precious yellow feathers under the wings, of which luxurious royal garments were manufactured—those were the industries on which they lived.

For the reasons common to all the native population of the islands, viz., the introduction of new germs of disease—syphilis, leprosy, tuberculosis, smallpox, etc.—this settlement gradually dwindled away, and in 1862 the few surviving members migrated to other localities. At present only patches of wild bananas, taro, and heaps of stones scattered in the forest indicate the places of former habitation and industry. I have heard, however, that as late as the seventies Kalakaua still levied a tax on olona fiber from the natives of Puna and Olaa districts, which fiber he sold at high prices to Swiss Alpine clubs, who valued it for its light weight and great strength.[48]

Throughout this period, subsistence fishing, ocean gathering, hunting, and forest gathering were still the primary livelihoods for the kua'aiana living in the Puna district. Despite strong economic and social forces pushing to disperse the 'ohana, Native Hawaiians still maintained strong family ties and obligations. They continued to look after the welfare of their relatives and friends. Native Hawaiians who had to move away to earn a living were periodically able to return to visit and find refuge among relatives and respite from the drudgery and alienating social conditions of wage labor. Some left their children to be raised by grandparents in the traditional rural setting rather than in a port town, thus perpetuating the practice of hānai or the raising of children by relatives.

In June 1873 the Boundary Commission conducted hearings to settle the boundaries of the privately held lands in the ahupua'a of Kea'au in the district of Puna. Uma was a *kama'āina* (native-born) expert witness. He described himself as a Native Hawaiian who had been born at Keauhou in Kea'au "at the time of the return of Kamehameha Ist from Kaunakakai, Molokai." He provided testimony that described the natural features and resources in the area and the traditional cultural and subsistence activities of Native Hawaiians in the district. According to Uma, the inland forest of Puna was used for bird catching and for the gathering of sandalwood and olonā. Uma also described caves that had been used for shelter during the wars between the Hawai'i chiefs:

> I have always lived there and know the boundaries between Keaau and Waikahekahe. My parents pointed them out to me when we went after birds and sandalwood. Waikahekahe Nui joins Keaau at the sea shore at Kaehuo-kaliloa, a rock that looks like a human body, which is between two points, the point on Waikahekahe is called Kaluapaa and the one on Keaau Keahu-okaliloa, thence the boundary runs mauka to place called Koolano, the pahoehoe on the North side is Keaau and the good ground where cocoanut trees grow is on Waikahekahe. In past days there was a native village at this place. Thence mauka to Haalaaniani (Ke Kupua) when the old road from Kalapana, used to run to Keaau thence the boundary runs to Wahikolae, two large caves, the boundary runs between them thence mauka, to another cave called—Oliolimanienie, where people used to hide in time of war . . . Keaau on the Hilo side of the road running mauka, thence to Kikihui, an old Kauhale [living compound] for bird catchers, thence to Hoolapehu, another old village, thence to Alaalakeiki, which is the end of Waikahekahe iki and Kahaualea joins Keaau. This place is at an old Kauhale manu [bird catcher's compound] . . . From the Hilo Court House to the Government School house, thence mauka to KeeKee; Kauhale kahi olona [olona fiber combing compound] in Olaa, the boundary is a short distance from the Government road, on the South East side . . . the sea bounds Keaau on the makai side. Ancient fishing rights, including the Uhu which was konohiki fish extending out to sea.[49]

Puaa was another kama'aina expert witness who testified on the boundaries of Kea'au. His testimony reveals areas in Kea'au where there were breadfruit trees, plots cultivated by Native Hawaiians, marshy areas, springs, and 'ōhi'a, orange, and banana trees:

> The boundary between Keaau and Waikahekahe is the land of, or place Keahuokaliloa, thence mauka along Waikahekahe to pahoehoe, on Hilo side of a place called Kukuikea (where the natives cultivate food, and where

bread fruit trees grow), thence to Hilo side of Waiamahu a large place that fills with water in the rainy season, thence to Koolano, the pahoehoe on the Hilo side of it is Keaau the soil is on Waikahekahe nui thence mauka along the road to Halaaniani, Keaau on the Hilo side of road; Halaaniani is a puupahoehoe, in a grove of ohia trees, called Keakui . . . below Kahopua-kuui's houses, to a place called Kilohana where Oranges are growing there the boundary of Keaau and Olaa leaves the Volcano road, and runs mauka above these Orange trees, thence to an ohia grove called Puaaehu, thence to Waiaele . . . A water spring with banana trees growing near it used to be an old kauhale.

Kenoi, originally from Kapapala in Kaū, provided testimony on the boundaries as he had learned them from companions with whom he went gathering in the forests. He spoke of going after the ʻōʻō bird in Keauhou; gathering sandalwood in Kahaualeʻa and at Puʻukea; and catching the ʻuwao at Namamokale, opposite Kauanahunahu. He also spoke of two ponds, Nawailoloa and Kilohana, on the road to Pānau from Palauhulu. Nailima, a kuaʻāina from Olaʻa, also provided testimony. He verified the accounts of those who went before him and also identified in his descriptive testimony a hill covered with puʻuhala by Kilohana, an old village at a place called Kaʻaipuaʻa, and a pond with aweoweo growing in the water at Waiaele on the old road from Olaʻa to Poʻohōlua. Waipo, a kuaʻāina from Waiākea, identified a small cave where natives worshiped idols at a place called Kawiakaʻawa and a place called Naʻauo, between Māwae and Waiaele, that people used to flee to and live in during times of war.

A description of the land use pattern and practices in Kapoho and Keahialaka in the late nineteenth century was recorded in a brief filed by attorneys Hitchcock and Wise and filed with the Boundary Commission for the Third and Fourth Circuits of Hawaiʻi on March 20, 1897. Of significance is the fact that where two ahupuaʻa were owned in common by the same family, in this case by Charles Kanaʻina and his son William Charles Lunalilo, the boundaries between the two parcels lost significance. The brief also speaks of an isolated section of land that belonged to no one and was therefore open to all, similar to the "Kamoku" in Hāmākua. In part it stated:

> The two ahupuaas of Kapoho, and of Keahialaka, were practically held by one family. By the great Māhele, Kapoho was confirmed to C. Kanaina, while Keahialaka was confirmed to his son W. O. Lunalilo. The influence remains that the laws and customs which in the case of adjoining ahupuaas

under different owners would have held and trespass, the one to the other thereby enjoined, were in this instance permitted to lapse. It is furthermore probable, and the presumption is given force by the subsequent isolation of Kaniahiku so-called that it was an Okana "a no man's land," similar to the Kamoku of Hamakua. This trend of the Puna coastline on both sides of the East Point with ahupuaas extending back rectangularly from the sea coast, would naturally bring about an irregular shaped remnant in the interior similar to those in the North Kohala District, and the upper Keauhou lands of Kona.[50]

In Puna, Joseph Nawahī, a founder of the Hui Aloha ʻāina (Hawaiian Patriotic League), had a strong following of royalists. On May 23, 1893, four months after the overthrow of the Hawaiian monarchy, Rufus A. Lyman, patriarch of the Lyman Estate, which now owns substantial landholdings in Keahialaka and Kapoho, wrote to his colleague, M. Whitney in Honolulu, suggesting that the provisional government open up government and Crown lands for homesteading by Native Hawaiians. He felt that such a gesture would win the support of Native Hawaiians for the illegal provisional government and undermine the influence of the royalist Joseph Nawahīokalaniopuʻu in the district:

> Here in Puna there are only three Crown Lands Olaʻa, Kaimu and Apua next to the Kau boundary. The Govt. lands are scattered all through District, and large tracts near the villages especially Opihikao, Kamaili, Kehena, and not under lease. And there are quite a number of young men there with families who own no land, who will probably remain in Puna and cultivate coffee, kalo, oranges, etc., if you get them settled on land they can have for homes for themselves.
>
> Nine of them have commenced planting coffee on shares for me.
>
> Puna has always been Nawahi's stronghold, and I want to see his hold on natives here broken. And I think it would help do it, if we can show natives here that the Govt. is ready to give them homes, and to improve the roads.

In 1894 the provisional government set up the Republic of Hawaiʻi, which instituted a program of opening up government lands for homesteading under the Land Act of 1895. In Puna, as Lyman had predicted in his letter to Whitney, homestead grants were quickly purchased and cultivated in coffee. Coffee acreage expanded from 168 acres in 1895 to 272.5 in 1899 in Olaʻa and Pāhoa.[51]

Puna, Territory of Hawaiʻi

Economic development in Puna centered on the scarcely populated inland forest areas around the towns of Pāhoa and Olaʻa in the twentieth century. A multiethnic plantation community also developed in and around these towns as immigrant Japanese, Puerto Rican, and Filipino laborers were imported to work on the developing sugar plantations. Hawaiian families continued to live along the coastal areas in lower Puna, particularly around Kalapana.

The Puna Sugar Company was established in 1900 in Kapoho. The lowland forest was cleared for cane fields, and railroads were built. Puna Sugar expanded around Pāhoa and Olaʻa.

At the turn of the century coffee was still an important agricultural industry in Puna. Cattle ranching was also significant. The Shipman family, a major landowner in the district, ran the Shipman Ranch in Keaʻau. Pineapple was started for export to California.

In 1908 the Hawaiian Mahogany Company erected a lumber mill in Pāhoa and sent out its first shipment of 20,000 ʻōhiʻa log ties to the Santa Fe Railroad. In 1910 the company became the Pāhoa Lumber Mill and obtained cutting rights to 12,000 acres of territorial forest in Puna.[52] Finally, in 1911 the territorial government designated 19,850 acres as the Puna Forest Reserve to protect it from logging. In 1928 the forest reserve was expanded to include a total of 25,738 acres.[53]

Charles Baldwin's *Geography of the Hawaiian Islands*, published in 1908, provides a glimpse of the Puna district at the turn of the century. Efforts to actively develop agriculture in the midst of old lava flows, seismic activity, and heavy rainfall included the cultivation of vanilla, tobacco, pineapples, rubber, and sugar cane.

TABLE 5 CENSUSES OF PUNA, 1900–1960

YEAR	POPULATION	SOURCE
1900	5,128	Twelfth U.S. Census: 1900
1910	6,834	Thirteenth U.S. Census: 1910
1920	7,282	Bureau of Health Statistics, Board of Health, pop. est.
1930	8,284	Fifteenth U.S. Census: 1930
1940	7,733	Sixteenth U.S. Census: 1940
1950	6,747	Seventeenth U.S. Census: 1950
1960	5,030	Eighteenth U.S. Census: 1960

The rainfall is so great in parts of the district that this lava has been rapidly decomposed, and the heaviest of forests are to be found, as in Olaa and the region about Pāhoa [the Puna Forest Reserve]. A large part of the soil of upper Olaa is ash which probably came from Kilauea; the great fertility of this soil is due to the decayed vegetable matter which has been added to it . . .

The Olaa section of Puna is a fine agricultural region, but, owing to the want of a market, small-truck farming does not pay. However, vanilla, tobacco, pineapples, and bananas grow well; and the rubber industry is destined to be an important one, as the climate is particularly well adapted to the growth of rubber trees. The cultivation of coffee in Olaa has been abandoned, as the trees did not thrive there.

All the lower lands of Olaa are planted with the cane of the Olaa Sugar Company. This is one of the largest plantations on Hawaii, and occupies nearly all of the available cane land of the Puna district, including the Kapoho and Pāhoa tracts . . .

A long section of the Puna coast, thirty or forty miles, shows evidence of having sunk: cocoanut trees are found below the tide level, or their dead stumps stand out in the sea.

At Kapoho there is a warm spring . . . Other interesting features of Puna are: the lava tree casts found in the forest above Kapoho; the bowlders strewn along the coast near Pohoiki by the great 1868 tidal wave; the heiau of Wahaula in farthest Puna.[54]

In 1913 the Hilo Board of Trade published a guidebook called *The Island of Hawai'i*, by Henry Walsworth Kinney, to promote tourism around the island. The Kīlauea Volcano and its spectacular sites, trails, and forested areas are prominently featured. Ola'a and Pāhoa were described as the centers of economic development for the Puna district:

The district of Puna may, for the sake of clearness, be divided into two sections, the Olaa region, the north half, and Puna proper. The former consists in the main of the great Olaa sugar plantation, and forest which has been partially cleared, while some tracts are used for cattle. The middle part of the district, with Pāhoa as the center, is used for extensive lumber operations. The remainder, Puna proper, is covered by forest and old lava flows, most of them covered with vegetation. In spite of its exceptional beauty and the fine opportunity it offers for seeing the typical Hawai'i, which is so rapidly disappearing in the march of progress, it is comparatively little known.[55]

Ranching and sugar plantations flourished at Olaʻa. ʻŌhiʻa and koa lumber operations were established at Pāhoa. Kinney described lower Puna as a traditional Hawaiian subsistence area. Kaimu and Kalapana were the main Hawaiian villages in lower Puna:

> At the beach the road enters first the village of KAIMU, exclusively Hawaiian, with a large grove of cocoanut trees surrounding a fine semi-circular sand beach. Care should be exercised in bathing on account of the undertow. Less than a mile further on, westwards, lies the village of KALAPANA, one of the largest Hawaiian villages in the Islands. There are no white inhabitants, and only a couple of Chinese stores . . . KALA-PANA still supports quite a large population, and is a very pretty village, having like all the Puna coast villages, a fine growth of cocoanuts, puhala and monkeypod trees. The landing is so rough that it is used now only for canoes.[56]

Kalapana's tourist attractions included Puʻu o Hakuma, a cave used as a place of refuge during war; the Niukukahi heiau; the ranch and Hawaiian village at Kahaualea; a mineral bathing pool called Punaluʻu; and the Wahaʻula heiau.

Kinney also described tourist attractions in Kapoho, including the Waia-Pelehonuamea crater, famous as the first residence of Pelehonuamea in Puna, and the three craters mauka of that, created as Pelehonuamea searched for a suitable home before reaching Kīlauea. Green Lake was said to be situated within a ring of five craters. Kūkiʻi heiau, the hot springs of Puna, and a pretty Hawaiian village called Koaʻe were also featured. Along the coast between Kapoho and Kaimu Kinney described Cape Kumukahi; the almost deserted Pohoiki village; Opihikao, with its hot-spring cave, and the small villages of Kamaile, Kehena, and Kaueleau.

Moʻolelo of Kalapana: The Territorial Years

The Kalapana Oral History Project, completed in 1990 by the University of Hawaiʻi at Hilo anthropologist Charles Langlas and student researchers, is a primary source of information about the life of Native Hawaiian kuaʻāina in Lower Puna during the territorial period. I have drawn upon this source, together with accounts by E. S. Craighill Handy and documents from the Volcano National Park archive, to describe the way of life of the kuaʻāina of Lower Puna.

Throughout the territorial years, the majority of the food of the kuaʻāina in Puna was produced at home. ʻUala (sweet potatoes), kalo (taro), and ʻulu (breadfruit) were the main staples. Seafood, especially fish, ʻopihi (limpet), and limu (seaweed), was the main protein. Chickens, pigs, and cattle were raised. Wild pigs and goats were hunted, and their meat was usually smoked. Some households kept cows for milk and even made butter. When cash was earned, special items from the store such as flour, sugar, tea, coffee, and rice could be bought.

Sweet potatoes were usually grown around the home. Families also grew chili peppers, onions, and sometimes pumpkins, watermelons, tomatoes, or cucumbers. Families in Kalapana usually had a taro patch in the uplands as far as the forest, which was as much as three or more miles from their house lots. Handy wrote that in 1935, when he toured Puna to appraise the old native horticulture, "one energetic Hawaiian of Kapaʻahu had cleared ʻōhiʻa forest, at a place called Kahoʻonoho about 2.5 miles inland, and had a good stand of taro, bananas, and sugar cane in two adjacent clearings."[57]

Pigs were allowed to run free, but to keep them tame and near the home, they were fed sweet potato vines and tubers after harvesting, papayas, mangoes, or breadfruit. Each family had its own way of marking its pigs by notching or slitting the ears or cutting the tail. Some pigs went wild and wandered up the Kīlauea mountain, even above the zone where the families cultivated taro. These were hunted with dogs.

The kuaʻāina in Kalapana utilized many methods of fishing during this period. Net fishing for ʻōpelu (mackerel) was the highest-yielding method. The fish was usually dried for later consumption or for sale. Aku was also caught for subsistence and for sale in season. As late as the 1930s, ʻōpelu fishing in Kalapana was conducted in accordance with traditional and customary rituals and was a community effort:

> The ʻōpelu season began in the summer months, after a first-fruits sacrifice: a fish from the first catch was placed on the kūʻula rock at the beach. The kūʻula rock was kept by a guardian, who brought it out for the ritual, and then took it away for safe-keeping. Traditionally the year was divided into two seasons, a period from approximately February to July, when aku could be caught and ʻōpelu was taboo, and a period from approximately August to

December, when 'ōpelu could be caught but aku was taboo. The opening of the 'ōpelu season was marked by a fish sacrifice.[58]

'Ōpelu fishing went from daybreak to evening. The canoes from a village generally went out together and kept each other in sight in case one should get into trouble. When they returned, people would be waiting to help carry the canoe up, and everyone would get a share of fish. Later in the day or at night the canoes might go out for 'u'u or kawele'a. On dark nights, if the fishermen went out, children would gather at the beach and keep bonfires of coconut leaves going to guide the fishermen back to shore. Until 1926 the nets were made of olonā from the wet uplands of Puna. After that they were replaced by store-bought cord.

A one-room house with a separate cookhouse was the usual style in Kalapana around 1900. By the 1920s several families still lived in such dwellings, but the majority of the families were already living in sizable multiroom board houses built in the Western style. Many families had also installed kerosene stoves in their houses. Since there was no running water in the Kalapana area, families had outhouses for toilets. Water barrels were used to collect water from the roof for drinking and cooking. In times of drought, they had to drink brackish water from the ponds. Brackish ponds were used for bathing, for doing laundry, for rinsing off saltwater after coming from the ocean, and for watering stock.

Through the 1920s and 1930s families still made their own poi from breadfruit or the taro they grew in the uplands. They usually made enough poi to last the whole week. After this, there was only a limited amount of daily cooking to do, mostly broiling fish on the fire or salting shellfish to eat with the poi. Sometimes the family might cook a pig in the imu, stew dried meat, or make rice over the fire or kerosene stove.

Weaving lauhala mats for home use and for sale was a large part of a woman's work during this period. Lauhala grew all along the coast, but women often went to Kehena to gather good-quality leaves.

Lū'au continued to be held for family gatherings to celebrate special occasions and life cycle events such as birthdays, weddings, anniversaries, and funerals. The lū'au for Christmas usually lasted through New Year's. 'Ohana relationships remained strong. Even the practice of hānai (adoption between family members) continued in Kalapana.

Through the 1920s and early 1930s relations with the outside were limited by distance and the difficulty of travel. The outside world was primarily represented in Kalapana in the form of schoolteachers, ministers from Hilo, Chinese stores (which sold goods from the outside), and campaigning political candidates. Automobiles were introduced during this time, and by the late 1930s most families had a car. Still, most people went to town only once or twice a month to shop for cloth, kerosene, and food items they didn't grow. Rice and flour were purchased in big bags. Since they seldom went to town, the kuaʻāina of Kalapana did not go to Western doctors and hospitals. Kalapana kuaʻāina relied on Native Hawaiian medicine, using herbal remedies for sickness and broken bones.

Even though cars became common in the 1930s, it was impractical to commute to work every day. Those who got a job outside the community usually relocated, even if the workplace was as close as Pāhoa. A few men stayed outside through the week and came back for the weekend. The men who lived in Kalapana usually combined subsistence farming and fishing for family food production with part-time work for cash—roadwork for the county and small-scale selling of vegetables, fish, or pigs. The county road from Kapaʻahu through Kaimu and up to Pāhoa was a one-lane gravel road. Nearly all the Kalapana men did roadwork for the county, breaking up rock into gravel. Each man worked an eight-hour day for $2, four or five days a month. The crew rotated so that all the members had a chance to work the same amount.

Additional cash could be made by selling extra ʻōpelu to the Chinese store owners to dry, or to be consumed fresh in Pāhoa. Some grew ʻawa in the uplands that was cut and dried and sold to a buyer from Hilo for export to Germany. Some husked and dried coconut to sell as copra to Chinese store owners. Sometimes Chinese drove from Hilo to buy pigs in Kalapana. As mentioned above, the women sold lauhala, weaving mats to fill orders from Hilo and Honolulu. They also sold smaller items such as hats and fans to sell to tourists. Children sometimes sold coconuts to tourists and posed for pictures. In 1918 the movie *Bird of Paradise* was filmed at Kaimu beach. Grass huts were built, and the people of Kalapana were paid to wander around in sarongs.

In the Kalapana village there were three churches—Catholic, Hawaiian Congregational, and Mormon. As discussed above, Fathers Walsh and Damien de Veuster established the Catholic Church in Kalapana. Since the time of Father Damien there has always been a resident priest in Puna and a strong Catholic congregation. During the term of Father Loots (1881–98) a small Catholic church was built at Kalapana village. In the twentieth century the main church and rectory were at Pāhoa, and the priest went to Kalapana to hold weekly services.[59]

In the 1840s the Congregationalists built a church at Kalapana and a meeting house in Kamoamoa. The first minister for the Kalapana under the Hawaiian Evangelical Association was Papapa Barenaba, who remained there from 1869 to 1873. After the 1868 earthquake and subsidence the Kalapana church was rebuilt. By 1905 a third church, called Mauna Kea, had been constructed on the same location. It was rebuilt again in 1930. From the nineteenth century through the present the Hawaiian Congregational churches held periodic conferences at the island level and the all-island level for discussion of church business. By the 1880s a feature of the conference was a song competition between the choirs of the various churches. In 1886 the Kalapana congregation won the competition and was presented with a silver pitcher and goblet by Princess Liliʻuokalani herself. The moʻolelo about this award has been proudly passed down from one generation to the next.

The Mormon church was built in Kalapana some time before 1910.

Hawaiʻi Volcano National Park

In 1932 a new force entered the lives of the Kalapana people. The Hawaiʻi Volcano National Park, urged on by the governor's office, the Hawaiʻi County Board of Supervisors, and prominent citizens, proposed expanding the park to include all the land from Apua over to Kaimu Black Sand Beach. The people in Kalapana strongly opposed the plan. Russell Apple interviewed Edward G. Wingate, who served as superintendent of the Hawaiʻi Volcano National Park at the time of the proposed acquisition. Wingate said that he supported the Native Hawaiians in Kalapana and felt it was wrong of the federal government and the park service to dispossess the Native Hawaiians of their homes, their land, and their traditional way of life. A compromise was reached. The Hawaiʻi Volcano National Park would expand to include the six ahupuaʻa of ʻApua, Kahue, Kealakomo, Panaunui, Laeʻapuki, and Kamoamoa; parts of Pūlama and Poupou; and Keauhou in the Kaʻū district. However, the lands from Kalapana over to Kaimu were deleted from the extension proposal.

Wingate was still concerned about negative impacts on the Kalapana Native Hawaiians' way of life of the road that was to be built to link the Chain of Craters road to Kalapana, all the way to Kaimu. He believed that the road would put pressure on the Native Hawaiians to sell their homes in Kalapana

TREE FERNS IN LAVA TUBE HAWAII NATIONAL

Figure 24 Tourists attracted to the volcano, its rainforest, and natural phenomena such as the Thurston Lava Tube continued to change the lives and livelihoods of the kuaʻāina of Puna during the Territorial period. 1925. Tai Sing Loo, Bishop Museum.

to developers or others and that their livelihoods, which were still dependent on the land and sea, would be destroyed. To make it possible for the Kalapana kuaʻāina to continue their way of living, he proposed that home sites be made available to them in the park extension so that the villagers could move into the park when they saw the need. In addition a fishing provision was included that allowed only Kalapana residents and those accompanied by a local guide to fish within the park extension. No Native Hawaiian was precluded from fishing in that area provided there was a local guide. This provision, according to Wingate, was "to protect the fishing for the people who lived from the sea and who lived from the land, to have some food source from the sea as some areas have been fished out." He also noted that serving as a guide would provide jobs and a source of a little cash income for the kuaʻāina in the district. Apple summarized Wingate's thinking as follows:

> A new village inside the Kalapana Extension was foreseen. The idea was
> a subsistence-type arrangement, with Hawaiians living in a traditional
> manner—fishing offshore and along the coast, houses near the shore and

Figure 25 Kuaʻāina of Puna established and maintained roads up to and within Volcano National Park and down to Kaimū Black Sands Beach in Kalapana. 1920s. Theodore Kelsey Collection, Hawaiian Historical Society.

agricultural plots inland. Exclusive fishing rights for those still living in Kalapana and for those living within the Extension were included.[60]

In 1938 the U.S. Congress passed the Kalapana Extension Act (52 Stat. 781 et seq.), which set an important precedent by including a provision to lease lands within the extension to Native Hawaiians and to permit fishing in the area "only by Native Hawaiian residents of said area or of adjacent villages and by visitors under their guidance." The special traditional subsistence lifestyle of the Native Hawaiians in Kalapana was acknowledged by the U.S. Congress, and measures were passed to protect it.[61]

Under the New Deal, federal programs created new jobs for the men of Kalapana. The federal government funded a county project to improve Kalapana Park and various road-building projects in Puna. The Civilian Conservation Corps (CCC) established a camp for young single men at the volcano. They cut trails, built stone walls, and were trained in carpentry skills. As military construction expanded in Honolulu in preparation for potential war with Japan, Honolulu became a boom town, attracting workers from the mainland and from neighboring islands. Many of the kuaʻāina of Kalapana moved there on the eve of the war.[62]

World War II and Puna

World War II had a profound effect on Hawaiʻi. In Puna, those who remained behind feared a Japanese invasion by sea. The coastline was watched and guarded by soldiers stationed in the Kalapana areas. Observation points were set up at Pānau and at Mokuhulu. The beach at Kaimu and Kalapana was strung with barbed wire to stave off an enemy landing. Initially the Kalapana people were not supposed to go through the wire, but eventually the soldiers let the people crawl through to fish or collect seafood at the beach. There was a nightly curfew, and blackout curtains were used so that not even a single glimmer of light could be seen by an enemy observing the area.

The 100 to 150 soldiers stationed in Kalapana were rotated every three months. Some camped in tents on Kaimu beach and Kalapana beach, some lived in the school cafeteria, and others lived in the gym and the priest's house.

During the war there were still kuaʻāina who grew taro in Puna, but many of them were in their sixties. By the end of the war they were getting too old to grow taro and make poi. Many younger men had left during the war, and many of those remaining in Kalapana got jobs on the outside, which left little time for taro. During the 1930s fewer canoes went out to catch ʻōpelu. The last canoe which went out from Kaimu was that of Simon Waiʻau Bill. When he got too old, in the late 1930s, he stopped fishing. Younger men were too busy going to school or going out to work to learn the technique of catching ʻōpelu. At Kalapana a couple of canoes continued going out even after the war. Eventually a boat ramp was constructed at Pohoiki, east of Kalapana, and the canoes were replaced by motorboats.

Other forms of subsistence production continued after the war, such as pole fishing from shore; gathering limu, opihi, and crab; and raising stock. Wild pigs were still hunted and remained an important source of meat. Native plants were gathered for herbal teas and medicine.

Statehood

In 1958, on the eve of statehood, the Puna district began to be parceled out in nonconforming subdivisions of raw land without any infrastructure. Tropic Estates bought 12,000 acres of land between Kurtistown and Mountainview and cut it up into 4,000 lots that were put on the market for $500 to $1,000 each. The project was named Hawaiian Acres.[63]

Royal Gardens was opened in Kalapana in the early 1960s. One-acre lots were sold for $995. The brochure for the development read in part:

> Along the southern shores of the Big Island, Hawaii, largest of the Hawaiian chain lies the historic and legendary lands of Kalapana. This site the setting for Royal Gardens, a fertile area directly adjacent to the Hawaii Volcano National Park with its spectacular attractions, yet only walking distance away from lovely beach and shore areas. Royal Gardens lots are all one acre in size, making it possible for the owners to have a small orchard or truck garden, or a magnificent garden, as well as a home and a haven for retirement.[64]

By contrast, the Bishop Museum study for the Kalapana Extension in 1959 described the coast nearest to Royal Gardens as follows: "Shoreline of low, black, lava cliffs, battered continuously by windward waves . . . This coast bears witness to the great volcanic forces underlying it through numerous earthquake-opened fissures, and to the violence of tidal waves through huge blocks of lava which have been ripped from the ocean cliffs and hurled inland."[65]

Actually, Royal Gardens land was 40 percent ʻaʻā (rough and broken lava rocks in tumbled heaps), 20 percent *pahoehoe* (solid thick sheets of lava, hard and smooth surfaced, with no soil covering), and 40 percent *'opihikao* (extremely rocky muck with pāhoehoe underneath). Water was scarce, with just a few widely scattered waterholes.[66]

Other nonconforming subdivisions similar to Hawaiian Acres and Royal Gardens were developed in Puna prior to adoption by the county of a comprehensive zoning ordinance. These included Eden Roc, Fern Forest Vacation Estates, Hawaiian Paradise Park, Hawai'i Beaches Estates, Aina Loa Estates, Orchid Land Estates, Leilani Estates, Nānāwale Estates, Vacation Lands, Kalapana Black Sands Subdivision, Kalapana Gardens, and Kalapana Sea View Estates. These subdivisions gradually attracted an in-migrant population of retirees, ex-military, and persons seeking an alternative lifestyle to urban centers in mainland United States.

Puna: A Cultural Kīpuka in the Late Twentieth Century

The landscape of Puna continued to be dominated by the seismic and eruptive phases of the Kīlauea volcano. Throughout the late twentieth century the landscape varied from the rocky shoreline, to barren lava fields, cultivated orchards, grassy plains, and dense rainforests. It included the Hawai'i Volcanoes National Park, large undeveloped nonconforming subdivisions, unsettled Hawaiian homelands, forest reserves, and small concentrations of population. The district was subject to heavy rainfall and periodically experienced severe flooding.[67]

The Puna district of the island of Hawai'i as a whole, and Lower Puna in particular, has been a rural area of Native Hawaiian cultural continuity. Of the 452 Native Hawaiians who lived in the Puna district in 1970, 77 percent or 350 lived in Lower Puna. In 1980, 1,334 Native Hawaiians lived in Puna, of whom 75 percent or 1,001 resided in Lower Puna. Between 1980 and 1990 the number of Native Hawaiians in Puna increased by 296 percent, to 3,953. For the first time, the majority of Native Hawaiians who lived in Puna resided outside Lower Puna. Only 38 percent lived in Lower Puna, while 62 percent lived elsewhere. This was due both to migration of Native Hawaiians into Puna from Hilo and other islands and to the displacement of Native Hawaiians from Lower Puna by volcanic flows out of the Kupaianaha lava lake.

Table 6 shows population trends in the district as a whole from 1970 to 2000.

As late as 2000, modern infrastructure for households and farm lots such as electricity, piped water, and sewage was still not available in many parts of Puna. Puna residents relied on generators, water catchments, centralized county water stands, and outhouses for their households.

There were four major water systems in the district: Olaa–Mountain View, Pāhoa, Kapoho, and Kalapana. Hawaiian Beaches had a privately owned water system. Glenwood and Volcano were not serviced by any water system and depended on roof catchment systems. There were no municipal sewerage systems in Puna. Most residents used cesspools and individual household aerobic treatment units. Aside from the primary routes, the majority of roads in the Puna district were substandard, and many were only cinder surfaced. Puna had thousands of nonconforming residential lots that lacked the basic improvements necessary for development or were being kept vacant for future speculation. Construction in the nonconforming subdivisions increased with strip residential development along the highways. There were three public-school complexes in the Puna District in the communities of Keaau, Mountain View, and Pāhoa.

Economically, Puna was primarily an agricultural district. Diversified agriculture prospered in the form of truck farming of lettuce, flowers, and cabbage in the volcano area; papaya groves in Kapoho; and flowers, principally anthuriums and vanda orchids, in the Mountain View, Pāhoa and Kapoho areas. Factors inhibiting the growth of these industries were a shortage of labor and housing, processing requirements, and plant disease. Vegetables and a variety of fruits, primarily oranges and tangerines, were grown throughout the district. Macadamia nuts were planted on the Hilo side of Kea'au. With the closing of the Puna Sugar Company in 1984, former sugar lands were sold to former workers to farm. They planted papayas, bananas, alfalfa, and trees for biomass. There were 197,900 acres zoned for agricultural use in Puna in 2000, but fewer than 50,000 acres were actively used for agriculture. The

TABLE 6 ETHNIC POPULATION OF PUNA, 1970–2000

ETHNIC GROUP	1970	1980	1990	2000
Hawaiian	452	1,334	3,953	9,325
Caucasian	1,237	5,078	9,515	22,010
Other non-Caucasian	3,465	5,339	7,313	NA
Total population	5,154	11,751	20,781	31,335

Sources: State of Hawai'i, Department of Business and Economic Development & Tourism, State of Hawai'i Counties and Districts, 1991; U.S. Census, 2000.

majority of agriculturally zoned areas were subdivided for large-lot residential purposes.

The major industrial activity in Puna was a large macadamia processing plant northeast of the sugar mill. Other industrial activities included a kim chee factory, quarrying of lava materials, slaughterhouses, bakeries, flower packaging, papaya processing and packing, and several cottage industries. These were primarily located around Keaʻau and Pāhoa, outside of lower Puna. There were no major government installations in the district.[68]

The rocky coastline, made up of sheer cliffs in many sections, was subject to tsunami inundation and subsidence. Inland areas were vulnerable to volcanic and seismic activity. These natural phenomena discouraged the development of major resorts or hotels in the district, although modest bed-and-breakfast establishments were established in Puna.

Native Hawaiian residents in the district supplemented their incomes from jobs or public assistance by engaging in subsistence fishing, hunting, and gathering for the households of their ʻohana. The fishermen, hunters, and gatherers utilized and exercised their traditional access to the ocean offshore of the Puna district and the adjacent mauka (upland) forest lands. The forest afforded access to middle-elevation plants and resources for Native Hawaiians who lived in each of the ahupuaʻa of the Puna district.

Native Hawaiians of the district utilized the forests of Puna from generation to generation to gather maile, fern, ʻieʻie, ʻōhiʻa, and other such native plants for adornment, weaving, and decoration. They also gathered plants such as koʻokoʻolau, māmaki, and noni for herbal medicine.

Due to the alteration and degradation of low- and middle-elevation forests in other parts of Hawaiʻi Island and the public status of the forests in Puna, Native Hawaiians from other parts of the island and from Oʻahu also regularly gathered liko lehua, maile, fern, ʻawa, and other native plants for hula and lāʻau lapaʻau (traditional Hawaiian herbal healing) purposes from this forest.

Puna Kuaʻāina in the Twentieth Century

Evidence that subsistence activities continued to be integral to the lives of the kuaʻāina of Puna is provided in three studies conducted between 1971 and 1994. A survey of the role of hunting in the Kalapana-Kaimu Native Hawaiian community was conducted in 1971 by the University of Hawaiʻi geography and anthropology departments and by the School of Public Health. The study revealed that hunting in the Puna Forest Reserve mauka of Kalapana-Kaimu yielded meat that comprised a significant amount of the regular diet of Native Hawaiian households in the area. Despite the fact that not every household had a hunter, many households benefited from hunting activities because the meat was shared among extended family members and friends.[69]

In 1982 the U.S. Department of Energy commissioned the Puna Hui 'Ohana, an organization of Native Hawaiian families in Puna, to conduct a survey of subsistence activities of Native Hawaiian 'ohana in Puna as part of a study to determine the social impact of developing geothermal energy in the district. The Puna Hui 'Ohana successfully surveyed an impressive 85 percent of the adult Native Hawaiians in lower Puna (351 out of 413 adult Native Hawaiians). The study found that 38 percent of those surveyed engaged in traditional subsistence hunting in the adjacent forests, 48 percent gathered medicinal plants, and 38 percent gathered maile in the nearby forests for household use.[70]

Interviews conducted in 1994 for the "Native Hawaiian Ethnographic Study for the Hawai'i Geothermal Project Proposed for Puna and Southeast Maui" with older and younger Native Hawaiian families in Puna documented a continuity of subsistence farming, hunting, fishing, and gathering and associated cultural customs and beliefs. This study focused on assessing the varied cultural impacts of geothermal energy development in Puna.[71]

As part of the study, Native Hawaiian families were asked to indicate the general location of trails, ancient sites, and areas of subsistence hunting, gathering, and fishing on a topographic map of the district. The map produced as a result of these 1994 interviews indicated that Puna kua'āina fished along the entire coastline of the Puna district and hunted primarily in the mauka forested areas. Plants were gathered throughout the entire district, both mauka and makai. Historic Puna trails were still used to travel from coastal communities up to the forest. The map also showed the cultural sites that the Puna kua'āina used and cared for.

The 1994 interviews confirmed that traditional subsistence activities were still an integral part of the way of life of the Puna kua'āina in the late twentieth century. Puna families engaged in subsistence when supplies such as fish and meat ran low. They also fished, hunted, and gathered for special 'ohana life-cycle occasions such as birthdays, weddings, graduations, and funerals.

The amounts harvested depended upon family size—that is, the larger the family, the greater the amount of subsistence resources required. Puna families stressed that one must never take more of a resource than what is needed and can be consumed. Most of the food consumed by Puna 'ohana still came

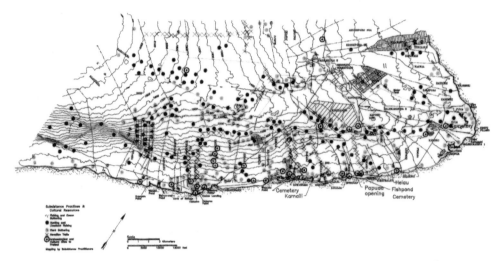

Map 3 In 1994 Puna residents mapped important cultural and natural resource areas and routes to access these areas. *Source:* Matsuoka et al., "Native Hawaiian Ethnographic Study," p. 101.

from some form of subsistence such as taro and sweet potato cultivated in their gardens; breadfruit gathered from their yards or lowland forest; fish and seafood harvested from the ocean; and wild pigs, goats, or cattle hunted in the forest. Selected staples such as rice, coffee, flour, sugar, and cooking oil were, of course, purchased in Hilo or other nearby towns.

The availability of subsistence resources varied by season. For example, certain species of fish, such as 'u'u and ahi, were more abundant during the summer months. Maile goes through periods of dormancy during dry months and regrowth during the rainy season. When a resource in a particular area dwindled because of overuse, a kapu or restriction on harvesting that resource was observed to allow for regeneration. Puna kua'āina would also weed an area or water the plants in the wild to enhance the regeneration of the resources.

Knowledge about where and how to carry out subsistence activities was passed down to the kua'āina living in Puna in the late twentieth century from previous generations. Each 'ohana respected the boundaries of their respective gathering and hunting areas. If someone wished to use an area outside of their own, out of respect they would usually ask permission.

Though most of the kua'āina identified themselves as Christians, they also held a set of beliefs that was consistent with traditional Hawaiian spiritual beliefs. They attended church on a regular basis, but they also prayed to Native Hawaiian deities as part of the regular protocol to succeed in their subsistence activities. They prayed for good luck before an activity and to express gratitude for a successful catch. They regularly acknowledged the presence of deities by asking permission to enter or take resources from their domain. On special occasions or for particular purposes they offered chants and ho'okupu or offerings to pay respect to the deities.

One particular deity that they honored with chant and ho'okupu was Pelehonuamea. The Puna families believed that Pelehonuamea protected and nurtured those who demonstrated respect for her. She could also harm those who showed her disrespect or acted improperly. The location and direction taken by some of the lava flows were interpreted by the Puna kua'āina as Pelehonuamea's way of letting the people know that they were not properly caring for the land. The flows covered over any damage to the land and restored it to a primal form.

Subsistence activities also helped to perpetuate the knowledge and memory of ancestors. One of the persons interviewed shared the following experience:

> When I pick flowers or medicine, I take the knowledge that my father taught me. What had to pick with, the whole process of knowing. There's a oneness—the whole mind and body has to be centered on the medicine and how it's gonna be used. You cannot think about anything else. It opens the channel, what you give out to that source. Be focused only on one thing, even making leis is the same concept. The whole time, while picking flowers, I was thinking about it . . . that's how my ancestors did it. That spiritualness is carried on from generation to generation.

Other forms of protocol were also observed. The Puna kua'āina did not talk openly about their plans prior to going out on an expedition. They believed that everything around them in nature had the ability to hear, and if whatever they were going to hunt or fish became aware of the intended expedition, the prey would escape or hide. Thus, if they referred to where they were going, they would use code words such as "holoholo" instead of fishing or hunting. In fishing, they did not take bananas with them and would give the first fish caught back to the ocean deities. They would also express gratitude to the deities after a successful subsistence expedition. The deities are believed to dislike anyone who is greedy or ungrateful and to have the ability to deprive such a person of future success in their expeditions if they took too much, did not share, or did not express gratitude.

In Puna, subsistence also served as a basis for sharing, gift giving, and trade. After a successful hunting or fishing expedition, the young men would make stops at the homes of family and friends, dropping off meat or fish along the way. By the time they reached home, they usually ended up with just enough to feed their immediate family. The kūpuna were particularly dependent upon this sharing network. For example, one of the kūpuna said that he taught his children how to hunt and fish and now they supply him with all that he needs.

Historic trails were generally used to access traditional subsistence gathering areas. The trails usually ran from the coastal communities where the kua-'āina lived, up into the forest. Four-wheel-drive vehicles replaced horses as the means of reaching subsistence areas. Vehicles were usually driven on dirt roads up to the point where the trail narrows and then they hiked the rest of the way.

Fishing and Ocean Gathering

Virtually every family in Puna engaged in fishing. While each person had his or her own special or favorite fishing spot, most fished the entire coastline from Kea'au to within the national park. The majority fished off of the rocky coastline or in shallow areas near shore. They threw net, laid net, whipped (cast), dunked (a kind of stationary fishing), and dove for fish.

Those who had boats fished either for subsistence or commercially one to two miles from shore for ahi and aku in the spring and summer. They also bottom fished at a depth of about 600 feet with hand lines. Some of the fishing grounds south of Kaimu were affected by the lava flows. For example, moi holes were destroyed when the lava altered the contour of the ocean floor. Visibility was also affected by the flow. Only ulua fishing seemed to remain unaffected.

In general, the fish caught were eaten raw, mixed with sea salt and limu, or cooked in a variety of ways—steamed, fried, or grilled. Occasionally, when a large amount of fish was caught, the fish would be dried for future use. Fish caught in remote areas, such as in the national park, were quickly cleaned and salted to dry to avoid spoilage during the long journey home without ice.

Ocean resources such as 'opihi, wana, hā'uke'uke, and limu are also gathered along the rocky shoreline of Puna. This is a hazardous undertaking. As a rule, Native Hawaiians are taught never to turn their backs to the ocean. The kua'āina also throw back their first catch, for example an 'opihi, as an offering for protection from the waves.

Gathering and Hunting

Puna kua'āina gathered plants for many purposes—food, medicine, tools, building materials, art, and adornment. Fruits were gathered in season as they ripened. Maile was gathered for special occasions such as birthday parties or graduations. Increasingly, the maile was found only in the forest at higher elevations, owing to commercial harvesting, development of subdivisions, and continuing volcanic eruptions. Occasionally the Puna families gathered resources for family members and close friends who moved to another part of Hawai'i or another island. Medicinal plants were once gathered throughout Puna. However, over the years development and volcanic activity have limited the growth of such plants to the forest reserve areas of the district. Those who engaged in lā'au lapa'au were dependent upon a healthy forest to gather native plants that still possessed the qualities and potency required for healing.

Puna kua'āina hunted wild pigs, goats, and cows from within the national park to Nānāwale. Some might go as often as every day or every other day in order to provide meat for their 'ohana. Everything caught was always shared with the broader 'ohana and older neighbors. Sharing the meat was tied to the belief that if one was generous with the catch, then the supply would always be there. Even if the catch was poor, the hunters still shared with others. Greed was believed to be punishable by poor hunting or bad luck. When the hunt was successful, the hunters generally thanked the 'āina.

The hunting methods used varied from guns to knives and dogs. Larger animals such as cows were shot and killed. Pigs and goats were usually chased and cornered by dogs and then stabbed and killed by the hunter. Animals were cleaned and dressed in the area where they were killed, and the meat was packed out by the hunters. Most of the time hunters were careful not to kill more than they could carry out.

The meat was usually smoked and cured. Most hunters had smokehouses in their back yards and used wood gathered from the forest or lava flows to smoke the meat.

Cultivation

Many kua'āina cultivated plants for food and materials around their houses or in tracts of land that required a long hike or travel by four-wheel drive. They grew taro, sweet potato, banana, breadfruit, coconuts, kukui (candlenut tree), papaya, lauhala, noni, ti leaves, and so on. The planting, harvesting, and preparing of taro was a family effort. 'Ohana with taro would gather about every three weeks to harvest taro, replant, and make poi. Individual families would thus go home with a generous supply of fresh poi to last until the next gathering. When ulu was abundant it was also cooked in the imu and pounded into poi. Sweet potatoes were also cooked in the imu and sometimes mashed and mixed with coconut milk for a dessert. Most families in Puna grew ti leaves in their yards. Traditionally, ti leaves were used as a charm to ward off evil spirits at the site where the leaves grew or to protect the person who would wear the charm. Ti leaves are also used to wrap fish and other food for steaming or cooking over an open fire or in an imu. Kukui nuts are also easily and customarily grown in yards. The nut is baked and used as a relish with Hawaiian salt to prepare raw fish. If the land around their house was not suitable for cultivation, then plots were cultivated in family land with better soil. Some families in Kalapana, for example, cultivated dry-land taro in Kamaili. Plots were even cleared in the forest for planting taro, sweet potatoes, and bananas.

Regeneration

At the end of the twentieth century, the Native Hawaiian community of Puna, particularly the lower part, remained distinct, geographically, culturally, and socially. A significant part of the population is descended from the first families who migrated there and settled in the district. They had a strong tradition of perseverance in a district that has been constantly changing and evolving.

In addition, young Native Hawaiian families were moving in increasing numbers into Puna from Hilo, Honolulu, and other neighboring islands. Beginning in 1958, most moved into the nonstandard subdivisions, which offered affordable homes for low- and moderate-income families. Yet despite the increase in the population, the opening of new subdivisions, and continuous eruptions by Pelehonuamea, Puna families still engaged in subsistence activities.

Pelehonuamea continued to manifest her presence in the Puna district through an active eruption that began on January 3, 1983, and continued into the twenty-first century with earthquakes, natural subsidence, and the steady flow of steam and natural gases out of the earth into the atmosphere.

When geothermal energy development for the generation of electricity threatened to destroy the Puna Forest Reserve, the kua'āina and Pele practitioners rallied together to protect the natural and cultural resources of the forest they and their ancestors had always utilized and protected. This challenge most clearly demonstrated the regenerative role of Puna as a cultural kīpuka. Testimony provided by kua'āina of Puna about their customary use of the forest convinced the circuit court judge and the judges of the Hawai'i State Supreme Court that Hawaiian cultural and subsistence beliefs, customs, and practices continued to be actively practiced in the Puna Forest Reserve. This resulted in a ruling of the Hawai'i State Supreme Court that more broadly defined the recognition of Native Hawaiian rights to access undeveloped private and public lands for cultural, religious, and subsistence purposes.

The ahupua'a of Kahauale'a, owned by the Campbell Estate, was originally targeted for geothermal energy development. When Pele began, on January 3, 1983, to continuously erupt at Kahauale'a from mauka to makai the State of Hawai'i offered the Puna Forest Reserve for the development project. In 1983 the Pele practitioners formed an organization they called the Pele Defense Fund. In 1985 they adopted a statement of the inherited beliefs that led them to oppose geothermal energy.

Pele Perspectives

1 Pele is the heart, the life of the Hawaiian religious beliefs and practices today.

2 Pele has always been and is today central and indispensable to Hawaiian traditional religious beliefs and practices.

3 Nowhere in the geographical Pacific except Hawai'i is there a recognized volcano-nature God but Pele.

4 Pele is the akua, and 'aumakua of Hawaiians today. Her blood relationships continue as shared traditions, genealogy and aloha for particular 'āina and places in Hawai'i. Pele is kūpuna and "tutu" to many Native Hawaiians.

5 Pele is the inspiration, strength and focus for those who are established in practices and performances of ancestral tradition and religion.

6 Pele influences daily spiritual and physical life activities, making it essential that Pele exist in pure form and environment.

7 Pele's person, her body-spirit, her power-mana, her very existence are the lands of Hawai'i. This 'āina is her, which she replenishes, nourishes, and protects. She is seen in special-alternate body forms, along with those of her sisters and brothers, their kino lau: the native fern, the native shrub, the blossoms of the native trees.

8 Pele is a living God. She is tangible. She has a home on Hawai'i. She has been seen by many living in Hawai'i. She causes earth quakes, tidal waves and lands to sink or surface from the ocean.

9 Pele is the magma, the heat, the vapor, the steam, and the cosmic creation which occur in volcanic eruptions. She is seen in the lava, images of her standing erect, dancing, and extending her arms with her hair flowing into the steam and clouds.

10 We know geothermal development will adversely affect and personally injure the sacred body of the God Pele, and that she would retaliate. We fear for the loss of our God, for the loss of the spirits of our ancestors, for the loss of the lives of our children, and for the loss of our places in Hawai'i.

11 We believe that geothermal development will unduly burden those who are the family of Pele, her guardians, her worshippers.

12 Geothermal development will severely impair those who depend on salient images of Pele, her viability, and her forests which are connections to the deity.

13 Geothermal development would impinge upon the continuation of all essential ritual practices and therefore also impacts the ability of training young persons in traditional religious beliefs and practices, and the ability to convey these to future generations.

14 Geothermal development will take Pele and diminish and finally delete her creative force, causing spiritual-religious, cultural, psychological and sociological injury and damage to the people who worship and live with Pele.

The Pele Defense Fund filed a suit to stop the exchange of the Puna Forest Reserve for Kahauale'a between the state of Hawai'i and the Campbell Estate (Pele Defense Fund v. Paty 79 Haw. at 442, 1992). Through the course of the court case, the kua'āina of Puna testified about their ongoing access to the Puna Forest Reserve for the hunting and gathering of resources. They explained the spiritual protocol followed out of respect for Pele and the multitude of ancestral deities dwelling in the forest.

Though unable to reverse the land exchange, the Pele Defense Fund won recognition of the rights of Native Hawaiians of Puna to access the Puna Forest Reserve for traditional and customary practices even under the private ownership of the Campbell Estate. The court case set a precedent for all Native Hawaiian rights of access by ruling that "Native Hawaiian rights pro-

Figure 26 The Pele Defense Fund led a broad movement to stop the development of geothermal energy to protect the Wao Kele o Puna lowland rainforest and protect the sacred realm of the family of Pele deities. 1990. Franco Salmoiraghi.

tected by Article XII. Section 7, may extend beyond the ahupua'a in which a Native Hawaiian resides where such rights have been customarily and traditionally exercised in this manner." Prior to this ruling, the rights of Native Hawaiians to access had been limited to the ahupua'a in which they lived.

The Pele case expanded the recognition of all Native Hawaiian rights and contributed to the regeneration of Native Hawaiian culture and religion throughout the Hawaiian Islands into the twenty-first century.[72] It also reaffirmed the continuing existence and belief in Pelehonuamea as the inspiration for new generations of Native Hawaiians from the rising of the sun at Kumukahi, Puna to its setting at Lehua, beyond Kaua'i.

❧ FIVE ❧

Moloka'i Nui a Hina:
Great Moloka'i, Child of Hina

Ho'i a'e o Wākea loa'a Hina	Then Wākea turned around and found Hina
Loa'a Hina he wahine moe nā Wākea	Hina was found as a wife for Wākea
Hāpai Hina iā Moloka'i, he moku	Hina conceived Moloka'i, an island
'O Moloka'i a Hina he keiki moku	Hina's Moloka'i is an island child.

—PAKU'I, IN FORNANDER, *Fornander Collection*, VOL. 4 (1916–17)

Na Kuluwaiea o Haumea he kāne,	Kuluwaiea of Haumea as the husband,
Na Hinanuialana he wahine	Of Hinanuiakalana as the wife
Loa'a Moloka'i, ke akua, he kahuna	Was born Moloka'i, a God, a priest
He pualena no Nu'umea	The first morning light from Nu'umea.

—KAHAKUIKAMOANA, IN FORNANDER, *Fornander Collection*, VOL. 4 (1916–1917)

CHANTS SUCH as these in the epigraph composed by Paku'i and Kahakuikamoana, which describe the conception and birth of Moloka'i by the Goddess Hina, are sources of the saying *Moloka'i Nui a Hina* (Great Moloka'i, child of Hina). They convey the image of Moloka'i as a child—small and fragile—that needs to be nurtured by the people who live there. Moloka'i, smaller than Hawai'i, Maui, O'ahu, and Kaua'i, has finite resources that must be cultivated and sustained. The kuaāina of Moloka'i trace their roots back to antiquity and the traditional responsibility they inherited to look after and care for the island and its resources.

Another important tradition of Moloka'i is summed up in the epithet "Moloka'i Pule O'o" (Moloka'i of the Powerful Prayer). The mo'olelo of the 'ohana Kame'ekua of Moloka'i, descended from the Kai'akea family of the

191

Moʻo clan, who they claim dates back to at least 800 BCE on Molokaʻi, is published as *Tales from the Night Rainbow*. It recounts how, around 1250 CE, the high priest Paʻao had gone back to his homeland in Tahiti to gather warriors to take over Hawaiʻi. When the Tahitian warriors attempted to invade Molokaʻi, the people of the island stood along the shoreline like a silent army. As the warriors attempted to beach their canoes, the people of Molokaʻi began to chant, starting softly until the chant grew into a mighty roar. Spears thrown by the invading warriors fell short. Men trying to go ashore fell back into the surf choking, unable to breathe.[1] The invasion failed. As the tale of their defeat spread, the island came to be known as Molokaʻi Pule Oʻo.

This saying is also rooted in a tradition that upholds Molokaʻi as the training center of the most powerful kahuna or priests in sorcery in all of Hawaiʻi. One of the most famous of the powerful Molokaʻi kahuna was the prophet Lanikaula, who lived in the sixteenth century. He was renowned for his ability to foretell the future and to give advice. His burial place, in a grove of kukui trees in East Molokaʻi, was revered as a sacred place from the 16th century through the early twenty-first century.

Figure 27 This young Hawaiian woman walking along the shoreline of Kapuaiwa Grove in Kalamaʻula is reminiscent of the saying *Molokaʻi Nui a Hina* (Great Molokaʻi, Child of Hina). 2004. Richard A. Cooke III.

The tradition of the Kalaipahoa Gods firmly established Moloka'i as a center of sorcery. According to the mo'olelo, there were trees at Maunaloa, Moloka'i, into which Gods had entered. When humans attempted to cut the trees, they died if the sap or even a small chip of the wood touched their skin. The Gods instructed Kāneiakama how to make offerings, approach the trees, and chop them in order to carve images of them. Kāneiakama managed to chop three blocks of wood from the trees and carve them into images he called Kalaipahoa, meaning carved with pāhoa axes. The stumps and branches left over from carving were thrown into the sea to protect humans from coming into contact with them and dying. The Moloka'i chiefs and kahuna who possessed the Kalaipahoa images became very powerful, famous, and feared throughout the islands. Kahekili secured control of the images when he became ruler of Moloka'i. Before he died he gave a little piece of one of the images to High Chief Kamehameha. After the Battle of Nu'uanu, Kamehameha himself assumed control of these godly images.[2]

The saying "Moloka'i, 'Āina Momona" (Moloka'i, Land of Plenty) honors Moloka'i as the land of "fat fish and kukui nut relish." The fat fish are raised in the numerous fishponds on the island. The "kukui nut relish," used to flavor the fish, refers to the lush and abundant resources of the island. These abundant resources, along with Moloka'i's strategic location between Maui and O'ahu, made it an island that the chiefs of Maui and O'ahu fought over, back and forth, to control.

"Moloka'i No Ka Heke" (Moloka'i is the greatest, the foremost) is a famous boast about the island of Moloka'i. It is the traditional rejoinder to Maui's boast of "Maui No Ka 'Oi" (Maui is the best). This saying reflects the pride that Moloka'i's people have in their island home. At the end of the twentieth century, this pride was reflected in the residents' praising Moloka'i as "the last Hawaiian island." In an impressive collaborative effort, the communities on Moloka'i combined efforts to designate the island a rural enterprise zone under the U.S. Federal Department of Agriculture in order to attract responsible investment to the island. The vision statement reaffirmed the Hawaiian values that are embraced by all of the people on Moloka'i, Hawaiian and non-Hawaiian alike. It stated in part:

> Moloka'i is the last Hawaiian island. We who live here choose not to be strangers in our own land. The values of aloha 'āina and mālama 'āina (love and care for the land) guide our stewardship of Moloka'i's natural resources, which nourish our families both physically and spiritually. We live by our kupuna's (elders') historic legacy of pule 'o'o (powerful prayer). We honor

our island's Hawaiian cultural heritage, no matter what our ethnicity, and that culture is practiced in our everyday lives. Our true wealth is measured by the extent of our generosity.[3]

The traditions of Moloka'i are still very much a part of the lives of the people who live on Moloka'i and care for it as their home.

Ruling Chiefs of Moloka'i

In the mo'olelo of Moloka'i, Kamauaua, a descendant of the Nanaulu line was recognized in the thirteenth century as the first ali'inui of the island.[4] In the fifteenth century Kahokuohua was one of the principal chiefs of Moloka'i. He was conquered by the chief of Hawai'i Island, Kalaunuiohua, in his drive to control all of the islands of Hawai'i. When Kalaunuiohua was defeated on O'ahu, Moloka'i was again ruled by its own chiefly line.

Later in the fifteenth century, Kihaapi'ilani assumed the chieftainship of Maui, Moloka'i, Lāna'i, and Kaho'olawe. For a period of time he lived in Waialua and worked with the Moloka'i chiefs to restore the fishpond walls and to lay out a road in West Moloka'i from 'Īloli to Mo'omomi. The roadway was lined with white shells and became known as Kealaakapūpū (pathway of the shells).

In the seventeenth century Moloka'i was ruled by Kalanipehu. His daughter married a chief of Puna who had moved to Moloka'i and was closely related to the ruling chiefs of Hawai'i. At the end of the seventeenth and in the early eighteenth centuries, internal conflicts among the Moloka'i chiefs led different sides to seek alliances from Maui and O'ahu and resulted in the loss of independent rule over the island.[5]

At the end of the first quarter of the eighteenth century, the chief Kuali'i of O'ahu allied with the Moloka'i chiefs of the districts from Kawela to Mo'omomi against the chiefs of the windward valleys. Though victorious, Kuali'i left the Moloka'i chief Paepae and his wife Manau in charge of the island, subject to his overall rule. Upon Kuali'i's death, his son and successor, Kapi'iohokalani, sought direct control over Moloka'i and invaded the island with a large force. The Hawai'i chief Alapa'inui, who was on Maui at that time with his army and fleet of war canoes, went to the aid of the Moloka'i chiefs and helped them defeat Kapi'iohokalani.[6] Rather than annexing Moloka'i, Alapa'inui instated the Moloka'i chiefs as rulers over Moloka'i. He also accompanied the Moloka'i chiefs to work out the terms of peace with the O'ahu chiefs.

On O'ahu, Kapi'iohokalani was succeeded by his son Kanahaokalani, who lived for only one more year. Upon his death, Peleioholani, a younger son of Kapiʻiohokalani, assumed the rule over Oʻahu. During his rule, he subjugated the chiefs of the windward valleys of Molokaʻi through the course of several expeditions. In the mid-eighteenth century the Molokaʻi chiefs killed a daughter of Peleioholani. He exacted revenge upon the island's chiefs and people and assumed direct rule over the island. Molokaʻi remained under the rule of the Oʻahu chiefs until the chief Kahekili of Maui conquered Oʻahu in 1785. Leaving Maui under the rule of his son Kalanikupule, Kahekili moved to Oʻahu to consolidate his rule.

In 1790, following his victory over Kalanikupule in the Battle of Kepaniwai in Iao Valley, Kamehameha moved on to Molokaʻi to prepare his invasion of Oʻahu and battle with Kahekili. After Kamehameha had killed High Chief Kiwalaʻō in the Battle of Mokuʻohai, the dead chief's mother, High Chiefess Kalola, his widow and sister High Chiefess Kekuʻiapoiwa, and his daughter High Chiefess Keʻōpūolani took refuge on Maui with High Chief Kahekili, the brother of High Chiefess Kalola. When Kamehameha invaded Maui, Kalola fled to Molokaʻi with her daughter and granddaughter. While making battle preparations on Molokaʻi, High Chief Kamehameha met with High Chiefess Kalola and asked to marry and be entrusted with the protection of the young chiefess Keʻōpūolani. She agreed to have him care for Keʻōpūolani but only after her own death. She died several days later. Rather than invade Oʻahu at this time, Kamehameha returned to Hawaiʻi to stop the abuse of his people and destruction of his lands in Waipiʻo, Hāmākua, Waimea, and Kohala by High Chief Keouakūʻahuʻula of Kaʻū. Kamehameha took Liliha and Keʻōpūolani with him to Hawaiʻi and eventually married Keʻōpūolani, who bore his successors, Liholiho Kamehameha II and Kauikeaouli Kamehameha III.

A year later, Kaʻeokulani, high chief of Kauaʻi, joined High Chief Kahekili to pursue and invade High Chief Kamehameha on Hawaiʻi at Waipiʻo Valley. On the way to Hawaiʻi, these chiefs and their armies landed on Molokaʻi and reclaimed the rule of the Maui chiefs over the island.

Upon their defeat in the Battle of Kepūwahaʻula at Waipiʻo, High Chief Kahekili returned to Oʻahu and left Chief Kaʻeokulani of Kauaʻi in charge of Maui. When High Chief Kahekili died in 1794, his son Kalanikupule was designated as his successor and ruler of Maui, Lānaʻi, Molokaʻi, and Oʻahu, although High Chief Kaʻeokulani remained in charge of Maui. Conflicts emerged and grew between High Chief Kalanikupule and High Chief Kaʻeokulani. When High Chief Kaʻeokulani decided to return to Kauaʻi, he stopped at Moloka'i to collect tribute, replenish his supplies, and take back the Kaua'i men who had been stationed there earlier.

As High Chief Ka'eokulani proceeded back to Kaua'i, he prepared to engage High Chief Kalanikupule in battle when he landed on O'ahu. The warriors of Kalanikupule fought against Ka'eokulani and his men off of Waimanalo, all along the Ko'olau coast of O'ahu and over to Waialua. The final battle was fought at Ponahawale in 'Ewa. High Chief Ka'eokulani was killed, and High Chief Kalanikupule became the sole ruler over Maui, Moloka'i, Lāna'i, Kaho'olawe, and O'ahu.

In 1795 High Chief Kamehameha, having secured his rule over Hawai'i, launched his campaign of conquest over the chiefs of the other islands. He first invaded and conquered Maui, then moved on to conquer Moloka'i, and from there he invaded and conquered O'ahu. Beginning in 1795 Moloka'i was ruled by the central government established by Kamehameha as the first Mō'ī or paramount chief and king of the Hawaiian Islands until the overthrow of the Hawaiian monarchy in 1893.

At contact in 1779, Captain James Cook estimated the population of Moloka'i to be 36,000, while his sailing master William Bligh estimated it at 20,000.[7] Kenneth Emory calculated the contact population at 10,500.[8]

Although the traditional chiefs of Maui and O'ahu valued Moloka'i for its bountiful fishponds, verdant fields of taro, and strategic location, Western trading vessels and whaling ships bypassed Moloka'i. They considered it a barren land with a sparse population, lacking adequate protected harbors or anchorages, fresh water, and provisions.[9] The limited freshwater resources and lack of harbors that made Moloka'i unsuitable for trade and agribusiness enterprises contributed to the perpetuation of traditional farming and fishing subsistence activities on the island throughout the nineteenth century and well into the twentieth. In light of these circumstances, the pace of cultural change due to Western influence during the nineteenth century was slower on Moloka'i than on the major Hawaiian islands. Throughout this period the Moloka'i Hawaiians maintained the traditional customs that complemented their traditional livelihoods.

Moloka'i in the Nineteenth Century

During the nineteenth century, the major impact of Western contact on Moloka'i was the decline of the population due to diseases and emigration. In 1804 the entire population of Hawai'i was infected by *ma'i oku'u* (either chol-

era or bubonic plague), and many died. David Malo estimated that throughout Hawaiʻi, one-half of the population succumbed to the disease.[10] Given
Molokaʻi's isolation from the port towns where the disease was introduced,
the kuaʻāina of Molokaʻi may not have been as widely exposed. However, the
first missionary stationed on Molokaʻi in 1832 estimated the population to be
8,000, and the *Missionary Herald*, which provided a more detailed survey, estimated the population at 8,700.[11] Assessment of the severity of the impact
upon the Native Hawaiians of Molokaʻi of introduced continental diseases,
and the maʻi okuʻu epidemic in particular, depends upon which estimate of
the population at contact one uses. If the estimate of Cook or Bligh is used,
then the impact of introduced diseases was extraordinary and tragic. If the
Emory estimate is used, then the decrease in the population may be attributed
more to emigration from Molokaʻi to Maui and Oʻahu, where commercial
activities and opportunities associated with the prosperous whaling industry
attracted many young Native Hawaiians from rural areas.[12]

In the fall of 1848 a measles epidemic killed one in every ten people on
Molokaʻi.[13] Molokaʻi's population also declined as many were attracted to
the centers of Western commercial activity at Lahaina and Honolulu. The
1849 census counted 3,429 persons on Molokaʻi.[14] Those who survived and
remained behind continued to cultivate taro and sweet potatoes and to gather
fish, shellfish, and other aquatic foods from the ocean and mountain streams.

In 1845 King Kamehameha III and the Council of Chiefs announced their
intention to initiate a series of changes, including the introduction of a system of private property, the naturalization of foreigners, the appointment of
foreigners to government positions and the imposition of taxes. On Molokaʻi,
1,344 residents signed a petition organized to oppose these changes:

> Greetings Honorable King of our ancestors from the time of the Gods (pō)
> down to us the descendants, as well as to the Kuhina nui of our Hawaiian
> Kingdom and all the aliʻi of you entire nation.
>
> The following is what we desire to request of you, our King, and our
> aliʻi under you in the legislature.
>
> 1 For the independence of your nation, King [Kamehameha] III, we do
>   not want the haole you have appointed over the Hawaiian government
>   to serve as officials.
> 2 We do not want haole to be made naturalized citizens.
> 3 We do not want you to sell any portion of your nation to haole.
> 4 Do not place confusing taxes upon your humble people [*huna lepo*—bits
>   of earth].

May these feelings of ours be shown to you, Your Majesty, and to our ali'i.
We sign our names.

The following is the total amount of names 1344

Aloha honorable one who has been appointed to the root of King Kamehameha II and King Kamehameha I.

Your humble servants, the commoners of your islands,

Given by Keaumaea, July 1845[15]

Through the course of the Māhele and the Kuleana Act, 636 awards for a
total of 2,332 acres were awarded to the maka'āinana of Moloka'i; ten awards
were granted to six ali'i, fifteen awards were granted to fifteen konohiki, and
four awards were granted to four foreigners. Three ahupua'a on Moloka'i
became Crown land, and thirty-six ahupua'a were designated as government
land.

Prominent among the ali'i who received land awards on Moloka'i was
Kekauonohi, who is described above as a recipient of land awards in Hāna and
Puna. She received four times the amount of land distributed to all of the
maka'āinana combined, a total of 10,341 acres in Kapualei (1,670 acres),
Kumu'eli (1,607 acres), Moakea (1,092 acres), and Naiwa (5,909 acres). William C. Lunalilo, who also received lands in Hāna and Puna, was awarded
1,168 acres in Waialua and 14,787 acres in Kawela. William Pitt Leleiohoku,
who also received land awards in Waipi'o and Puna, as discussed above, was
awarded 3,921 acres in Kamalō. Julia Alapai Kauwa, who also received land in
Hāna, received ahupua'a part 5 in Honomuni. Victoria Kamāmalu, who was
discussed above as having received lands in Puna, received an ahupua'a in
Hālawa. Enoka Kuakamauna, who was a konohiki for Hoapilikāne and Hoa-
piliwahine on Moloka'i, received 401 acres in Keopuka Uuku; 168 acres in
Ahaino 2, and 72 acres in Wailau.

According to the 1850 census, 3,540 persons lived on Moloka'i. In 1845,
1,344 Native Hawaiians had petitioned against the sale of land, yet only 636
awards were granted. The petition indicates that at least 1,344 persons on
Moloka'i knew of the proposed changes to the land system. Did the majority
of these petitioners (708) decide to boycott the process and not submit an
application? Did those among the petitioners who did not apply succumb to
illness or disease? Were half of the 1,344 persons from the same household so
that only one person would have submitted an application for an award? Perhaps all of these factors combined to help to account for the low number of
applicants for lands on Moloka'i. An analysis of this petition, which is pre-

sented in Appendix III, shows that 268 names on the petition match the names of persons who received Land Commission awards.

The pattern of land awards on Molokaʻi reflects a concentration of Native Hawaiian families in Manaʻe or east Molokaʻi, from Kalamaʻula, along the south and southeast section of the island up to the boundary with Hālawa Valley. Of the Molokaʻi Land Commission awards to makaʻāinana, 69.7 percent or 443 of the awards were located in east Molokaʻi, which represented 77 percent of the land awarded or 1,791 acres. The 1853 population map for Molokaʻi developed by John Coulter reflects the same pattern of concentration of the population in the ahupuaʻa of East Molokaʻi.

The second area of significant concentration of Native Hawaiians on Molokaʻi was the windward valleys of north Molokaʻi, from Hālawa and over to the Kalaupapa peninsula. Native Hawaiians living in the windward valleys received 29.7 percent or 189 of the Molokaʻi land awards, which represented 22 percent of the lands awarded or 522 acres.

No awards were given to makaʻāinana in west Molokaʻi, and only four awards were given to makaʻāinana in central Molokaʻi, for a total of 19.23 acres.

Traditional economic activities were pursued on these kuleana lands primarily at a subsistence level for household consumption and exchange with extended family members and neighbors. During this period, east Molokaʻi, or Manaʻe, sustained the bulk of the island's population with its fertile lands and numerous fishponds. Kanepuʻu, a Hawaiian writer for the newspaper *Ke Au Okoʻa*, toured Molokaʻi in 1867 and praised Manaʻe as having good lands and providing the people who lived there with a pleasant life. His detailed

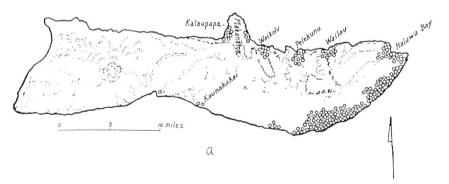

Map 4 The Coulter 1853 map shows a population of 3,540 for Molokaʻi, with 2,700 persons living in Manaʻe. o = 20 persons. *Source: Coulter, Population and Utilization of Land and Sea,* p. 21.

account of the east end included descriptions of the rich resources of Manaʻe Molokaʻi for subsistence economic activities:

> Moakea to Honouli—Good place to live and grow sweet potatoes and dry land taro.
>
> Honoulimaloo—dry . . . only sweet potato and dry land taro grows, not enough water for wet land taro.
>
> Honouluwai—many taro patches from lowlands to uplands . . . life there is pleasant.
>
> Kumimi and Moanui—dry and dreary plain cut by ridges. Some taro patches on side adjoining Honouliwai. Some taro patches at Moanui.
>
> Waialua—taro patches on every side stretching from shore to inland. Good place to live. Many hala trees along the banks of the streams. A large stream, but not as large as Moaula.
>
> Poniohua and Puelelu—kula lands that are irregular on the mountain-ward side. Wet patch taro grows in the upland while dry land taro and sweet potato thrive in the lowland. At this place begins the patches in which springs bubble up. Poniohua has a taro patch that had been dug up at large mounds in the center where bananas, sugar cane, sweet potatoes . . . and so on had been planted while taro grew below in the water.
>
> Kainalu to Ahaino-iki—whole district fertile . . . plants grow well.
>
> Kailiula, Ahaino nui—uala and kalo . . . fishponds . . . fertile soil.
>
> Kupeke and Pukoo—fertile, but dry and hot.
>
> Punaula and Mapulehu—good land. Mapulehu has a wide plain and large valley.
>
> Ualapue—a good land, filled with taro patches and a pond.[16]

At Hālawa and Waialua, surpluses of taro and fish were steadily produced and sold to markets at Lahaina and Honolulu. George Bates, who visited Hālawa Valley in 1853, described the beauty of Hālawa and the commercial production of taro which he observed:

> The valley of Hālawa . . . is the finest scene on Molokai. The traveler stumbles on its brink unawares. At a depth of nearly twenty-five hundred feet below him, the whole scene is spread out before him . . . scores of taro beds, and a number of dwellings, and the romantic river are all seen in a single glance; . . .
>
> The cultivation of taro is carried on here on a large scale. It is raised chiefly to supply the Lahaina market. I was informed by Mr. Dwight [a

missionary on the island] at Kaluaʻaha, that the entire amount raised for sale and home consumption was valued at $15,000 to $20,000. The valley of Hālawa is the richest spot on the island.[17]

Thus, where it was possible, Molokaʻi Hawaiians had an active interest in earning cash to acquire a variety of introduced material goods. Moreover, political and economic changes under the constitutional monarchy required payment in cash of property, income, and poll taxes. Additional economic activities to earn cash included the gathering of kukui nuts for oil (through 1858); of *pepeiaoakua*, a fungus considered a delicacy by the Chinese, for export to San Francisco and China; and of *pulu*, the silky fiber of a native fern found in Molokaʻi forests that was used to stuff pillows and mattresses. Some Molokaʻi Hawaiians also participated in short-lived, small-scale enterprises. During the 1849 Gold Rush, some Hawaiians cultivated potatoes for export to California. During the Civil War, cotton was grown and exported from Molokaʻi. The mission station grew grapes. Coffee was cultivated at Kalaʻe. Rice was grown in the windward valleys. Hawaiians experimented with the cultivation of tobacco. An attempt to grow sugar on a large scale began in 1872.[18]

The major enterprise established on the island on a permanent basis was the ranching of cattle, sheep, and goats on a large scale by Kamehameha V as well as by small farmers. Dairies were also set up and produced butter and milk. Ranching was the major "industry" on Molokaʻi until the establishment of pineapple plantations beginning in 1923.[19]

Indicative of both the decline of the population and the minimal influence of foreigners during the nineteenth century is the 1896 census figure, which showed that there were 2,132 Hawaiians living on Molokaʻi and only 175 non-Hawaiians.[20]

The Establishment of Kalawao and Kalaupapa

The history of Kalawao County, including Kalaupapa on Molokaʻi, was distinct from that of the rest of Molokaʻi. In January 1865 the legislature passed "An Act to Prevent the Spread of Hansen's disease," which gave the kingdom's board of health the authority to segregate and isolate persons who contracted Hansen's disease (leprosy).[21] In September 1865 the board of health acquired over 700 acres of land in Waikolu and Waiʻaleʻia valleys for the express purpose of isolating victims of Hansen's disease. Later, in 1865, they also acquired Kalawao. These lands were selected for their geographic features. Access to them by land and by ocean was difficult, and they were self-contained areas that had previously provided fifteen to twenty families with sufficient resources for their subsistence. According to the 1866 board of health report:

> The tract was extremely well situated for the purpose designed. It is difficult of access from the sea; has no roads passing through it into other districts; is supplied with water by two running streams; has a large area of kalo land; enjoys the advantage of the constant trade wind; has ample grazing lands; and possesses a soil capable of raising vegetables of all different kinds adapted to these islands in the greatest abundance.[22]

Hawaiians who lived in these valleys were given a settlement of $1,800 and government lands in east Moloka'i in exchange for their land and homes. Several hundred people relocated to Kainalu and Waialua on the southeastern coast of Moloka'i.

As the number of persons with Hansen's disease increased, the board of health continued to expand the isolation area. In 1866 the board acquired Makanalua Valley.

Moloka'i became famous as the "Lonely Isle" because of the Hansen's disease settlement at Kalawao-Kalaupapa. However, the settlement operated as a world unto itself, quite separate from the rest of the Moloka'i residents. There was little contact between the settlement and the rest of the island, with the exception of the windward valleys of Hālawa, Wailau, and Pelekunu, whose residents provided the settlement with pa'i'ai and seasonally gathered salt at the peninsula.[23]

The following lament chant conveys the loneliness and grief of those Hawaiians who contracted Hansen's disease and were rounded up like animals and banished to Kalawao and Kalaupapa. It was composed by Ka'ehu, a renowned hula master of Kaua'i who contracted Hansen's disease and was sent to Kalawao, where he died.

Lohe ana kauka aupuni	Report reached the government doctors
Ho'ouna ke koa maka'i	Who sent military soldiers
Hopuhopu 'ia mai kohu moa	Caught were we like chickens.
Alaka'i i ke ala kohu pipi	Led along the road like cattle.
Kū ana imua o ka Papa Ola	We confronted the Board of Health.
Papa ola 'ole o nei ma'i	A board promising no cure for this disease.
Ki'ei wale mai na kauka	The doctors just peered at us
Halo ma'ō ma'ane'i	Peering this way and that

Kuhi a'e nā lima i Lē'ahi	Fingers pointed toward Lē'ahi
"Hele 'oe ma Kalawao"	"You go to Kalawao"
Lālau nā koa Aupuni	Military soldiers seized us
Halihali ia kai kauwapo	Fetched us to the wharf
Ho'ili nā pio a pau	All prisoners were sent aboard
Ka luahi ia a ka ma'i lēpele	Victims of leprosy
Hiki ke aloha kaumaha no	Great grief and sadness possessed us,
I ka 'ike 'ole i ka 'ohana	For we had not seen our families
Ka waimaka ho'i ka 'elo'elo	Tears poured like raindrops
Ho'opulu i ka papalina	Wetting the cheeks[24]

In 1873, after 600 people had been banished to Kalawao, the government purchased the Kalaupapa Peninsula, excluding the eastern portion. Despite the expansion of the settlement, several people continued to live on their kuleana lands on the peninsula. While they lived there, the kuleana holders provided hiding places, food, and lodging for the healthy friends and relatives of the Hansen's disease exiles.[25] In 1895 the Board of Health claimed these kuleana through condemnation proceedings and evicted the holders for health reasons.

Although the board of health had expected the Hansen's disease victims to fish and farm for their day-to-day sustenance, the board realized within the first year that the exiles were too ill, demoralized, and debilitated to provide for their own needs. Beginning in 1866 the legislature appropriated monies to purchase food and supplies. In 1868 a hospital building, a schoolhouse, and quarters for the young boys and young girls were constructed by the kingdom. By 1872 more homes had been built, and the weekly rations included five pounds of meat and twenty-one pounds of pa'i'ai, most of the latter purchased from Hālawa, Wailau, and Pelekunu. Nevertheless, conditions in the settlement were miserable. The Hansen's disease victims complained in letters to relatives about the lack of health care, the separation of husbands from wives, poor and insufficient food, the scanty supply of clothes, the difficulty they had obtaining rations when they were ill, and complete lawlessness.[26] In response to the complaints of friends and relatives of the victims of Hansen's disease, King Lunalilo instituted a number of reforms during his brief one-year reign in 1874. The same year Father Damien began to live and work among the suffering lepers of Kalawao.

From 1874 through 1889, through the efforts of Father Damien and his supporters, conditions gradually improved. In November 1888 the Sisters of

Charity, led by Mother Marianne, also began to tend and care for the Hansen's disease victims at Kalawao.[27] By 1900, when Hawai'i became a territory, vast improvements had been completed. By this time most of the exiles lived on the Kalaupapa Peninsula, where the climate was drier and the dock accessible. Access to clean fresh water, a constant problem, had become available with the extension of water pipes to Kalaupapa. Life for the Hansen's disease patients at the settlement was bittersweet during the early years of the territorial period.

Moloka'i in the Territorial Period

During the territorial period, the population of Moloka'i continued to decline until the Hawaiian Homesteading Program started in 1922 and pineapple plantations were established in 1923. In 1900, not counting Kalawao the population of Moloka'i was 1,327. The population of Kalawao was comparable at 1,177. In 1910 the population of Moloka'i, again excepting Kalawao, hit its lowest point at 1,006, while the population of Kalawao dropped to 785. The 1920 population figure outside of Kalawao rose by only eleven, to 1,117.[28] It is estimated that up to this point 96 percent of the population of Moloka'i outside of Kalawao was concentrated in the area east of Kamalō and the windward valleys.[29] During this period population declined primarily because of the emigration of people to other islands, particularly O'ahu, to seek jobs and gain access to material goods not available on Moloka'i.

The Hawaiian Homes Program and the pineapple industry attracted people to Moloka'i beginning in 1922. By the time of the 1930 census, there were 4,427 people living on Moloka'i. This represented an increase of 148 percent over the 1920 figure. Of the total population, 1,869, or 42 percent, were Hawaiian or part Hawaiian. The east end of Moloka'i continued to be an area of concentration. Of 971 inhabitants of the southeast coast and the windward valleys, 566, or 58 percent, were Hawaiian or part Hawaiian. Owing to the establishment of the Hawaiian Homesteading Program, Pala'au-Ho'olehua became another area where Hawaiians concentrated. Out of its 1,031 inhabitants, 826, or 80 percent, were Hawaiian.[30]

Cattle ranching was the major industry on Moloka'i until 1923, when pineapple began to be grown on a large scale on land leased from Moloka'i Ranch. Although Moloka'i Ranch was the major operation, there were also smaller ranches along the southern coast. At the west end, Moloka'i Ranch developed a paddock system for cattle, gradually fencing in the open range. They hunted down the wild herds of deer and goats; started control measures against guava, lantana, and pāmakani; introduced new grasses; and started a breeding program using Devon bulls.

In 1904 the ranch had 5,598 head of cattle, 13,918 sheep, 298 horses, 272 pigs, and 1,614 colonies of bees. Then, in 1917, the ranch decided to gradually abandon sheep herding in favor of cattle raising because beef earned a better return than sheep and because sheep diseases were a perennial problem.

Table 7 compares the raising of sheep and cattle on Moloka'i from 1900 through 1930.

Moloka'i Ranch also started apiaries on its land in 1901. In 1904 the first harvest of honey was sold commercially. Between 1904 and 1909 Moloka'i honey was sold to the United States and Australia. From 1909 to World War I most of the honey was marketed to Germany through H. Hackfeld and Company. When the German market closed during World War I, Moloka'i began to export its honey to California. Moloka'i was the largest producer of honey in the world in 1919, when the ranch had 2,250 colonies of bees producing 2,946 cases of honey and 80 cases of beeswax. It grossed as much as $21,000 in one year alone. In 1937 the industry folded when all of the bees became infected with American foul brood.[31]

The ranch employed males from ten to twenty years of age, according to a Native Hawaiian informant, Albert Kahinu. He lived on Moloka'i until 1902, then moved to Honolulu, returning to Moloka'i at age 18 in 1912. To him, the work was hard, but the cost of living was reasonable. The highest wage was about $30 a month, and the employees received subsistence supplies twice a month. Moreover, there was an abundance of fish to supplement the income from the ranches. According to Kahinu, "Living at that time was very friendly . . . all the fish you want . . . you can get in the sea, you can kick the fish with your feet, in those days. Ka i'a ka wāwae o Hīlia—The fish that can be kicked at Hīlia."[32]

It was attempted to raise sisal on barren spots on the southeast shore, but

TABLE 7 HEAD OF SHEEP AND CATTLE RAISED ON MOLOKA'I, 1900–1930

YEAR	CATTLE	SHEEP
1900	6,354	15,800
1910	6,213	7,915
1920	8,140	3,643
1930	7,623	225

the venture failed owing to high overhead and the low-price sisal from Mexico, a major producer of the fiber. At Puko'o frogs were raised commercially for export. The Duvauchelle family of Puko'o hunted, killed, and processed sharks for engine oil, which they sold to the Pioneer Mill at Lahaina.[33] Puko'o was the social center for Mana'e during the first three decades of the twentieth century. The main post office was located there and had a wharf that serviced the residents of the area.

Other minor industries included boat construction and guitar making. At Hālawa, Wailau, and Mana'e, hats woven out of native materials such as lauhala, makaloa, and coconut leaves were produced for sale. Lauhala mats were also woven for household use and for sale.[34]

Charles Baldwin provided a good overview of commercial economic activities on Moloka'i:

> The larger part of the island is devoted to cattle raising. Taro is grown in Pelekunu and Wailau for the leper settlement. Sisal is also grown in places.
>
> Formerly there were a great many fish ponds within the barrier reef along the southern shore of the island, but many of these ponds are not

Figure 28 Kūpuna Albert and Lani Kahinu were photographed by L. R. Sullivan in 1920 and interviewed by Mary Kawena Pukui in 1961. Coincidentally, this couple raised a cousin of my father's whose mother died in childbirth. 1920. Sullivan Collection, Bishop Museum.

now, as there is no market for the fish, and the inclosing walls have been allowed to fall to pieces. Some fish are sent to Lahaina and Honolulu.[35]

Despite the diversity of commercial enterprises that were pursued at east Molokaʻi, subsistence farming of taro and sweet potatoes and fishing continued to be the mainstay of the 900 or so Hawaiians who lived along the southern coast and in the windward valleys of Molokaʻi.

Up through World War II Molokaʻi was a marginal rural area with a small, predominantly Native Hawaiian population. The population was concentrated in kuleana lands in the eastern part of the island, the windward valleys, and the Kalawao Hansen's disease settlement. The establishment of the Hawaiian Homes Program and the pineapple industry did not transform life for Hawaiians living on the eastern end of Molokaʻi. These economic enterprises did, however, introduce new forces and influences into the central and western parts of the island that had previously been sparsely populated and devoted to ranching. By World War II Molokaʻi was an island with four distinct communities—the Native Hawaiian subsistence farmers and fishermen of east Molokaʻi and the windward valleys, the Native Hawaiian homesteaders of Kalamaʻula and Hoʻolehua, the Hansen's disease patients at Kalawao-Kalaupapa, and the immigrant laborers at Kualapuʻu and Mauna Loa. The following sections describe the distinctive character of each of the communities where Hawaiians were predominant.

Manaʻe: East Molokaʻi

East Molokaʻi includes the southern coast east of Kaunakakai as well as the windward valleys on the north end of the island. However, it is the southeast coast that is commonly referred to as Manaʻe. Manaʻe consists of a narrow coastal plain of fertile alluvial lowlands and numerous freshwater springs. Gentle slopes, gulches, and narrow valleys lead inland to the east Molokaʻi mountains, where the peaks are usually shrouded by clouds and waterfalls flow down sheer cliffs. The mountain rains percolate into the water lense and in some places emerge along the coast and shore as springs. They also feed intermittent streams that keep the valley recesses lush with native plants.

The coastline of Manaʻe is protected by a barrier reef that extends more than one mile out to sea. This extensive reef makes the ocean calm along the shore. The ocean is the backyard of most of the families living in east Molokaʻi. Its proximity, calmness, and shallow depths provide easy access to the ocean's resources.

Of Moloka'i's fifty-three fishponds, thirty-five fringe the southeastern shore. J. N. Cobb listed eighteen fishponds as being in active use for commercial purposes in his report *The Commercial Fisheries of the Hawaiian Islands*. The fishponds ranged in size from 1 acre to 54.5 acres and totaled 293 acres altogether.[36] Within these ponds Mana'e Hawaiians raised mullet, awa, aua, kākū, āholehole, 'o'opu, eels, shrimp, squid, and crab.[37] The mullet from the 'Ualapu'e, Nī'aupala, Pipi'o, Puko'o, and Kūpeke ponds were noted for their fatness and were especially popular in Lahaina. In an account of Hawaiian fishing lore by Kahaulelio that ran in *Nūpepa Kū'oko'a* from February through July 1902, the author said that the Lahaina people ran and leaped and hurried to get mullet from those particular Moloka'i ponds, because to delay meant returning empty-handed. He also provided instructions on how to catch the fish from these ponds:

> In fishing, go just before daylight, with nets having meshes of two finger's [*sic*] width in the hands of Hulu, laumana and others. The breezes blow strongly and while still shivering with cold, plunge into the icy water. With one or two drawings of the net, the boat is filled, the sails set with Lahaina as the goal. At this time it is still dark and light comes when Kekaa is reached or Lahaina itself. When you open the belly of the mullets of these ponds, the fat within is like that of a hog and does resemble it in every way.[38]

Forty ahupua'a, averaging two square miles each, make up Mana'e.[39] Kua-āina living in these ahupua'a had access to ocean and mountain resources as a part of their inherited kuleana rights, and they utilized the resources of their region on a regular basis, hunting wild deer, goats, pigs, turkeys, ducks, and pheasants and gathering fruits, nuts, vegetables, vines, materials for twine, native plants for healing, and flowers for special occasions.

From the ocean, shellfish, seaweed, squid, lobsters, crabs, and other reef life were gathered. The Mana'e Hawaiians not only harvested the many fishponds that fringed their shore, they also fished at greater depths by net, diving, and trolling. In the valley streams they caught 'o'opu and 'ōpae.

Mana'e kuaāina also raised animals and crops on their kuleana land. Most families raised domestic pigs, one or two head of cattle, and some chickens. Almost every household owned a horse as its major means of transportation. They cultivated the traditional Hawaiian staples of taro, sweet potato, and breadfruit. They also planted onions and watercress and other introduced vegetables and fruits in their gardens.

Figure 29 A classic kua'āina and farmer of Moloka'i. Circa 1912. Ray Jerome Baker, Hawaiian Historical Society.

All these foods, both cultivated and gathered, provided the Mana'e kua-'āina with a healthy daily diet. These foods were usually jointly gathered, cultivated, and shared among the 'ohana. Throughout Mana'e several households commonly lived together on the kuleana land of the 'ohana. Food obtained through hunting, gathering, or fishing was also given as gifts or exchanged for other types of food or services with neighbors. Sometimes it was sold for cash to buy additional provisions.[40]

In 1931 Handy surveyed Moloka'i and wrote up his observations about east Moloka'i in volume 1 of *The Hawaiian Planter*. He described a method of planting taro in mounds that was unique to east Moloka'i. His account documents the extensive cultivation of taro and sweet potatoes by the people of Mana'e from 1900 through 1930:

> Wet taro was seen at Keawanui, Puko'o, Kawaikapu, Waialua, Honouliwai,
> and Pohakupili. My short visit to Molokai in 1931 did not allow time for
> any exploration. At Kamalo I observed and photographed a method of taro
> cultivation said to have been common along this coast in ancient times. In
> flat swampy ground earth is heaped up into long mounds 3 or 4 feet high
> and about 3 feet broad on top, each mound surrounded by water left stand-
> ing in the ditches created by digging out and heaping up the earth. The
> taro is planted around the lower margins of the mounds near the water;
> sweet potatoes are planted on top. This method of swamp-land planting
> finds its counterpart in the old style of mounding (termed kipikipi) prac-
> ticed in Waiakea, Hawaii.[41]

The kupuna informant Peter Namakaeha said that lehua, nohu, piko ke'o-ke'o, piko 'ele'ele, and pi'iali'i taro varieties were planted at Kalama and 'ōhi'a. Some was pounded into pa'i'ai for consumption by the 'ohana, and some was sold.[42] Handy also wrote about his 1931 tour of south Moloka'i: "In 1931, potato patches were seen at various places near the road along the south coast, and Hawaiians said that many parts of the kula land used to be planted with both sweet potato and dry taro. It is safe to assume that potatoes were grown all along this coastal plain fringed with fishponds from Waialua to Punakou."[43]

In 1961 Daniel Pahupu, a kupuna informant, shared his mana'o about life in Mana'e with Mary Kawena Pukui of the Bishop Museum. "Before, loa'a no ke kalo, ai no ke i'a alo la—Just get the taro, the meat is right there in front. The land was not kapu, therefore we never lacked anything, but now, ea hemahema—the spirit is lacking."[44] Namakaeha, a respected fisherman from

Honouliwai, also summed it up nicely: "I have everything. What more I want? No island beat Molokaʻi. We have everything . . . Whereas some islands you don't get everything. I live one of the best life."[45] In short, east Molokaʻi provided Hawaiians with an abundance of natural resources which more than adequately fulfilled their food needs.

The Windward Valleys

Windward Molokaʻi has seven major ahupuaʻa, each averaging six square miles.[46] The valleys are separated from each other by high tablelands that extend from the east Molokaʻi mountain range out to the coast, where they drop dramatically down to the ocean. The walls of the valleys are steep and ascend as high as 1,500 to 2,000 feet. Beaches, rocky and inaccessible by boat except during the summer months, are found only at the mouths of the valleys.[47] The uplands are usually cloaked in fog and saturated by rain. Sizable streams flow year round in each valley. The narrow valley bottoms were settled by early Hawaiians who planted taro in terraces.

In 1916 the Bishop Museum ethnographer Kenneth Emory toured the windward side of Molokaʻi and observed

> cliffs, several thousand feet high; promontories, bold and razor-edged; deep gorges rushing down to the sea, all in the wildest confusion, and covered with a beautiful mantle of variegated green, except where the cliffs were sprayed with salty foam. And one of the added charms of this was the beautiful waterfalls that waved their glossy threads down the face of the cliffs.
>
> Waterfalls, peaceful vales, lagoons hidden under dark caverns, tropical birds floating above, vines swaying in the wind, every form and color of beauty lay revealed in the grand precipice above us, filling half the space between horizon and zenith.[48]

The windward valleys generously furnished their inhabitants with water to irrigate taro terraces; edible fruits and root crops; plants for healing; fibers for cordage; freshwater oʻopu fish, ʻōpae, wī, and hīhīwai; and an ocean teeming with fish, seaweed, and shellfish. Each of the windward valleys abounded in native plants that provided for the day-to-day needs of the kuaʻāina. ʻAwa usually grew in the wet uplands. Breadfruit, sugar cane, arrowroot, and bananas were raised on the borders of the taro patches and the sloping ground. Gourds for containers grew in warm, damp spots near the sea. Olonā provided fiber for lines and nets, and the wauke for tapa grew in the uplands. Yams grew in the lower forest zone. These cultivated plants were complemented by numerous forest plants that supplemented the diets of the Hawaiians of the windward valleys, as well as flowers for adornment and decoration.[49]

Pelekunu, Wailau, and Hālawa are the valleys about which accounts are available. The descriptions of the lifestyle and livelihoods of the families in those valleys shed light on the living conditions of kua'āina along Moloka'i's windward shore during the first three decades of the twentieth century. According to the Native Hawaiian informant Daniel Napela Naki, who was born in Wailau, raising taro and fishing were the primary enterprises of the families who lived in Wailau, Pelekunu, and Hālawa. These activities were pursued not merely to meet the subsistence needs of the local families. Poi and fish from these valleys were also sold to the settlement at Kalaupapa and the urban center of Lahaina. Fred Tollefson, a kupuna of Norwegian descent who learned to speak fluent Hawaiian growing up on Moloka'i, recalled how the pa'i'ai, or pounded taro, from Wailau, Pelekunu, and Hālawa was wrapped in ti leaves and the bundles floated in to the shores of Kalaupapa from offshore boats.

James Poaha described the interrelationship between the windward valleys and the Kona or leeward coastal plain as similar to the mauka-makai pattern of exchange that was traditionally practiced among the native Hawaiians:

> A fishing place . . . that was the livelihood of those who lived here before [leeward side]. The people who lived on the leeward side, and those who lived on the wet/water lands would bring pa'i'ai and take fish from here. From Hālawa, Pelekunu, and Wailau.
>
> Poi came from those places—as pa'i'ai wrapped in ti leaf. The outer cord to bind was made of sisal. One bundle was 40 pounds. The monetary value was only 75 cents. When those bundles were brought over, each one got out his poi board. When they carried the pa'i'ai from Wailau it was the back which bore the load. The food was carried on the backs. Such great patience they had . . . Much patience.[50]

In addition to exchanging fish, the residents on the kona side produced salt and exchanged it with the people from the windward side.

Pelekunu

In 1916 Kenneth Emory's group toured windward Moloka'i and landed in Pelekunu Valley. Emory provided *Mid-Pacific Magazine* with a rare description

Figure 30   Kūpuna James and Mary Poaha were photographed with their children, James Jr., Ambrose, Agnes, Eva, and Margaret, by L. R. Sullivan in 1920. The couple was interviewed by Mary Kawena Pukui in 1961. 1920. Sullivan Collection, Bishop Musuem.

of life in that remote windward valley. There were nine rather dilapidated, old-fashioned, and crudely built houses scattered along the crescent-shaped bay. Along the front of the village and a little back from the beach was an ancient stone wall. To the rear of the village and squeezed into the narrow valley far back were rudely cultivated taro patches that were almost neglected. There were no roads, stores, or shops—only houses and people with the bare comforts of civilization, such as kerosene lamps, tin and iron ware, matches, and so on. Emory was impressed with the hospitality of the people: "Though these people had just enough to keep them alive, everything of their's [sic] that we could use was our's [sic] while we stayed there. The little school house was our's for the night, and they brought us poi, dried fish, and felt hurt when we most emphatically refused one of their few hogs, the most highly prized of all their possessions."[51]

Harriet Ne, a kupuna who had spent the first six years of her life, from 1915 to 1921, with the last eight families to inhabit Pelekunu Valley, was interviewed in 1979. She provided vivid glimpses into the lifestyle and livelihoods of the people there. According to her, everyone usually got up at dawn to make maximum use of the sunlight. The valley was so narrow that the sun did not shine very long.[52]

Poi was the staple food of the Pelekunu families. The production of this basic necessity, according to Ne, was a collective enterprise of each family in the valley. The eight families who shared the resources of Pelekunu Valley were closely bound in their day-to-day lives. For example, every family needed poi on a daily basis, and the families rotated the responsibility for producing the weekly supply of poi for the whole valley. According to Ne, the men would get up early, cook breakfast, and go to the taro patches. The children ate, cleared the breakfast table, and then followed the fathers to the patch, where they would tie the pulled taro into bundles, carry the bundles to the stream to be washed, and then take them to the community shed where the taro was to be cooked. After cooking, the taro was cooled on a big net, and everyone gathered around to peel off the skin. The clean taro was placed on the community poi board, which was seven feet long and about two and a half feet wide. Men on both ends and sometimes in the middle would pound the taro into poi. When finished, the poi was given out to each family. They received enough to last them the whole week, when the next family would take over the work of pounding poi.[53]

Pelekunu was rich in natural foods, and gathering plants and shellfish was a basic feature of life in the valley. Ne explained that the name of the valley refers to the smell of freshwater shellfish that dries up and dies on stream rocks:

> Hihiwai is a beautiful shellfish, and it's very tasty and it lives under the great big rocks in the fresh water streams. But early in the morning, they all come up, crawling up to the top of the rock to breath [*sic*] the sunlight and it takes them hours to get to the top of the rock. By the time the sun comes up, they're stranded up on the top of the rock in the hot sun, so they all die there, because they can't get back to their water homes fast enough, and so when they die on the top of the rock they become smelly and that is what Pelekunu means, it means smelly and it got it's [*sic*] name from the smelly shellfish that dried up on the rock.
>
> So what the children did, they took their little baskets and stuff, by the way, the baskets are made from the Makaloa weed (sedge plant) which grew wild in Pelekunu, and they would gather the Hihiwai while their mothers would be doing their laundry and the fathers would be preparing their breakfast.[54]

In addition to the resources of the valley, the ocean provided a plentiful supply of food. The major source of protein was fish from the ocean. The only meat they ate was *honu* (turtle), which frequented an offshore island and swam in on a certain tide. When the people in the valley felt a certain wind blowing in from Maui, they knew that the turtles would be swimming toward land. They would get their spears and go down to the beach to catch the honu. Whoever caught big honu would share with the others. Pelekunu was also noted for its blue *uhu* (fish), which swam off of a certain point. The boys used to climb on a ridge above the point and dive into the ocean when they spotted the distinctive fish's blue color.[55]

During World War I Pelekunu was almost completely depopulated. According to Daniel Napela Naki, Pelekunu was the first of the valleys to be abandoned. When Jennie Wilson married Johnnie Wilson, mayor of Honolulu, in 1920, she left the valley to live with her husband. She had been the schoolteacher until the school was phased out in 1915, and she had also served as the postmistress for the valley. Everyone else also moved out of the valley about the same time.[56] According to Ne, Jennie Wilson had continued to teach the children of the valley even after the school had closed. When she left, many of the families decided to move out of Pelekunu so that their young children could attend a regular school. In addition, the windward valley taro farmers lost the contract to provide pa'i'ai to Kalaupapa, outbid by Honolulu taro growers. This cut the Pelekunu taro farmers off from a major source of income. Some moved to Honolulu and others to the other side of Moloka'i, where they continued to farm. A few applied for and received Hawaiian homestead lands at Ho'olehua.[57]

Wailau

According to Emory, Wailau was very similar to Pelekunu. It had a peaceful Hawaiian village along the crescent-shaped bay, taro patches behind the village, and countless ridges leading up to the precipitous valley walls. Another traveler to Wailau in 1921 was impressed with the natural resources around the stream, which provided residents with ample and easily attainable food: "They hurried into the stream and in no time returned with some lehua-eating 'o'opu and hīhīwai shellfish. A fire was lit, the ti-leaf wrapped fish laid on it and when cooked we ate lunch. We ate heartily of ho'io fern leaves, shrimps, the lehua-eating 'o'opu fish of Pi'ilani, the wī and hīhīwai shell-fish, so numerous in this stream."[58]

Daniel Napela Naki, born in Wailau, recalled the livelihood of the people there in an interview with Mary Kawena Pukui in 1961. According to him, fishing and taro were the main work. The valley provided them with most of their basic needs. However, when they needed provisions such as salt, coffee, flour, crackers, kerosene, and household or garden tools and supplies, the residents of Wailau would hike out and back in through the ridge above Mapulehu on the leeward side of the island. Access into the valley from the ocean was possible only during the calm summer months. Otherwise, they would hike in and out of the valley, a journey of three to four hours if they were burdened with a lot of supplies or two and a half hours if they were traveling light.[59]

The native kūpuna informants from Wailau boasted of the abundance of food that the valley provided for the Hawaiians who lived there. The taro was so plentiful that they did not grow any sweet potatoes there, as was common in other parts of Moloka'i. In speaking about the extensive system of taro patches in the Wailau of his youth, Naki referred to the old Hawaiian proverb "Aia no i'a malalo, aia no i'a maluna" (there is food below and there is food above).[60] There was plenty in the stream—hīhīwai, 'o'opu, 'ōpae—and in the ocean. Even in the taro patches the pūpū lo'i, which is similar to escargot, was raised. Sugar cane was cultivated on the banks of the taro patches.

Another kupuna from Mana'e, Amoy Duvauchelle, recalled how she stayed in Wailau for one month when she was seven years old. She distinctly remembered the ʻoʻopu, hīhīwai, ʻopihi, mountain apples, and white and yellow gingers of the lush valley.[61] Emma Apana, who was born in Wailau in 1892, recalled how full her net would get whenever she went to catch ʻōpae. She described how the ocean provided an abundance of ʻopihi, paiʻea and ʻaʻama crabs, squid, ʻōʻio, moi, and āholehole.[62] Mr. Kaopuiki remembered catching akule, moi, halalū, and all kinds of fish there.[63] The problem with getting fish from the ocean was that boat launchings and landings were safe only during the summer months. Thus, most of the fish were caught near the shore through diving and the use of nets. For this reason, the Wailau Hawaiians frequently exchanged their paʻiʻai for fish with the residents living on the kona side of the island. The Hawaiians also utilized all of the various native plants in the valley to develop a well-rounded diet. Naki described how even the pōpolo plant and potato leaves were baked in ti leaves in place of meat and eaten.[64]

The only basic necessity they lacked was paʻakai, or Hawaiian salt. Because the sun shone on the valley floor for only a few hours a day due to the steep vertical cliffs, there was no place to dry out the ocean water for salt. The residents would gather salt from Kalaupapa during the summer months or buy it from Kaunakakai when they hiked out for provisions.[65]

Naki was raised speaking Hawaiian and pidgin English. He recalled that Hawaiians knew how to heal themselves with native plants and lamented the reliance on pills and injections due to the disappearance of these plants and their use. Maile hōhono was used as a laxative. The oʻo moa, which grows sometimes on the hapuʻu, was cooked with potatoes, pounded together, and made into small balls for a cathartic. Koʻokoʻolau was the original Hawaiian tea. Uleulehala was good for expectant mothers, and the ʻilima flowers were used as a purgative.[66]

In summing up life in Wailau, Naki used the phrase "Hala no ia la" (and so passed the days). Life was pleasant, and the days passed easily. After World War I there were about four families living in Wailau. The school had closed by 1920, and the last family left the valley in 1937. The majority of families who left Wailau moved to Manaʻe.

Hālawa

The ethnohistoric literature on Molokaʻi singles out Hālawa as the wealthiest taro-growing valley on Molokaʻi. It has been excavated and studied as a classic example of irrigated agricultural adaptation in the Hawaiian Islands.[67] In the early 1900s Chinese moved into Hālawa to grow rice, but they abandoned the paddies as well as their water buffalo when cheaper California-produced rice took over the market.[68]

Through the end of the period under review, Hālawa continued to be occupied and taro continued to be grown for subsistence and sale. Handy's 1931 survey of Molokaʻi described the extent to which taro was cultivated there:

> At the eastern end of Molokai the beautiful valley of Hālawa with its broad flats is one of the few localities where taro is cultivated intensively by Hawaiians today. In 1931 only the lower terraces were planted, the taro being grown partly for subsistence and partly for sale. Since that time events have transpired which favor a revival of subsistence planting and perhaps the rehabilitation of the abandoned terraces.[69]

As late as 1935 Hālawa had a population of ninety people. They continued to produce taro for markets in Kaunakakai and Honolulu. In fact, it was not until the tsunami of 1946 that the population of Hālawa significantly decreased. The tsunami destroyed homes and devastated the two major irrigated taro pond field complexes, ending the commercial production of taro at Hālawa.[70]

John Akina was born in Hālawa in 1896, and his wife, Edith, was born there in 1906. In 1961 they were interviewed by Mary Kawena Pukui. The Akinas explained that everyone in Hālawa, as at Pelekunu and Wailau, worked together to cook taro in the imu, clean it, and pound it into paʻiʻai to sell. The people of Hālawa used pieces from a cracked pōhue or Hawaiian ʻumeke gourd to scrape and clean the taro and fed the peelings to their domestic chickens and pigs.[71] Rebecca Uahinui, born in Hālawa in 1891, named some of the varieties of taro raised in Hālawa: aʻapu, uli, ʻeleʻele, piʻialiʻi, lehua, and mana. She also spoke of the collective labor needed to produce paʻiʻai.[72]

At Hālawa, as at Pelekunu and Wailau, many kinds of marine and aquatic foods from the fresh mountain stream and the ocean could be caught. Mrs. Uahinui recalled the abundance of ʻalamihi crabs, ʻopihi, ʻōpelu, ʻāweoweo, hinalea, and manini caught in the ocean; and ʻoʻopu and ʻōpae caught in the stream.[73] According to John Akina, ʻaʻama crabs were especially plentiful when the ocean was calm. He also remembered seeing a lot of ʻōʻō and ʻiʻiwi birds in the valley as a young boy. He blamed the mongoose for killing off the native birds in the valley.[74]

Like Pelekunu and Wailau, Hālawa lacked a source of salt. Thus, the residents got their salt from Kalaupapa. In the summer months when the ocean was calm and the salt would gather on the flat beach rocks at Kalaupapa, the people would venture out by boat to Kalaupapa to gather salt. Kalaupapa was noted for its clean, high-quality salt.[75]

Mana'o Aloha 'Āina o Nā Kūpuna

"Hala no ia la" (so passed the days) was the phrase most often repeated by the kupuna of Moloka'i in Pukui's interviews of them in 1961 and 1964. These interviews were conducted in Hawaiian with Moloka'i Hawaiians who grew up between 1900 and 1930. In the interviews, the Moloka'i Hawaiians talked about the way of life in east Moloka'i. They revealed a persistence of cultural values, beliefs, and practices. The phrase "Hala no ia la" was usually spoken as a final comment in reference to the abundance of natural foods available to them on Moloka'i, how pleasant life was, and how easily the days passed from one to the next.

Sarah Wahineka'apuni Naoo was native to Honouliwai. She exemplified the intimacy that Hawaiians maintained with the land. At Pukaulua beach, Sarah knew where the different varieties of limu, such as līpa'akai, limu kohu, līpoa, and manuwea, flourished, their use, and how to clean and prepare them properly. She knew the types of fish, shellfish, and crabs that gathered in the different sections of the beach, their habits and niches, and when and how best to catch them.[76] Each of the surrounding boulders that formed the distinctive features of the landscape had descriptive names. For example, a rock that resembled a person sitting and observing the sea was called Pōhakuloa. Another rock at Pukaulua was named Pōhaku Puka.

Sarah was also familiar with the life cycle of the freshwater o'opu which lived in the Honouliwai stream. According to Sarah, they ran in season during September. They came down from the upland when there was plenty of water, but when the water was white they wouldn't come. The fishermen went at night to catch the o'opu. When they caught more than needed for the household, Sarah's 'ohana would sell the o'opu in the market.

Sarah Naoo had lived in close harmony with the 'āina for a lifetime, and the 'āina provided her with a large part of her food. She assured Mary Kawena Pukui of the richness of life in east Moloka'i: "'A'ole 'ike mau i ka hale kū'ai. Kahi o Moloka'i Nei, 'a'ole pilikia. Hele hulihuli ma kahakai, ka pīpipi, papa'i, 'ōhiki" (No constant visits to the store. This part of Moloka'i, here, no trouble. Go searching at the beach . . . pīpipi, crab, 'ōhiki).[77]

Sarah Ka'ai'a Kalima of Kalua'aha also shared her mana'o. She spoke of the fragrant limu ʻeleʻele that grew at Kaluaʻaha, where freshwater springs bubbled up on the shore. The ʻalamihi and ʻaʻama crabs were also plentiful.[78]

The kupuna were steeped in Hawaiian folklore, and it formed an integral part of their identity as Hawaiians of Molokaʻi. Pukui offered an interesting comment about the importance of the knowledge about place-names during one of the interviews:

> No ke aloha no, paʻa ka inoa o ka makani, a me ka ua, pehea aku la. Minamina mākou ke inoa ʻāina o nalowale, o like auanei me Oʻahu. Ulu mai ko Oʻahu ka namu ano ʻē.

> [It was out of love, they gave and remembered the names of the wind, the rain and whatever else. We hate to lose the place-names, lest it become like Oʻahu. Oʻahu is growing with peculiar foreign speech.][79]

Knowledge about the place-names and the traditions behind them was significant to the people of Molokaʻi. It informed them about their ancestors, described their adjustment to the natural environment on Molokaʻi, and explained their cultural beliefs and practices. In their day-to-day experience, it was commonplace for them to feel spiritual forces at work behind the natural phenomena they observed.

Sarah Kalima shared her understanding of the various epithets for Molokaʻi listed at the beginning of this chapter. Sarah affirmed that *Molokaʻi Nui a Hina* meant Molokaʻi the Great, Child of Hina, because, according to legend, Hina gave birth to Molokaʻi. Sarah also described the cave of Hina in the Kaluaʻaha district as having flat stones and maidenhair growing in it. In front of the entrance grew a kukui tree. According to the ancient Hawaiians, when Hina went there to bathe, she would pray and the cave would fill with water. The famous old saying was that no one had really seen Molokaʻi until they had seen the cave of Hina. In Sarah's youth, the cave was maintained, and people would visit it with hoʻokupu or offerings.[80]

According to Sarah, Molokaʻi Pule Oʻo (Molokaʻi of the Powerful Prayer) referred to the traditional practices of ʻanāʻanā that Molokaʻi was famous for. As an example of how Molokaʻi acquired that reputation, Sarah told the story of how Kamehamehaʻailūʻau of Maui conquered Molokaʻi and drove the original people inland. The people of Molokaʻi resented the taking of the shores. When they were commanded to prepare a lūʻau for the subjects of Kamehamehaʻailūʻau, the people pounded the ʻauhuhu plant used to stun fish and mixed it with the sweet potato poi served at the feast. All of Kamehamehaʻailūʻau's people died except his steward, who lived to tell the tale and spread the reputation of Molokaʻi Pule Oʻo.[81]

According to Sarah Kalima, "Molokaʻi I Ka Oʻo Lāʻau" was yet another famous saying. It referred to the poles used to steer and propel canoes through the shallow waters of the reef that extends over a mile from Manaʻe's shore. "Molokaʻi Kuʻi Lāʻau" referred to the kuʻi hula step that was reputed to have originated on the island.

Regarding the place-names of Molokaʻi, Waldemar Duvauchelle and Zellie Duvauchelle Sherwood each shared the story of how loulu palms started to grow on the small island off Wailau. A young chief successfully used the broad leaves of the loulu to fly from the cliffs above Wailau to the island in order to win the hand of the ruling chief's daughter in marriage. Ever since that time loulu palms grew on the small island. They also both told the story of Keana-puhi, the ocean cave at Wailau that is large enough to accommodate a forty- or fifty-foot sampan. The guardian of the cave fought with and defeated a Shark God on that side of the island. Anapuhi forced the Shark God to guarantee that no human would be attacked by a shark in the waters between Wailau and Hālawa. There is no record of anyone ever having been attacked by a shark in the ocean there.[82]

Sarah Kalima explained how the stones for building the ʻOpeahina fishpond and the ʻIliʻiliʻōpae heiau were carried over the mountains from Wailau. She said that one can hear the music of those who built the fishpond and the heiau on the night of the Kāne moon. The menehune builders play the ʻūkēkē and the drum on those nights. According to Kalima, the guardian of Hono-uliwai is the shark ʻaumakua Kauhuhu, who eats only human wrongdoers. She talked of Ka Puʻu Neʻe o Hāʻupu, the hill that was lifted up by a turtle until it was killed by a supernatural man.[83]

Zellie Sherwood shared her version of how the prophet Lanikaula was killed by the jealous kahuna of Lānaʻi, who burned and prayed over Lanikaula's excrement. He was buried by his sons in his famous kukui grove above Hālawa. She remembers seeing the grave when she was young, before the area was bulldozed.[84]

Tollefson, Kaopuiki, and Poaha all talked of the kioea sea bird, which frequents the reefs and shore off Manaʻe. They spoke of this bird as "Ka manu kahea i ka lawaiʻa" (the bird that calls to the fishermen). It was believed that when the birds called out it was time to put out the canoes and go fishing. The bird was migratory and frequented Manaʻe during the kona wind season, which coincided with good fishing conditions.[85]

Grace Hagerman said that she often heard and saw spirits. As a child she remembered hearing the *huaka'ipō* or night marchers. She shared a story about going fishing in a pond, not knowing that she had begun to menstruate. She felt a creeping sensation in one cheek, then felt her hair being yanked, and suddenly realized that going into the pond in her condition had offended the spirit guardian of the pond.[86]

It seemed natural to Mitchell Pau'ole that they experienced problems with caterpillars in the area of Pu'u Pe'elua or Caterpillar Hill. According to legend, a supernatural caterpillar that could turn into a man was burned alive by the family of the woman he had married. In the fire he burst into hundreds of caterpillars, and to this day there are many caterpillars in that area.[87]

Both Waldemar Duvauchelle of Puko'o and Daniel Naki of Waialua recalled that akule stopped frequenting the ocean between Puko'o and Waialua for nineteen to twenty years prior to the time they were interviewed in 1961. Duvauchelle explained how the akule disappeared after an old man had used a *kū'ula* stone, or Hawaiian Fishing God stone, to pray for the fish to come into Puko'o. One day there were so many fish, they couldn't catch all of them fast enough. The fish began to die off for lack of oxygen in the water. The people tried to chase the fish out of the pond, but many still died. Since that day, no akule returned to Puko'o, and Duvauchelle had not seen any akule from the time he was young until 1961. The kū'ula stone disappeared after the old man died.[88]

Naki attributed the disappearance of the fish to problems between the fishermen. According to him, the fishermen kept grumbling among themselves, wishing each other bad luck, and the fish could hear this. One day the fish simply disappeared. According to Naki, no fish were seen in the area for nineteen years.[89]

It is evident that the native informants who spent the early years of their life on Moloka'i between 1900 and 1930 lived as close to the land and ocean as their ancestors had prior to the arrival of Cook. They continued to live upon the lands of their ancestors and to cultivate taro, sweet potatoes, bananas, sugar cane, and so on. However, even in the remote districts, they had better tools and equipment available to them, such as iron rather than wooden 'ō'ō, hoes, shovels, and saws. Also, unlike their pre-contact ancestors, they cultivated the land as much for commercial enterprise as for household use. They also grew a variety of introduced cash crops and foreign plants for home consumption and for sale.

The Moloka'i Hawaiians continued to fish the fishponds, the mountain streams, and the ocean as their ancestors had done in ancient times. In most cases they drew upon knowledge acquired from their elders about the habits and habitats of the fish as well as the ocean and its daily and seasonal changes. Although they used similar methods of fishing, they also used better boats, tools, and equipment such as motorized boats, nylon nets, snorkels, and goggles.[90] In hunting, there were more introduced animals and fowl than had been available prior to European contact, and methods of hunting had changed under foreign influence as well.

Despite being punished in school for speaking Hawaiian, children continued to speak the mother language in households that were composed of the ʻohana.[91] This was the case in Manaʻe as well as the windward valleys. Within the ʻohana, many generations lived together, and thus the young continued to learn the Hawaiian language and traditions from their grandparents and elders.

Finally, Hawaiians often expressed their love and appreciation for the land in chants and songs. Songs about places often explained the history and traditions connected with selected districts, serving to record the significance of important and sacred places. The song "Nani Hālawa," written by David Kalaʻau and sung for Mary Kawena Pukui by Same K. Enos, recounts the significance of various districts of Molokaʻi:

Nani Hālawa Waiho mai	Beautiful Hālawa lay out there
Me ka wailele o Moaʻula	With the Moaʻula waterfall
Wai kau mai i ka pali	Water suspended there on the cliff
Wai kaulana o ka ʻāina	Famous water of the land
Kaulana Waialua ka hela i ka laʻi	Famous Waialua spread out calmly, peacefully
Kehakeha i ka uka o Pakaikai	Proudly standing in the upland of Pakaikai
Ilaila ʻohu ʻoi loua nui	There in the thick fog
Home noho a ka lani mehameha	Home lived by the chief Kamehamehaʻailūʻau
Kaulana Kainalu i ka ʻehu a ke kai	Famous Kainalu in the spray of the sea
Me ka wai huʻi koni o ka wai kapu	With the cold tingling water of the sacred water
Ilaila hoʻi au i ʻike i iho ai	There, indeed, I came to know
I ke ʻala o ka līpoa	The fragrance of the līpoa limu[92]

Unlike the families of East Molokaʻi, change was the dominant pattern of life between 1900 and 1930 for the Hansen's disease patients at Kalawao-

Kalaupapa and the areas where the Hawaiian Homes Commission sponsored settlements beginning in 1922.

Kalaupapa and Kalawao

In 1900 there were 1,177 people in the settlement. By 1910 this number had decreased to 785, of whom 624, or 80 percent, were Native Hawaiian. By 1920 the population at Kalawao had decreased to 667, of whom 589, or 88 percent, were Native Hawaiian. By 1930 there were only 605 residents at Kalaupapa, of whom 400, or 66 percent, were Native Hawaiian.

Life in Kalaupapa between 1900 and 1930 was a vast improvement over the days when Father Damien ministered to the basic needs of the exiles. Board of Health services and programs steadily expanded during this period with support from the U.S. federal government. The patients led active lives—socially, physically, and politically. Yet they still suffered the pain of being separated from family and loved ones, bore the shame of general social ostracism, and endured long-term physical deterioration from Hansen's disease.[93] According to a Hawaiian male patient who had gone to Kalaupapa in 1920: "We are like people anyplace else. We love, marry, drink, murder, commit suicide, fight. We have all the human drama. We are everything you are on the outside. Just like that—life is life."[94]

From 1900 through 1929 the residents of Kalaupapa formed social clubs and participated in church activities. There were six churches in Kalaupapa during this period—two Protestant, two Catholic, and two Latter-Day Saints (Mormon). The Kalaupapa Settlement had assembly halls, a bandstand, a race track, a baseball field, shooting ranges, athletic clubs, debating societies, two small brass bands, and glee clubs.

In 1908 a children's nursery for the healthy infants of afflicted parents was opened at Puahi at the base of the pali that leads out of Kalaupapa. Parents were allowed to visit their children on Wednesdays and Sundays if they received a permit. A Hawaiian who lived at Kalaupapa for sixty-seven years explained how painful it was to be separated from his children after they were born to him and his wife:

> You know, the babies that were born inside here were not allowed to stay with their parents. After the babies were born, the law said they had to be taken away to the baby nursery in Kalaupapa . . . We would try to keep the babies as long as we could, but most times, we kept them only until morn-

ing. Then we would carry them to the nursery . . . They allowed the children to live one year inside Kalaupapa nursery. There we could see them only through thick glass, but no can touch! Then after one year, they were removed. They were either hanai by family members, or "issued" out for adoption by the Board of Health.

It was so hard to give up your children like that . . . they never took good care of them, yet they would not let us care for our own children, even when we knew they were sick. It was hard. You love them, and then they are taken away, just like we were taken away.[95]

Nevertheless, such a policy was necessary to protect the health of the child and was ultimately in the interest of the parents as well. An alternate policy would have been mandatory sterilization of the patients, which would have denied the patients their right to have offspring at all.

Residents of Kalaupapa caught fish to supplement their food rations. Under the sponsorship and supervision of the Board of Health, they raised livestock; ran a dairy until the drought of 1909; operated a poi factory, a laundry, a saw mill, a slaughterhouse, and an ice-making plant; and raised crops, including taro, sorghum, alfalfa, pumpkins, and papayas. Those who worked in these enterprises were paid wages by the territorial government. In 1901 a resident opened a private store at Kalaupapa. In 1902 a dry goods store and a grocery store opened at Kalawao. A bakery and a fish market opened in 1904. In 1905 a Hui Hoʻoʻikaika Kino (Group to Develop Strong Bodies) contracted with the Board of Health to cultivate all available land in Puahi in taro. One-third of the output was to go to the board, and two-thirds could be sold at market rates.[96]

In 1930 a committee appointed by the governor, Lawrence M. Judd, to study Hansen's disease made a number of recommendations that, when implemented, marked the end of an era for Kalaupapa. The pivotal recommendation was the second one: "The adoption of a policy whereby there would be no further involuntary transfers of patients to Kalaupapa." This ended the policy of punitive segregation of Hansen's disease patients and ended Kalaupapa's stigma as a penal institution. The committee recommended improvements at Kalaupapa totaling $200,000. It also recommended improvements at the Kalihi Hospital in order to accommodate a total of 350 patients. Land acquisition and improvements at Kalihi were to cost $375,000.[97]

According to the report, there were 760 known cases of Hansen's disease in Hawaiʻi as of June 30, 1930. Moreover, the number of those afflicted had averaged 760 since 1910, with the number of deaths from Hansen's and the number of new cases being relatively equal.[98]

The committee felt strongly that hospitalization was the most effective way to control the spread of Hansen's disease but recognized that efforts to institutionalize the patients at Kalaupapa would "result in failure from lack of cooperation on the part of the inmates, and would create a hiatus of mental unrest, something that should be carefully avoided." For that reason, they recommended no additional transfers to Kalaupapa and a concentration of expanded health-care facilities at the Kalihi hospital.[99]

Nevertheless, an extensive program to rehabilitate and revitalize the facilities at Kalaupapa and to construct new facilities for water and electricity was initiated in 1931. The legislature appropriated $400,000 in 1931 for public works projects at the settlement and an additional $200,000 in 1932. According to the Judd Committee report, these improvements were aimed at adding to the happiness of the patients and their dependents. The policies Judd initiated marked the beginning of a new era in the Kalaupapa settlement.[100]

In ending this overview of the conditions in Kalawao from 1900 through 1930, I would like to close with the observations of a blind, disabled Hawaiian who was among the last to be involuntarily banished to Kalaupapa in 1930. He reflects the pride and dignity that the victims of Hansen's disease upheld in spite of their lifelong suffering and affliction. He also describes the reliance and love that the patients developed for each other as an 'ohana:

> No, I'm not bitter about this disease. I have been here at Kalaupapa since I was twelve. Maybe I'm lucky. I never think about it too much. I get three square meals a day here. I get care from the nuns and the nurses. I have my talking books and I listen to my big band music . . . Like the other patients, they caught me at school. It was on the Big Island. I was twelve then. I cried like the dickens for my mother and for my family . . . They sent me to Honolulu, the Kalihi Receiving Station, real fast. Then they sent me to Kalaupapa. That's where they sent most of us. Most came to die. So, I stay here . . . Me, I've got the heart problem and stomach ulcers. I'm blind and I can't walk. Then I get side effects from the sulfone drug medicine. Still, maybe I'm lucky. In Kalaupapa, we are all in the same boat; we help one another. We are one family, all the same, with love in our heart . . . with aloha for each other. Oh, we fight between ourselves, like in any family, but we are all in it together here. There is no where else for us to go.[101]

In 1941 sulfone drugs were shown to effectively treat and arrest the disease, and after treatment patients who so chose could reintegrate into society. For most, however, Kalaupapa was their place and their home. They chose to live out their lives at the settlement with others who had become ʻohana to them.

Hawaiian Homesteading: ʻĀina Hoʻopulapula

In 1921 the Hawaiian Homes Commission was established by the U.S. Congress through the efforts of the Aha Hui Puʻuhonua o Nā Hawaiʻi, the territorial legislature, and Hawaiʻi's delegate to Congress, Prince Jonah Kūhiō Kalanianaʻole. The purpose of the commission was to manage and administer 200,000 acres of the original Crown and government lands of the Kingdom of Hawaiʻi for the rehabilitation of Native Hawaiians who were of half or more Native Hawaiian ancestry. The lands were to be leased out as agricultural homesteads for ninety-nine years for $1 a year.

The first commissioners included the governor of Hawaiʻi, Wallace R. Farrington, and his four appointees—Kalanianaʻole, Akaiko Akana, Rudolph Duncan, and George Cooke.[102] During the first five years of the program, operations were to be experimental and limited to Molokaʻi lands and selected tracts on Hawaiʻi island. In 1922, the Hawaiian Homes Program was established on Molokaʻi, where it continued for another eight years. The commission brought together Hawaiians from all of the major islands to start a new community that would revitalize the Hawaiian people. They selected applicants who were at least half Hawaiian in ancestry, had an aptitude for farm work, and were of good character.

The homesteaders who settled on Molokaʻi came from Honolulu, rural Oʻahu, Maui, Hawaiʻi, Kauaʻi, and Molokaʻi. The men had worked as stevedores, laborers, farmers, carpenters, engineers, mechanics, truck or tractor drivers, foremen or superintendents, clerks or salesmen, firefighters, and mail carriers. The settlers also included a dentist, a fisherman, a cowboy, a blacksmith, a welder, a boilermaker, a plasterer, and a music instructor. The women were primarily homemakers, but there were also a trained nurse and a hotel cafeteria worker among them. They were Mormon, Catholic, and Protestant. Some had graduated from the Kamehameha Schools, and some had only sixth-grade educations. Some were fortunate enough to have moved with their brothers and sisters to Molokaʻi, but the majority were unrelated to one another.

The lands allotted to the Hawaiian Homes Commission on Moloka'i were second-class pastoral lands. In 1918 they were valued at $1 per acre, and the government had rented them out for 5 cents an acre.[103] On the positive side, the Moloka'i lands consisted of deep-red fertile soil. From September through February, the wet season, there was enough rain to grow crops without irrigation. Thus, Moloka'i's primary growing season coincided with the winter season, when mainland-grown vegetables and fruits were usually scarce in Hawai'i markets. The pineapple plantation camps and the Moloka'i Ranch provided an accessible local market for fresh produce and animal feed. The Honolulu market was only sixty miles away by ocean. However, the Moloka'i lands also had serious drawbacks. They lacked sufficient water for domestic use throughout the year and for growing during the dry season from March through August. Strong winds blew across them throughout the year, and they were infested with pests and diseases.[104]

In November 1921 the commissioners toured all the Moloka'i lands allotted to them with their agricultural experts and engineers. They selected the coastal flats at Kalama'ula as the location for the first homesteading settlement and chose plots at Kala'e, Malehua, and Kalama'ula for demonstration farm projects.[105]

Beginning in January 1922 commission engineers and agriculturalists surveyed the land, constructed roads, and developed water for irrigation and domestic use from the Waihi'i spring and other springs in Kalama'ula. The Kalama'ula lands were subdivided into twenty-three lots and a 2,100-acre community pasture. By the time that homesteaders were ready to move in, a storage dam and two 10,000-gallon storage tanks were constructed to provide 2.5 million gallons a day from the spring and the well.[106]

In January 1922, before any homesteaders were on the land, the first demonstration farm was started at Kala'e in upper Kalama'ula. The Commission planted Guam corn and New Era pigeon peas and raised chickens. The plot was located on an exposed, windswept hillside. During the first growing season, rainfall was below average—the season was the driest since the drought of 1908—and there was no equipment to cultivate the crop after the initial planting. Nevertheless, the demonstration project succeeded in producing 400 sacks of corn from fifteen acres and a large crop of pigeon peas from two acres. The project also hatched and raised 500 chickens.[107]

The demonstration farm at lower Kalama'ula was located on an old swamp. The soil packed easily and, without irrigation, was inclined to bake into large, tough blocks. The commission planted alfalfa, sweet potatoes, beans, corn, and

Figure 31 Kapuaiwa Coconut Grove is in the heart of Kalamaʻula, where the first Hawaiian homesteads were established on Molokaʻi. Circa 1920s. Tai Sing Loo, Bishop Museum.

vegetables.[108] As soon as the homesteaders moved onto the land, the demonstration project was phased out in favor of having the settlers carry out the trial work on their own land in consultation with the commission's experts.[109]

The third demonstration farm in Malehua experimented in pineapples and forage crops for fattening of livestock. Initially it was planted in corn, and then, beginning in 1923, pineapples were grown. Eventually it too was phased out.[110]

By February 1923 thirteen homesteaders were on their lots and hard at work.[111] Homesteaders cut down the kiawe trees covering their land and burned all the brush. The commission assisted them by pulling out the tree stumps with a tractor. After the land was cleared, the homesteaders plowed their lots using commission equipment.[112] Homesteaders lived in tents and makeshift shelters for a short period while building permanent homes on their lands. They worked from daybreak to nightfall to build their homes, clear their land, and plow and plant it. They called Kalamaʻula's homesteading area Kalaniana‘ole Settlement, in honor of Prince Jonah Kūhiō Kalaniana‘ole, who had been instrumental in getting the U.S. Congress to establish the Hawaiian Homes Commission and who had passed away on January 7, 1922. By the end of the first year, in 1923, the commission filed a report:

> There are present (February 11th) 13 homesteaders on the ground and actually at work. With the exception of the greater part of the clearing, they are doing their own work. All are enthusiastic, working hard, and from present indications, bound to succeed. Men, women and children all work. For the majority, time, such as eight or ten hour days, matters little. They lead the regular farmer's life—sunup to sundown. Pending the final clearing of the low lands, and the completion of the flume line, many have cleared portions of their rocky upper lands.[113]

By summer 1924 the Hawaiian homesteaders were harvesting sweet potatoes, watermelons, corn, cucumbers, bananas, tomatoes, and alfalfa. Homestead tomatoes controlled the Honolulu market. A net return of nearly $2,000 was made from a field of two and a half acres. The alfalfa yielded one ton per acre and brought in $30 to $35 a ton when baled. Homesteaders were able to produce ten alfalfa crops a year and thus earn $300 to $350 per acre, per year. At the same time they raised 835 hogs and 2,308 chickens. There were 127 head of cattle on the homesteads, 114 horses, 17 mules, and a few goats, raised on an experimental basis. The project was hailed as the "Molokaʻi Miracle."[114]

Expanding upon the successful homesteading experience at Kalamaʻula, the commission opened the Palaʻau-Hoʻolehua area for homesteading in 1924. Seventy-five families settled in Hoʻolehua between 1924 and 1926, eight went in 1928, and forty-eight arrived in 1929.[115]

The Hoʻolehua families planted large quantities of corn, pumpkins, melons, tomatoes, cucumbers, sweet potatoes, squash, and peanuts to sell. They also raised vegetables for home consumption such as beans, onions, and cabbage, as well as livestock.[116] Farming at Hoʻolehua was difficult owing to high winds, several droughts, and infestation with pests and blights. It required a substantial financial outlay and constant care, including spraying. Marketing of the crops was also problematic.[117] However, the progress they made was impressive.

In September 1926 the Maui County Evangelical Association held its semi-annual meeting at Kaluaʻaha, Molokaʻi. Henry Judd, editor of *The Friend*, reported favorably on the progress they observed at Kalamaʻula and Hoʻolehua:

> To those who had been acquainted with Molokaʻi as it was a few years ago, it was also a new experience to witness the transformation that has been wrought both on the makai lands, where a large area formerly in kiawe forest is now under active cultivation, and on the mauka lands, where old pasturage is now being plowed up, houses erected and vigorous efforts being made to establish the eighty-two homesteaders in a successful venture in farming.
>
> Away from the deleterious influence of the slums of Honolulu, Hilo and other crowded places, located on the broad acres of Molokai's rich fields, there is every chance for the Hawaiian people to come into their own, to revive the old traditions of farming practiced on the island of Molokai itself as well as on other islands of the group.
>
> To one who had not visited Molokai for four years, it was a revelation to observe the great amount of hard work that has been done in both sections of this rehabilitation project. It will continue to be an object of much interest to this observer and will be watched with the confident hope that success will crown the efforts of the Hawaiian people themselves to be rehabilitated in body, mind and estate and—most important of all—in spiritual life and power.[118]

Gertrude and Mitchell Pauʻole, who moved to Hoʻolehua from Honolulu in 1925, were interviewed in 1961 by Mary Kawena Pukui about their pioneering efforts at Hoʻolehua. Gertrude Pauʻole shared the following experiences about leaving Honolulu and settling at Hoʻolehua:

> We came on the ship, *Likelike* in 1925, January. We left on the 6th. We got here on the 7th. If we didn't work hard . . . no more nothing. We don't see meat. We don't see apple. My children eat the tomato and the cucumber as fruits. We grow the pumpkin and fix poi. I had to put on one stocking, two stocking and three stocking. Cold this place. No more nothing. Just lantana and māniania. And we had a one by twelve.
>
> When we left Honolulu we sold all my things. The money we used to buy food—palaoa, sugar and all those things. Hard to buy food here . . . because he wasn't working. After he found work it was $59 a month. We had a quarter acre head cabbage, peanuts, watermelon. We lived on the peanuts. We bagged them up and stored them in the warehouse and when we want food we go to the store and sell them. $15 a bag . . . that's plenty.
>
> No irrigation—just depend on the rain. We had forty acres. Just like you gamble. You plant. If the rain gonna fall then all right. No rain, you lose all what you had.[119]

In 1926 Hoʻolehua homesteaders entered into contracts with Libby, McNeill & Libby to plant pineapples on homesteaders' land. Planting of pineapples began in 1927, and the first crop was harvested in 1929. Initially, the planting of pineapples proceeded in conjunction with the cultivation of other crops. In 1927–28 the homesteaders harvested 42 tons of sweet corn, 2 tons of peanuts, 200 tons of field corn, 22 tons of tomatoes, 22 tons of pumpkins, 13 tons of watermelon, 3 tons of cantaloupes, 6 tons of Irish potatoes, 2 tons of cucumbers, and 2 tons of sweet potatoes. They collectively grossed $13,670 from that harvest.[120] However, the trend of growing pineapples under a plantation system, in conjunction with the major pineapple corporations—Libby, McNeill & Libby and California Pineapple Company—was a development that eventually replaced diversified agricultural enterprise on individual plots.

The reasons for turning to large-scale pineapple production were understandable and primarily related to the harsh natural conditions, especially the lack of water from rainfall or irrigation. The spring water from Kamehameha V Spring at Kalamaʻula had a high salt content. When the water evaporated, large amounts of salt remained in the soil. By 1930 the soil at Kalamaʻula was unfit for raising crops. The settlers there asked for lots in Hoʻolehua where they could have pineapple grown under contract to the pineapple companies, and their request was granted in 1931. Also, pests had increasingly become a major problem in the homesteaders' crops. These conditions made it difficult to predict yields and therefore prevented homesteaders from entering into contracts that could have assured systematic and profitable marketing of their crops. Prices for produce often fluctuated depending on the supply. At times the return was barely enough to cover the costs of production.[121] These problems were summarized by a commission employee for Felix Keesing, who conducted a study of homesteading on Molokaʻi in 1935 for the territorial legislature:

> We cannot tell what produce the homesteaders are going to have in this
> climate, hence cannot enter into any contracts in Honolulu. Our inability
> to anticipate the yield, found out by bitter experience, is the key to our
> marketing troubles. Where homesteaders have quit producing, it has not
> been their lack of interest, but rather the uncertainty of getting a return.[122]

In light of these difficulties, pineapple production provided a welcome alternative to diversified agriculture for the Hawaiian homesteaders of Molokaʻi. The contract guaranteed $23 per ton of harvested pineapples. In 1929, fifty-four homesteaders earned $32.30 per ton of harvested pineapple, for a total of $121,902 or an average of $2,257 per family. In 1930, sixty-two families earned $303,059 or an average of $4,888.[123]

Most of the homesteaders felt that if it were not for the pineapples, they would not have been able to meet their financial obligations or earn a living on their homesteads. The pineapple crop brought in a substantial income for the homesteaders during the depression years. Prior to the pineapple contracts, homesteaders had begun to seek outside employment as a dependable source of income while they struggled to keep up with the care of their crops. The pineapple crops kept the homestead land in active and profitable agricultural production.[124]

In the initial years, when the pineapple was planted on individual plots of land on a rotation basis in checkerboard fashion, many of the homesteaders weeded and cared for the crop on their individual lot. However, beginning in 1931 the block system was used to plant the pineapple in order to reduce labor costs and infestation by mealy bugs. At that point the majority of homesteaders hired Korean and Filipino workers to care for their portion of the crop, or they opted to pay the plantation work gangs to do it. By 1936 nearly all the Kalanianaʻole settlers worked their pineapple lands, but only a few of the

Hoʻolehua settlers did so. According to Keesing, the pineapple contracts provided the homesteaders and the companies with mutual benefits. The companies were given use of good land without having to pay rent or taxes, and the homesteaders received credit, expert management training, and assured market, and an immediate financial return for work done.[125]

In an interview with Pukui in 1961, Harry Hanakahi explained why the homesteaders turned to the farming of pineapples:

> We built our home. We paid 5 percent interest on $3,000 loan to build a house. We paid big interest. But we had hoʻomanawanui til the pineapple came. If no pineapple, we would have quit the land. They ain't going to live on that land there. No water. Dry land. They would have quit.
>
> We planted alfalfa. Planted tomatoes. Then nobody buy in Honolulu. Was not in demand. What we going do. People don't know how to pick. Some only half ripe, some too ripe. Then, were not in demand over there. What we going do? The Commission tell us, your tomatoes are rotten, you can't get nothing. We got discouraged. We raised 200 pigs. Everybody have pig. Then plague came—pneumonia. All wipe us out. Dying everyday.[126]

Gertrude Pauʻole explained to Pukui how they spent the money that they received from the first pineapple crop: "When we had the first pineapple money we paid all our debts. We didn't buy radio, we didn't buy one thing. Only we looked first was kaukau [food] because hard to get food here. Was hard, but the children enjoy—always happy."[127] Mitchell Pauʻole described why they decided to plant pineapples and what they did with subsequent pineapple earnings:

> Our life here was very difficult. But we had the hope that some day our condition would be improved. And during the year 1927 the question of using our land for pineapple planting was then discussed. And it was during that time that those homesteaders here went into planting pineapple and in 1929, those who went in planting pineapple got their first earning in 1929. The earning that we earned then, not like what we earning today. The earning then ran into the thousands of thousands of dollars. And because of that, we had our first earning, then the condition was made much better. Our extension and the furniture were bought with those earnings, in cash.[128]

In 1927, after the five-year experimental period the U.S. Congress had established had passed, the territorial legislature conducted an investigation into homesteading at Kalamaʻula and Hoʻolehua. The *Honolulu Advertiser* sent a reporter to accompany the Senate committee that inspected the Molokaʻi homesteads. His article was printed in March:

> Molokai homesteaders ask for nothing more than an even chance to make good on the lands that they have taken up under the terms of the Hawaiian rehabilitation scheme. They make no exorbitant demands—only a request for adequate water that they may irrigate their land and grow crops with which to conduct a profitable farming business. They are happy and contented now despite the fact that the year 1926 brought but 12 to 19 inches of rainfall on Molokai and consequently, without artificial irrigation, the way was beset with many difficulties and setback. The project is a success and will repay the territory a hundred-fold once conditions are created that will give these ambitious sons and daughters of the soil an even chance to make good at their new profession.[129]

The territorial senators were impressed with the hard work and perseverance of the Hawaiian homesteaders, who worked cooperatively with each other for the overall success of the project. Homesteaders frankly recounted the hardships they had endured during the drought of 1926. For example, Kenneth Auld, a graduate of Punahou and the University of Hawaiʻi who settled his family at Hoʻolehua, explained how he and his family had struggled to save two acres during the dry spell and manage to break even. Despite feeling discouraged, he and his family decided that they would be patient: "Everyone here is happy and hopeful. I am confident that in five years we will be in a permanently sound condition."[130] Although actual progress from a strictly agricultural standpoint had been limited by the unfavorable climate, the territorial senators were nevertheless encouraged by the sight of whole families working together, tilling the soil, side by side, for the success of their own farms. Before the regular session of 1927 adjourned, the territorial legislature passed Joint Resolution no. 1, which declared the experiment to be a success and requested the Secretary of the Interior to approve the activities of the commission and to extend the work of the commission to all of its designated lands on all of the islands.[131]

In April 1927 the Secretary of the Interior, Hubert Work, toured Molokaʻi to assess the progress of the Hawaiian Homes Commission for the U.S. federal government. Impressed with the progress of the homesteaders, he urged Congress to approve and expand the commission's work. Through the joint efforts of Work; Victor Houston, Hawaiʻi's delegate to Congress; and Governor Wallace R. Farrington, Congress voted to extend the work of the commission and passed amendments to the Hawaiian Homes Commission Act that were signed by President Calvin Coolidge on March 7, 1928.[132]

Mitchell Pauʻole proudly described the welcome given by the homesteaders to the Secretary of the Interior:

> After the first five years, this homestead project was then declared a success. The Secretary of Interior, Mr. Work made a trip to Molokaʻi with commissioners who were then on board. We brought what we had planted as a hoʻokupu. So he saw what we really had done with those five years. Sugar cane and everything you can think of. Each one of the homesteaders brought. We presented a hoʻokupu to him at the homestead office. And it was then that it was declared a success.[133]

The Homestead Commission's report to the 1931 legislature pointed to general social and economic indicators of its success. It noted that from 1910 through 1930 the numbers of Hawaiians increased from 36,000 to 43,000. Savings deposits of Hawaiians during the same period increased from $232,329 to $2,339,000. Personal property of Hawaiians also increased from $1,259,000 to $2,669,000.[134]

Reports about the Hawaiian Homesteading Program on Molokaʻi up through 1930 continued to be favorable and supportive despite criticisms from certain planter interests that had opposed the establishment of the program in the first place. One such report was published in a six-part series in the *Star-Bulletin* from October 4, 1930, through October 10, 1930. The articles were written by Wallace R. Farrington, a former governor and chairman of the Hawaiian Homes Commission who was publisher of the *Star-Bulletin* in 1930. Farrington first visited the Kalanianaʻole Settlement and was impressed with the perseverance of these pioneer homesteaders:

> Here the Hawaiians under the Hawaiian Homes law, demonstrated what they could do. They did well. A long and interesting story could be told of their struggles. Some of them are not through struggling, but the good work of keeping up the homes and the small farms is going on.
>
> These people have the largest number of problems to meet of any that have gone on the land under the Hawaiian Homes law. Some have proved that they can make a success of the diversified farming, raising chickens and doing general truck gardening that is most adaptable to the land on this lower level. Others have suffered discouragement and gained much experi-

ence. All, however, are keeping up their places, maintaining their families, and they look well and happy, despite the fact that they are not in the class with the larger financiers of the Hoolehua pineapple section.[135]

At Hoʻolehua Farrington was most impressed with the hard work performed by the women, whom he considered to be the backbone of the homesteads. According to Farrington, the women not only bore the children and did the heavy housework, they also went into the fields and worked next to the men and were not embarassed to wear old clothes. He commented, "I do not recall a single report of extraordinary expenditures of new wealth, where the women of the family have been referred to as the ones who are luxuriously spending much of the money."[136]

In his articles, Farrington addressed rumors and criticisms that he had frequently heard. One such criticism was that the homesteaders worked in outside jobs rather than solely on their farms. Farrington defended that practice:

> Because some of these people are engaged in other activities than their farms, an occasional inquirer comes along to say that they are not homesteaders. It is hard to understand, however, why anyone should complain if, for instance, one of these homesteaders finds employment as wharfinger at Kaunakakai, a very important position. Another finds employment as territorial game warden. Another teaches school. The women folk of these families stay at home and look after the garden and the crop, and the children. The men of the family are capable in their position. Someone must do the work they are doing. Kaunakakai is growing, the pineapple industry is making a very busy center of the south side of the island. It seems entirely reasonable and proper that homesteaders who are equipped to fill positions on the wharf, or elsewhere, or even in the supervision of road construction, should take this work while the members of their families are carrying on the small farm at home.[137]

Farrington challenged those who promoted the notion that homesteaders did not work. He acknowledged that the Hawaiian homesteaders were not experts in growing pineapple and that some worked harder than others. However, he pointed out that in any group of people it was normal for some to work harder than others. The most important fact was that a high percentage of women and children, boys and girls, worked in the fields: "Men and women have the clean, hard hands that can only be made by hard toil."[138]

How homesteaders handled their pineapple profits was another focal point of criticism. Charges of wasteful spending on "luxuries" such as automobiles or trucks and investments into risky businesses were frequently made. In defense of the homesteaders, Farrington wrote:

> Frequent reference is made to the unusual luxuries bought by these people. I doubt if they buy any more of the unusual things than do the general run of humanity.
>
> If you have wanted some particular thing all your life, and after years of hard work you have enough money to buy it, what do you do?
>
> If you have been foolish at some time in your buying career, should you be too critical when others show about the same percentage of folly as yourself? [139]

As to investments in uncertain business ventures, Farrington seemed to think that the homesteaders had been persuaded to invest in the Hawaii Lumber Company by some very experienced salesmen. They had also followed the unwise leadership of one of the agricultural experts of the commission, who had invested $2,000 in the company. He felt certain, however, that they had learned not to invest in new, high-risk businesses:

> The gist of this new education is that it usually pays a little fellow, who has not time to study up on the details of the prospects, to stay out of new corporations. Usually, a new corporation has to go through a period of experience, mistakes and troubles that are the result of competition, adjustment of new personnel, lack of organization and a multitude of other things that absorb money but do not pay dividends to the stockholders. So the prospect seems fair that as some of the homesteaders are rather anxious to get out of the Hawaii Lumber Co., they will also be slow in taking up with cooperative enterprises that are experiments. [140]

Farrington was also impressed with the Pioneer Day lū'au. The celebration had been postponed for a month because the homesteaders were too busy harvesting their crops. He made special note of the fact that no intoxicating liquor was consumed and that the party was a wholesome family affair despite the fact that the pineapple checks had just been distributed on the previous night.

Overall, Farrington's assessment of Ho'olehua was summed up in the fifth article of his series:

> If Hoolehua is not a place where real human, spiritual and material values of great worth exist and are being renewed and further developed, I do not

know where an American community can be found that will fill such a qualification.

The critics may complain all they please and the doubtful ones may be as dubious as they like, the fact remains that these people have prosperous homes, they are at work, they are learning to be more skilled in agriculture, they are interested, they are taking care of their children, they are behaving themselves as well as average humanity and a good sight better than many of the critics. They are growing in health, happiness and good citizenship. If that is not a good investment I do not know what is.[141]

The turning point in the Hawaiian Homesteading Program on Molokaʻi came in 1931. By that time pineapple had taken firm root on the homestead lots, the first pineapple checks had been received, and homesteaders were bound to ten-year contracts. At that point, the block planting program was initiated to arrest the infestation of the crops by insects and diseases. In 1931, homesteaders raised public charges that the Hawaiian Homes Commission had mismanaged their affairs and exposed them to exploitation from salesmen and creditors. In response to these charges, Governor Lawrence Judd appointed a special commission to investigate the complaints and criticisms against the Hawaiian Homes Commission and to make recommendations on how to improve management of the program.[142]

The special committee was chaired by Princess Abigail Kawananakoa and made up of Charles Chillingworth, Lang Akana, John C. Lane, and Oscar P. Cox. They visited the homesteads, talked with the settlers, held public meetings to discuss the problems, and studied the records and reports of the commission. In its final report the committee charged the Hawaiian Homes Commission with failure to guide the homesteaders and claimed that: (1) homesteaders were being exploited, (2) no supervision or advice was being provided on modern methods to protect and conserve the pineapple fields, (3) the commission lacked interest in the program, (4) there was no spirit of comradeship and fellowship between the commission and the homesteaders, (5) one commissioner had not attended meetings for a year, and (6) the commission had spent more money on the community hall than was necessary.

The committee recommended that the rehabilitation program be extended to those Hawaiian homelands being leased to non-settlers. It also recommended that the Kalanianaʻole settlers be allowed to take up leaseholds in the upper pineapple lands while retaining a residence lot at Kalanianaʻole. In addition, the committee suggested that homesteaders be allowed more than sixty head of cattle in the community pasture, where a paddock system would be introduced. The committee also recommended that homesteaders be put on a budget. Finally, the committee sought removal of the executive secretary and the agriculturalist for not performing their duties.[143] The response to and implementation of the committee's report was left to the commission, which adopted some but not all of the recommendations as policy.

By 1936 the pineapple payments were distributed through the commission, which provided advice to the homesteaders on how to budget their income to steadily pay off debts over time as well as to maintain enough income for immediate family expenses.[144]

Kamaʻāina O Molokaʻi

On the homesteads, the holdings were spaced far apart and did not engender a feeling of community. Nevertheless, the homesteaders shared what little they had with one another and developed new social networks. Felix Keesing quotes one of the old-timers as telling him: "When we came there were just a few houses. There were no autos or pineapples and only a trail to Kaunakakai. We all lived together like one big family. What was yours was mine and mine yours with no thought of pay. Now that is lost. When the big money came the friendship between us broke. Everyone is now for himself."[145]

Mitchell and Gertrude Pauʻole also recalled the sharing and help given to one another during the early days of the settlement. Because they helped each other in their time of need, the homesteaders considered each other sisters and brothers. Gertrude Pauʻole said, "We call each other brother or aunty until today. So that is the happiness of the homestead here."[146]

Homestead life was not all work and struggle. Among the recreational activities enjoyed by the homesteaders were planting flower gardens, automobile drives, horseback riding, pool, volleyball, baseball, and orchestras. The whole community gathered together to celebrate May Day, Kūhiō Day, Labor Day, and an annual fair.[147] In 1927 the commission renovated a barn to use as a community hall for meetings, and community gatherings.[148] Most of the homesteaders participated in churches—Mormon, Hawaiian Protestant, Roman Catholic, Ke Akua Ola, and Christian Scientist.[149]

In September 1924 Maui County opened a four-room schoolhouse on Hawaiian Homes land near the Kamehameha V coconut grove. There were seventy school-age children on the homesteads in 1925.[150] Most homestead children married children of other homesteaders. Kinship bonds helped to gradually cohere the homestead community over the years. As the homesteaders became permanently established and their families matured, single-family households expanded into ʻohana. Relatives from other islands stayed for extended periods of time with homestead families. Adult children, single and married, continued to live with their family on the homestead land.[151]

Although they developed informal social networks of cooperation and support, the homesteaders were unable to form a permanent farming cooperative. In 1923 the Kalanianaole settlers formed the First Hawaiian Homes Cooperative Association. The Hoʻolehua farmers formed a similar association. Both eventually dissolved. The commission commented on this phenomenon in its 1925 report to the Hawaiʻi legislature:

> At present the greatest obstacle to cooperative marketing by the home-steaders is their failure to realize that they must share their losses as well as their gains. The homesteader whose individual contribution to a ship-ment goes through without damage cannot as yet understand why he should be assessed for a portion of the loss occasioned by a less fortunate member of the cooperative organization.[152]

Felix Keesing commented on this issue in his 1936 report. According to him, certain homesteaders had better crops or considered themselves to have worked harder and felt penalized when returns where shared. Before long, homesteaders began to market part or all of their produce outside of the cooperative and undermined the association. Commercial enterprise replaced cooperative work.

The homestead communities founded to establish Hawaiians as commercial farmers were distinct from the subsistence farmers and fishermen of Manaʻe and the windward valleys. Once their homestead lands were converted to pine-apple production, the homesteaders were integrated into and dependent upon a cash economy based on wage earning and marketing of cash crops. Their primary source of food was the store, rather than the ocean, gardens, valleys, and mountains. However, as the Hawaiian homesteaders became kamaʻāina to Molokaʻi, they also hunted, fished, and gathered from Molokaʻi reefs, streams and forests.

Over time, they sank roots into the land as they raised families. Their children grew up with, and some even married, lineal descendants of the original Hawaiian families in the surrounding districts. The homesteaders' ʻohana net-work expanded to incorporate new relatives and friends, and the homestead communities cohered and evolved into important centers for the Hawaiian community with new cultural and social patterns of interaction. As they experienced the natural phenomena of Moloka'i, they began to learn the ways and traditions of the Moloka'i people. Thus in 1961, when Mary Kawena Pukui interviewed homesteaders and their descendants, most were able to share a deep knowledge of Moloka'i's place names, mele, myths, and legends. Mitchell Pau'ole, one of the most prominent of the homesteaders, who gained a reputation as the honorary mayor of Moloka'i, probably spoke for most of the pioneer homesteaders when he told Pukui: "And so the homestead life has been a wonderful life for each one of us, regardless of the hardship but we endured all of that by having that spirit of ho'omanawanui and be with it. We took up homesteading with the spirit that we were coming to make the best of it and we stuck with it until this day. We made our home here and we will be buried here."[153] Thus, the Hawaiian homesteaders established themselves on the 'āina of Moloka'i and opened a new chapter in the history of Hawaiians on the island. Their achievements, however, were important in establishing a Hawaiian Home Lands Program for Hawaiians on every island. A beautiful and popular song written to praise the beauty of Kalama'ula, Moloka'i, and to honor it as the location of the first Hawaiian Homes Settlement provides a fitting end to this section:

A he sure maoli no, ea	Sure indeed
Me ke onaona, ehe	With the soft fragrance
Me ka nani—Kalama'ula	With the beautiful—Kalama'ula
'Āina ua kaulana	Land made famous
I ka ho'opulapula	Because of the homesteading or rehabilitation
Me ka nani—Kalama'ula	With the beautiful—Kalama'ula.

Moloka'i at the End of the Twentieth Century

As in the other districts previously discussed, life on Moloka'i was affected by World War II and the 1946 tidal wave. During the war, 3,000 men were stationed on Moloka'i to defend the island from any attack. Young men left Moloka'i to fight in the war and to work at the lucrative jobs at Pearl Harbor.[154]

The tidal wave hit Kalaupapa and the area from Hālawa to Puko'o with the greatest force. Waves on the north shore measured fifty-eight feet. As at Waipi'o, the destruction of many homes, taro patches, and gardens led the families of Hālawa to move to other sections of Moloka'i.

Throughout the postwar period the economy of Moloka'i was sustained by two major pineapple companies, Dole and Del Monte, and by ranching. Studies of the economy of Molokaʻi from 1970 through 1994 documented the continuing importance of subsistence fishing, hunting, gathering, and farming as part of the livelihoods and culture of the Molokaʻi kuaʻāina. Molokaʻi persisted as a model of a community-based island economy rooted in subsistence where the kuaʻāina pursued traditional livelihoods.

In 1970 the University of Hawaiʻi Departments of Anthropology and Geography and the School of Public Health sponsored research in human ecology on Molokaʻi. The report, published as *Molokaʻi Studies: Preliminary Research in Human Ecology,* noted that the exchange of wild food in east Molokaʻi was based on the abundance of natural food resources of the area and the frequency of interaction of the residents.[155] The report noted that if tourist activities were expanded, they would encroach on traditional gathering spots. A resulting decline in supply of wild foods, coupled with a lessened interest in gathering due to competing forms of entertainment and increased demands on time, would effect a decrease in wild food exchange.

Maui county developed the Molokaʻi Community Plan in 1981 to guide future decisions about development on the island of Molokaʻi. Included in the plan was the East End Policy Statement, which determined that East Molokaʻi should retain its rural character. It encouraged development of aquaculture and restoration of the many fishponds on that part of the island.

Also in 1981, the Urban and Regional Planning Program of the University of Hawaiʻi conducted a study that examined the major values of the community so that policy decisions about alternative energy developments could be grounded in the residents' preferred way of life. It was published as the *Molokaʻi Data Book: Community Values and Energy Development.*[156] The study indicated that the "preferred way of life on Molokaʻi" was closely associated with rural living, Hawaiian culture, slow pace, everybody knowing everybody, family togetherness, and living off the land. Tourism, development, and higher prices were inconsistent with the preferred way of life on the island.

A study of traditional Hawaiian land use in 1982 investigated the feasibility of locating a small traditional Hawaiian community on conservation lands in the remote Pelekunu Valley on Molokaʻi.[157] The elements of the project included self-sufficiency; use of low-technology, low-energy-consumption, labor-intensive, self-built structures; diversified subsistence farming and fishing; and the maintenance of Hawaiian culture. "Residential subsistence," emphasizing residential use of homestead parcels while at the same time encouraging and integrating "backyard" agriculture, was suggested in a 1983 study for the Kalamaʻula Hawaiian homestead.[158] A report by the University of Hawaiʻi's Department of Urban and Regional Planning, *Contemporary Subsistence Lifestyles in Hawaiʻi: Implication for State Policy*, recommended in 1985 that the state legislature fund a more detailed study of subsistence on Molokaʻi as a case study for other rural Hawaiian communities. That same year another study, *An Economic Development Strategy and Implementation Program for Molokaʻi*, recommended support for developing fisheries on Molokaʻi. It concluded:

> Fishing on Molokaʻi continues to play a strong part in the Hawaiian culture; it suits the rural lifestyle of the Island; and it accepted as an appropriate type of resource use for economic development. For generations, the Native Hawaiian population survived largely on food harvested from the sea. The wide reef that fringes the southern shore of Molokaʻi supported extensive subsistence fisheries, and shoreline fishponds were used to age and fatten several species.[159]

The study pointed out that a lack of jobs and ready cash for groceries forces many Molokaʻi families to depend on the ocean for subsistence. It also stated that many Molokaʻi residents own fishing gear or boats, and the majority of families have ready access to fresh seafood through family members, relatives, and friends.

In 1987 the last pineapple company closed its operations. That same year a tuberculosis epidemic led to the decision to eradicate all the cattle on Molokaʻi. Molokaʻi General Hospital geared down its operations, limiting births to delivery by midwives. At 20 percent, Molokaʻi's unemployment rate was three times the state's average. Many small businesses shut down. In response to this economic crisis, the state opened the Molokaʻi office of the Department of Business and Economic Development and Tourism (DBEDT) in 1987 and set up the Molokaʻi Interdepartmental Task Force. The task force noted that "increased consideration should be given to alternate approaches supportive of subsistence activity as an integral, preferred way of life for many Molokaʻi residents." A special loan program was set up to stimulate small businesses, particularly in the areas of agriculture, fisheries, and culture. The Molokaʻi DBEDT tried to enhance subsistence activity on Molokaʻi while introducing mainstream economic development programs such as industrial parks, a slaughterhouse, and an ice-making plant.

To stimulate the fishpond industry, a model project was initiated in 1989 at ʻUalapuʻe fishpond in Manaʻe by Maui county and the state of Hawaiʻi. In 1990 the Molokaʻi Office of the Department of Business and Economic Development and Tourism sponsored development of the "Master Plan for ʻUalapuʻe Ahupuaʻa: Blending Traditions & Technology." The plan was designed to protect the vital water resources of the fishpond by proposing a management plan for the resources of the entire ahupuaʻa. The nonprofit Molokaʻi-based group Hui o Kuapā developed a plan for establishing a finfish hatchery in December 1991.

The University of Arizona started a demonstration project in 1991 for the cultivation of seaweed in a fishpond managed by a Native Hawaiian land trust. Based upon its success, the program has now expanded into commercial production and is providing training to interested community members.

In 1993 the Governor's Task Force on Molokaʻi Fishpond Restoration identified 74 fishponds ranging in size from less than an acre to 73 acres, with the majority located on the southeast side. Moreover, it found that the island of Molokaʻi, with a protected reef extending over 14,000 acres, is blessed with a very high percentage of restorable fishponds. The task force recommended that the state provide the money needed to establish the fish hatchery as proposed by Hui o Kuapā. The task force also recommended that the state appropriate additional funds for the repair of ten fishpond walls, community training and research, and a Molokaʻi Fishpond Commission to implement a long-term plan for the restoration and revitalization of the fishponds on Molokaʻi. In the same year, a fishermen's cooperative made up of forty fishermen who produce an estimated 60–70 percent of the island's commercial fish landings opened an ice house.

The Governor's Molokaʻi Subsistence Task Force was set up, in response to concerns raised by a group of hunters, to review all subsistence activities on Molokaʻi, including hunting, and to make recommendations for policies to protect and enhance subsistence on the island. Over the years, a number of activities contributed to the degradation of the natural environment of Molokaʻi. Offshore reefs and oceans were impacted by pollution, erosion, and soil runoff from resorts, residential development, and ranching. Sand from the west end of Molokaʻi was mined and shipped to Oʻahu to make cement to build the freeways and hotels and to replace lost sand at Waikiki Beach. Gravel and rocks from east Molokaʻi were used in freeway construction on Oʻahu. Ranching on the east end contributed to deforestation, erosion, and runoff. Once-productive fishponds were allowed to fill with silt, and the walls fell into disrepair following tsunamis and storms. Overharvesting of marine resources relied upon for subsistence was a growing problem. Traditional resources such as the turtle could not be used for subsistence under new federal regulations. Wild-life such as deer, goats, pigs, and birds were abundant on privately owned lands but were too scarce to be hunted on public lands.

Nevertheless, the study, completed in 1994, concluded that many families on Moloka'i, particularly Hawaiian families, continued to rely upon subsistence fishing, hunting, gathering, or cultivation for a significant portion of their food. A random sample survey of the families on Moloka'i revealed that 28 percent of their food was acquired through subsistence activities. Among Native Hawaiian families the survey found that 38 percent of their food was derived from subsistence activities. The families reported receiving food through subsistence activities at least once a week. Virtually every person surveyed believed that subsistence was important to the lifestyle of Moloka'i.[160]

Availability of the natural resources needed for subsistence was essential to Moloka'i households, where the unemployment rate was consistently higher than on other islands and a significant portion of the population depended upon public assistance. In March 1993, the unemployment rate of 8.1 percent on Moloka'i was higher than the statewide rate of 4.7 percent. With regard to public assistance, in 1990, 24.4 percent of the Moloka'i population received food stamps, 12 percent received Aid to Families with Dependent Children, and 32.5 percent received Medicaid. According to the U.S. census for 1990, 21 percent of the families on Moloka'i had incomes that fell below the poverty level of $12,674 for a family of four. The ability to supplement meager incomes through subsistence was very important to maintaining the quality of life of families on the island through 1994.

Subsistence was also critical to the persistence of traditional Hawaiian cultural values, customs, and practices. Cultural knowledge, such as about place-names; fishing ko'a; methods of fishing and gathering; or the reproductive cycles of marine and land resources were passed down from one generation to the next through training in subsistence skills. The sharing of foods gathered through subsistence activities continued to reinforce good relations among members of extended families and with neighbors.

Without subsistence as a major means for providing food, Moloka'i families would have been in a dire situation when agribusiness phased out. Subsistence provided families with the essential resources that compensated for low incomes and a means of obtaining food items that were prohibitively costly. Food items such as fish, lobster, crab, limu, and deer meat that are normally obtained through subsistence were generally unavailable or were very costly in stores. In this respect, subsistence not only provided food, it also ensured a healthy diet critical to the prevention of illness.

A primary reason for the persistence of subsistence practices on Moloka'i through 1994 was the continued availability of renewable natural resources. In turn, while years of macroeconomic strategies wreaked havoc on Hawai'i's natural environment and endemic species of flora and fauna in urban areas and on plantations, subsistence practices allowed the natural resources in rural communities like on Moloka'i to persist.

On Moloka'i, subsistence was a viable sector of the economy that continued to function alongside the sugar and pineapple plantations and the ranches. Hawaiian extended families commonly supplemented their incomes with subsistence fishing and hunting. Unfortunately subsistence was generally not recognized as a bona fide economic sector by Western economists. In the face of economic decline in Hawai'i, such as with the phasing out of agribusiness, decisions were generally made that promoted new economic development based on linear progress toward capital accumulation. This usually came in the form of tourism.

Moloka'i provides a rare example of how residents adapted to changing economic circumstances without massive external intervention. Historical

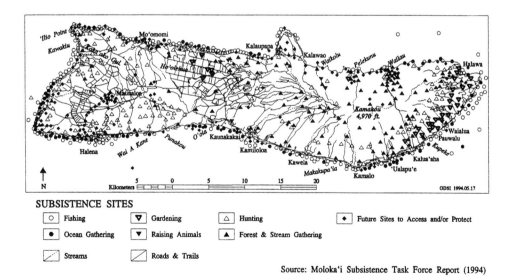

SUBSISTENCE SITES

○ Fishing	▽ Gardening	△ Hunting	◆ Future Sites to Access and/or Protect
● Ocean Gathering	▼ Raising Animals	▲ Forest & Stream Gathering	
Streams	Roads & Trails		

Source: Moloka'i Subsistence Task Force Report (1994)

Map 5 In 1993 subsistence practitioners on Moloka'i mapped the locations of their various subsistence activities. *Source:* Matsuoka, McGregor, and Minerbi, "Governor's Moloka'i Subsistence Task Force," pp. 3, 77.

accounts indicate that when agribusiness closed on Molokaʻi, subsistence became a more vital aspect of the economy.[161] Through community-based efforts, residents organized to successfully stave off tourism development while promoting values related to community and family integrity. Subsistence and other community-based endeavors were considered the forces that bound the social elements necessary for cultural perpetuation together. Subsistence was not a replacement economy but a tradition that survived after macroeconomic strategies (i.e., plantations and ranches) failed.

Indicative of the continuing significance of subsistence to the people of Molokaʻi at the end of the twentieth century was a rural empowerment grant application which succeeded in attracting $2.5 million to the island over a ten-year period. Designed by a broad cross section of the island, the vision statement quoted at the opening of this chapter was adopted for the island's economic development in the twenty-first century. It continued with the following insights:

- We envision strong ʻohana (families) who steadfastly preserve, protect and perpetuate these core Hawaiian values.
- We envision a wise and caring community that takes pride in its resourcefulness, self-sufficiency and resiliency, and is firmly in charge of Molokaʻi's resources and destiny.
- We envision a Molokaʻi that leaves for its children a visible legacy: an island momona (abundant) with natural and cultural resources, people who kōkua (help) and look after one another, and a community that strives to build an even better future on the paʻa (firm) foundation left to us by those whose iwi (bones) guard our land.[162]

The plan outlined community-based economic projects that would make sustainable use of the islands' resources. These included watershed protection, a native plant nursery, taro production, aquaculture development, and a community land trust.[163]

The vision statement and economic development plan reflected the ongoing significance of Native Hawaiian cultural values and subsistence practices to the people of the "Last Hawaiian Island" of Molokaʻi as a major cultural kīpuka of modern Hawaiʻi. The central role of the Molokaʻi kuaʻāina in regenerating Native Hawaiian culture during the Hawaiian renaissance will be discussed in chapter 6.

SIX

Kahoʻolawe: Rebirth of the Sacred

I have my thoughts, you have your thoughts, simple for me, difficult for you. Simply . . . the reason is . . . I am a Hawaiian and I've inherited the soul of my kūpuna. It is my moral responsibility to attempt an ending to this desecration of our sacred ʻāina, Kohe Mālamalama O Kanaloa, for each bomb dropped adds further injury to an already wounded soul.

—GEORGE HELM, "Reasons for Fourth Occupation of Kahoʻolawe,"
January 30, 1977

IN THE 1970s the island of Kahoʻolawe stirred the ancestral memory of Native Hawaiians and inspired the first cultural renaissance in Hawaiʻi since the islands came under American control in 1898. Throughout the twentieth century, the United States colonized Hawaiʻi through political, social, economic, and military institutions. World War II transformed the way of life in Hawaiʻi and led to the development of new political and economic alliances.[1] In 1959 U.S. colonial policy culminated with statehood for Hawaiʻi.

When Hawaiʻi became a state, tourism grew to be the main industry for the islands' economies. American progress seemed to be overdeveloping the islands and replacing the Native Hawaiian and local way of life. However, in an extraordinary convergence of events, the island of Kahoʻolawe became a focal point of a major political movement challenging American control of Hawaiʻi. Surprisingly, rather than leading to fuller assimilation of Native Hawaiians into American society, statehood sparked a reassertion of Native Hawaiian rights and a revitalization of Native Hawaiian language, culture, and spirituality. The island of Kahoʻolawe served as the dynamic catalyst for this unexpected native rights movement.

George Helm was one of the Native Hawaiian leaders whose vision shaped the movement. He was born and raised on Molokaʻi as a kuaʻāina. Together with other young men and women from the island they roused the Molokaʻi kūpuna to guide a movement to stop the bombing of Kahoʻolawe. From Molokaʻi, these young men and women also reached out to kuaʻāina and kūpuna from Hāna and the rest of Maui, Hawaiʻi, Lānaʻi, and Kauaʻi to join in the effort. Their outreach extended to Native Hawaiians at the University of Hawaiʻi and political activists on Oʻahu. However, it was the kuaʻāina from Molokaʻi and Hawaiʻi's rural communities who started the movement for Kahoʻolawe and nurtured it into a uniquely Hawaiian movement. They successfully involved multiple generations—from kūpuna, or elders, to mākua, or the adult parent generation, as well as ʻōpiʻo from the university and high schools. Kahoʻolawe became a primary site of cultural regeneration through the aloha ʻāina projects initiated by the kuaʻāina from Hawaiʻi's cultural kīpuka. Indeed, it is through Kahoʻolawe that we can best understand and appreciate the significant interrelationship between the knowledge and experience of the kuaʻāina from the various cultural kīpuka of the islands and the contemporary revival of Native Hawaiian culture and religion.

In March 1977 Helm and Kimo Mitchell, a kuaʻāina of Hāna, were mysteriously lost in the ocean off of Kahoʻolawe during a protest of the bombing of Kahoʻolawe. The movement for which they had become martyrs grew into an islands-wide movement that not only succeeded in stopping military use

Figure 32 A view of Kahoʻolawe looking over the top of the island from the southern cliffs reveals one of the quiet moods of this sacred island. 1994. Franco Salmoiraghi.

of Kahoʻolawe in 1990, but also sparked the revitalization and impressive ren-aissance of Hawaiian culture, music, navigation, arts, agriculture, and aqua-culture.

Conventional History of Kahoʻolawe

Kahoʻolawe, the smallest of Hawaiʻi's major islands, consists of forty-five square miles of volcanic craters, hills, valleys, rugged cliffs, and sandy shore-lines, with nearshore reefs and deep ocean channels. It lies eight miles south of the second largest island of Maui.

In the late eighteenth century goats were introduced to the island and allowed to go feral. In the nineteenth century the Hawaiian monarchy used the island as a penal colony to which they banished political rivals, adulterers, and Catholic converts. In 1858 the island was leased for sheep ranching. Over-grazing by goats and sheep destroyed the natural flora and left the island bare and vulnerable to the erosive forces of wind and rain. Reforestation efforts in the early twentieth century introduced noxious alien species of trees, grasses, and shrubs to sustain cattle ranching, which further degraded the island's ecosystem.[2]

At the dawn of World War II the island was taken over by the U.S. Navy for live-fire ordnance exercises and combat training. Kahoʻolawe came to be called the "most shot-at" island in the Pacific. By September 1945 150 Navy pilots, the crews of 532 major ships, and 350 Navy, Marine, and Army shore fire control officers had trained at Kahoʻolawe. Another 730 service members had trained in joint signal operations on the island. During the Korean War Navy carrier planes used Kahoʻolawe to practice airfield attacks and strafing runs on vehicle convoys and other mock North Korean targets. In 1965, dur-ing the cold war, a one-kiloton nuclear explosion was simulated on the island when the U.S. Navy detonated 500 tons of TNT. During the Vietnam era, Navy and Marine Corps planes practiced attacks on surface-to-air missile sites, airfields, and radar stations. By the time of the Gulf War, live fire training on the island was reduced as the Navy shifted its primary training to other state-of-the-art electronic target ranges.[3]

The Cultural Significance of Kahoʻolawe Is Revealed

In January 1976 Native Hawaiians staged an occupation of Kahoʻolawe as a means of drawing national attention to the desperate conditions of Native

Hawaiians.[4] A bill to grant Native Hawaiians monetary reparations for the illegal overthrow of the Hawaiian monarchy by U.S. naval forces was pending in Congress. Two young men from Moloka'i—Noa Emmett Aluli, M.D., and Walter Ritte—were in the one boat that made it past the Coast Guard blockade and actually landed on the island. While the Navy arrested the protesters, Ritte and Aluli remained hidden. Having stayed behind, they roamed the island for two days before being discovered and arrested. Not only did they witness vast destruction around the island, they also felt the presence of a deep spiritual force. Kaho'olawe revealed to them that it was not just a barren target island.

Seeking an explanation of their spiritual epiphany on Kaho'olawe, Aluli and Ritte sought out Native Hawaiian kūpuna to share their memories of Kaho'olawe. They recruited Helm and drew upon the kua'āina of Moloka'i, Hāna, and Hawai'i.

Moloka'i kūpuna such as Aunty Mary Lee, Aunty Clara Ku, Aunty Lani Kapuni and Aunty Harriet Ne revealed that Kaho'olawe had served as a refuge for Native Hawaiian spiritual customs and practices and that it was a center

Figure 33 Moloka'i kūpuna revealed that Kaho'olawe was a sacred place dedicated to Kanaloa, the Hawaiian god of the ocean. Shown here are Aunty Barbara Hanchett, Aunty Lani Kapuni, Aunty Clara Ku, Aunty Mary Lee, and Aunty Rose Wainui (front). 1974. Franco Salmoiraghi.

for training in the arts of non-instrument navigation involving the sighting of heavenly bodies. Uncle Harry Kūnihi Mitchell of Ke'anae, Maui, shared the chants and mo'olelo about Kaho'olawe he had learned from his kūpuna. He interpreted the meaning of the island's place-names. Aunty Alice Kuloloio and her 'ohana spoke of their tradition of fishing, gathering limu, and subsisting upon the abundant marine resources of the ocean surrounding the island. Aunty Edith Kanaka'ole of Hilo, Hawai'i, advised the young men to organize their work in stopping the military use of Kaho'olawe in a Hawaiian manner: as an 'ohana for the island rather than as an association.

Through the course of this spiritual journey, an entirely new image of Kaho'olawe as a sacred island emerged. The Native Hawaiian kūpuna revealed that the island had originally been named Kanaloa, for the Native Hawaiian god of the ocean. Hawaiian ancestors respected the island as a physical manifestation of Kanaloa. It is the only island in the Pacific named for a major god. Kaho'olawe was also named Kohemālamalama o Kanaloa, which can be translated as "the shining birth canal of Kanaloa" or "the southern beacon of Kanaloa." Both names link the island to its role as a traditional center in the training of way-finding between Hawai'i and Tahiti. Mastery of the art of navigation required a complete spiritual and intellectual immersion in the natural elements of ocean, wind, currents, stars, moon, and sun. One must come to know the nature and characteristics of the Hawaiian god of these elements, Kanaloa, to become a master way-finder and travel across his magnificent body form, the vast ocean. Kaho'olawe provided the ideal location to immerse oneself within the natural elements related to sailing and navigation that Native Hawaiians honored as Kanaloa.

Mo'olelo o Kanaloa

Native Hawaiians first settled Kanaloa some time around 1000 CE. They built their homes in its valleys, fished its waters, and farmed its slopes. At Pu'u Moiwi they hewed stone adzes out of basalt veins at the second largest such quarry in the Hawaiian Islands. They also crafted basaltic glass cutting tools, carved petroglyphs, and built fishing shrines and temples to sacred deities.

Early Native Hawaiian settlers constructed sixty-nine coastal fishing shrines around the island to mark separate fishing grounds for distinct varieties of fish that thrive in the ocean offshore. In addition, there are numerous inland shrines which also appear to have a connection to fishing. The ocean surrounding the island has continued to be accessed by fishermen from Maui for fish, seaweed, limpets, and other forms of marine life for subsistence and medicinal uses. The coral reefs surrounding Kanaloa are in a pristine condition relative to the reefs off heavily populated areas of our islands. There is still a wide variety and abundance of fish and marine life in the reefs and ocean around Kanaloa. Seabirds live in cliffs and rocky islets on the leeward side of the island.

The following chant, "Oli Kūhohonu o Kahoʻolawe Mai No Kūpuna Mai" (Deep Chant of Kahoʻolawe from Our Ancestors) was composed by early Native Hawaiians for Kanaloa. Harry Kūnihi Mitchell learned it from his kūpuna. Mitchell's ancestors settled at Honuaʻula on Maui and fished and gathered marine life in the ocean and along the shorelines of both Honuaʻula and Kanaloa. The family moved to Keʻanae, Maui after a lava flow in Honuaʻula displaced them. Nevertheless, they continued to visit Kanaloa, gather marine life from its shoreline, and fish in the surrounding ocean. The chant connects Kanaloa to navigators returning from a transpacific voyage.

Wehewehe mai nei kahi ao	Dawn is breaking.
Kū mai nā waʻa kaulua	Two double-hulled canoes are sighted.
Pūē ke kanaka mai ka waʻa mai	The men cheer from the canoe.
Kūkulu ka iwi o ka ʻāina	Land is sighted.
ʻAilana Kohemālamalama	To your left it is like heaven all lit up
Hoʻohiki kēia moku iā Kanaloa	We dedicate this island to Kanaloa.
Akua o ka moana ʻili, moana uli	God of the shallow and deep ocean
Ke holo nei me ke au kāhili	We are running in an erratic current.
ʻŌhaehae mai ka makani	The wind is blowing from all directions.
ʻAlalā keiki pua aliʻi	The chief's child is crying [Alalā is also the name of the channel between Kahoʻolawe and Maui].
Ka piko hole pelu o Kanaloa	The island of Molokini is shaped like the navel of Kanaloa.
Kahua pae ʻili kīhonua āhua	The channel between Molokini-Kanaloa and Maui Kahiki Nui is shallow.
Puehu ka lepo o Moaʻula	Dust is spreading over Mount Moaʻula.
Puʻuhonua moʻokahuna kilo pae honua	Gathering place of the kahuna classes to study astronomy.
Pōhaku ahu ʻaikūpele kāpili o Keaweiki	Stone of deep magic of Keaweiki
Kau lī lua ka makani ke hae nei	The wind is chilly
Kāwele hele nei ʻo Hineliʻi	Light rain is falling

Nāpoʻo ka lā i Kahikimoe	The sun is setting toward Kahiki.
Nue mai ke ao Lanikau	The glow after the sunset is like the colors of the rainbow
Kapu mai ka honua kūpaʻa loa	The world seems to be standing still.
Pau ka luhi ʻana o ka moana	We shall no more labor on the ocean.
Manaʻo hālana pū I ke Akua	My thoughts are enlightened toward God.
He aloha pili kaʻu no kēia ʻāina	My love for this land will always be deep within my heart.
Aloha nō ka mana o nā kūpuna	I love the knowledge and power of my ancestors.

The chant reveals four ancient names for Kanaloa: Kohemālamalama, meaning "to your left and lit up like heaven"; Hineliʻi, "light rain"; Kahiki Moe, "the sun sets in Kahiki"; and Kanaloa, name of the Hawaiian and Polynesian god of the ocean, ocean currents, and navigation. A fifth name combines two of these into Kohemalamalama o Kanaloa, "the southern beacon of Kanaloa." The more recent name, Kahoʻolawe, can be translated as "to take and to embrace."

According to Hawaiian tradition, the name Kanaloa singles out the entire island as a wahi pana since it is the only island in the Pacific named after and dedicated to a major Polynesian god. The name Kohemālamalama o Kanaloa can also be interpreted as meaning "the shining birth canal of Kanaloa." This identifies the island as a traditional puʻuhonua.

Creation myths for Kanaloa also reinforce its significance as a wahi pana. The island, like Hawaiʻi, Maui, Kauaʻi, Niʻihau, and Oʻahu, was born of Papa and Wākea. Two chants by composers of the time of Kamehameha give similar accounts of the birth of the island by Papa.

The chant by Kaleikuahulu gives the following version:

> Papa was weakened at the birth of the island Kanaloa.
> It was born beautiful as a birdling and a *naiʻa* [porpoise],
> It was the child born of Papa.
> Papa forsook her husband and returned to Kahiki;
> Returned to Kahiki she lived at Kapakapakaua.[5]

The chant by Pakui records the birth as follows:

| Kaahea Papa iā Kanaloa, he moku, | Papa was prostrated with an island, Kanaloa, |
| I Hānauia he pūnua he naiʻa, | Who was born as a birdling; as a porpoise; |

255

He keiki ia nā Papa i Hānau,	A child that Papa gave birth to,
Ha'alele Papa ho'i i Tahiti,	Then Papa left and went back to Tahiti,
Ho'i a Tahiti Kapakapakaua	Went back to Tahiti at Kapakapakaua.[6]

David Malo provides a creation chant that attributes the birth of Kanaloa to Papa and Wākea and describes the island as being red, a traditionally sacred color. The part of the chant referring to the birth of the island reads as follows:

Lili-'ōpū-punalua o Papa	The womb of Papa became jealous at
iā Ho'o-hoku-ka-lani.	its partnership with Ho'ohokulani
Ho'i hou o Papa noho iā Wākea.	Papa returned to live with Wākea.
Hānau, o O'ahu, he moku,	Born was O'ahu, an island,
Hānau o Kaua'i, he moku,	Born was Kaua'i, an island,
Hānau o Ni'ihau, he moku	Born was Ni'ihau, an island
He 'ula 'ā o Kaho'olawe.	Glowing fiery red was Kaho'olawe.[7]

Chants of Pele, Hawaiian god of the volcano, and her family of deities reinforce the significance of Kanaloa as a wahi pana and pu'uhonua. Pele was born in Kapakuela. Her husband, Wahieloa, was enticed away from her by Pelekumuhonua. Pele traveled in search of him. With her came the sea, which poured from her head over the land of Kanaloa. This is said to be the first time that the sea is brought to Kanaloa. Her brothers chant at this phenomenon:

> A sea! a sea!
> Forth bursts the sea,
> Bursts forth over Kanaloa,
> The sea rises to the hills.[8]

According to the rest of the chant, the sea floods the land three times, then recedes. The floodings are called the sea of Kahinali'i, the mother of Pele.

Kepelino provides the following account of how Pele brought the sea to Hawai'i at Kanaloa:

> It is said that in ancient times the sea was not known here. There was not even fresh water, but with the coming of Pe-le the sea came also. It was thus that Hawaii got the sea. Her parents gave it to her and she brought it in her canoes to the land of Pa-ku-e-la and thence to the land of Ka-na-loa, and at this place she poured the sea out from her head. That is how Hawaii got its sea. But when the sea burst forth her brothers chanted:

A sea! a sea!
The sea bursts forth,
The sea bursts forth on Ka-na-lo-a
The borders of the sea reach to the hills,
Gone is the restless sea,
Twice it breaks forth
Thrice it breaks forth,
The sea borne on the back of Pe-le.[9]

The brother of Pele who navigates for the family in their voyage through the Hawaiian chain of islands is Kamohoaliʻi, the principal male shark god. There are two sites on Kanaloa that are associated with Kamohoaliʻi. The first is Lua o Kamohoaliʻi, or the abyss of Kamohoaliʻi. This is one of four puʻuhonua for Kamohoaliʻi in Hawaiʻi.[10] It is located in a deep cave that opens onto the ocean on the northeast side of the island. No one has explored it in modern times. In the story of Laukaʻieʻie, Kamohoaliʻi, and his shark people are said to be living at Kanaloa. This is likely to have been at the site identified on maps as Kahua Hale o Kamohoaliʻi, or the house foundation of Kamohoaliʻi in the central portion of the island.[11] Shrines to Kamohoaliʻi have been rediscovered on the cliffs above Kanapou Bay, which is a breeding ground for sharks.

The Fornander account of Puʻuoinaina, the legendary moʻowahine who lived on Kanaloa, refers to the island as a sacred land. According to the myth, "This daughter of theirs was placed on Kahoolawe; the name of Kahoolawe at that time, however, was Kohemalamalama; it was a very sacred land at that time, no chiefs or common people went there."[12]

Kanaloa's status as a wahi pana is also related to its role as a training center in the art and science of navigating transpacific voyages using the stars for way-finding.

Kanaloa as a Training Center for Way-Finding

Kanaloa, both the god and the island, figured prominently in the long voyages between Hawaiʻi and Tahiti. Moaʻulaiki at the *piko* or central part of the island was the location of a traditional training school for navigators. Moaʻula is a place-name associated with a place in Tahiti. There are other places in Hawaiʻi named Moaʻula—the waterfall in Hālawa Valley on Molokaʻi; the falls, stream, ridge, and heiau in Waikolu on Molokaʻi; a heiau in Waipiʻo Valley on

Hawai'i Island; a gulch in Ka'ū on Hawai'i Island; and a heiau in Kīpapa Gulch on O'ahu. Moa'ula was one of the powerful kahuna priests associated with Kanaloa. An important feature of this site is a bell stone that was broken in half and carried to this point in two parts and put back together. The split in the rock is oriented north to south. The ancient name of the rock is Pōhaku Ahu 'Aikūpele Kāpili o Keaweiki" (the put-together rock that kneads the knowledge of the mo'okahuna priest Keaweiki). The kahuna, Keaweiki, was associated with the school for training in astronomy and navigation at Moa'ulaiki. At Moa'ulaiki are found the foundations of a platform used for the navigational school and of a house for the kahuna who instructed the students in navigation. Moa'ulaiki affords a panoramic view of the islands of Lāna'i, O'ahu, Moloka'i, Maui, and Hawai'i, all the interconnecting channels, and the currents that run through them. It was and remains an ideal site for astronomical observation in relation to the surrounding islands and channels.

Oral traditions identify Lae o Kealaikahiki as the major point of departure for Hawaiians leaving for Tahiti in the thirteenth century. The name translates as Point of the Pathway to Tahiti. The Hawaiians probably waited here for the ideal moon, wind, and other signs to launch their voyages to Tahiti in the strong southerly Kealaikahiki Channel and current. Members of the voyaging canoe Hōkūle'a estimate that they could have saved five days sailing if they had left from here rather than from the Big Island.[13] While in the Kealaikahiki Channel, the crew also noted that if the stern of Hōkūle'a is aligned with Pu'u o Hōkū, Moloka'i, on the northern horizon and the north star above it in the heavens, then the bow of the canoe is aimed directly at the point between two stars that marks the location of Tahiti.

The Hōkūle'a crew also noted that Kanaloa lies one mile north of 20°30' latitude, making it the closest land mass to the latitudinal center of the main Hawaiian Islands. Memorizing the image of the Southern Cross from sea level near this latitudinal center is critical for navigators learning how to find Hawai'i on their voyage home. Thus, Kanaloa and Lae o Kelaikahiki itself were ideal locations for the training of navigators. A platform has been recently constructed at Lae o Kealaikahiki for the training of new generations in non-instrument navigation.

Just above the high-water mark, inland from Lae o Kealaikahiki, is a traditional compass site made up of four large boulders. The lines formed by the placement of the stones mark true north, south, east, and west, as has been verified by placing a compass in the center of the stones. Jutting out from the shoals just south of Lae o Kealaikahiki is another key navigational marker, both traditional and contemporary. On the charts it is identified as Black Rock. The traditional name for it is Pōhaku Kuhi Ke'e I Kahiki ("the rock that points the way to Tahiti"). The rock was an important marker for boats sailing along the western side of Kanaloa because it indicated how far the shoals extended into the channel. It mysteriously disappeared in 1984.

The legend of Mo'ikeha, chief of Kaua'i, who sent his son Kiha to bring his other son, La'amaikahiki, back to Hawai'i places Kanaloa as the centerpiece in navigation between Hawai'i and Tahiti. Fornander offers the following translation of the La'amaikahiki account:

> As the place [Kahikinui, Maui] was too windy, Laamaikahiki left it and sailed for the west coast of the island of Kahoolawe, where he lived until he finally left for Tahiti. It is said that because Laamaikahiki lived on Kahoolawe, and set sail from that island, was the reason why the ocean to the west of Kahoolawe is called "the road to Tahiti."
>
> After Laamaikahiki had lived on Kahoolawe for a time, his priests became dissatisfied with the place, so Laamaikahiki left Kahoolawe and returned to Kauai. Upon the death of Moikeha [his father] the land descended to Kila, and Laamaikahiki returned to Tahiti.[14]

The tradition of the migratory chief Tahitinui also refers to Kealaikahiki as central to the voyage between Hawai'i and Tahiti. Fornander writes:

> After Hawaii Loa was dead and gone, in the time of Ku Nui Akea, came Tahiti-nui from Tahiti and landed at Ka-lae-i-Kahiki (the southwest point of Kahoolawe, a cape often made by people coming from or going to Tahiti). Tahiti-nui was moopuna of Ki, Hawaii Loa's brother, and he settled on East Maui and died there.[15]

In the account of the voyage of Wahanui, a chief of O'ahu, who went to Kahiki, they sailed from O'ahu to Haleolono on Moloka'i, then on to Kaunolū on Lāna'i, and finally left for Kahiki by way of Kealaikahiki. According to Samuel Kamakau:

> Wahanui was a chief of O'ahu who went to Kahiki. With him were Kilohi the kilo, who knew the stars, Moopuaiki the kahuna, and the crewmen. They sailed from O'ahu and landed at Haleolono on Moloka'i. Early in the morning they sailed by Kaholo on Lana'i and by broad daylight were passing Kaunolu Cape. A little to the southeast of there is Apua Cape, where lived a man called Kaneapua . . . After repeated attempts to sail, Kaneapua

was given a place on the canoe, and they sailed for Kahiki by way of Ke-ala-i-kahiki at Kahoʻolawe.[16]

Peter Buck concluded through his research that Kealaikahiki was the primary departure point for voyages to Tahiti:

> The point of departure for the south was the passage between Kahoolawe and Maui which was named Ke Ala i Kahiki (The Course to Tahiti). In a translation from Kamakau, Alexander (1891b) refers to the southern sailing directions. Hokupaa, the North Star, was left directly astern; and when Hokupaa sank below the northern horizon on reaching the Piko o Wakea (the Equator), Newe became the guiding star to the south. No sailing directions were given for the return voyage to the north.[17]

Two known accounts also place Kealaikahiki as a point of landing in Hawaiʻi after the long journey from Kahiki. Placing Kealaikahiki as a point of arrival would coincide with the oral tradition related in the chant from Harry Kūnihi Mitchell, "Oli Kūhohonu o Kahoʻolawe Mai Nā Kūpuna Mai." Samuel Kamakau, in *Ka Nūpepa Kūʻokoʻa* of January 12, 1867, wrote about the coming of the gods. A recently published translation of the article provides an account of the arrival of Kanaloa to Hawaiʻi by way of Kealaikahiki on Kanaloa:

> According to the moʻolelo of Kane and Kanaloa, they were perhaps the first who kept gods (ʻo laua paha na kahu akua mua) to come to Hawaiʻi nei, and because of their mana they were called gods. Kahoʻolawe was first named Kanaloa for his having first come there by way of Ke-ala-i-kahiki. From Kahoʻolawe the two went to Kahikinui, Maui, where they opened up the fishpond of Kanaloa at Lua-laʻi-lua, and from them came the water of Kou at Kaupo.[18]

Kamakau's account of the legend of Kūkanaloa again identifies Kealaikahiki on Kanaloa as a point of arrival to Hawaiʻi from Kahiki:

> In the wanana and pule and mele of Ka poʻe kahiko, it is said that Kukanaloa came during the time of Kakaʻalaneo . . . It is said that Kukanaloa ma landed in Waiheʻe from Ke-ala-i-kahiki; Kiwi was the spot where they came ashore, and Kahahawai the place where they panted and stammered.[19]

The fishing resources of Kanaloa also elevate the island as a traditional place of significance to the fishermen of the surrounding islands of Lānaʻi, Molokaʻi, and Maui.

In the Ocean of Kanaloa

The primary evidence of the rich and varied fishing resources of the waters surrounding Kanaloa is the location of the sixty-nine fishing *ko‘a*, or shrines, around the island. The first settlers may have been attracted to Kanaloa from Maui by the fishing resources and decided to make a home there. Ko‘a were used by fishermen to mark and develop their fishing grounds. The first fish caught were given as offerings on the ko‘a upon the men's returning from a day of fishing as gratitude for the guidance of the shrine. The ko‘a serve as land markers for ocean fishing grounds. In some cases the fish were fed at certain grounds to assure that they would be plentiful in those designated areas, and the ko‘a serves as a land marker.

Kū‘ula, the patron of fishing, is honored at the fishing ko‘a. He is represented on the shrine as an upright stone. Pieces of coral or ko‘a are usually placed on the shrine to represent Hina, the wife of Kū‘ula. The practices honoring Kū‘ula were introduced in Hawai‘i by his son A‘ia‘i. Beckwith offers an explanation of the Kū‘ula custom:

> The god lived as a man on earth on East Maui in the land called Alea-mai
> at a place called Leho-ula (Red-cowry) on the side of the hill Ka-iwi-o-Pele
> (the bones of Pele). There he built the first fishpond; and when he died he
> gave to his son Aiai the four magic objects with which he controlled the
> fish and taught him how to address the gods in prayer and how to set up
> fish altars. The objects were a decoy stick called Pahiaku-kahuoi (kahuai),
> a cowry called Leho-ula, a hook called Manai-a-ka-lani, and a stone called
> Kuula which, if dropped into a pool, had the power to draw the fish thither.
> His son Aiai, following his instructions, traveled about the islands establish-
> ing fishing stations (ko‘a) at fishing grounds (ko‘a aina) where fish were
> accustomed to feed and setting up altars (kuula) upon which to lay, as
> offerings to the fishing gods, two fish from the first catch.[20]

One of the early shrines built by A‘ia‘i in Hawai‘i was on Kanaloa at Haki-oawa. It is described as a square-walled Kū‘ula like a heiau, set on a bluff looking out to the sea.[21] The following is an account of how A‘ia‘i constructed the shrine on Kanaloa:

> Thus was performed the good work of Aiai in establishing ku-ula stations
> and fish stones continued all around the island of Maui. It is also said that
> he visited Kahoolawe and established a ku-ula at Hakioawa, though it differs
> from the others, being built on a high bluff overlooking the sea, somewhat

like a temple, by placing stones in the form of a square, in the middle of which was left a space wherein the fishermen of that island laid their first fish caught, as a thank offering. Awa and kapa were also placed there as offerings to the fish deities.[22]

In 1902 the Hawaiian-language *Nūpepa Kū'oko'a* published a series of articles titled "He Mau Kuhikuhi No Ka Lawai'a Ana" (Fishing Lore) by A. D. Kahaulelio, who had been trained as a fisherman by his parents and grandparents. Kahaulelio's grandparents were born in Keone'ōi'o, Honua'ula, Maui, and then moved to Lahaina. Kahaulelio fished inshore and in the deep sea for a living. He and his grandparents were very familiar with the ocean around Kanaloa. His articles in *Nūpepa Kū'oko'a* provide extensive information about the fishing resources around Kanaloa. He described the boundary of the more than 100 fishing grounds that he frequented between Lāna'i, Kanaloa, Ukumehame, and Lahaina:

> From the cape of Hawea at Kaanapali running directly to the cape of
> Hema on Lanai, close to Maunalei; then to the cape of Kamaiki on Lanai;
> thence directly to the cape of Paki (the same as the cape of Kelaikahiki) on
> Kahoolawe; thence to the cape of Kukui on Kahoolawe then straight to the
> cape of Papawai are the places that are well known and have been fished in
> by your writer, in sunshine, in rain and in the winds that rage and blow
> into a terrific gale.[23]

Kahaulelio described in detail the methods used for catching some of the various species of fish caught off Kanaloa—*mālolo, weke, ulua*, and uhu. He also gathered he'e and 'opihi from the reefs and coast of the island. According to Kahaulelio, mālolo were numerous at Kanaloa and sold for $20 a canoe-load at Lahaina. He fished for weke with a net and with fishhooks. On dark nights he did *ku'iku'i* fishing for ulua with his father along the hilly and rocky coast of the island. They used paka eel for bait and a stout wooden pole and three-ply *olonā* cord. To catch uhu near the beaches of Kanaloa, Kahaulelio used a kind of bamboo pole that was also used to catch aku, with hā'uke'uke, wana, and ina sea urchins as bait. According to Kahaulelio, the fishing ground on the seaward side of Kealaikahiki called Laepaki was one of the most productive of the three deep-sea fishing grounds of Kanaloa.[24] Kahaulelio wrote at length about the big *'opihi makaiauli* of Kanapou Bay:

> It is at that large stream facing Honuaula. The opihi are as large as the
> bowls found in shops, not large ones, but the smaller ones. Goat meat could

be boiled in opihi shells and the twenty-five cents worth of beef bought in Lahaina could be cooked entirely in the opihi shells of that locality, not the opihi dived for, but that which clung to the sea cliffs. Your writer was there for a week without vegetable food, living only on water, fish, opihi and goat meat. That is how I discovered that that was the place of large opihis.[25]

In his articles, Kahaulelio related the legend of Puʻuiʻaiki, who left Kohala on a small canoe and was swamped in the middle of the ʻAlenuihāhā Channel. Feeling sorry for Puʻuiʻaiki, the prophet Moaʻula, who lived at Moaʻula on Kanaloa, sent the *opihi makaiauli* to rescue him. After grasping the ʻopihi, Puʻuiʻaiki was swallowed whole by a shark. Puʻuiʻaiki used the ʻopihi to scrape away at the flesh of the shark, and after three nights and days the shark landed at Kanapou Bay and died. Puʻuiʻaiki came out of the shark, his head now bald and shiny from having been inside the shark, and rested on the beach. He survived an attempt by some fisherman of the island to stone him and was rescued by the prophet Moaʻula. The story provides a vivid description of the marine life, the native plant vegetation, and the freshwater sources around Kanapou Bay and reinforces Kahaulelio's own experience of being able to live on the island for a week relying upon those same resources.[26]

The Sea and the Land

There are other place-names on the island that identify additional marine resources utilized by Hawaiians who lived on the island. Honokanaiʻa is the traditional name for what is called Smuggler's Bay. It means "the dolphin harbor." Dolphins are frequently observed playing in the offshore waters of this bay. A bay between Honokanaiʻa and Kealaikahiki near what is called Smuggler's Bay is named Honukanaenae, meaning "tired turtle." This was where the turtles came to rest and to lay their eggs. It is not currently used as a nesting spot by turtles, probably because of the military encampment located in the vicinity.[27]

Koʻele Bay is said to refer to a variety of large tough ʻopihi.[28] The easternmost and westernmost points of Kuheʻeia Bay are the sites of fishing koʻa and bear names referring to the white *hilu* fish and the red hilu fish, respectively. The eastern point is Laehilukea, "white hilu point." The western point is Laehiluʻula, "red hilu point." Kuheʻeia itself means "squid grounds."[29]

Laepuhi means "eel point." Laeokuakaʻiwa means "the point where the frigate bird roosts." Nālaekoholā, the name of the two outermost points of Ahupū Bay, means "humpback whale points."[30]

An islet off of the southern coast of Kanaloa is called Puʻu Koaʻe, meaning "hill of the tropical bird." Seabirds that feed daily off deep-sea fish guide fishermen to schools of fish in the open ocean and can be followed back to landfalls.

Between 1400 and 1600 CE, Native Hawaiians opened agricultural plots inland and planted sweet potatoes and dry-land crops. By the middle of the seventeenth century, the northeast portion of the island at Hakioawa emerged as the largest settlement on the island. The people built many house sites, two major heiau, and several koʻa there. The population began to decline in the eighteenth century due to inter-island warfare and the introduced diseases that had affected the other Hawaiian Islands. In particular, High Chief Kalaniopuʻu of Hawaiʻi invaded Kanaloa in one of his battles against High Chief Kahekili for control over Maui, Lānaʻi, and Kanaloa and many of the residents perished. In 1793 Captain George Vancouver gave Kahekili a gift of goats, which he sent to Kanaloa to graze and multiply. The goats ultimately reproduced into thousands of animals that roamed the island, denuded it of its vegetation, and caused severe erosion and destruction of the island's natural resources.

Kanaloa and Aloha ʻĀina

The contemporary rediscovery of Kahoʻolawe as a sacred island dedicated to Kanaloa led to a revival of the traditional Hawaiian value of aloha ʻāina, or love and respect for the land. Ancestral memories of the kūpuna focused upon aloha ʻāina as the Hawaiian value at the core of traditional spiritual belief and custom.

According to the kūpuna, Native Hawaiians respect, treasure, praise, and worship the land and all natural elements as deities and the source of universal life. At one level, family genealogies link contemporary Hawaiians to astronomers, navigators, planters, fishermen, engineers, healers, and artisans. These ancestors settled Hawaiʻi and constructed great walled fishponds, irrigated taro terraces, dry-land agricultural systems, heiau, and family settlements. At a deeper level, beyond these human forebears, ancestral chants trace Hawaiian origins to such great gods as Papa Hānaumoku, the earth mother and birth mother of the Hawaiian Islands; Wākea, the sky father; Kāne, the springs and streams; Kanaloa, the ocean; and Pele, the volcano. Hawaiians are genealogical descendants of the earth, sea, sky, and natural life forces.

Acknowledgment of such ancestry thus places a responsibility upon contemporary Native Hawaiians to protect the land and all of its resources in one's lifetime and for the lifetimes of future generations. This is the moral responsibility that George Helm spoke of in the epigraph to this chapter. In addition, aloha 'āina embodied several layers of responsibility. At one level, it meant protecting the physical sustainability of Hawaiian lands and natural resources. At another level, it meant organizing and rallying for Hawaiian native rights and sovereignty to achieve the political standing necessary to protect the 'āina. At the deepest level, it meant a spiritual dedication to honor and worship the gods who were the spiritual life of these forces of nature.

Gradually, the movement that developed to protect Kanaloa from continued military bombing and combat exercises grew to be more pro-Hawaiian than anti-American. It embraced the environmental, political, and spiritual meaning and practice of aloha 'āina.

For fourteen years, from 1976 through 1990, the Protect Kaho'olawe 'Ohana led Native Hawaiians and the general public in protests to end the desecration of Kaho'olawe/Kanaloa. A series of illegal occupations of the island led to arrests and lengthy and expensive court defenses. Members were sentenced to imprisonment or were barred from ever returning to the island. In some instances 'Ohana members were ostracized by family, friends, and the broader community for their activism. The hardest loss was the tragic disappearance of George Helm and Kimo Mitchell, in March 1977, in the waters surrounding the island during their protest of the bombing.

In 1980, as the result of a civil suit filed in 1976 by Helm, the Protect Kaho'olawe 'Ohana reached an out-of-court settlement with the U.S. Navy, called a consent decree. The Navy was mandated to conform to the National Historic Preservation Act and to survey and develop a plan to protect historic sites, complexes, and features on the island. Under the Environmental Protection Act, the Navy was mandated to stop bombing the island for ten days of each month, to limit their bombing and shelling to the central third of the island, to clear two-thirds of the island of surface ordnance, to eradicate the feral goats, and to begin soil conservation and revegetation programs. In compliance with the American Indian Religious Freedom Act of 1978, the Protect Kaho'olawe 'Ohana was acknowledged to be Ke Kahu O Ka 'āina or Steward of the Land and allowed access to the island for religious, cultural, and educational activities for four days in ten months of each year. This served as a critical turning point in the struggle to restore Kanaloa to the people of Hawai'i. Several members of the 'Ohana criticized the consent decree as an unacceptable compromise because it meant joint use of the island with the U.S. Navy and therefore an acknowledgement of their presence and use of the island. In protest, they resigned from the organization. Those who remained in the 'Ohana viewed the consent decree as an interim measure to relieve the island of full-scale, year-round bombing. Isolating the bombardment to a third of the island meant that two-thirds of the island could begin the healing process, being cleared of surface ordnance and replanted with grasses and trees.

Under the consent decree, the 'Ohana began to resettle and heal Kanaloa. An average of sixty participants were taken to the island each month to work with the 'Ohana on erosion control and revegetation projects. The 'Ohana established a permanent base camp on the northeast side of the Island at Hakioawa as well as three temporary camps along the north side at Kūheʻeia and Ahupū and on the west side at Keanakeiki. Hiking trails were cleared, water catchments installed, and soil conservation and revegetation projects initiated. Ancestral shrines and temples were rededicated, and new cultural sites, such as a traditional meeting house, a hula platform, and a memorial for kūpuna who had passed on, were established. Beginning in 1982 the 'Ohana revived the annual celebration of the Makahiki or harvest ceremonies in honor of Lono, the Hawaiian god of agriculture. Strategically, the consent decree established the 'Ohana as the steward of Kanaloa and significantly expanded the network of support for permanently ending all military use of the island.

Within the framework of this moʻolelo, the relevance of these developments is that these various projects and the manner in which the Protect Kahoʻolawe 'Ohana conducted its work were designed and guided by kuaʻāina from Maui, Lānaʻi, Kauaʻi, Molokaʻi, and Hawaiʻi. Harry Mitchell, the Kūkahiko 'ohana, and the Lind 'ohana of Maui shared their knowledge of the bays, points, currents, and channels surrounding Kanaloa and how to safely navigate them. They also guided the 'Ohana in how to anchor in the bays and land upon the shores of the island that lack moorings, piers, or docks. Their knowledge of the fishing grounds and marine resources was utilized in securing food for those who ventured to Kanaloa to help stabilize its natural and cultural resources. The Maui kuaʻāina provided guidance on how to prepare to enter the ocean surrounding Kanaloa and how to pack to survive on the island. Everything brought to the island is floated through the ocean and landed by swimming it to participants who form a line from the shore out into the waves. Those who go to Kanaloa bring sufficient supplies of fresh water and cook their food on propane burners and in traditional imu. It is an amazing experience in living with the 'āina, one that transforms the lives of those who make the open ocean crossing. Harry Mitchell, who endured the ultimate sacrifice of losing his son Kimo for the life of Kanaloa, walked the island with 'ohana members, pointed out each significant cultural site, explained its purpose and function, interpreted the name given to it by our ancestors, and shared the mo'olelo associated with it. These were recorded in video and produced by the 'ohana to educate the wider public and new generations of students about the historical cultural importance of Kanaloa.

Maui families also shared their knowledge of the historic connection of Haleakalā on Maui to Kanaloa. Harry Mitchell spoke of an underground lava tube that connects Kanaloa to Haleakalā in the same way an umbilical cord connects a fetus to its mother and noted that the island is shaped like a fetus. The kūpuna described a long cloud, Keaoloa, that formed daily above the forests of Ulupalakua on the slopes of Haleakalā and extended across the Alalā-keiki Channel to Moa'ulanui on Kanaloa, across the island and the Kealaika-hiki Channel to Lāna'i, and across the Kaiokalohi Channel to Ho'olehua on Moloka'i. This cloud was the principal source of rain for the island of Kanaloa throughout most of the year, when the northeast trade winds prevailed. When the forests on Haleakalā were cleared for pasture, the cloud stopped forming over 'Ulupalakua, and the rain stopped falling on Kanaloa for the greater part of the year.

Figure 34 The annual Makahiki ceremony on Kaho'olawe includes a procession to the top of the island to open the ceremonies in November and a procession across the island to close the ceremonies in January. 1987. Franco Salmoiraghi.

'Ohana of Lāna'i provided guidance in how to cross the Kealaikahiki Channel to the western shores of Kanaloa from their island. They shared their experience and knowledge about restoring the dry-land forests and soils of Lāna'i, which of those of all the islands are the closest in type and condition to those of Kanaloa. The dry-land forest at Kanepu'u on Lāna'i remains a model for the restoration of Kanaloa's flora and natural resources.

'Ohana of Kaua'i shared their traditions and knowledge of fishing and gathering and the transmigrations throughout the island chain that connected Kaho'olawe to the families of all of the islands.

The kua'āina of Moloka'i organized the groups who visited to work as an 'ohana in practicing the values of *aloha kekāhi i kekāhi*, or love and respect for each other, and *laulima*, or cooperative work. They organized the work projects in fulfillment of aloha 'āina and *mālama 'āina*, or care for the land. Hui Ala Loa, which was the predecessor and parent organization of the Protect Kaho'olawe 'Ohana, served as a model in how to organize multiple generations—both the mākua and the 'ōpi'o—under the leadership of the kūpuna.

Through the leadership of Noa Emmett Aluli and Colette Machado of Moloka'i, the 'Ohana remained rooted in the founding principles of aloha 'āina, kūpuna leadership, 'ohana or collective decision making and action, accountability to the grassroots kua'āina, and a clear focus on healing and restoring the life of Kanaloa itself. The 'Ohana navigated the treacherous political times and steered clear of centering the organization in Honolulu, where opportunistic Native Hawaiian leaders desired to use Kaho'olawe to advance their own political agendas and the abstract goal of political sovereignty and independence. The 'Ohana continued to follow the philosophy of George Helm—"follow your na'au, but do your homework"—which made it a committed organization of political action guided by an informed and sophisticated strategy. Moreover, the Moloka'i kua'āina kept alive the memory and vision of George Helm for Kaho'olawe to be regreened and restored as a pu'uhonua for the Hawaiian culture, so that the sacrifice of Helm's life would not be in vain.

Before George Helm died he and Aluli founded the Kohemālamalama o Kanaloa/Protect Kaho'olawe Fund. Together, Aluli and Machado linked the Protect Kaho'olawe Fund (PKF) to national funding groups supportive of Native American culture, land rights, and sovereignty, among them the Seventh Generation Fund, the Tides Foundation, and the Gerbode Foundation. The Protect Kaho'olawe Fund board included representatives of grassroots communities on every island and therefore did more than raise money for the work of stopping the bombing of Kanaloa and restoring its cultural and natural resources. The fund also helped establish and fund grassroots organizations engaged in aloha 'āina land struggles on Kaua'i, Maui, Lāna'i, Moloka'i, and Hawai'i, continuing to expand the network of support for Kanaloa.

In the 1980s the PKF helped the Hāna Pōhaku on Maui raise funds for self-sufficiency projects in taro cultivation and fishing, research into protecting their land from federal condemnation for a national park, and protection of their water rights from diversion for hotels. The Hui Ala Nui o Makena on Maui was assisted by the PKF in the research and legal work to keep access to the Makena coastline open for fishing and gathering by local people.

On Kaua'i, the fund assisted the Niumalu-Nawiliwili Tenants Association to develop an alternative land use plan that included their new homes. For Lāna'i, monies were raised for research of kuleana lands and water concerns. Hui Ala Loa on Moloka'i received assistance for its litigation and organizing

Figure 35 On October 22, 1990, President George H. W. Bush stopped the bombing and all ordnance delivery exercises on Kaho'olawe. The amphibious exercises shown here did not involve ordnance and were the last military exercises conducted on the island in 1993. 1993. Franco Salmoiraghi.

work to protect that island's cultural, natural, and agricultural resources from overdevelopment.

On the island of Hawai'i, the PKF assisted the Mālama Ka 'Āina Hāna Ka 'Āina community organization to get monies to develop a plan to settle Hawaiian Home Lands at King's Landing by families desiring to pursue traditional Hawaiian subsistence livelihoods instead of building standard residential houses on lots. Ka 'Ohana O Kalae at South Point worked with the PKF to receive monies for a community curatorship program to protect the historic sites and rich natural resources of the Ka'ū district from industrial development. Efforts of Pele practitioners to protect her and the Kīlauea volcano and rainforest from geothermal development were initially funded by grants to the Protect Kaho'olawe Fund until the Pele Defense Fund branched out from the PKF.

In summary, the Protect Kaho'olawe Fund, under the leadership of Aluli and Machado, served as a launching pad for much of the practical work of aloha 'āina in the 1980s and the early 1990s. The work to protect Hawaiian ancestral lands from development; to perpetuate traditional Hawaiian spiritual relationships to the land, including religious ceremonies; and to continue traditional subsistence economic activities was established and persisted and grew through the efforts of the various community-based organizations affiliated with and supported by the Protect Kaho'olawe 'Ohana and Fund.

Kua'āina from Hawai'i organized the building of a *hale halawai* or meeting house, bringing in 'ōhi'a logs and grass for thatching from the forests and pastures of their island. Fishermen from Hawai'i brought their skills to provide subsistence for people while they were staying on Kanaloa. The Kanaka'ole 'ohana of Hawai'i provided the chants and the ceremonies to celebrate the Makahiki and to reopen cultural sites, as well as to build new sites and dedicate them.

The reestablishment of the Makahiki and other Native Hawaiian cultural and religious ceremonies and practices on Kanaloa was the most significant outcome of the movement to stop the bombing of Kanaloa. These ceremonies and practices reconnected a generation of Native Hawaiians with their ancestors and their soul as a people. The revival of these religious ceremonies deserves special attention. It was inspired and guided by Edith Kanakaole, her daughters Nalani and Pualani, her son-in-law Edward Kanahele, her son Parley Kanaka'ole, and the Edith Kanakaole Foundation of the island of Hawai'i that was founded in her honor.

Rebirth of the Sacred

From the outset, Helm and Aluli followed the guidance of the kūpuna who counseled them by acknowledging and including the ancestral spirits of Kanaloa in the effort to stop the bombing and heal the island. Kahuna Sam Lono and Emma DeFries of Oʻahu conducted a ceremony in 1976 at Hakioawa to ask permission of the ancestral spirits of the land to open the religious sites on the island to receive hoʻokupu or offerings. In 1979, John ʻĀnuenue Kaʻimikaua of Oʻahu and Molokaʻi and his *hālau hula* or school of hula conducted a ceremony to give life to the land by burying offerings of food in the ground and dances of *hula kahiko*. Papa Paul Elia of Molokaʻi offered a prayer to the ancestral gods for strength, organization, and protection of the land. At that time Aunty Emma DeFries did a *hoʻuwēʻuwē* or lamentation chant for the ʻāina acknowledging the neglect of the island which caused its devastation. Other kūpuna who committed their *mana* for the respect and return of the ancestral spirits and the Native Hawaiian gods of nature to Kanaloa included Aunty

Figure 36 George Helm helped found the movement to stop the bombing of Kahoʻolawe, for which he gave his life a few months after this photo was taken. The movement to stop the bombing of Kahoʻolawe sparked the Hawaiian renaissance and the movement for Native Hawaiian sovereignty. 1977. Bishop Museum.

'Iolani Luahine, Uncle Sam Hart, Aunty Luka Naluai, Uncle Henry Lindsey, and Aunty Gardie Perkins.[31] In 1981 the 'Ohana asked Aunty Edith Kanaka-'ole and her daughter Nalani Kanaka'ole of Hālau o Kekuhi to train them in how to conduct a Makahiki ceremony. The 'Ohana wanted to place the healing and regreening of the island under the care of Lono, Hawaiian god of agriculture and productivity.

Hālau o Kekuhi and the Edith Kanaka'ole Foundation are the most influential force in the revitalization of sacred ceremonies and rituals on Kanaloa and in contemporary Hawai'i as a whole. Aunty Edith Kanaka'ole was trained in the hula by her mother, Mary Ahi'ena Kanaele Fujii, who was born in the 1880s and raised in the *hula kapu* or sacred hula in the Puna district of Hawai'i.[32] Hālau o Kekuhi, according to its Web site, "is celebrated for its mastery of the 'Aiha'a style of hula and chant . . . a low postured, vigorous, bombastic style of hula which springs from the eruptive volcano persona, Pele and Hi'iaka."[33] It is "a traditional classical dance company" rooted in "seven generations of family practitioners" and leaders in hula and oli. The Edith Kanka'ole Foundation was founded in the summer of 1990. Its purpose is to heighten indigenous Hawaiian cultural awareness and participation through educational programs that maintain and perpetuate the teachings, beliefs, practices, philosophies, and traditions of Edith and Luka Kanaka'ole and their ancestors, including Edith's mother, Ahi'ena, her great-uncle Lonokapu, and Luka's father and mother, Ioana Kanaka'ole and Haleaka Kaleopa'a.

In January 1982 the Protect Kaho'olawe 'Ohana conducted what may have been the first public Makahiki ceremonies in honor of the Akua Lono since High Chief Kekuaokalani conducted the Makahiki ceremonies before going into battle in defense of the Hawaiian religion in 1819, in the year of the 'Ai Noa or Abolition of the Kapu. The purpose of the ceremonies was to attract the akua, Lono, to Kanaloa in the form of rain clouds to soften the earth and ready it to receive young plants to revegetate the island. Every year since 1982 the 'Ohana has opened the Makahiki season in November after the appearance of the Makali'i or Pleiades constellation on the horizon at sunset and has closed the Makahiki season in January or late February. Edith Kanaka'ole and Nalani Kanaka'ole prescribed the ho'okupu, ten offerings including various *kino lau* or body forms of the akua. They advised the 'Ohana in the crafting of an *akua loa* or image of Lono. Nalani Kanaka'ole composed the chants of prayer to Lono. The Edith Kanaka'ole Foundation described the central chant:

This Lono chant concentrates on the kinolau or body forms of Lono which are the manifestations that encourage growth. The prayer is a formula used in many traditional chants that is; recognizing and addressing the great Gods of the elements, followed by an account of their creations, then an enumeration of offerings, a statement of the body forms of the deities and finally the reason for the prayer. The need in this case is to ensure vegetation and growth on the island. The very last line releases the formal communication with the God. This is the FIRST formal prayer chant composed for a formal modern day Makahiki ceremony.[34]

In May 1986 Pualani Kanakaʻole Kanahele and Edward Kanahele were asked by the Protect Kahoʻolawe ʻOhana to design a ceremony for the Akua Kanaloa. The biennial RIMPAC naval exercises were scheduled to culminate with the joint ship-to-shore shelling of the island by U.S. and Canadian naval forces after forty-five days of joint naval maneuvers from California to Hawaiʻi. After years of protest, the ʻOhana resolved to enlist Kanaloa himself in the effort to protect his kino lau from the bombing and in the effort to restore the island to the people of Hawaiʻi. The ceremony was designed to be small and private. The central chant asked Kanaloa to give strength and skill to those united in the goal of protecting and giving life to the island. The hoʻokupu of heʻe (octopus), a kino lau of Kanaloa, could not be eaten by those involved in the ceremony. This ceremony provided focus and inspiration to those involved in the ongoing work to stop the bombing and restore the life of the island.

In 1982 Kumu Hula Hokulani Holt Padilla of Maui, a member of the Protect Kahoʻolawe ʻOhana, decided to build a *pā hula* or hula platform at Hakioawa so there would be a formal arena for the hula practices on Kanaloa. Over the course of five years, many people who came to Kanaloa on an access visit with the Protect Kahoʻolawe ʻOhana contributed their aloha and hard work to build up the platform. During the opening of the Makahiki in November 1987, the pā hula was dedicated to Laka and named Kaʻieʻie in a ceremony led by Kumu Hula Hokulani Holt Padilla with the participation of Kumu Hula Pualani Kanakaʻole Kanahele and Kumu Hula Kealiʻi Reichel.

A chant composed by Pualani Kanahele for the healing ceremony described below, "He Koʻihonua No Kanaloa He Moku," chronicled the origin and history of the island and provides a poetic summary of the process of reviving religious ceremonies on the island:

Ua ala Hawaiʻi mai ka moehewa nui	The Hawaiian woke from the nightmare
Hoʻomaopopo i ke keiki iʻa a Papa	Remembered was the child of Papa
ʻO Kanaloa	O Kanaloa
Ke moku hei Haumea	The sacred land of Haumea
ʻO Kohemālamalama	O Kohemālamalama
Ke Kino o Kamohoaliʻi	The body form of Kamohoaliʻi
E hoʻōla kākou iā Kahoʻolawe	Save Kahoʻolawe
Ola i ka lani a Kāne	To live in the heavens of Kane
Ola i ke kai a Kanaloa	To live in the sea of Kanaloa
Ua Kaheaʻia ʻo Lono i ka makahiki hou	Lono was summoned for a new year
Ma ka Hale Mua o Lono i kahea ʻia ai	At the Hale Mua of Lono, he was called,
Ua Kanaloa ʻo Kanaloa i Kohemālamalama	Kanaloa was reconfirmed to Kohemālamalama
Puka hou aʻe ka mana o Kanaloa	The energy of Kanaloa was revitalized
Ua kani ka leo pahu i ka Mālama o Hoku	The voice of the drum sounded in the care of Hoku
Kuwawā i ka houpo a Laka	Resounding in the bosom of Laka
Ua ala ʻo Laka ma Kaʻieʻie i Kanaloa	Laka awoke at Kaʻieʻia at Kanaloa.

The revival of sacred ceremonies on Kanaloa is what distinguished the Protect Kahoʻolawe ʻOhana as a pro-Hawaiian and cultural organization. As the ʻOhana and its political struggle and practical restoration efforts evolved, cultural protocol and religious prayer proved to be an essential element in shaping and defining their efforts. Ultimately, perseverance and this holistic approach proved successful.

The Bombing Stops

Finally, on October 22, 1990, after a decade of persistent, dedicated, and focused work for Kanaloa under the consent decree, the bombing of Kahoʻolawe stopped. The Democratic senator from Hawaiʻi, Sparky Matsunaga, passed away in office in April 1990. The National Republican Party and President George Bush himself urged Congresswoman Patricia Saiki to run for the deceased senator's seat as part of the national campaign to win a Republican majority in the U.S. Senate. According to Saiki's Native Hawaiian campaign manager, Andy Anderson, Bush asked the congresswoman what it would take for her to get elected. She said it would take a miracle for her as a Republican to get elected from the Democratic state of Hawai'i. Asked what such a miracle might be, Anderson and Saiki's campaign staff suggested that stopping the bombing of Kaho'olawe would win her the support of the general public in her bid for the U.S. Senate.[35] In an interview on November 11, 2003, at the time the U.S. Navy transferred control of access to the island, Saiki described her conversation with the president:

> He said, "What can I do for you to give you a hand here, to help with the state and get your election looked at positively?" I said, "No. 1, you've got to stop the bombing of Kahoolawe. It is an island that has been devastated by the impact exercises. Although the exercises are very worthy, it is an assault and an insult to the Hawaiian people."[36]

Bush directed the Secretary of Defense to immediately discontinue use of the island for bombing and target practice a day before he set out from Washington to campaign for the congresswoman in Hawai'i.[37] Jet bombers scheduled to make a bombing raid on Kaho'olawe that morning were grounded.

In order to keep his competitive edge in the race for the U.S. Senate seat, Saiki's challenger, Democratic Congressman Daniel Akaka, worked with Democratic Senator Daniel Inouye to do more for Kaho'olawe/Kanaloa than Saiki and Bush had done. In November 1993 the U.S. Congress passed and President Bill Clinton signed an act that recognized Kaho'olawe/Kanaloa as a national cultural treasure and stopped the use of Kanaloa for any military training for two years and 120 days. It also established the Kaho'olawe Island Conveyance Commission to make recommendations for the future use of the island. This was a more significant and permanent measure. A presidential memorandum could be rescinded or overridden at any time in the future, unlike a Senate bill that had been passed into law. This shifted the balance of support in favor of Congressman Akaka, who was first elected to the U.S. Senate in November 1990. The Conveyance Commission recommended that title to the island be turned over to the state of Hawai'i and that the Congress appropriate $400 million to conduct a ten-year omnibus ordnance clean-up of the island. On May 9, 1994, the U.S. Navy formally returned the island to the state of Hawai'i in ceremonies at Palauea, Maui, across the channel from Kanaloa. Under a specific Hawaiian law, Hawai'i Revised Statutes Chapter 6K, the island will eventually be turned over to a sovereign Hawaiian entity. It states in part, "The resources and waters of Kanaloa shall be held in trust as part of the public land trust; provided that the State shall transfer management and control of the island and its waters to the sovereign native Hawaiian entity upon its recognition by the United States and the State of Hawai'i."[38] This measure set a precedent for Native Hawaiian sovereignty in that the state of Hawai'i acknowledges that there will be a sovereign Native Hawaiian entity and that repatriated federal lands can be part of the land base of the sovereign entity.

A unique feature of the approach taken by the Kaho'olawe Island Conveyance Commission to arrive at its recommendations and complete its final report was a special cultural ceremony held in August 1992 at Hakiowa. "E Kaho'olawe, E Ho'omau Ana Hou I Ka Mauli Ola," a healing ceremony for the land, ocean, and people of Kaho'olawe, was the name and purpose of the event. It was organized by the Edith Kanaka'ole Foundation in coordination with the Protect Kaho'olawe 'Ohana and the Conveyance Commission. The central feature was the construction of a *mua* or memorial platform to honor the kūpuna who had dedicated their lives to the healing of the island. Government leaders from the federal, state, and county governments and from the Office of Hawaiian Affairs were invited to sit on the mua with kūpuna from each island and the leaders of the Protect Kaho'olawe 'Ohana. Each was served the ceremonial drink 'awa by Parley Kanaka'ole, the *kahu* or leader of the ceremony, and in receiving the drink each was asked to make a decision and commit to doing whatever was in their power to heal the island of Kaho'olawe. The Edith Kanaka'ole Foundation composed special chants to open the ceremony at dawn and to acknowledge the genealogy of the decision makers and kūpuna upon their stepping onto the mua, a genealogical history of the island, and chants in honor of George Helm and Kimo Mitchell. The opening dawn chant, called "E Ala E," has become a popular chant throughout the islands as a protocol for starting the day in a Hawaiian frame of mind.

This cultural ceremony affirmed support for the recommendation of the commission to Congress to permanently end military use of the island, turn title over to the state of Hawai'i, and appropriate $400 million to clear the island of ordnance and begin the healing and restoration of the island's cultural and natural resources.

The Native Hawaiian Cultural Renaissance

Kanaloa also sparked a broader cultural revival, one that reverberated throughout the Hawaiian Islands from 1976 through the 1990s and challenged other institutions of American colonization.

A general cultural renaissance developed as the number of *hālau hula* or schools that teach traditional Hawaiian dance and chant expanded and the number of dancers of both Hawaiian and non-Hawaiian ancestry increased. Hawaiian music gained new popularity and new songs, styles, and rhythms were created. Lā‘au lapa‘au, traditional herbal and spiritual healing practices, were recognized as valid and significant. Traditional Hawaiian healers began to train a new generation in the Hawaiian healing arts.[39]

Of international significance, traditional navigational skills were revived through transpacific noninstrument navigation in traditional Hawaiian sailing canoes such as the *Hōkūle‘a*, the *Hawai‘i Loa*, and the *Makali‘i* were accomplished. These voyages spread the Hawaiian cultural renaissance throughout the Pacific—from the Marquesas to Tahiti and the Cook Islands, New Zealand, Australia, and Rapa Nui (Easter Island).

As Native Hawaiians from all of the islands continued to visit Kanaloa and to become involved in the struggle to stop military use of the island, they also carried back to their home islands the message of aloha ‘āina. Where resort or industrial developments threatened to expand into the rural districts that had served as the last strongholds of Native Hawaiian custom, belief, and practice, communities began to organize to protect their lands and natural resources and Hawaiian way of life, many with the support of the Protect Kaho‘olawe Fund.

Native Hawaiians on Moloka‘i continued to organize as Hui Ala Loa to stop resort development that threatened to divert limited water resources away from community-based economic development and to destroy subsistence resources.

Native Hawaiians in Ka‘ū organized against plans to launch rockets from Hawaiian Home Lands at South Point and to develop a spaceport at Kahilipali and Palina Point. They argued that these massive projects would destroy Native Hawaiian cultural sites in the district, bring in newcomers, and transform the Native Hawaiian way of life.

As discussed in chapter 4, practitioners of the Hawaiian volcano goddess Pele on the island of Hawai‘i organized against geothermal energy development in the Wao Kele o Puna rainforest of Puna. Industrialization of the volcano threatened to destroy the largest expanse of lowland tropical rainforest in the United States. The Pele practitioners asserted that geothermal energy would desecrate and destroy the life force and manifestations of their deity.

Native Hawaiians of Maui organized against sprawling resort development that blocked access to the beaches of Makena for subsistence fishing and gathering of marine resources. Hawaiians on all islands organized to protect their traditional burial grounds from destruction by various forms of development, a movement sparked by the controversy at Honokahua in Maui, where over 1,000 graves were dug up and relocated to build a Ritz-Carlton Hotel.

In 1983 a group of University of Hawai'i professors and native speakers of Hawaiian from Ni'ihau formed Pūnana Leo, to develop Hawaiian language immersion preschools. In 1984 the first Pūnana Leo school opened, and by 1995 the nine Pūnana Leo Hawaiian Immersion preschools had a total enrollment of 181 students. In addition, Pūnana Leo began to work toward rescinding the law that mandated that English be the only medium of instruction in public schools. In 1987, after an absence of 100 years, the Hawaiian language began again to be a medium language of instruction in the public schools. By the 1999–2000 school year Ka Papahana-Kaiapuni Hawai'i (public education Hawaiian Language Immersion Program) had approximately 1,750 students enrolled in eighteen schools. The Hawaiian language has been rescued from extinction and continues to grow and expand as the language of choice for Native Hawaiians.

When the last sugar plantation in leeward O'ahu shut down in the 1990s, taro farmers on windward O'ahu petitioned the Hawai'i State Water Commission to stop diverting the waters of the Wai'āhole and Waikāne streams to the 'Ewa plains. Thanks to their efforts, only half of the water is now diverted, and the other half is allowed to flow into the Wai'āhole stream. Native stream life returned, marine life in Kane'ohe Bay became more abundant, and farmers reopened taro terraces that had lain dry and overgrown with brush for decades. A new generation of Hawaiian and local youth from windward O'ahu began to pursue livelihoods involving the cultivation of taro, as their grandparents had done.

Throughout these struggles it became increasingly apparent that Native Hawaiians lacked official legal standing to adequately protect Native Hawaiian lands and resources. Moreover, developments that occurred on state or federal government lands exploited the original Crown and government lands of the Hawaiian Kingdom to which Native Hawaiians maintained vested rights of inheritance that were never surrendered. Thus, Native Hawaiians began to seek political solutions to effectively protect the lands and resources essential for the perpetuation of spiritual and cultural customs, beliefs, and practices.

Native Hawaiian Sovereignty and Recognition

Under the U.S. Constitution, indigenous Native American tribes are recognized as domestic dependent nations, with inherent powers of self-governance and self-determination, for which the U.S. federal government sustains a trust responsibility.[40] This status has been extended to Eskimos, Aleuts, and Native Alaskans under the Alaskan Native Claims Settlement Act. However, other ethnic and racial minorities within the fifty U.S. states do not enjoy the status of nationhood, they do nor do they have the right of self-governance and self-determination, and the federal government does not have a trust responsibility for them. The status of Native Hawaiians as an indigenous people within the currently defined boundaries of the United States has been recognized through various policies.

From 1906 through 1998 the U.S. Congress, in effect, recognized a trust relationship with the native people of Hawaiʻi through the enactment of 183 federal laws that explicitly included Native Hawaiians in the class of Native Americans.[41] Some of the laws extended federal programs set up for Native Americans to Native Hawaiians, while others represented recognition by the U.S. Congress that the United States bore a special responsibility to protect Native Hawaiian interests.[42] Although the operational policy of the U.S. Congress has been to exercise a trust responsibility with Native Hawaiians similar to that which Congress has with Native Americans, the laws passed extended an implicit rather than explicit and formal recognition that Native Hawaiians are a sovereign people with the right of self-governance and self-determination. Without such an explicit law, Native Hawaiians may not be eligible to receive the special benefits, entitlements, and protection the U.S. Congress extended to them beginning in 1906.

The U.S. Supreme Court, in the case of Rice v. Cayetano, ruled on February 23, 2000, that elections for the trustees of the State of Hawaiʻi Office of Hawaiian Affairs (OHA), in which only Native Hawaiians were allowed to vote, used unconstitutional race-based qualifications.[43] The majority of the members of the court ruled that the Native Hawaiian OHA election violated the Fifteenth Amendment of the U.S. Constitution, which states that the right to vote cannot be denied on account of race or color.[44] Subsequently, in the November 2000 election for OHA trustees, all registered voters, regardless of Native Hawaiian ancestry, were allowed to cast votes and to run for these offices.

The U.S. Supreme Court, in its ruling, stated that Native Hawaiians have a shared purpose in the Islands with the general public and that the Constitution of the United States has become the heritage of all the citizens of Hawaii, including Native Hawaiians. In addition, the court raised questions about whether Native Hawaiians are in fact a distinct and unique indigenous people with the right of self-governance and self-determination under U.S. law or are instead an ethnic or racial minority not eligible for such rights.

In the ruling, a majority of the Supreme Court justices also raised, but did not resolve, four fundamental questions regarding the status of Native Hawaiians. May Congress treat the Native Hawaiians as it does the Indian tribes? Has Congress in fact determined that Native Hawaiians have a status like that of Indians in organized tribes? May Congress delegate to the State of Hawai'i the authority to preserve that status? Has Congress delegated to the State of Hawai'i the authority to preserve that status?[45] A negative answer to any of these questions could result in a determination that Native Hawaiians do not qualify under U.S. law for the rights and protection afforded other indigenous peoples within the fifty states. The majority of the Supreme Court Justices also seemed to open the door to future legal challenges on the status of Native Hawaiians when it stated:

> It is a matter of some dispute, for instance, whether Congress may treat the native Hawaiians as it does the Indian tribes. Compare Van Dyke, The Political Status of the Hawaiian People, 17 Yale L. & Pol'y Rev. 95 (1998), with Benjamin, Equal Protection and the Special Relationship: The Case of Native Hawaiians, 106 Yale L.J. 537 (1996). We can stay far off that difficult terrain, however.[46]

Suddenly, the status, rights, and entitlements Native Hawaiians had enjoyed throughout the twentieth century could be legally challenged out of existence. Moreover, the Supreme Court ruling seemed to contradict the policy of the U.S. Congress toward Native Hawaiians.

Hawai'i's congressional delegation, led by Senators Daniel Akaka and Daniel Inouye, drafted and introduced legislation (called the Akaka Bill) to explicitly and unambiguously clarify the trust relationship between Native Hawaiians and the United States. Although the bill failed to pass from 2000 to 2006, Hawai'i's congressional delegation will continue to introduce similar bills until one passes. Such a bill would formally and directly extend the federal policy of self-determination and self-governance to Native Hawaiians as Hawai'i's indigenous native people. The legislation would provide a process for recognition by the United States, under the Secretary of the Department of Interior, of a Native Hawaiian governing entity.[47]

Lessons of Stewardship from Kanaloa

Kanaloa is important as an example of the role played by kua'āina from cultural kīpuka in the perpetuation and revival of Native Hawaiian culture. Through Kanaloa, kua'āina shared their understanding and experience related to traditional concepts of wahi pana, aloha 'āina, and lōkāhi, popularized as core practices in the stewardship of Hawai'i's land, ocean, and natural resources.

Upon receiving title to the island of Kaho'olawe, the State of Hawai'i set up the Kaho'olawe Island Reserve Commission (KIRC) to manage the island and its surrounding waters, out to two miles, as a Native Hawaiian cultural reserve. The commission adopted a vision statement that reads in part:

> The kino (body) of Kanaloa is restored . . . Na po'e Hawai'i (the people of Hawai'i) care for the land in a manner which recognizes the island and ocean of Kanaloa as a living spiritual entity. Kanaloa is a pu'uhonua (spiritual refuge) and wahi pana (sacred place) where Native Hawaiian cultural practices flourish.
>
> The piko (navel) of Kanaloa is the crossroads of past and future generations from which the Native Hawaiian lifestyle spreads throughout the islands.[48]

This vision statement encompasses the physical and spiritual restoration of Kanaloa, both the island and the god. It projects activities on the island that revolve around restoration. The isolation of the island provides a historic opportunity to revegetate it with native plants. It also envisions a protected marine sanctuary that can serve as a pool for restocking marine life for the ocean in and around Maui nui. The statement presents Kanaloa as a cultural learning center where traditional cultural and spiritual customs, beliefs, and practices of Native Hawaiians such as way-finding, fishing, and healing can flourish and spread out to all the islands. Native Hawaiian culture exists nowhere else in the world, and Kanaloa will play a role its perpetuation.

In order to implement this vision, the KIRC worked with the Protect Kaho'olawe 'Ohana and the Edith Kanaka'ole Foundation to develop traditional kua'āina stewardship principles for guiding the development of a land use plan for the island.[49] First among these principles is that the ahupua'a is the basic unit of Hawaiian natural and cultural resource management. An ahupua'a runs from the sea to the mountains and contains a sea fishery and beach, a stretch of kula or open cultivable land, and, higher up, the forest. The court of the Hawaiian kingdom described the ahupua'a principle of land use in the case *In Re Boundaries of Pūlehunui*, 4 Haw. 239, 241 (1879) as follows:

> A principle very largely obtaining in these divisions of territory [ahupua'a] was that a land should run from the sea to the mountains, thus affording to the chief and his people a fishery residence at the warm seaside, together with products of the high lands, such as fuel, canoe timber, mountain birds, and the right of way to the same, and all the varied products of the intermediate land as might be suitable to the soil and climate of the different altitudes from sea soil to mountainside or top.

The entire island was on ahupua'a of the moku or district of Honua'ula. The island was divided into twelve watersheds or 'ili. Restoration of the island will start at the central point of the island and proceed down to the ocean, 'ili by 'ili, recognizing the integral relationship between soil disturbance, water flows, wind, erosion, and runoff.

A second important principle is that the natural elements—land, air, fresh water, ocean—are interconnected and interdependent. From the ocean rise clouds that drench the land with rain, which recharges the island's water table or flows across the landscape in streams or rivers. The rivers and springs ultimately flow back to the beaches and into the ocean. Cultural land use management must take all aspects of the natural environment into account. The atmosphere where clouds form is an integral link in the cycle of life. Ho'ailona or prophetic natural signs and omens appear in the atmosphere and help guide and validate Hawaiian practices.

Hawaiians consider the land and ocean to be integrally united and that these ahupua'a also include the shoreline as well as inshore and offshore ocean areas such as fishponds, reefs, channels, and deep-sea fishing grounds. The sixty-nine fishing ko'a that had been constructed on the island were also markers for offshore fishing grounds. These fishing grounds are also part of 'ili and must be considered in restoration activities on the island.[50]

A third important principle of Native Hawaiian stewardship is that of all the natural elements, fresh water is the most important for life and needs to be considered in every aspect of land use and planning. The Hawaiian word for water is *wai*; the Hawaiian word for wealth is *waiwai*. In Hawai'i, water is the source of well-being and wealth, and the wealth of the land is based upon the amount of fresh water available upon it.

A fourth important principle is the acknowledgment that Hawaiian ancestors studied the land and the natural elements and became very familiar with the land's features and assets. Ancestral knowledge of the land was recorded and passed down through place-names, chants, and legends that name the winds, rains, and features of a particular district. Hawaiians applied their expert knowledge of the natural environment in constructing their homes, temples, cultivation complexes, and irrigation networks. Hawaiian place-names, chants, and legends inform Hawaiians and others who know the traditions of the cultural and natural resources of a particular district. Insights into the natural and cultural resources inform those who use the land how to locate and construct structures and infrastructure so as to have the least negative impact upon the land. In planning for the land, ancestral knowledge about the land and its natural resources should be gathered in order to allow for sustainable use of its resources.

A fifth principle recognizes that an inherent aspect of Hawaiian stewardship and use of cultural and natural resources is the practices of aloha ʻāina and mālama ʻāina, or respect and conservation of the land to ensure the sustainability of natural resources for present and future generations. These rules of behavior are tied to cultural beliefs and values regarding respect of the ʻāina, the virtue of sharing and not taking too much, and a holistic perspective on organisms and ecosystems that emphasizes balance and coexistence. The Hawaiian outlook that shapes these customs and practices is lōkāhi, or maintaining spiritual, cultural, and natural balance with the elemental life forces of nature.

Taken together, these principles, learned through the collaboration of kuaʻāina, scholars, Native Hawaiian activists, and planners in projecting future uses of Kanaloa, provide an excellent foundation for the stewardship of the Hawaiian Islands as a whole.

In recognition of the important lessons of Kanaloa for the stewardship of our Hawaiian Islands, the Bishop Museum partnered with Community Development Pacific and the Protect Kahoʻolawe ʻOhana to develop an exhibit, Kahoʻolawe: Ke Aloha Kūpaʻa I Ka ʻāina, Steadfast Love of the Land. Photographs featured in the exhibit were also published in a book, *Kahoʻolawe, Nā Leo O Kanaloa: Chants and Stories of Kahoʻolawe*. Through photo murals, framed photos, cultural and military artifacts, videos, interactive displays, and computer simulations, the story of Native Hawaiians' love and care for the land was told through the moʻolelo of Kanaloa. The exhibit opened at the Bishop Museum in January 1996 and eventually traveled to all the major islands— Maui, Lānaʻi, Hawaiʻi, Kauaʻi, and Molokaʻi. Nearly 187,000 people, especially students from various public and private schools, learned of the importance of caring for the natural and cultural resources of the Hawaiian islands through the exhibit.

In 2001 the exhibit was reorganized for a national exhibit at the Arts and Industries Building of the Smithsonian Institution at the National Mall in Washington, D.C. Renamed "Kahoʻolawe: Rebirth of a Sacred Hawaiian Island," it opened on June 5, 2002. By the time the exhibit closed on September 2, 2002, 304,037 visitors had viewed the it. The national exhibit took the visitor behind the tourist and Hollywood images of Hawaiʻi and related the trials and tribulations of living on islands with fragile ecosystems. Kanaloa provided a model of how a community can successfully combine efforts with biologists and technical experts to restore premium natural resources and respect the cultural beliefs, customs, and practices of an indigenous people. The exhibit also depicted a chronology of the historical relationship of Native Hawaiians to the U.S. government up through the congressional legislation that would have recognized the sovereignty of Native Hawaiians. To help interpret the exhibit to a national audience, fifty-five persons who had connections to Hawaiʻi and were living in the Washington, D.C., area were trained as docents. Public programs on celestial way-finding, Native Hawaiian storytelling, and songs of Native Hawaiian political resistance were organized to expand upon the information presented in the exhibit.

The exhibit reaffirmed that Kanaloa has been reborn in the hearts and minds of Native Hawaiians as a sacred island. It connects Native Hawaiians to their ancestral spirits, as described in the passage by the Hawaiian scholar Edward Kanahele quoted in chapter 1.

Kanaloa is such a place for all Native Hawaiians. Moreover, it is a place where non-Hawaiians too can experience the Native Hawaiian culture that is at the core of the Hawaiian Islands.

Kanaloa and the People of Hawaiʻi

Throughout the years of the struggle to stop the bombing and reclaim Kanaloa as sacred Hawaiian land, the broader multiethnic local community also rallied in support of the effort as their own. The Protect Kahoʻolawe ʻOhana is not exclusively Native Hawaiian and includes distinguished leaders who are of local Asian and Caucasian ancestry. Because Native Hawaiians comprise only 20 percent of the Hawaiʻi population, the success of the movement to protect Kanaloa was made possible only through the support of the broader local community. Hawaiian and non-Hawaiian political leaders alike, such as Senator Daniel K. Inouye, Senator Daniel Akaka, Congressman Neil Abercrombie, Congresswoman Patsy Mink, former Congresswoman Patricia Saiki, and Governor John Waiheʻe, played important roles in ending the bombing and the authorization of $400 million for the clean-up and restoration. Among the thousands who have visited the island with the Protect Kahoʻolawe ʻOhana since the 1980 consent decree made it possible have been Native Hawaiians and non-Hawaiians alike.

Everyone who wants to embrace and experience Native Hawaiian culture is welcome to go to Kanaloa and work on projects to heal her natural and cultural resources. Kanaloa reconnected a generation of Hawaiians to their ancestral soul. Throughout the years of access to the island, it has been shown that Kanaloa can also connect non-Hawaiians for whom Hawaiʻi is home to Native Hawaiian culture. Through the experience on Kanaloa, Native Hawaiian values and way of life are being spread throughout the Islands. The final verse of the chant composed by Pualani Kanakaʻole Kanahele on the history of the island seems a fitting note on which to end this chapter:

Ua hōʻea ka lā hoʻihoʻi ea	The day for sovereignty is at hand
Ka lā hoʻihoʻi moku	The day to return the island
Ka lā hoʻihoʻi mana kūpuna	The day to return the ancestral influence
Aia i ka Mua Haʻi Kūpuna e Hānau nei	It is at the Mua Haʻi Kūpuna where it is born
E kanaloa ʻia ana i ka piko o kapae ʻāina	To be established in the navel of the islands
He ʻāina kūpaʻa no nā Hawaiʻi	A steadfast land for the Hawaiians
E ola ka Mua Haʻi Kūpuna	Give life to the Mua Haʻi Kūpuna
A mau loa i ka lani a Kāne	Forever in the heavens of Kāne
A mau loa i ke kai a Kanaloa	Forever in the sea of Kanaloa.[51]

⭒ SEVEN ⭒

Ha'ina Ia Mai: Tell the Story

I OPENED THIS mo'olelo with a personal journey in an attempt to land on the island of Kanaloa with Uncle Harry Mitchell. I finally crossed the channel and landed on Kanaloa in November 1984. Through Kanaloa and Mitchell I was introduced to the kua'āina of our islands and led back to my ancestral soul as a *kanaka 'ōiwi*.[1] Through Kanaloa I have participated in the annual Makahiki ceremonies to Akua Lono, beginning in 1986, as well as ceremonies in honor of Akua Kanaloa and Akua Kāne.

My involvement with Kanaloa led me to focus my scholarly research on the cultural kīpuka of our islands among the kua'āina who protected the sacred nature of nā kanaka 'ōiwi and of the islands of our lives. This research endeavor gave the responsibility to me as a kanaka 'ōiwi to first place this work at the service of those who shared their knowledge with me. In Hawaiian we have a saying: "Aloha mai no, aloha aku" (When aloha is given, aloha should be returned). The kua'āina in the various cultural kīpuka described in this book shared their knowledge and experience with me with aloha, and I have strived to return their aloha by applying the information I gathered to our efforts to protect the natural and cultural resources and subsistence lifestyles of their communities. This has to a large degree postponed the publication of this work, but I believe it was necessary to first make sure that the traditional knowledge of the kua'āina was given back to them to protect their well-being and quality of life. My own purpose in publishing this work is to promote the critical significance of these cultural kīpuka for the perpetuation of kanaka 'ōiwi culture and, hopefully, to inspire public efforts and the formation of public policies that will protect these cultural kīpuka.

Sustainable use of Hawai'i's natural and cultural resources is a core concept for planning the future of Hawai'i, and Native Hawaiian stewardship principles can play a significant role in achieving sustainability for the Islands. These, in combination with the traditional principles associated with the subsistence practices of kuaʻāina in cultural kīpuka described in this moʻolelo, are important in protecting Hawaiʻi's precious cultural and natural resources.

The subsistence practices described in this book's chapters on Waipiʻo, Hāna, Puna, Molokaʻi, and Kanaloa can serve as a foundation for the design of sustainable use of Hawaiʻi's resources. As we move into the twenty-first century it is critical to acknowledge the importance of protecting these cultural kīpuka and the natural and cultural resources, which are critical to the subsistence practices of the kuaʻāina of these districts—not only for the kuaʻāina and their descendants, but also for Hawaiʻi's multicultural society as a whole.

Waipiʻo

Of all of the cultural kīpuka covered in this book, Waipiʻo is the only place where I did not conduct oral histories or engage in community-based work. Here I relied upon the unpublished field notes of Stella Jones from her ethnographic work there, sponsored by the Bishop Museum in 1931. I also mined the comprehensive oral history interviews of the Ethnic Studies Oral History Project staff, collected in *Waipiʻo Mano Wai: An Oral History Collection*, vols. 1 and 2. Most recently my colleague Luciano Minerbi, a professor in the University of Hawaiʻi at Mānoa's Department of Urban and Regional Planning, conducted a planning practicum with the taro farmers, landowners, educators, and residents of Waipiʻo Valley in the fall of 1999. The technical report provided me with an update on the production of taro in the valley and the cultural education projects centered in the valley.

Waipiʻo Valley flourishes as an important Native Hawaiian center that sparks and nourishes our cultural imagination. The valley made news in 1994 when the sacred kaʻai or sennit burial caskets believed to contain the bones of High Chief Līloa and High Chief Lonoikamakahiki were taken from the Bishop Museum and apparently returned to a burial cave in Waipiʻo Valley. As discussed in the chapter on Waipiʻo, these kaʻai were removed in 1829 from the Hale o Līloa by Kuhina Nui Kaʻahumanu after her conversion to Christianity. The Bishop Museum had planned to place the kaʻai in the Kalākaua crypt at Mauna Ala in Honolulu, while Native Hawaiians from Hawaiʻi Island had asked permission to instead inter the kaʻai in Waipiʻo Valley. Before any formal action was taken, the kaʻai were removed, and it is believed that they were taken back to their place of origin—Waipiʻo Valley.

In March 2004, the State Water Commission ruled that the Lalakea Ditch, which had diverted the Lalakea and Hakalaoa Streams to irrigate Hāmākua coast plantations for eighty years, could be dismantled.[2] On June 29, 2004, the stream flow was fully restored and once again there were two Hiʻilawe falls instead of only one. The stream restoration is being studied by Bishop Museum scientists in collaboration with students from Hawaiʻi Island middle schools.[3] The restoration of these Waipiʻo streams will set a precedent. The only other case of restoration of stream waters was on windward Oʻahu in the case of the Waiāhole, Waianu, and Waikāne streams, but these streams have only been partially restored.

Waipiʻo Valley is one of the most gorgeous and picturesque ahupuaʻa in our islands. Its cultivated taro pond fields conjure memories of traditional Hawaiʻi, and it is one of the few places that now flourishes as a Native Hawaiian cultural and educational center, with programs offered by the Edith Kanakaʻole Foundation and Kanu O Ka ʻāina Charter School. The Bishop Museum may one day return its land to a Native Hawaiian land trust in support of the cultural and educational programs in the valley. The entire valley is protected within the coastal zone wherein any development requires a special management area permit, including an assessment of impacts upon Native Hawaiian subsistence, cultural, and religious practices. Waipiʻo Valley is an important cultural icon in the hearts and minds of Native Hawaiians and local people as a traditional and contemporary center of Native Hawaiian culture and taro production. All of these factors combined will contribute to its perpetuation as a cultural kīpuka.

Hāna

The rugged and luxuriant Hāna district of Maui, with its deep, verdant valleys, glistening waterfalls cascading down to the sea, and magnificent mountain slopes disappearing into billowing clouds, is alluring and enchanting. However, until my first visit to Keʻanae-Wailuanui with Harry Mitchell, as described in the opening of this moʻolelo, I never really experienced its special qualities, nor did I learn the moʻolelo of the Hawaiian ʻohana who provided stewardship of this land from generation to generation. In subsequent visits with Mitchell he often reminisced and shared stories of the land and of his youth as we drove along the coast, from valley to valley, past stream after stream, to his taro lands in Keʻanae-Wailuanui. One weekend, in April 1988, in order to assist me with the Hāna chapter for my dissertation, Mitchell drove me from Kahului to Keʻanae-Wailuanui and on to Hāna, through Kīpahulu, Kaupō, Nuʻu, Kahikinui, Kanaio, and ʻUlupalakua, down Haleakalā and back to Kahului to share the moʻolelo of his ʻāina and his own connection to each place. The landscape, for me, was no longer just a beautiful place to look at, swim in, hike through, and enjoy. Mitchell's moʻolelo brought the ʻāina to life with the spirit of our ancestors, the kuaʻāina who lived on the land for generations, and their descendants who continue to care for it today. The land was alive with resources that had fed the generations of ʻohana who nurtured the land, embraced and cared for it as a part of their ʻohana, and relied upon it for subsistence. Mitchell and his ancestral knowledge had led me onto the path of the kuaʻāina who held sacred the life of the land and the resources of the land.

In addition to the interviews with Mitchell, I also discovered interviews conducted by Mary Kawena Pukui, in Hawaiian and English, with kūpuna of Hāna, Kīpahulu, Kaupō, and Nuʻu in May 1960. These are reposited in the Audio-Recording Collection of the Anthropology Department of Bishop Museum. Some of these interviews were transcribed and translated, and some were not. The purpose of the interviews was to record and document the original Hawaiian names of places on each of our islands. The collection is an invaluable treasure, and I was honored and privileged to be the first scholar allowed access to them in 1987. For Hāna, there were fifty-five half-hour taped interviews with thirty kūpuna. A translation by Pukui of Thomas K. Maunupau's article about his trip to Kaupō, published in the *Nūpepa Kūʻokoʻa* of June 15, 1922, was another valuable source of information for Kaupō.

In 1994 I had a chance to contribute to the protection of Keʻanae-Wailuanui and give something back to Mitchell's community. I worked on a study with Group 70 and Cultural Surveys Hawaiʻi that resulted in a report titled "Kalo Kanu O Ka ʻĀina: A Cultural Landscape Study of Keʻanae and Wailuanui, Island of Maui." Mitchell had passed away in 1990, but his spirit guided my work. I conducted interviews with thirteen kuaʻāina of Keʻanae-Wailuanui who ranged in age from twenty-seven to ninety-four. I felt so privileged to be able to interview kūpuna Enos Akina, who was ninety-four; kūpuna Helen Nakanelua, eighty-three; kūpuna Mary Kaauamo, eighty-two; kūpuna James Hueu, eighty; kūpuna Maggie Alu, seventy-nine; and kūpuna Apolonia Day, seventy-two. The knowledge they and the younger mākua of Keʻanae-Wailuanui shared with me was invaluable.

The purpose of the study was to develop a policy for Maui County and the State of Hawaiʻi to protect historical cultural landscapes in Hawaiʻi, such as Keʻanae-Wailuanui. In January 1993 the Hawaiiʻi State Legislature established a task force on cultural landscapes within the Department of Land and Natural Resources. In 1994 the task force completed its work by providing descriptions and typologies of cultural landscapes in Hawai'i: (1) abandoned villages or agricultural systems; (2) taro-producing areas; (3) sugar lands; (4) ranches; (5) fishing areas; (6) religious and legendary sites; (7) fishponds; (8) traditional gathering areas; and (9) entire islands. The task force recommended that a model project focusing on the Ke'anae-Wailuanui community be funded to develop specific guidelines on how to protect historical cultural landscapes in Hawai'i.[4] The Maui County General Plan and the Hāna Community Plan recommended that Maui county retain the cultural identity of the Hāna region and promote only those economic activities that are environmentally benign and compatible with the cultural sensitivities of the area. Federal funds were available to Maui county to fulfill the purposes of the National Historic Preservation Act to designate protection of national historic cultural landscapes, and Maui county decided to use these federal preservation monies for a study to recommend measures to protect the cultural landscape of Ke'anae-Wailuanui.

From the oral history interviews that I conducted, I was able not only to document the rich cultural heritage of the 'ohana who live in Ke'anae-Wailuanui, but also to generalize patterns of traditional subsistence custom and usage among the kua'āina of the ahupua'a. These patterns have served as a template for comparison in other cultural kīpuka. I have been able to build and expand upon this model to document and protect subsistence customs and practices and the natural resources upon which kua'āina throughout the cultural kīpuka of our islands rely. In subsequent studies to document and map Native Hawaiian cultural and natural resources used for cultural, religious, and subsistence purposes, I incorporated the cultural information from the Ke'anae-Wailuanui study.

Boundaries

The information provided to me by the kua'āina of Ke'anae-Wailuanui helped me understand that there are actually two intersecting areas that make up a cultural landscape—the core area and the broader area of traditional cultural practices. The core area includes land used for residence, areas of taro cultivation, irrigation networks, and associated settlement and circulation systems.

The broader traditional cultural practices area usually coincides with the traditional ahupua'a and moku. It includes all of the zones needed for the people to gather, hunt, and fish for subsistence, cultural, and religious purposes. In many cases, the areas utilized by 'ohana for gathering, hunting, and fishing may have extended beyond the ahupua'a into other areas of the moku or district or another part of the island. One must rely upon the ʻohana of the area who are subsistence practitioners to describe the boundaries of the traditional cultural practices area.

Often environmental impact studies focus only on impacts on natural and cultural resources within the core cultural practices area. However, it is important to broaden the scope of such studies to include the expanded cultural use area of the entire ahupuaʻa and moku.

Landscape Components

Through the Keʻanae-Wailuanui study, I learned that the cultural landscape is composed of physical elements that manifest the technological and cultural basis of human use of the land through time.

The components of a Hawaiian cultural landscape include (1) areas of taro cultivation; (2) other areas of cultivation; (3) circulation networks; (4) buildings, structures, nonstructural facilities, and objects; (5) clusters (defined as groupings of buildings or features that result from function, social tradition, climate, and other influences); (6) internal boundaries; (7) an irrigation ditch system, including roads and tunnels; (8) archaeological and historic sites; (9) open areas; (10) small-scale elements; (11) viewing points; and (11) cultural resources and use areas. Of these components, I focused on the cultural resources and use areas in the Keʻanae-Wailuanui district and in subsequent studies.

First, there are wahi pana such as heiau, shrines, burial caves and graves, and geographic features associated with deities and significant natural, cultural, spiritual, or historical phenomena or events. Edward Kanahele offered the following description of wahi pana: "The gods and their disciples specified places that were sacred. The inventory of sacred places in Hawaiʻi includes the dwelling places of the gods, the dwelling places of venerable disciples, temples, and shrines, as well as selected observation points, cliffs, mounds, mountains, weather phenomena, forests, and volcanoes."[5]

Secondly, streams and springs are important as habitats for native species of marine life, for taro cultivation, and for domestic uses.

Third, shorelines, reefs, and nearshore and offshore ocean resources are important for gathering of foods and medicines and for conducting cultural and spiritual customs.

Fourth, forests are important for hunting pigs and other animals; for gathering plants used for medicine, foods, ceremonial adornment, and ritual offerings; and for conducting spiritual rituals.

Fifth, domains of 'aumakua or ancestral deities are particular natural and cultural features where Hawaiians renew their ties to ancestors through experiencing natural phenomena and witnessing *ho'ailona* or natural signs.

Sixth, trails and dirt roads are indispensable for affording access to the cultural resources and use areas, both mauka to forests and streams and makai to streams and the ocean.

Though I have expanded upon this essential list in subsequent studies, these served as an important starting point in developing a systematic community-based approach to identifying and documenting the wide range of cultural and natural resources relied upon for cultural, religious, and subsistence activities.

The most exciting aspect of the study for me was to document the unbroken continuity of cultural and subsistence beliefs, customs, and practices in a thriving, predominantly Native Hawaiian community at the end of the twentieth century. The kua'āina of Hāna persist in their way of life despite newcomers, illegal drugs, and economic challenges. As the intensity and pace of change increases within a global economy, public policies will be needed that provide funding, regulation, and enforcement to protect the Native Hawaiian way of life in Hāna.

Puna

I spent most of my summers as a child and through college with my grandparents in Waiākea on the edge of Hilo, Hawai'i. My parents owned papaya fields and hala forest land in 'Opihikao in the Puna district adjacent to a small ranch owned by my mother's brothers. I spent many summer days in Puna, both at 'Opihikao and also at Puna's wondrous black sands, rugged lava rock coastline, warm pools and springs, mysterious lava tubes, awesome volcanic craters, and spectacular eruptions. Puna is an essential and dynamic place that helps define my life and identity as kanaka 'ōiwi.

My formal research into Puna took shape around the "Native Hawaiian Ethnographic Study for the Hawai'i Geothermal Project Environmental Impact Study" that I conducted with Jon Matsuoka of the School of Social Work and Luciano Minerbi of the Department of Urban and Regional Planning. This was the first Native Hawaiian cultural impact study conducted for a major federal project in Hawai'i since it began to be required as part of an environmental impact study. We decided to design the study as a template for subsequent cultural impact studies and thus set ourselves a high standard. Although the study areas included both Puna and East Maui, my role was to conduct the ethnographic study of Puna and the Pele beliefs, customs, and practices in conjunction with Matsuoka, Kumu Hula Pualani Kanakaʻole Kanahele, and a Pacific Islands Studies graduate student, Noenoe Barney-Campbell. This final report served as an excellent model of how to model and conduct a cultural impact study. It formed the basis of the Puna chapter in this book, and I patterned the chapters on Waipiʻo, Hāna, and Molokaʻi on the same model.

The federal and state governments and the private investor terminated the Hawaiʻi Geothermal Project before the entire Environmental Impact Study was completed and published by Oak Ridge National Laboratory. The archaeological assessment was stopped in its initial phase. However, since the cultural impact study component that we were responsible for was already completed, Oak Ridge printed and distributed it to the informants, government agencies, and public and university libraries. This book is the first time much of the information gathered for the ethnographic study will be published and made available to a larger audience. We shared our model for the conduct of a cultural impact study with the Hawaiʻi Office of Environmental Quality Control, and it was incorporated into their official guidelines on how to conduct such studies as part of an environmental impact study.

The ethnographic study of Puna began with an examination of the traditional cultural significance of the district. The place-names for the district and the ʻōlelo noʻeau or descriptive proverbs and poetic sayings for which the area is famous were found and interpreted. Descriptive chants for the area were researched, translated, and interpreted. A special review of the Pele chants for the district was conducted in order to identify significant sites and cultural use areas. Combined, these sources provided valuable insights into the cultural resources and features for which the area was known and the overall role of this area in the traditional cultural practices and customs of Hawaiians. Each of the chapters describing the cultural kīpuka opens with a discussion of the ʻōlelo noʻeau and chants descriptive of and unique to that particular ahupuaʻa, moku, or island.

Traditional moʻolelo record what the Native Hawaiian ancestors observed as the primal natural elements and the important natural and physical features and natural resources of the landscape. They provide, in story form, a description of the natural environmental setting in which the early Hawaiians settled and established themselves. The primal natural elements were depicted as manifestations of Hawaiian deities, and the myths and chants relate which natural elements dominated the landscape and the lives of the early Hawaiians. Research by archaeologists complements the traditional moʻolelo with material evidence and artifacts of the record of human settlement. Archaeological studies have increased over the years as part of required environmental impact studies conducted for proposed development. These reports are available at the University of Hawaiʻi at Mānoa's Hamilton Library and the Hawaiʻi State Historic Preservation Department. An inventory of these reports is available at the State Historic Preservation Department. The traditional moʻolelo for each of the cultural kīpuka follows the discussion of the ʻōlelo noʻeau and chants.

For the period of ruling chiefs, early contact with European and American traders and the establishment of the Hawaiian monarchy, the four published Native Hawaiian scholars of the early nineteenth century—David Malo, Samuel Kamakau, John Papa Ii, and Kepelino—provide excellent accounts.[6] Abraham Fornander's *Collection of Hawaiian Antiquities and Folk-lore* is also important. Documents range from the journals of explorers and missionaries to government records of the Kingdom of Hawaiʻi—such as the census, tax records, indices of land awards, record of Native Testimony to the Board of Commissioners to Quiet Land Titles, and the Boundary Review Commission proceedings—and Thrum's *Hawaiian Annual*.

For the territorial period, from 1898 through statehood, visitor guide books, magazines, newspapers, monographs such as Handy's *Native Planters in Old Hawaiʻi*, and documents in the archives of the State of Hawaiʻi and various museums are excellent resources. For Puna, the Hawaiʻi Volcano National Park Headquarters Library had documents and records particular to the district. Oral history and key informant interviews are important sources of information about the lifestyle and livelihoods of the Puna Hawaiians. For Puna, I drew upon the Kalapana Oral History Project and interviews by Russell Apple.

For the post-statehood period, I searched for contemporary studies and also conducted my own oral history interviews in every area except Waipiʻo Valley. In the summer of 1970 the University of Hawaiʻi at Mānoa Departments of Geography and Anthropology and the School of Public Health collaborated on human ecology studies in North Kohala and Puna, work preceded by a similar study on Molokaʻi by the Department of Anthropology. These studies include surveys of subsistence activities in each of these areas and provide a useful baseline of data for comparison of these activities over time into the twenty-first century.

In 1982 the U.S. Department of Energy commissioned a study by the Puna Hui 'Ohana, an organization of Hawaiian families in Puna, as a prelude to a proposal to develop plants for producing electricity from geothermal energy. This study also surveyed the subsistence activities of the families in the Puna community and provides useful data for comparison with the earlier University of Hawai'i study as well as subsequent ones. A similar study was conducted on Moloka'i in 1981 and published in the *Moloka'i Data Book: Community Values and Energy Development* by the Department of Urban and Regional Planning. There was nothing comparable for Hāna or Waipi'o.

For the geothermal ethnography, Jon Matsuoka and I conducted key informant interviews in 1994 with members of Native Hawaiian 'ohana who had lived in the Puna district for several generations. As a unique feature of the interviews, informants were asked to identify areas of subsistence, cultural, and religious use on a topographical map of the district. The data gathered were analyzed and organized into a report on the customs, beliefs, and practices of the Puna Hawaiians.

The interviews revealed that there is still a wealth of ancestral knowledge that has been kept alive and is practiced by Hawaiian families in Puna. Moreover, the living culture is constantly undergoing growth and change. Certainly the ethnohistories of places such as Puna, Hāna, and Moloka'i can be developed from a wide variety of written sources. Nevertheless, cultural impact studies, in order to be complete, need to go beyond the written record and include interviews with key informants who are members of Hawaiian 'ohana and traditional hālau (cultural groups) who live in the area and have established a relationship of stewardship for the cultural and natural resources of the area. For Puna, the rich ethnohistorical written sources were complemented by interviews and focus group discussions and participatory mapping with Hawaiian families, members of hālau, and cultural groups. All the information gathered, written and oral, was combined into the final report on the impact of geothermal energy development on the cultural beliefs, customs, and practices of the Puna Hawaiians.

At the same time that the ethnographic study was being conducted, the Pele Defense Fund was preparing its case to protect the traditional and customary rights of Native Hawaiians in the Wao Kele o Puna Forest (Pele Defense Fund v. Paty 79 Haw. at 442 [1992]).[7] When the case was heard in August 1994, key informants that were interviewed for the geothermal ethnographic study testified as witnesses. I also presented testimony based upon the key informant interviews, including the topographic map of Puna on which the informants had noted with pasted-on dots the location of their subsistence hunting, fishing, and gathering areas, cultural sites, and trails. This testimony and that of the key informants laid the foundation for a ruling that set a precedent for Native Hawaiian gathering rights in Puna and throughout the islands.

Moloka'i

I first began to visit Moloka'i in 1975 as a class project for the ethnic studies course on Hawaiians that I teach at the University of Hawai'i at Mānoa. Colette Machado, a good friend and former student who had returned to her home island, welcomed the students so they could be educated about the cultural significance of Moloka'i and learn about the political struggles of the homesteaders for water and of the kua'āina for access. The idea was for us to be inspired to do research and organize support for Moloka'i when we went back to O'ahu. Colette helped to arrange places for us to camp, vehicles to transport baggage from the airport, and community speakers to educate the students.

Through Colette I met people of Moloka'i who were members of both Hui Ala Loa and the Protect Kaho'olawe 'Ohana—Noa Emmett Aluli, Judy Napoleon, Joyce Kainoa, and John Sabas. I already knew George Helm from high school; he went to the all-boys' St. Louis High School on O'ahu at the same time I attended the all-girls' sister school, Sacred Hearts Academy. We were both in a co-ed choral group started by Kumu John Lake for the students from our schools.

Over the years of visiting Moloka'i, I grew to appreciate the grassroots community of Moloka'i who were guided by their kūpuna in a lifelong commitment to protect the Hawaiian way of life on Moloka'i and on Kaho'olawe. My connections to Moloka'i and Kaho'olawe were intertwined, although my first actual visit to Kaho'olawe was ten years after my first visit to Moloka'i.

Throughout the years I gave support to community issues on Moloka'i. When I wrote my dissertation on cultural kīpuka, I decided to research the history of the kua'āina of Moloka'i as a prime example of an entire island that had been bypassed by the mainstream of economic and political change. In this, the interviews of forty-eight kūpuna by Mary Kawena Pukui in 1961 and 1964, preserved on eighty-three half-hour tapes in the Bishop Museum's Audio-Recording Collection, served as my primary source. I also used a 1941 unpublished manuscript by Southwick Phelps on the cultural resources of the island and George Cooke's book about Moloka'i Ranch. For the section on the experiences of early Hawaiian homesteaders, I also used the Mary Kawena Pukui's taped interviews, together with manuscripts and reports on the establishment of the Hawaiian Homes Commission and its program of homesteading on Moloka'i.

In 1993 I worked with Jon Matsuoka of the School of Social Work and Luciano Minerbi of the Department of Urban and Regional Planning and a committee of Moloka'i kua'āina, state officials and representatives of Moloka'i Ranch to develop the "Governor's Moloka'i Subsistence Task Force Report." In June 1993 we worked with the task force to conduct a random sample survey of the Moloka'i community regarding the extent and importance of subsistence activities on Moloka'i. In July and August 1993 the task force conducted focus groups with subsistence fishers, hunters, and gatherers in Kaunakakai, East End, Mauna Loa, and Ho'olehua, as well as with island-wide commercial fishermen and lā'au lapa'au practitioners. One of the key features of these focus groups was participatory mapping of subsistence hunting, fishing, and gathering areas, as well as trails, on a topographic map of the island. It was the first time we had used this method; its success led us to use it again in our Puna Cultural Impact Study.

The Moloka'i Subsistence Task Force met through September and October 1993 to balance the findings of the random sample survey and the input from the focus groups to propose policies and recommendations for the community to review. The task force held a community meeting in November 1993 and received additional recommendations, which were incorporated into a final report in December 1993. I outline this process to convey the breadth of input from the community that was demanded by the task force in order to complete the final report. Of any community that I have worked with, the Moloka'i community is the most committed to finding ways to control its own destiny, and it values the community process in order to derive and design a community-based initiative.

As noted in chapter 5, the survey and the focus groups confirmed that Moloka'i continued to be a rural island where the kua'āina engaged heavily in subsistence farming, fishing, hunting, and gathering. Among the random sample group surveyed across the entire island, informants stated that 28 percent of their food comes from subsistence. Among the Native Hawaiian families surveyed, informants stated that 38 percent of their food come through subsistence activities. Respondents reported obtaining food acquired through subsistence activities approximately once a week.

Through the study, the Moloka'i kua'āina hoped to impress the policymakers and economists that subsistence needed to be acknowledged as an important sector of the economy—as important as the market sector and the government sector. Economic planning for Moloka'i and other rural communities needed to factor in subsistence and the impact on the natural resources relied upon for subsistence. This report was not meant to sit on a shelf and gather dust. It was used immediately to introduce and justify legislation to designate the northeast coast of Moloka'i, from Nihoa Flats in the east to 'Ilio Point in the west, as a community-based subsistence fishing management area under the Hui Mālama o Mo'omomi. The legislature granted communities throughout the islands the ability to designate subsistence fishing management areas and established Moloka'i's northeast coast as a pilot project from 1995 to 1997. The community worked vigorously with the Department of Land and Natural Resources to adopt management rules for the pilot project that would be incorporated as general rules for community-based subsistence fishing management areas throughout the Islands. However, after the pilot project ended, the department failed to follow through on the general rules. Numerous rural communities throughout the state would like to collaborate with Hui Mālama o Mo'omomi to protect invaluable nearshore fishing grounds throughout the state from overfishing and depletion.

The study also formed the basis of testimony in water allocation cases for the Kamiloloa Aquifer regarding the potential impact increased drilling and withdrawal of water by Moloka'i Ranch would have on the subsistence resources both on land and on the nearshore reefs. The Department of Hawaiian Home Lands also responded to the study by placing management of Hawaiian Home Lands hunting grounds under the management of the Moloka'i homesteaders.

In 1998 the Moloka'i community embarked on a major effort to boost the island's economy. They applied to the Department of Agriculture for a rural empowerment zone grant. There were hundreds of community meetings, and I assisted in synthesizing the community's goals, objectives, and economic projects throughout the process. Although the Moloka'i community did not get the empowerment designation, in 1999 the federal government designated it an enterprise community (EC). It will receive $250,000 per year for ten years, a total of $2.5 million, to partner with private entities and government agencies to leverage additional monies for forty identified economic development projects. In 2003 the community incorporated as Ke Aupuni Lōkahi to carry out the projects and programs as an enterprise community.

Designed by a broad cross section of the island for the purposes of the grant, the Ke Aupuni Lōkāhi Enterprise Community is guided by an outstanding vision statement, quoted in chapter 5 on Molokaʻi, to guide the island's economic development in the twenty-first century. The statement on Community Values elaborates upon the meaning of the vision statement. It explains that the vision statement reflects the concept of aloha ʻāina and the belief that the land or ʻāina is alive and must be respected, treasured, nurtured, and protected if it is to be productive. Hawaiians believe that in return for good stewardship, the land sustains the people who care for it. The sacred and dependent relationship between the land and the people sustained Molokaʻi for a thousand years, and the vision statement affirms aloha ʻāina as the bedrock value upon which Molokaʻi's economic recovery will be founded:

> Throughout the centuries before western explorers arrived, Molokaʻi people knew every different wind, rain and cloud formation by its own given name. Fish were never taken out of season. Prayer rituals accompanied every step of farming, from planting to harvest. Fresh water sources were stringently protected, and an abundance of water was regarded as the highest symbol of wealth. In return for their protection of the land, the people of Molokaʻi became renowned for their ability to produce abundant quantities of food, and the island acquired the name ʻāina momona, abundant land. The Vision Statement expresses our community's belief that we can only restore this island's legendary productivity if we become more vigilant guardians of its resources.[8]

By the time of the 1998 grant project, I commuted weekly to Molokaʻi and was a part-time resident of Hoʻolehua. In January 2003 Ke Aupuni Lōkāhi set up a special committee to engage in a community-based master land use planning process for the Molokaʻi Ranch, which is incorporated as Molokaʻi Properties Limited (MPL). For more than 100 days and with a total of 300 participants, five committees considered hundreds of planning issues that would affect the lives of the people of Molokaʻi. I participated in the Cultural Issues Committee. During the summer of 2004 the proposed plan was completed, and a process of facilitated and community meetings began. Under the plan, MPL will donate 26,000 of the 65,000 acres it owns to the Molokaʻi Land Trust. These lands generate annual rental revenues of $250,000, which can be used to fund the operations of the land trust. An additional 29,000 acres will be permanently protected in an agricultural and rural reserve and under existing conservation easements. In return, MPL seeks community support to develop 200 luxury home lots on the last pristine shoreline on Moloka'i, along Lā'au Point. The community is in the process of weighing the benefits and drawbacks of the overall package.

In January 2004 Ke Aupuni Lōkahi Moloka'i asked me to conduct a Moloka'i Responsible Tourism Study. I launched the study in January 2005. My task was to interview and hold focus group discussions with Moloka'i business operators, subsistence farmers and fishermen, community organizations, community contacts for sports and high school events, and Ke Aupuni Lōkahi in order to design a five-year visitor plan. The plan follows community guidelines for stewardship of the island's environmental, cultural, and infrastructure resources. The challenge is to develop tourism on Moloka'i while still upholding Moloka'i's renown as "the last Hawaiian island," which is the reason why families continue to live on Moloka'i and why visitors are attracted to its shores.

As the Ke Aupuni Lōkahi initiatives and the Moloka'i Ranch planning indicate, the Moloka'i community is still intent on shaping its own destiny, keeping Moloka'i Hawaiian, and actively engaging the community in planning its own future. Moreover, the community constantly leans upon its traditional strengths, reflected in the famous sayings for the guidance and direction of Moloka'i. These are described in the following closing thoughts for Moloka'i:

> The saying, "Moloka'i Nui A Hina" or Great Moloka'i, Child of Hina, affirms that Moloka'i, like a human child, was born to a mother and father: Wākea, god of the sky, and Hina, goddess of the moon and weaver of the clouds. This traditional legend of origin establishes that the island of Moloka'i, like a child, is small and fragile—unlike a large continent. The resources of an island are finite, and these finite resources need to be nurtured by the island's "family" if the people are to be strong, healthy, and prosperous. Many of the people of Moloka'i trace their roots on the island back to antiquity, making the island an integral part of their ancestral family. Moloka'i's modern-day stewards have a special responsibility to care for the island as they would care for a member of their own family—a responsibility bequeathed to them by Hina, birth mother of this island.
>
> "Moloka'i Pule O'o," island of powerful prayers, is another traditional name for Moloka'i. In ancient times this name inspired fear and respect throughout Hawai'i, because it was based on the island's reputation as a

training ground for the most powerful priests in the islands. Legends say that the people of Molokaʻi could drive invading armies from their shores by simply uniting in prayer. This name recognizes Molokaʻi as an ancient center for learning, and honors the spiritual strength of Molokaʻi's people, and their historic sovereign control over the island. Although Molokaʻi is not self-governing today, as discussed below, her people are nevertheless respected for their ability, thus far, to protect the Hawaiian culture, subsistence lifestyle and the natural resources upon which they are dependent. Their feat has been accomplished by combining an intimate knowledge of the island's resources with strength of character and fearless determination to deal with threats to their environment and lifestyle. The enduring description of Molokaʻi as "the last Hawaiian island" affirms the success of the community in protecting the Hawaiian way of life as the core of the island's multi-ethnic, close-knit society.

ʻĀina Momona: Land of Plenty: Before Western contact, the economy of Molokaʻi was agricultural and centered on inshore aquaculture, the cultivation of various crops, fishing, hunting and gathering. As a result of the industry of her people, Molokaʻi, with its extensive protected reefs and fishponds, gained a reputation as the land of "fat fish and kukui nut relish." The "fat fish" came from Molokaʻi's fishponds and the waters surrounding the island. The mention of "kukui nut relish" refers to the lush resources of the land. The island as a whole was popularly called "ʻĀina Momona" or "Land of Plenty" in honor of the great productivity of the island and its surrounding ocean.[9]

Kanaloa

And now, I will close this moʻolelo where I opened it, with my connection to Kahoʻolawe / Kanaloa. As mentioned above, I finally made the ocean crossing to Kanaloa in November 1984 with Uncle Harry Mitchell, a group of my students from the ethnic studies "Hawaiians" course, and the Luʻuwai family. At first, I didn't feel the spirit of the island. There was too much to do, between cooking, hiking, keeping track of my students, and thatching the Hale Halawai. When it was time to leave, not everyone could fit on the boat and a small group of eight or ten of us stayed behind an extra day and night to wait for another boat to pick us up. It was then, when it grew quiet except for the natural sounds of the wind and the surrounding ocean, that I sensed the spirit of the land. And in the evening, when the kuaʻāina from Hawaiʻi and Maui and Moloka'i opened up and talked story around the campfire, I felt the presence of our ancestors in their stories.

When I went back to O'ahu, the island kept calling inside me to return and to get involved in the struggle to stop the bombing. I did return and continued to return, as I will for the rest of my life. I have been steadfast in the work to stop the bombing and to heal the wounds of the island. And I began to honor Lono in the Makahiki and Kanaloa in private offerings of ho'okupu. The chapter on Kaho'olawe reflects my research and my experience with the many members of the 'Ohana and those who have visited its shores and been touched by the island. Although tremendous gains have been made in healing the island, many obstacles remain and we in the 'Ohana must remain vigilant and steadfast and work in partnership with the Kaho'olawe Island Reserve Commission, which has the financial, personnel, and political resources to establish and protect Kanaloa as a cultural reserve.

Though title to Kaho'olawe/Kanaloa was transferred to the State of Hawai'i in May 1994, the U.S. Navy retained control over access to the island in order to conduct an omnibus cleanup of the island from November 10, 1993, through November 11, 2003. After fifty years of use as a military weapons range, Kaho'olawe/Kanaloa's 28,800 acres were contaminated with shrapnel, target vehicles, and unexploded ordnance. The U.S. Navy signed an agreement with the State of Hawai'i to clean up 30 percent of the island's subsurface of ordnance. In 1993 the U.S. Congress appropriated $460 million for the U.S. Navy to fulfill this obligation. The U.S. Navy contracted Parsons-UXB Joint Venture to conduct what is acknowledged to be the largest unexploded-ordnance remediation project in the history of the United States. Over 10 million pounds of metal, 370 vehicles, and 14,000 tires were removed from the island and recycled. However, rather than clearing 30 percent of the island to a depth of four feet, the Navy contractor cleared only 2,650 acres (9 percent) of the island's subsurface. Another 19,464 acres (68 percent) of the island's surface was cleared of ordnance, but 6,686 acres (23 percent) of Kanaloa has not been cleared at all. Disturbingly, the U.S. Navy can guarantee only that it is 90 percent confident that 85 percent of the ordnance in the 2,650 acres or 9 percent was cleared of ordnance to a depth of four feet.

What does this mean? Access to our beloved island will continue to be limited to the "cleared" areas, which have the highest priority for cultural activities and revegetation projects. These include Hakioawa and Hakioawa Iki, where the 'Ohana maintains its primary base camp, has restored heiau and shrines, and has established new cultural sites. Moa'ulanui, where the KIRC has established its staging area for the revegetation of the island, is accessible. Moa'ulaiki, the traditional center for the training of navigators in traditional way-finding arts, had the highest priority for clearance. Honokanai'a was the central staging area for the clean-up and the center of the communications system, and was one of the first areas cleared of ordnance. Kealaikahiki, from which long voyages between Hawai'i and Kahiki were launched, was identified as an ideal site for contemporary training in celestial navigation and cleared. In October 2004 a special platform for navigators to observe the position of the North Star and Southern Cross over the horizon relative to the piko or central point of Kealaikahiki was constructed and dedicated by Master Navigator Mau Pialug, representatives of each of the Hawaiian voyaging canoes, the Protect Kaho'olawe 'Ohana, and the KIRC.

The adjoining beach at Keanakeiki, where the closing ceremonies for the annual Makahiki are conducted, will continue to be accessible. Kūhe'eia, center of the ranching operations in the early twentieth century; and Kaulana, site of the kingdom's prison settlement and school and an ideal planting area; and Ahupū, another ranching site and location of the island's largest petroglyph field and obsidian glass quarry, were all cleared. Honoko'a, location of several fishing shrines and the landing place of King Kalākaua when he visited the island, was cleared so that the fishing traditions of the island could be practiced there and passed on. In addition, a cross-island road and trails link Hakioawa and Kuhe'eia to the central part of the island over to Honokanai'a and out to Kealaikahiki and Keanakeiki. Portions of a round-the-island trail were cleared, such as at Kanapou Bay and its surrounding cliffs, where there are observation points to read the weather and the natural elements. Even the uncleared areas can be accessed by small groups and with escorts who are trained to detect and handle unexploded ordnance. Activities will continue to focus on the healing and restoration of the cultural and natural resources of Kanaloa and reviving Native Hawaiian spiritual and cultural customs and practices. The limited clearance of ordnance means that the island will not be open for general recreational or commercial activities, nor for resorts, golf courses, or subdivisions.

Is this the end? Under state law, when the Navy transferred control of Kanaloa to the state, it was to be held in trust for transfer to the sovereign Hawaiian entity when it is reestablished and recognized by the federal and state governments. The 'Ohana is committed to holding the Navy accountable for clearing more of the island as our use and needs expand so that the island can ultimately be returned to the sovereign Hawaiian entity for safe and meaningful use as a cultural reserve.

I choose to end this moʻolelo with the words of Noa Emmett Aluli from the foreword of *Kahoʻolawe Nā Leo o Kanaloa* because they reflect my own thoughts and experiences as we have shared our lives and aloha with Kanaloa and the ʻohana who remain connected to this island and to all our islands:

> On Kahoʻolawe, we've been able to live together as Hawaiians. We've been able to practice the religion and to carry on the traditions we've learned from our kūpuna, our elders. In doing this, we connect to the land, and we connect to the gods. We call them back to the land and back to our lives . . . We commit for generations, not just for careers. We set things up now so that they'll be carried on. We look ahead together so that many of us share the same vision and dream. To our next generations we say, Go with the spirit. Take the challenge. Learn something. Give back.[10]

❧ APPENDIX I ❧

1851 Petition from Puna Native Hawaiians to Extend the Deadline to File a Land Claim

PUNA

O makou ka poe makaainana o Puna nei, ke noi aku nei makou i ka aha olelo

1 O ko makou mau kuleana i komo ole i loko o na Lunahoona, e hookomo koke ia mai me ka uku ole,

2 E waihoneole ia na kula me ka Alodio ole ia

3 Ona aina aupuni i haawi wale ia i ka poe makemake maoli i ka hana

4 E pau ka noho nui 'ana o na kanaka ma ka hale hookahi

5 E hoola ia ke kanawai o ka poe palaualelo

6 E pau ka male ana o ka luahine me ka mea opiopio pela ou no ka ele ma kule me ka mea opiopio

PUNA

We are the common citizens of Puna and we petition the legislature that:

1 That our kuleana that have not been entered with the Land Commissioners be immediately entered without fees.

2 That the kula areas be left untouched without be owned in fee simple.

3 That government lands be given only to those who really want to work.

4 That people not be allowed to occupy a single house in large numbers.

5 That a law dealing with laziness be brought up.

6 That marriages between old people and young people be abolished.

(TRANS. W. H. WILSON, OCTOBER 5, 1977)

Number of Males Who Paid Taxes in Puna in 1858

		OVER 20 YEARS OF AGE	UNDER 20 YEARS OF AGE
1	Apua	4	1
2	Kealakomo	32	15
3	Panau Nui	15	4
4	Paunau Iki	1	
5	Laepuki	33	6
6	Kamoamoa	3	
7	Pulama	9	
8	Kahaualea	36	4
9	Kapaahu	12	
10	Kupahua	6	1
11	Kalapana	87	7
12	Kaimu	60 over 25	5
13	Ua Kona	1	1
14	Kehena	32	6
15	Keekee	3	1
16	Kamaili	10	1
17	Kaueleau	3	1
18	Kanane	22	5
19	Opihikao	13	1
20	Iililoa	4	1
21	Kauaea	33	1
22	Malama	5	1
23	Kaukulau	3	
24	Keahialaka	11	
25	Pohoiki	33	1
26	Oneloa	6	
27	Ili kipi kaa Inaina Papoi kou	1	
28	Laepaoo	4	

		OVER 20 YEARS OF AGE	UNDER 20 YEARS OF AGE
29	Pualaa	5	1
30	Kapoho	49	8
31	Kula	47	8
32	Puua	12	3
33	Koae 1	30	7
34	Koae 2	9	1
35	Kanekiki	1	1
36	Halepuaa	22	4
37	Kahuai	8	
38	Waawaa	8	
39	Honolulu	3	1
40	Waiakahiula	31	3
41	Keonepoko	3	
42	Halona	4	
43	Popoki	2	
44	Makuu	37	7
45	Keaau	56	15
46	Olaa	85	8

Moloka'i, Petition of July 2, 1845

HE PALAPALA HOOPII NA KA POE MAKAAINANA

Molokai, hoouna ia ku i ka malama o Julai, 1845.

Aloha nui ka Moi hanohano o ko makaou mau kupuna mai ka po mai a hiki mai ia makou i na keiki. Pela no ke Kuhina nui o ke Aupuni Hawaii nui, a me na lii o kou aupuni a pau. Eia ko makou manao noi aku ia oe e ko makou Moi a me ko makou mau alii malalo ou maloko o ka ahaolelo.

1 No ke kuokoa ana o kou aupuni e ka Moi III aole o makou makemake e noho luna na haole au i hoonoho ai maluna o ke Aupuni Hawaii.
2 Aole o makou makemake e hoohiki na haole i kanaka (Hawaii).
3 Aole o makou makemake e kuai aku oe i kekahi apana aina o kou Aupuni i na haole.
4 Aole e kauia ka Auhau pohihihi i kau poe huna lepo.

Ma keia mau manao o makou a hoike aku la ia ia oe e ka Moi a me kou poe alii.
Ke kakau nei makou i ko makou mau inoa malalo iho.
Eia ka huina o na inoa (1344*)

Aloha ka mea hanohano i hoonohoia ma ka mole o ka Moi Kamehameha II a me ka Moi Kamehameha I.

Na kou poe Kauwa makaainana huna lep o kou Paeaiana
Na Keaumaea i haawi aku.

PETITION BY THE COMMON PEOPLE OF MOLOKA'I

Moloka'i, Sent in the month of July, 1845

Greetings Honorable King of our ancestors from the time of the gods (pō) down to us the descendants, as well as to the Kuhina nui of our Hawaiian Kingdom and all the ali'i of your entire nation.

The following is what we desire to request of you, our King, and our ali'i under you in the legislature.

1 For the independence of your nation, King (Kamehameha) III, we do not want the haole you have appointed over the Hawaiian government to serve as officials.

2 We do not want haole to be made naturalized Hawaiian citizens.

3 We do not want you to sell any portion of your nation to haole.

4 Do not place confusing taxes upon your humble people (huna lepo—bits of earth).

May these feelings of ours be shown to you, Your Majesty, and to your ali'i.

We sign our names.

The following is the total amount of names 1344.*

Aloha honorable one who has been appointed to the root of King Kamehameha II and King Kamehameha I.

Your humble servants, the commoners of your islands,

Given by Keaumaea

[TRANS. W. H. WILSON, AUGUST 10, 1977]

1 Lokane	2 Kulau	3 Kapuhenehone	4 Kaikaina
5 Kalaukaa	6 Kalaumano	**7 Mahi**	8 Naihe
9 Owao	10 Kaakau	11 Lae	12 Kaapuiki
13 Makalilio	14 Kauipuniho	15 Wahine	**16 Kalia**
17 Kaheewahine	18 Kuakea	19 Kaneinei	**20 Kaheana**
21 Kalawaia	22 Nalua	23 Peleleleu	24 Kaunahi
25 Hoaehae?	26 Kawalua	27 Pookee	28 Kauokuu
29 Maiawa	30 Kaakau	**31 Paaluhi**	32 Kalele
33 Uwe	34 Kauwehia	35 Kahualii	36 Kokoniho
37 Kaiwiahuula	**38 Kailianu**	39 Haipu	40 Laakapa
41 Molokai	42 Makana	43 Kekiiokalani	44 Petero
45 Kawaa	46 Kahookuu	47 Kaleoku	48 Kawaaliilii
49 Kaila	50 Kaula	51 Keanoalii	52 Pauloa
53 Kaapolani	**54 Amalu**	55 Kamailuna	56 Kuaili
57 Naleilehua	58 Kauhimahalupe	59 Kauao	**60 Kama**
61 Paana	**62 Akahi**	63 Wahineaukai	64 Hamakaia
65 Lahana	66 Pihanui	67 Kaleiwahine	68 Kahaomaneo
69 Kuaana	70 Kaena	71 Papu	72 Kaehukanakaliilii
73 Muoouo	74 Kealakai	75 Nakahili	76 Kaikapu
77 Kamakaunui	78 Kawaalauioili	79 Kau	80 Kealo
81 Kailikole	**82 Kau**	83 Puapua	84 Daniela
85 Upai	86 Ukuala	87 Kahaikupuna	**88 Mahoe**
89 Kioi	**90 Kaiwipalaoa**	**91 Kapahi**	92 Kamamaka
93 Kamoku	94 Kamaiahulu	**95 Kalikelike**	**96 Kama**
97 Kalama	98 Kalahale	99 Kaehumakalani	100 Kauwe

101 Kamalino	102 Kalawe	103 Kalepale	104 Kaialau
105 Kaahi	106 Kaluaokamoku	**107 Kekahuna**	108 Kekolohe
109 Kekahuna 2	**110 Keliikanakaole**	111 Timoteo	112 Pua
113 Kuli	114 Kumaikalala	115 Laukua	116 Laa
117 Helekaihuelani	**118 Lono**	119 Lupua	120 Malia
121 Mahaole	122 Mahiai	123 Manoa	124 Maa
125 Meeau	**126 Nahuaai**	127 Kaakau	128 Naeole
129 Kaole	130 Keawekane	**131 Kalua**	**132 Waimea**
133 Mahi	134 Kekaha	135 Kaii	136 Naahu
137 Kaohilo	138 Kani	139 Kuokoa	140 Pehu
141 Pehu 2	142 Apuia	**143 Kaaea**	144 Kamokuahiole
145 Kuahamano	146 Puna	147 Kaneliilii	148 Kamoku
149 Piha	150 Keaka	151 Paanoio	152 Pualoha
153 Pinea	154 Nahoalawelawe	155 Kailaa	156 Keahi
157 Kanepauloa	158 Kaimu	159 Paku	160 Haleloa
161 Kalama	**162 Naono**	163 Pua	164 Kapohuli
165 Lonopuawela	**166 Pilaliohe**	**167 Keawe**	168 Malue
169 Kekahuna	170 Okou	171 Kauluahewa	172 Nalaukau
173 Kauhai	174 Kaaulaukini	175 Hanapilo	176 Koele
177 Kauwelani	**178 Kalua**	179 Kala'	180 Pahaha
181 Kuheleloa	**182 Ehu**	183 Alaala	**184 Pulehu**
185 Mahu	186 Palahuli	187 Palena	188 Kawiino
189 Ailepo	190 Kau	**191 Kuanea**	192 Keaweeli
193 Naeleele	194 Keaweelie	**195 Kahaka**	**196 Opunui**
		(+1 grant)	
197 Nanoha	198 Aewai	199 Palahe	200 Manuai
201 Kilauakea	**202 Kamai**	203 Nainea	204 Kamaunu
205 Kanakaole	206 Kanaau	207 Kaneaikai	208 Hihipalani
209 Kuhiheauau	**210 Kamai**	211 Pupule	**212 Kahaule**
213 Luha	214 Pehipolani	**215 Kahaule 2**	216 Kekupuwale
217 Kanunu	218 Hilea	**219 Naili**	220 Maoma
221 Kanakake	222 Kanakaloa	**223 Kapule**	**224 Paele**
225 Aea	226 Kailikea	227 Kahuaono	**228 Haole**
229 Kaanaana	230 Kaleikau	231 Kaaimoku	**232 Kaka**
233 Nalii	234 Kahuliaikau	235 Luhia	**236 Elemakule**
237 Kaiamalani	**238 Kale**	239 Heleonalama	240 Opae
241 Nakukulani	**242 Paele**	243 Kapua	244 Waikonale
245 Uilama	246 Kamai	**247 Kaniau**	**248 Kuapa**
			(+1 grant)

249 Oopa	250 Kanakaole	251 Kaahui	252 Meahole
253 Akaaina	254 Halama	255 Wahalumilumi	256 Maikai
257 Maikuli	258 Kaiu	**259 Makaole**	260 Kaiahauna
261 Kamaka	**262 Kalino**	263 Kokaehe	264 Kaaiaiamoku
265 Oleole	266 Upai	**267 Nakaula**	268 Kamakaalua
269 Kahaulepo	270 Kaheana	**271 Nalu**	**272 Mahoe**
273 Koloka	274 Ika	275 Wahineaela	276 Ana
277 Ohina	278 Kauwiki	279 Kaakau	280 Elisai
281 Ualanui	282 Kunui	283 Kanui	284 Mokeha
285 Molia	286 Kaaikapuu	287 Kaoha	288 Uihaai
289 Naopu	290 Paiahi	291 Puapuu	292 Heneriaka
293 Paaluhi	**294 Hihia**	295 Puahiohi	296 Kawaihua
297 Lepelua	298 Kawaipi	299 Kaai	300 Laie
301 Loiloi	302 Kaakua	303 Nakai	**304 Keawe**
305 Kuheleloa	**306 Kahue**	**307 Kalua**	**308 Kaina**
309 Naiole	310 Kanoho	311 Kanioi	**312 Mahoe**
313 Hopu	**314 Kaaikaula** (+1 grant)	315 Kalualoa	**316 Kapalena**
317 Kuaea	**318 Awala**	319 Inoino	320 Kealakahi
321 Hawaii	322 Kaiwi	323 Kekua	**324 Namaile**
325 Kaualo	326 Aikino	327 Wahalepo	328 Daniela
329 Kelaukila	330 Kamala	**331 Kane**	332 Kaniho
333 Kanakanui	334 Kaoha	335 Kahua	336 Kanakaole
337 Waimoe	**338 Penopeno**	339 Naonohi	340 Kama
341 Lima (+1 grant)	342 Kanene	**343 Kauhanui** (+1 grant)	**344 Nahoiha**
345 Kauhi	**346 Kapule**	347 Kanui	348 Kaaukai
349 Kahapana	350 Kaai	351 Kanoao	352 Kaheiki
353 Kahiawa	354 Kukeaa	355 Palapala	356 Kapai
357 Ihi	358 Mulihele	**359 Lawelawe** (+1 grant)	360 Aoao
361 Kanakaole	362 Kekolohe	363 Naili	364 Kawaiwai
365 Halualani	366 Ohule	**367 Kikoikoi**	368 Naili
369 Kahooaha	370 Pauahi	371 Kameheu	**372 Kawainui** (+1 grant)
373 Keanini	**374 Paele**	375 Kaaea	376 Ku
377 Keleau	378 Makaila	379 Kapaiwahea	**380 Kaili**
381 Kahaiola	**382 Luia**	383 Opapa	384 Kauahooloku
385 Mose	**386 Kuhoe**	387 Nakoholua	388 Malaihi

389 Kikau	**390 Kahookano** (+1 grant)	**391 Kaiamoku**	**392 Namakaelua**
393 Maalahia	394 Kauaawa	395 Kanehaole	**396 Kaluau**
397 Kaleo	398 Kukahana	399 Kuaana	**400 Kewalo**
401 Kekahuna	**402 Kapu**	**403 Nahia**	404 Nahale
405 Pupule	406 Mahu	407 Mauoha	408 Laa
409 Moewaa	410 Paahao	**411 Lolo**	**412 Pupuka**
413 Puaa	414 Kekau	415 Kamaunu	416 Kupololu
417 Nuipoohiwi	418 Lani	419 Luka	420 Hooipo
421 Pio	422 Kaolelo	423 Kaninau	424 Ika
425 Pupuka	426 Malao	427 Kapae	428 Muouou
429 Lolo	430 Kahili	431 Kahunui	432 Kepaa
433 Kahilina	**434 Puali**	435 Keneau	436 Kane
437 Kailaa	438 Kaakau	439 Ilikealani	440 Hawea
441 Kaluahine	**442 Ohule**	443 Puaahaliu	**444 Kanemanaole**
445 Opu	446 Ehu	**447 Haole**	**448 Kauku**
449 Nalaalaau	450 Kulohaaina	**451 Kauhi**	452 Solomona
453 Kealia	454 Kaui	455 Aberakama	**456 Mahina**
457 Piipii	458 Makalii	459 Kaohia	460 Umauma
461 Lulii	462 Paahao	**463 Kaili**	464 Wahineaukai
465 Pahoa	466 Kawakea	**467 Kahalau**	468 Pau
469 Poke	470 Pueaina	471 Honu	472 Kahue
473 Paele	474 Lakaba	475 Kahaohuli	476 Aukupu
477 Naupa	478 Maeikaukane	479 Nakaoolelo	480 Wahinekoliola
481 Ninihua	**482 Halulu**	**483 Hulu**	484 Napaepae
485 Kauhi	486 Piiaimoku	487 Nakaa	488 Kahuha
489 Paaluhi	490 Ioane	**491 Aukai**	492 Iopa
493 Pukuhe	494 Oopa	**495 Ihu**	**496 Ueuele**
497 Hemahema	498 Haipu	**499 Kamakahi**	500 Keliihooleia
501 Kaohimaunu	502 Kalele	503 Kaheana	**504 Kaiue**
505 Kalaauala	506 Kahukanokoliilii	507 Kualualii	**508 Kila**
509 Kaiakea	**510 Kawelo**	511 Kahiau	**512 Luuloa**
513 Mahiai	514 Makaihuia	515 Moaku	516 Nawaaloloa
517 Pulehi	**518 Pohuehue**	519 Waha	520 Mahiai
521 Mahina	522 Napihelua	523 Kahalekai	524 Hokai
525 Naonealaa	526 Namakakaia	527 Kamai	**528 Kameheu**
529 Kulani	530 Namakaokeawe	531 Kewalo	532 Kelakela
533 Kaloa	**534 Opuloa**	535 Kalauahea	536 Haole

537 Paikaniau	**538 Kakii**	539 Nahuaai	540 Nahuaai
541 Kuohau	542 Inoino	543 Haa	544 Kahau
545 Inui	**546 Mahoe**	547 Kanalualii	548 Aweka
549 Kuaeau	550 Uwelani	551 Ualani	552 Aloi
553 Kuai	554 Kane	555 Moi	556 Kumaikalala
557 Kalawe	558 Kau	559 Kaluaokamoku	560 Kekahuna
561 Naliikawaa	562 Ouwe	563 Wahineino	564 Keakui
565 Nuka	566 Makaino	567 Alaala	568 Wahinekapu
569 Kaumaka	570 Wahinealii	571 Paku	572 Kepaa
573 Naleilehua	574 Iliwai	575 Kekaha	576 Kamakahelei
578 Kapuli	579 Hanaloa	580 Kaakua	581 Lihue
582 Makahoohano	583 Kaiwi	584 Mahu	585 Waimea
586 Kolia	587 Kaeha	588 Laukua	589 Kalahale
590 Aukai	591 Kaumakua	592 **Kaianui**	593 Kalokane
594 Kaipuniho	595 Naihe	596 Kaikaina	597 Manoa
598 Uluhoa	599 Mahi	600 Kalaumano	601 Kua
602 Owau	603 Kahakukaalina	604 Imahiai	**605 Kuloa**
606 Kuanea	607 Kanalualii	608 Kepaa	609 Inui
610 Kaluau	**611 Kahoowaha**	612 Wahinealii	613 Kaumaka
614 Mahiai	615 Kuohao	616 Kawahahei	617 Nahuaai
618 Pioe	619 Aloalo	620 Aukai	621 Wahinekapu
622 Luina	623 Kaha	624 Makaino	625 Kealohi
626 Nawahine	627 Ponoino	628 Kelakela	629 Kahaleolani
630 Waihinalo	631 Kai	632 Lona	633 Pehu
634 Kahuakailuhi	635 Kamanohelii	**636 Mahoe**	637 Pohaku
638 Mahoe	639 Hea	640 Puaohi	**641 Kahiko**
642 Kalua	643 Lea	644 Paiuma	645 Hikihewa
646 Kelono	647 Keanoalii	648 Kalanahea	649 Kahalau
650 Kaili	651 Kale	652 Kaloa	**653 Kaiwinui**
654 Kaianui	**655 Kahinu**	656 Hoki	657 Kaie
658 Namakaokaia	659 Namealoaa	660 Laakapu	661 Namakaokeawe
662 Kalani	663 Kameheu	664 Kamaka	665 Kaha
666 Wahahee	667 Maui	668 Pakaha	669 Kahue
670 Kaia	671 Umi	672 Keliikuewa	673 Ukuula
674 Naomi	675 Pukuinui	676 Maleka	**677 Kiekie**
678 Alapai	**679 Keawa**	680 Niho	681 Pupule
682 Kahoomaika	683 Kapalo	684 Pulehuhua	685 Kanui
686 Kehuluaulani	687 Kaialau	688 Hinaele	689 Kiula

690 Kaumu	691 Maihuki	692 Keliiaukai	693 Lakalo
694 Kahuna	695 Paahao	696 Kanawi	697 Kuaai
698 Kamakahoo-hano	699 Malae	700 Lehua	701 Kau
702 Poopuu	703 Paahao	**704 Upai**	705 Kahaule
706 Naone	707 Kualawa	708 Napae	**709 Kuku** (+1 grant)
710 Kauwe	711 Paulaulaiki	712 Kaikulani	713 Kanuku
714 Oiai	715 Kaahaialii	716 Kalualohi	717 Paakua
718 Kekaha	719 Hanaloa	720 Kuaeou	721 Ilo
722 Haole	723 Nalehua	724 Naonealaa	**725 Naholowaa**
726 Wahineaea	727 Haipu	728 Ikaa	**729 Makapo**
730 Puana	731 Kapa	732 Kaialau	733 Kalaipaka
734 Nakalina	735 Healani	**736 Aki**	737 Mueau
738 Kekahuna	739 Lono	740 Kalahale	741 Kaukaliu
742 Papalana	743 Kuli	744 Kama	745 Kama
746 Kapiolamau	747 Paahao	748 Paoloa	749 Puapua
750 Waiale	**751 Kahananui**	752 Kaaiau	753 Halulu
754 Puamana	755 Iliwai	756 Luahine	757 Pauma
758 Kauaeau	759 Kaupuna	760 Nuuu	761 Holi
762 Hakii	763 Kama	764 Kaumakae	765 Kaa
766 Kumu	767 Kua	768 Kalua	769 Peihalu
770 Heke	771 Luhulu	772 Naoka	773 Wahineine
774 Kali	775 Keakui	**776 Puu**	777 I
778 Alalo	779 Halawai	780 Kaale	781 Amuamu
782 Naowa	783 Nohunohu	784 Palema	785 Auwaepaa
786 Kumahoe	787 Oehu	788 Paku	789 Ahi
790 Makaula	791 Kapaahu	792 Kuala	**793 Kowilikopaa**
794 Apua	795 Pahi	796 Hoohano	797 Kane
798 Nahaka	799 Kaehana	800 Kea	801 Moloku
802 Hakuole	**803 Kawelo**	**804 Puupuu**	805 Pipi
806 Kaule (+1 grant)	807 Kuapuu	**808 Kamauoha**	**809 Paele**
810 Kahue	811 Kahaaweai	**812 Kuluwaimaka**	813 Kahuine
814 Hulihee	815 Kuhihewa	**816 Nahoaai**	817 Kahu
818 Kawelo	**819 Muolo**	**820 Hilo**	821 Paele
822 Paele 3	**823 Kaheiau**	824 Kaheaaku	825 Koemakaia
826 Pala	**827 Ihu**	828 Keanui	**829 Paele 4**

830 Kaululaau	831 Onei	**832 Hua**	833 Paiwi
834 Kapale	835 Kalaeone	**836 Mauku**	837 Kuanoni
838 Wawae	839 Kupuwale	840 Nukai	841 Waiki
842 Mahoe	843 Kaumauina	844 Miki	845 Kawai
846 Keo	847 Paumanao	848 Nauaua	849 Lauae
850 Paakea	851 Kaaiia	852 Kanae	853 Kumuhonua
854 Mahoe	855 Kuaiwa	856 Kauwanui	857 Auweka
858 Aa	859 Inoino	860 Imahiai	861 Ikoa
862 Opuloa	863 Ualani 1	864 Ualani 2	865 Ualani 3
866 Uuoe	867 Uu	868 Haa	869 Haole
870 Haole 2	871 Kealani	872 Kaahui	**873 Kaahu**
874 Kahue	875 Kakii	876 Kahipa	877 Opanui
878 Kaea	879 Kaanui	880 Poonui	881 Minamina
882 Kekahuna	883 Kaniau	884 Kanikau	885 Kukapu
886 Wahinehue	**887 Kaukini**	888 Wahinehue	889 Namilo
890 Naimihale	**891 Keala**	892 Kaae	893 Kahula
894 Makaole	**895 Kaialiilii**	896 Kaililua	897 Nakao
898 Kaolala	899 Piko	900 Keha	901 Nahooikaika
902 Nakeokeo	903 Kaheananui	904 Kaiwa	905 Naanana
906 Kahaaheo	907 Kekua	908 Kawelowahine	909 Paiwa
910 Kahapu	911 Maneo	912 Mahiai	**913 Moo**
914 Kanakaole	915 Kualii	916 Kaulana	917 Pahia
918 Kekuinaa	919 Kahikanaka	920 Kakani	**921 Naoo**
922 Waialua	923 Nahaupia	924 Kekahuna	925 Nikipala
926 Nakala	**927 Kepio**	928 Kekahuna	929 Kaai
930 Kaakau	931 Kahai	932 Kainui	933 Wahauwia
934 Opiopio	935 Kahina	936 Waianu	937 Nakihei
938 Loika	939 Ohimai	940 Mukoi	941 Maihu
942 Paalou	943 Kahioumae	944 Nakai	945 Kekuewa
946 Ieremia	947 Kahoeua	948 Naki	949 Kaupalolo
950 Kauia	951 Pimoa	952 Kanahele	**953 Mahoe**
954 Kamai	955 Kaai	**956 Napela**	957 Kahue
958 Hawaii	959 Makapo	960 Kapukila	**961 Kahema**
962 Nakahuna	963 Kaiaiki	964 Kaunuino	965 Kukanalua
966 Pauahi	967 Palama	968 Upai	969 Keaa
970 Naahuelua	**971 Kanewanui**	**972 Kaneheana**	**973 Kaneakua**
			(+1 grant)

974 Pokepa	975 Maiola	976 Koihoomoe	977 Paana
978 Pahio	**979 Keawe**	**980 Kukoa**	981 Kaukaukapa
	(+2 grants)		
982 Kalilikane	983 Kauhi	984 Solomona	985 Iosepa
986 Kaia	**987 Lolo**	988 Kaailaau	989 Kaneelele
990 Iimona	991 Ahulili	992 Kaniu	**993 Kapopule**
994 Koowahie	995 Kanakanui	996 Kaeku	997 Poohina
998 Heehua	999 Pali	1000 Puhikea	1001 Kaialawaia
1002 Daniela	1003 Waialoha	1004 Naohe	1005 Paauao
1006 Kaihe	1007 Kaakau	1008 Palima	1009 Palima 2
1010 Kanae	1011 Ukunui	1012 Upai	1013 Makuai
1014 Pukuha	1015 Kaihumua	1016 Omino	1017 Kaloulu
1018 Puli	1019 Haole	1020 Kanui	1021 Puhaumea
1022 Kaheleino	**1023 Kalamaikai**	1024 Kumalaua	1025 Kaha
1026 Paipaiku	1027 Naoha	1028 Kawehena	1029 Loheau
1030 Kaialuau	1031 Mahoe	**1032 Hanunu**	1033 Palapu
1034 Hainoa	1035 Kauiki	**1036 Keaki**	1037 Kamoku
		(+1 grant)	
1038 Naonea	1039 Ai	**1040 Kahiapaiole**	1041 Kalapauila
1042 Hapuku	**1043 Uaiaholo**	1044 Kikoopaoa	**1045 Kaluau**
(+1 grant)			(+3 grants)
1046 Kekipi	1047 Luaka	1048 Hololoa	**1049 Kahoohalahala**
1050 Kalaihae	1051 Kuaana	1052 Kaiu	1053 Kalaeone
1054 Kalua	1055 Kanui	1056 Kaai	**1057 Kahui**
1058 Kaiwa	1059 Kawelo	1060 Kakau	1061 Pueo
1062 Kaelehiwa	1063 Iai	**1064 Kaleo**	1065 Geogi
		(+1 grant)	
1066 Wahie	1067 Makalawelawe	1068 Naiakapu	1069 Kaiheelua
1070 Huewaa	1071 Kepio	**1072 Naope**	1073 Puaanui
1074 Mahoe	1075 Keaka	1076 Maheai	1077 Kahana
1078 Puuone	**1079 Piikoi**	**1080 Mai**	1081 Moo
1082 Wailele	1083 Koiole	1084 Kai	1085 Kanakaole
1086 Kalili	1087 Mu	**1088 Aki**	1089 Kamohai
1090 Puailelewale	1091 Kupa	**1092 Kanakaokai**	1093 Laa
		(+1 grant)	
1094 Kala	1095 Kaholopo	1096 Kahaipu	1097 Mai
1098 Kenaumoku	1099 Naone	1100 Kalahili	1101 Amalu
1102 Kaluaoko	1103 Kelohe	1104 Lai	1105 Manamana

1106 Debora	1107 Moo 1	1108 Moo 2	1109 Papalua
1110 Paele	1111 Kamakolu	1112 Makali	**1113 Kaanaana**
1114 Kanakaole	1115 Waa	1116 Kaona	**1117 Hoe**
1118 Kai	1119 Kamili	1120 Keahiaena	1121 Kamai
1122 Kuhilani	1123 Noa	**1124 Nahuina**	1125 Nahuka
1126 Nalu	**1127 Pakaka**	1128 Paumano	1129 Paouahi
1130 Naonea	1131 Kaialiili	**1132 Lili**	**1133 Ikeole**
1134 Nauele	**1135 Pule**	1136 Kaili	**1137 Kaheaku**
1138 Uhai	1139 Kaokako	1140 Kaaihue	1141 Kaholopo
1142 Aola	1143 Kamauoha	1144 Ukehaui	**1145 Kauakahi**
			(+2 grants)
1146 Kikau	1147 Nopahi	1148 Kekaowai	1149 Kekaowai
1150 Nika	1151 Moo	**1152 Haena**	1153 Loita
1154 Hoolulu	1155 Debora	**1156 Makalohi**	1157 Makolu
1158 Kahula	1159 Kaiawaawa	1160 Kaoloa	1161 Kahaawepala
1162 Kauhihai	1163 Kaheananui	1164 Kapela	1165 Kaiwi
1166 Kaikaalele	1167 Kaoihia	1168 Kekui	1169 Kupanihi
1170 Lilia	1171 Lihue	1172 Moewale	1173 Mareka
1174 Nakoana	**1175 Naehuelua**	1176 Niau	1177 Wahapuaa
1178 Kealoha	1179 Kualana	1180 Kawaianuhea	1181 Kekoo
1182 Naaiholei	1183 Kekini	1184 Kalakia	1185 Geogi
1186 Laa	1187 Keikiama	**1188 Aki**	1189 Kapahi
1190 Kaha	1191 Kapuahiauli	1192 Poopuu	1193 Keaka
1194 Kaapuiki	1195 Palauaiki	1196 Naone	1197 Kahaule
1198 Kamuku	1199 Kamamaka	1200 Kaiwipalana	1201 Upai
1202 Lukua	1203 Mahiai	1204 Keliikanakaole	1205 Keliikanakaole
1206 Kehuliaulani	1207 Kanaau	1208 Kahee	1209 Kaahanui
1210 Ilihune	1211 Uhilau	1212 Kaaehule	1213 Ehu
1214 Kaakau	1215 Kawelowahine	1216 Helenihi	1217 Kupuna
1218 Kuapuu	1219 Paaluhi	1220 Nahaomama	1221 Nooui
1222 Lea	1223 Hilihewa	1224 Kelono	1225 Kahiko
1226 Pehu	1227 Kanaauohelii	1228 Kahela	1229 Pohaki
1230 Poihe	1231 Waihinalo	1232 Kahalolani	1233 Kealo
1234 Kaha	1235 Nawahine	1236 Kini	1237 Kaaukai
1238 Nuhi	1239 Paakiki	1240 Kaheewahine	1241 Waiole
1242 Kalama	1243 Kau	1244 Kolia	1245 Niho
1246 Nakua	1247 Kaiwini	1248 Kahananui	1249 Pelelao
1250 Kaunahi	1251 Kalawaia	1252 Kaheana	1253 Pua

1254 Noa	1255 Kaahu	1256 Nalua	1257 Hoaeae
1258 Poonui	**1259 Maiaawa**	1260 Awailua	1261 Poohee
1262 Kalikelike	1263 Kalele	1264 Kakau	1265 Paaluhi
1266 Kale	1267 Kaaiai	1268 Nalauha	**1269 Nainaelua**
1270 Makaole	1271 Uwe	1272 Kaneiahula	1273 Kaaipuhi
1274 Kaiwiahuula	1275 Kokoniho	1276 Kahuailio	1277 Limahanaiau
1278 Kalawehau	1279 Makana	1280 Molokai	1281 Kahula
1282 Kanui	1283 Pinui	1284 Muoone	**1285 Aki**
1286 Nahoomana	1287 Poonui	1288 Moi	1289 Kaupo
1290 Kaakau	1291 Kawelowahine	1292 Kapuna	1293 Paloe
1294 Kuapuu	1295 Paialuhi	1296 Upai	1297 Pupule
1298 Kahele	1299 Kawauki	1300 Naouealaa	1301 Kahee
1302 Uhilau	1303 Naholowaa	1304 Kaahanui	1305 Mae
1306 Ilihune	1307 Makapo	1308 Kaaepule	1309 Kehuluaulani
1310 Kaahilila	1311 Kuka	1312 Ehu	1313 Kanakaole
1314 Kahaikukuna	1315 Waimea	**1316 Mahu**	1317 Naou
1318 Kalia	1319 Kaeha	1320 Aukai	1321 Maakua
1322 Kaimakua	1323 Naainaelua	1324 Nakua	1325 Nalehua
1326 Naliikoa	1327 Nuhi	1328 Puna	1329 Kuana
1330 Pakaikua	1331 Puanana	1332 Ohikulani	1333 Kahoʻowaha
1334 Kapahi	1335 Napae	1336 Kauwe	1337 Poopua
1338 Namai	1339 Kaahu	1340 Kahinu	1341 Kaiwilana
1342 Kewalo			

*Two names are missing. The 268 names that match names of persons who received Land Commission Awards through the Māhele and Kuleana Acts are shown in **boldface.**

Source: Hawaiʻi State Archives, ser. 222, box 2, folder 3.

1. The primary sources for this monograph are oral histories. As a historian I also draw upon available written documents, records, newspapers, and monographs for each cultural kīpuka. However, since most written accounts of Hawai'i focus on the major islands and centers of trade, written sources for these rural communities are limited; oral history sources complement and enhance the history or mo'olelo of these districts and the kua'āina who lived there from generation to generation.

2. In Mary Kawena Pukui and Samuel H. Elbert, *Hawaiian Dictionary* (Honolulu: University of Hawai'i Press, 1975), *kua'āina* is translated as "person from the country, rustic; of the country, countrified, rustic. Lit. back land."

3. Eric Enos, an educator who reopened taro patches in the uplands of Wai'anae on the slopes of Mount Ka'ala, speaks of kua'āina as backbone in the video *He Makana No Nā Kumu: A Gift to the Teachers of Hawaiian Students*, produced by Diane Kahanu and Nā Maka o Ka'Āina, 1991.

4. Noa Emmett Aluli, family physician to 'ohana on the island of Moloka'i and one of the founders of the Protect Kaho'olawe 'Ohana, speaks of kua'āina as those who bend their backs to work the land.

5. Daniel Pahupu, interview by Mary Kawena Pukui, March 9, 1961, Mana'e, Moloka'i (Audio-Recording Collection, Department of Anthropology, Bernice Pauahi Bishop Museum).

6. Ibid. The Audio-Recording Collection, Anthropology Department, Bernice Pauahi Bishop Museum, was a major source of information for this mo'olelo. The collection was published in Mary Kawena Pukui, Samuel H. Elbert, and Esther T. Mookini, *Place Names of Hawaii* (Honolulu: University of Hawai'i Press, 1984). The Moloka'i information was also included in Catherine Summers, *Molokai: A Site Survey*, Pacific Anthropological Records 14 (Honolulu: Bernice Pauahi Bishop Museum, 1971).

7. This version of the chant and the translation is in Pualani Kanakaole Kanahele, "Ka Honua Ola / The Living Earth" (unpublished ms., funded by the Center for Hawaiian Studies at the University of Hawai'i at Mānoa from the State Foundation on Culture and the Arts), pp. 101–3.

8. Andrew Lind, *An Island Community: Ecological Succession in Hawaii* (New York: Greenwood Press, 1968), pp. 102–3.

9. The general patterns noted here are based upon data and sources referred to and discussed in the chapters on Waipiʻo, Hāna, and Molokaʻi.

10. E. S. Craighill Handy and Elizabeth Green Handy with Mary Kawena Pukui, *Native Planters in Old Hawaii: Their Life, Lore, and Environment* (Honolulu: Bishop Museum Press, 1972), p. vi.

11. Rubellite Johnson, *Kumulipo: Hawaiian Hymn of Creation*, vol. 1 (Honolulu: Topgallant, 1981); *The Kumulipo: An Hawaiian Creation Myth*, trans. Queen Liliʻuokalani (Kentfield: Pueo Press, 1997).

12. Handy, Handy, and Pukui, *Native Planters in Old Hawaii*, p. 64.

13. *Kahoʻolawe, Nā Leo O Kanaloa: Chants and Stories of Kahoʻolawe* (Honolulu: ʻAi Pōhaku Press, 1995).

14. Sitiveni Halapua, "Sustainable Development: From Ideal to Reality in the Pacific Islands," paper prepared for the Fourth Pacific Islands Conference of Leaders, Tahiti, French Polynesia, June 24–26, 1993, sponsored by the East-West Center, Honolulu.

15. Davianna Pōmaikaʻi McGregor, "Kupaʻa I Ka ʻĀina: Persistence on the Land" (Ph.D. diss., University of Hawaiʻi, 1989).

16. I have also conducted an ethnographic study of the ahupuaʻa of Waiāhole, Waikāne, Hakipuʻu, and Kahana on Oʻahu as the foundation for testimony I prepared for the Waiāhole Water Case before the Hawaiʻi State Water Commission. Waiāhole and Waikāne were the focus of a significant struggle by resident Hawaiian and local farmers and fishermen in the 1970s to retain the lands in agriculture and sustain the rural Hawaiian and local lifestyle characteristic of cultural kīpuka. In my study I concluded that these valleys are still cultural kīpuka, but their location on the island of Oʻahu and proximity to the city of Honolulu place them at risk of being transformed into suburbs of Honolulu. The conscious efforts of the new generation of Hawaiian kuaʻāina in these valleys to farm taro and to sustain the near-shore fishponds and fishing grounds and to reestablish the natural flow of the stream waters of these valleys away from diversion networks and tunnels and toward leeward Oʻahu will sustain these rural valleys as cultural kīpuka.

17. These periods are discussed and summarized in Patrick V. Kirch, *Feathered Gods and Fishhooks: An Introduction to Hawaiian Archaeology and Prehistory* (Honolulu: University of Hawaiʻi Press, 1985); Patrick V. Kirch, *Legacy of the Landscape: An Illustrated Guide to Hawaiian Archaeological Sites* (Honolulu: University of Hawaiʻi Press, 1996); and Malcolm Naea Chun and Matthew Spriggs, "New Terms Suggested For Early Hawaiian History," *Ka Wai Ola O OHA* (February 1987): 4. Other sources for dating these periods are Abraham Fornander, *Fornander Collection of Hawaiian Antiquities and Folk-lore: The Hawaiians' Account of the Formation of Their Islands and Origins of Their Race, with the Traditions of Their Migrations as Gathered from Original Sources*, ed. Thomas G. Thrum, Bernice Pauahi

Bishop Museum Memoirs, vols. 4–6 (Honolulu: Bishop Museum, 1916–20); Martha W. Beckwith, *Hawaiian Mythology* (Honolulu: University of Hawai'i Press, 1970); Samuel Kamakau, *Ruling Chiefs of Hawaii* (Honolulu: Kamehameha Schools Press, 1961); Samuel Kamakau, *Ka Po'e Kahiko: The People of Old*, Bernice Pauahi Bishop Museum Special Publication 51 (Honolulu: Bernice Pauahi Bishop Museum Press, 1964); Samuel Kamakau, *The Works of the People of Old*, Bernice Pauahi Bishop Museum Special Publication 61 (Honolulu: Bernice Pauahi Bishop Museum Press, 1976); and David Kalākaua, King of Hawaii, *The Legends and Myths of Hawaii: The Fables and Folklore of a Strange People* (Tokyo & Rutland, Vt.: Charles E. Tuttle, 1973).

18. Ross Cordy, *Exalted Sits the Chief: The Ancient History of Hawai'i Island* (Honolulu: Mutual, 2000), pp. 104–9.

19. Samuel Kamakau, *Tales and Traditions of the People of Old: Nā Mo'olelo a ka Po'e Kahiko*, ed. Dorothy B. Barrere, trans. Mary Kawena Pukui (Honolulu: Bishop Museum Press, 1991), p. 112.

20. Kamakau, *Tales and Traditions*, p. 136. See also Thomas G. Thrum, Hawaiian Folk Tales (Chicago: McClurg, 1921); Thrum, *More Hawaiian Folk Tales* (Chicago: McClurg, 1923); W. D. Westervelt, *Legends of Ma-ui* (New York: AMS Press, 1979).

21. E. S. Craighill Handy and Mary Kawena Pukui, *The Polynesian Family System in Ka-'u, Hawai'i* (Tokyo and Rutland, Vt.: Charles E. Tuttle, 1976), pp. 5–6.

22. At the time of Cook, 1778–79, Kalaniopu'u controlled Hawai'i island, while Kahekili controlled Maui, O'ahu, Moloka'i, Lāna'i, Kaho'olawe, Kaua'i, and Ni'ihau.

23. T. K. Earle, *Economic and Social Organization of a Complex Chiefdom: The Hale‘a District, Kaua'i, Hawai'i*, Anthropological Papers of the Museum of Anthropology, University of Michigan, No. 63, 1978 (unpublished ms.); Caroline Ralston, "Hawaii, 1778–1854: Some Aspects of *Maka'āinana* Response to Rapid Cultural Change," *Journal of Pacific History* 29, no. 1 (January 1984): 23.

24. On O'ahu, the ahupua'a were bounded on each side by mountain ridges. On Maui, the ahupua'a were bounded on each side by streams. On Hawai'i, cinder hills or *pu'u* were used as boundary markers.

25. Handy, Handy, and Pukui, *Native Planters in Old Hawaii.* For a detailed description of traditional Hawaiian land divisions see David Malo, *Mo'olelo Hawai'i*, trans. Nathaniel B. Emerson as *Hawaiian Antiquities*, Bernice Pauahi Bishop Museum Special Publication 2 (Honolulu: Bishop Museum Press, 1951).

26. Mary Kawena Pukui, *'Ōlelo No'eau: Hawaiian Proverbs and Poetical Sayings*, Bernice Pauahi Bishop Museum Special Publication 71 (Honolulu: Bishop Museum Press, 1983), p. 198.

27. Ibid., no. 1149, p. 125.

28. Kamakau, *Ruling Chiefs*, pp. 1–21; Marion Kelly, *Majestic Ka'u: Mo'olelo of Nine Ahupua'a*, Department of Anthropology Report Series 80–2 (Honolulu: Bishop Museum Press, 1990); Pukui and Green, "*Nā Ali'i*," pp. 74–77, 131–33.

29. Pukui, *'Ōlelo No'eau*, no. 1150, p. 125.

30. David Malo, "Causes for the Decrease of the Population in the Islands," trans. with comments by Lorrin Andrews, *Hawaiian Spectator* 2, no. 2 (1839): 125.

31. Kirch, *Legacy of the Landscape*, p. 6.

32. The estimate from Cook's voyage was 400,000. A recent study places the precontact population as high as 800,000; see David Stannard, *Before the Horror* (Honolulu: University of Hawai'i Press, 1989).

33. Handy and Pukui, *The Polynesian Family System*, pp. 234–35.

34. Malo, "Causes for the Decrease," p. 125.

35. Ralph Kuykendall, *The Hawaiian Kingdom* (Honolulu: University of Hawai'i Press, 1968), 1:29–60.

36. Kamakau, *Ruling Chiefs*, pp. 219–28; Kalākaua, *Legends and Myths*, pp. 429–46; Marshall Sahlins, *Historical Metaphors and Mythical Realities: Structure in the Early History of the Sandwich Islands Kingdom* (Ann Arbor: University of Michigan Press, 1981), pp. 55–64; William Davenport, "The Hawaiian 'Cultural Revolution': Some Economic and Political Considerations," *American Anthropologist* 71 (1969): 1–20; A. L. Kroeber, *Anthropology* (New York: Harcourt, Brace, 1948).

37. Kanakaole Kanahele, *Ola Honua*.

38. Kamakau, *Ruling Chiefs*; Kuykendall, *Hawaiian Kingdom*.

39. The excerpt is from "Nā Kumukanawai O Ka Makahiki 1839 A Me Ka 1840," reproduced in Ka Ho'oilina, "The Legacy: Puke Pai 'ōlelo Hawai'i," *Journal of Hawaiian Language Sources* 1, no. 1 (March 2002): 32–33. Note that the journal translates *pae 'āina o Hawai'i nei* as Sandwich Islands, but I've translated it more precisely as Hawaiian archipelago.

40. Ibid., pp. 40–41. I changed the translation to more accurately reflect the Hawaiian. I wrote "from Hawai'i to Ni'ihau" instead of "from one end of the Islands to the other"; the Hawaiian stated, "It belonged to the people and the chiefs in common," although the journal translation changed the word order so that it reads "It belonged to the chiefs and people in common."

41. Office of the Commissioner of Public Lands, *Indices of Awards Made by the Board of Commissioners to Quiet Land Titles in the Hawaiian Islands* (Honolulu: Star-Bulletin Press, 1929), p. 2.

42. Ibid., pp. 3, 14.

43. Ibid., pp. 3, 15.

44. Louis Cannelora, *The Origin of Hawaii Land Titles and of the Rights of Native Tenants* (Honolulu: Security Title Corporation, 1974).

45. Ibid.; Jon J. Chinen, *The Great Māhele: Hawaii's Land Division of 1848* (Honolulu: University of Hawai'i Press, 1958), p. 8.

46. Office of the Commissioner of Public Lands, *Indices of Awards*.

47. Ibid.; Chinen, *The Great Māhele*, p. 8.

48. Study by Marion Kelly cited in Neil Levy, "Native Hawaiian Land Rights," *California Law Review* 63, no.4 (July 1975): 856.

49. Prince Jonah Kūhiō Kalaniana'ole, "The Story of the Hawaiians," *Mid-Pacific Magazine* 21, no. 2 (February 1921).

50. Hawai'i Revised Statutes, sec. 7-1 (1985).

51. Kuykendall, *The Hawaiian Kingdom*; Davianna McGregor, "Voices of Today Echo Voices of the Past," in *Mālama: Hawaiian Land and Water*, ed. Dana Naone Hall (Honolulu: Bamboo Ridge Press, 1985).

52. William Goodale, "The Hawaiian as Unskilled Laborer," *Hawaiian Almanac and Annual* (1914): 183.

53. *Ka Nūhou*, May 23, 1873.

54. U.S. Department of State, *Papers Relating to the Mission of James H. Blount, United States Commissioner to the Hawaiian Islands* (Washington: Government Printing Office, 1893; also referred to as "Blount Report"), pt. 2, p. 5.

55. U.S. Congress, House Report No. 243, "Intervention of United States Government in Affairs of Foreign Friendly Governments," 53rd Congress, 2d sess., December 21, 1893 (Washington: Government Printing Office, 1893); U.S. Congress, Senate Committee on Foreign Relations, "Hawaiian Islands," in *Report of the Committee on Foreign Relations with Accompanying Testimony and Executive Documents Transmitted to Congress from January 1, 1893 to March 19, 1894*, vols. 1–2 (Washington: Government Printing Office, 1894 [also referred to as "The Morgan Report"]); U.S. Congress, Senate Committee on Foreign Relations, *Report No. 227*, "Report from the Committee on Foreign Relations and Appendix in Relation to the Hawaiian Islands, February 26, 1894," 53d Congress, 2d sess. (Washington: Government Printing Office, 1894); U.S. Department of State, "Blount Report."

56. Robert M. C. Littler, *The Governance of Hawaii: A Study in Territorial Administration* (Stanford, Calif.: Stanford University Press, 1929).

57. U.S. Congress, "Congressional Debates on Hawaii Organic Act, Together with Debates and Congressional Action on Other Matters Concerning the Hawaiian Islands," 56th Congress, 1st sess., 1899–1900, *Congressional Record* 33, pts. 1–8.

58. McGregor, "Kūpa'a I Ka'āina." The Big Five are C. Brewer, Theo H. Davies, Cas-

tle & Cooke, AmFac, and Alexander and Baldwin. Lawrence Fuchs, *Hawaii Pono: A Social History* (San Diego: Harcourt, Brace & World, 1961); Noel Kent, *Hawaii: Islands under the Influence* (New York: Monthly Review Press, 1983); Andrew Lind, *An Island Community: Ecological Succession in Hawaii* (Chicago: University of Chicago Press, 1938).

59. McGregor, "Kūpaʻa I Kaʻāina."

60. Eckbo, Dean, Austin, and Williams, with Morris Fox, consultant, "H-3 Socio-Economic Study: The Effects of Change on a Windward Oahu Rural Community" (unpublished report, Honolulu, 1973).

NOTES TO CHAPTER TWO

1. Colin Lennox, "A Report to the Trustees of the Bernice P. Bishop Museum on the Resources of Waipiʻo Valley, Island of Hawaii: Their Past and Present Uses and an Analysis of the Problems Facing their Fuller Use in the Future," unpublished manuscript (1954), Bernice Pauahi Bishop Museum Library, p. 3; Alfred E. Hudson, "Archaeology of East Hawaiʻi, 1930–32," unpublished manuscript, Bernice Pauahi Bishop Museum Library, pp. 132–34.

2. Samuel H. Elbert and Noelani Mahoe, *Na Mele o Hawaiʻi Nei: 101 Hawaiian Songs* (Honolulu: University of Hawaiʻi Press, 1978), pp. 49, 94.

3. Martha Beckwith, *Hawaiian Mythology* (Honolulu: University of Hawaiʻi Press, 1970), p. 155.

4. Ibid.

5. Ibid., pp. 86, 122.

6. Ibid., pp. 350–51.

7. Ibid., p. 142; Westervelt, in *Paradise of the Pacific*, June 1906, p. 10.

8. Roger Rose, *Reconciling the Past: Two Basketry, Kaʻai, and the Legendary Liloa and Lonoikamakahiki* (Honolulu: Bernice Pauahi Bishop Museum Press, 1992).

9. Beckwith, *Hawaiian Mythology*, pp. 353, 357–58, 509–10.

10. Fornander attempted to place the legendary chiefs of the migratory period and thereafter in specific years. He dated Pilikaeaea at 1090. Fornander, *Fornander Collection*, vol. 6, pt. 2, pp. 312–16.

11. Abraham Fornander, *An Account of the Polynesian Race, Its Origins and Migrations, and the Ancient History of the Polynesian People to the Times of Kamehameha I*, vol. 2 (London: Trubner, 1880), p. 73.

12. Malo, *Moʻolelo Hawaii*, pp. 251–54.

13. Ross Cordy, in *Exalted Sits the Chief: The Ancient History of Hawaiʻi Island* (Honolulu: Mutual, 2000), using 20 years per generation, rather than the 30 years per generation used by Fornander, placed Pili's reign at 1320 CE. He dated Kahaʻimoeleʻa to 1460–80, Kalaunuiohua to 1480–1500, Kihanuilulumoku to 1560–80, and ʻUmialīloa to 1600–1620.

14. Handy, Handy, and Pukui, *Native Planters in Old Hawaii*, pp. 534–35; Beckwith, *Hawaiian Mythology*, pp. 389–92; Kamakau, *Ruling Chiefs*, pp. 1–21.

15. Kamakau, *Ruling Chiefs*, pp. 19–20.

16. Cordy, *Exalted Sits the Chief*, p. 200.

17. John F. G. Stokes, *Heiau of the Island of Hawai'i: A Historic Survey of Native Hawaiian Temple Sites* (Honolulu: Bernice Pauahi Bishop Museum Press, 1991), pp. 159–62.

18. Ibid., p. 151.

19. Stephen L. Desha, *Kamehameha and His Warrior Kekuhaupi'o*, trans. Frances N. Frazier (Honolulu: Kamehameha Schools Press, 2000), pp. 275–89.

20. Stokes, *Heiau*, p. 160.

21. Desha, *Kamehameha*, pp. 299–301.

22. William Ellis, *Journal of William Ellis, Narrative of a Tour of Hawaii, or Owhyhee; With Remarks on the History, Traditions, Manners, Customs and Language of the Inhabitants of the Sandwich Islands* (Honolulu: Advertiser, 1963), p. 256.

23. Ibid., pp. 365–66.

24. Kamakau, *Ruling Chiefs*, p. 285.

25. Rose, *Reconciling the Past*, p. 11.

26. Hudson, "Archaeology of East Hawaii," pp. 141–42, 151–53.

27. Cited in Handy, Handy, and Pukui, *Native Planters in Old Hawaii*, p. 534.

28. Dorothy Barrere, comp., "The King's Māhele: The Awardees and Their Lands," unpublished bound manuscript, 1994 (Hamilton Library, University of Hawai'i at Mānoa). Information on the ali'i of the māhele is drawn from this manuscript.

29. Office of the Commissioner of Public Lands [OCPL], *Indices of Awards Made by the Board of Commissioners to Quiet Land Titles in the Hawaiian Islands* (Honolulu: Star-Bulletin Press, 1929), pp. 3–7, 17–18, 432–36.

30. Cited in Hudson, "Archaeology of East Hawaii," p. 142, and in Ethnic Studies Oral History Project [ESOHP], *Waipi'o Mano Wai: An Oral History Collection*, 2 vols. (Honolulu: Ethnic Studies Program, University of Hawai'i at Mānoa, 1978), p. C-23.

31. ESOHP, *Waipi'o Mano Wai*, p. C-23.

32. Ibid., p. C-24.

33. Ethel Damon, *Father Bond of Kohala: A Chronicle of Pioneer Life in Hawaii* (Honolulu: The Friend, 1927), p. 209.

34. Lennox, "Report to the Trustees," pp. a, 4.

35. Cited in Handy, Handy, and Pukui, *Native Planters in Old Hawaii*, p. 534; printed in *Paradise of the Pacific*, May 1895, p. 67.

36. Lennox, "Report to the Trustees," p. 24.

37. Glenn Petersen, "Taro Farming in Waipio Valley on the Island of Hawaii," in *North Kohala Studies: Preliminary Research in Human Ecology*, ed. R. Warwick Armstrong

and Henry T. Lewis (Honolulu: University of Hawai'i Press, 1970), p. 26; Stella Jones, "Field Notes on Waipi'o, 1931," from an informant called Kahimoku. These are unpublished field notes for work by Jones sponsored by the Bishop Museum and are located in the Bernice Pauahi Bishop Museum Library.

38. Lennox, "Report to the Trustees," p. 24.

39. *Pacific Commercial Advertiser*, June 27, 1906, p. 5.

40. Kalani and Sam Kaaekuahiwi, in Jones, "Field Notes on Waipi'o, 1931."

41. Sam Kaaekuahiwi, in Jones, "Field Notes on Waipi'o, 1931."

42. David Makaoi, interview by Vivien Lee and Yukie Yoshinaga, February 9, 1978, Nu'uanu, O'ahu, ESOHP, *Waipi'o, Mano Wai*, p. 844.

43. ESOHP, *Waipi'o, Mano Wai*, p. i, Appendix I.

44. Kalani in Jones, "Field Notes on Waipio, 1931"; Lennox, "Report to the Trustees," pp. 24–25.

45. Mrs. Kapahu in Jones, "Field Notes on Waipi'o, 1931."

46. Lennox, "Report to the Trustees," p. 25.

47. Petersen, "Taro Farming in Waipio Valley," p. 26.

48. U.S. Bureau of the Census, *Fifteenth Census of the United States: 1930, Occupation Statistics Hawaii* (Washington, D.C.: Government Printing Office, 1932), table 22, p. 70. The census provides an enumeration by election precinct. The election precincts are identified in Hawai'i State Archives, "Governors' Proclamations, 1926–1930," pp. 6–21, 128–47.

49. David Makaoi, February 9, 1978, ESOHP, *Waipi'o, Mano Wai*, p. 850.

50. Ibid., pp. 847–48, 850–52; Rachel Thomas, April 8, 1978, ESOHP, *Waipi'o, Mano Wai*, pp. 1015–17.

51. Ted Kaaekuahiwi, interview by Vivien Lee and Yukie Yoshinaga, March 13, 1978, ESOHP, *Waipi'o, Mano Wai*, pp. 395–96; William Kanekoa, April 7, 1978, ESOHP, *Waipi'o, Mano Wai*, pp. 700–701; David Makaoi, February 9, 1978, ESOHP, *Waipi'o, Mano Wai*, pp. 853–54.

52. Ted Kaaekuahiwi, March 13, 1978, ESOHP, *Waipi'o, Mano Wai*, pp. 392–94, 397–98; David Makaoi, February 9, 1978, ESOHP, *Waipi'o, Mano Wai*, p. 858.

53. David Makaoi, February 9, 1978, ESOHP, *Waipi'o, Mano Wai*, p. 858.

54. Jones, "Field Notes"; Rachel Thomas, interview by Vivien Lee and Yukie Yoshinaga, April 8, 1978, Kukuihaele, Hawai'i, ESOHP, *Waipi'o, Mano Wai*, pp. 1010–11.

55. Sam Kaaekuahiwi in Jones, "Field Notes," and Jones' own observations.

56. Sam Kaaekuahiwi in Jones, "Field Notes."

57. Sam Kaaekuahiwi in Jones, "Field Notes."

58. Nelson Chun, interview by Vivien Lee and Yukie Yoshinaga, March 11, 1978, Honoka'a, Hawai'i, ESOHP, *Waipi'o, Mano Wai*, p. 174.

59. David Makaoi, February 9, 1978, ESOHP, *Waipiʻo, Mano Wai*, p. 861; Ted Kaaekuahiwi, March 13, 1978, ESOHP, *Waipiʻo, Mano Wai*, pp. 400–402.

60. Jones, "Field Notes."

61. Comment on fertilizer: Nelson Chun, March 11, 1978, ESOHP, *Waipiʻo, Mano Wai*, p. 174.

62. David Makaoi, February 9, 1978, ESOHP, *Waipiʻo, Mano Wai*, pp. 844–45.

63. Sam Kaaekuahiwi in Jones, "Field Notes."

64. David Makaoi, February 9, 1978, ESOHP, *Waipiʻo, Mano Wai*, p. 854.

65. Ibid., pp. 842, 857–58.

66. George Farm, interview by Vivien Lee and Yukie Yoshinaga, April 4, 1978, Kukuihaele, Hawaiʻi, ESOHP, *Waipiʻo, Mano Wai*, 301–2.

67. Jones, "Field Notes"; Fannie Hauanio Duldulao, interview by Vivien Lee and Yukie Yoshinaga, March 14, 1978, Kukuihaele, Hawaiʻi, ESOHP, *Waipiʻo, Mano Wai*, p. 275.

68. Ted Kaaekuahiwi, March 13, 1978, ESOHP, *Waipiʻo, Mano Wai*, pp. 403–5; Rachel Thomas, April 8, 1978, ESOHP, *Waipiʻo, Mano Wai*, pp. 1020–21.

69. David Makaoi, February 9, 1978, ESOHP, *Waipiʻo, Mano Wai*, p. 854.

70. Leslie Chang, interview by Vivien Lee and Yukie Yoshinaga, June 4, 1978, Hilo, Hawaiʻi, ESOHP, *Waipiʻo, Mano Wai*, pp. 86–87; William Kanekoa, interview by Vivien Lee and Yukie Yoshinaga, April 7, 1978, Kukuihaele, Hawaiʻi, ESOHP, *Waipiʻo, Mano Wai*, p. 702; David Makaoi, February 9, 1978, ESOHP, *Waipiʻo, Mano Wai*, pp. 869–70.

71. David Makaoi, February 9, 1978, ESOHP, *Waipiʻo, Mano Wai*, p. 961.

72. Leslie Chang, June 4, 1978, ESOHP, *Waipiʻo, Mano Wai*, pp. 90–91.

73. Hawaiʻi State Archives, Land Matters, Public Lands Petitions File, Naleilehua to Governor Carter, January 1, 1904.

74. In 1947 the people of the valley asked the county to widen the road, but the county did not want to spend the estimated $10,000–$15,000 that it would cost. The road was wide enough for mules and for narrow-based four-wheel-drive vehicles. Lennox, "Report to the Trustees," pp. 64–66.

75. Fannie Hauanio Duldulao, March 14, 1978, ESOHP, *Waipiʻo, Mano Wai*, p. 297.

76. Leslie Chang, June 4, 1978, ESOHP, *Waipiʻo, Mano Wai*, pp. 91–92; David Makaoi, February 9, 1978, ESOHP, *Waipiʻo, Mano Wai*, pp. 868–69.

77. Jones, "Field Notes."

78. Daughter-in-law of Mrs. Kanekoa in Jones, "Field Notes."

79. Fannie Hauanio Duldulao, March 14, 1978, ESOHP, *Waipiʻo, Mano Wai*, p. 276.

80. Ibid.

81. Daughter-in-law of Mrs. Kanekoa in Jones, "Field Notes."

82. Jones, "Field Notes."

83. David Makaoi, February 9, 1978, ESOHP, *Waipiʻo, Mano Wai,* p. 863.

84. Fannie Hauanio Duldulao, March 14, 1978, ESOHP, *Waipiʻo, Mano Wai,* pp. 271, 274.

85. Ibid., pp. 272–73.

86. David Makaoi, February 9, 1978, ESOHP, *Waipiʻo, Mano Wai,* p. 842.

87. Ibid., p. 859.

88. Ted Kaaekuahiwi, March 13, 1978, ESOHP, *Waipiʻo, Mano Wai,* pp. 412–15.

89. ESOHP, *Waipiʻo, Mano Wai,* p. C-28.

90. *Paradise of the Pacific,* June 1948, p. 11.

91. Lennox, "Report to the Trustees," pp. a, 4.

92. University of Hawaiʻi Land Study Bureau. "Preliminary Survey of Resource Development and Rehabilitation Opportunities in Waipiʻo Valley, Island of Hawaiʻi," Special Study Series, L.S.B. Report 1, January 1960.

93. R. Warwick Armstrong and Henry T. Lewis, eds. *North Kohala Studies: Preliminary Research in Human Ecology* (Honolulu: University of Hawaiʻi Press, 1970).

94. *Honolulu Star-Bulletin,* March 12, 1964.

95. *Honolulu Star-Bulletin,* November 17, 1972.

96. ESOHP, *Waipiʻo, Mano Wai,* pp. C-31–C-32.

97. Department of Urban and Regional Planning, University of Hawaiʻi at Mānoa, "Waipiʻo Valley: Towards Community Planning and Ahupuaʻa Management," technical report (Fall 1999), p. 17.

98. *Honolulu Star-Bulletin,* November 10, 1963.

99. Ibid.

NOTES TO CHAPTER THREE

1. Pukui, *ʻŌlelo Noʻeau,* no. 460, p. 55.

2. Curtis J. Lyons, "Land Matters in Hawaiʻi," *The Islander,* no. 2 (Honolulu, 1875), p. 111.

3. Jocelyn Linnekin, *Children of the Land: Exchange and Status in a Hawaiian Community* (New Brunswick, N.J.: Rutgers University Press, 1985); Leonard Lueras, *On the Hana Coast: Being an Accounting of Adventures, Past and Present, in a Land Where the Hand of Man Seems to Rest Lightly* (Honolulu: Emphasis International, 1983); Bob Jones, "Kaulana na Pua/Famous Are the Children" [KGMB news special], 1987.

4. Thomas K. Maunupau, *Nūpepa Kūʻokoʻa,* June 15, 1922, trans. Mary Kawena Pukui (Hawaiian Ethnographic Notes), Newspapers 1922–24, Bernice Pauahi Bishop Museum Library. After I used this version for my dissertation it was published as Thomas K. Maunupau, *Huakai Makaikai a Kaupō, Maui: A Visit to Kaupō, Maui, as published in Ka*

Nūpepa Kū'oko'a, *June 1, 1922–March 15, 1923*, ed. Naomi Noelanioko'olau Clarke Losch, trans. Mary Kawena Pukui and Malcolm Naea Chun (Honolulu: Bernice Pauahi Bishop Museum Press, 1998), pp. 103–4.

5. W. M. Walker, "Archaeology of Maui," unpublished manuscript (Bernice Pauahi Bishop Musuem, 1931), pp. 34–35; Beckwith, *Hawaiian Mythology*, pp. 226–37.

6. Beckwith, *Hawaiian Mythology*, p. 230.

7. Martha W. Beckwith, ed., *Kepelino's Traditions of Hawai'i*, Bernice Pauahi Bishop Museum Bulletin 95 (Honolulu: Bernice Pauahi Bishop Museum; New York: Kraus Reprint, 1971), p. 229.

8. Beckwith, *Hawaiian Mythology*, p. 64.

9. Handy, Handy, and Pukui, *Native Planters in Old Hawaii*, p. 510.

10. Beckwith, *Hawaiian Mythology*, p. 65.

11. Ibid., pp. 99–100.

12. Julia Naone, interview by Mary Kawena Pukui, May 3, 1960, Hāmoa, Kīpahulu, Maui (Audio-Recording Collection, Department of Anthropology, Bernice Pauahi Bishop Museum), no. 85.6.

13. Julia Naone, interview by Mary Kawena Pukui, May 3, 1960, no. 85.4; Josephine Kauakeaohana Roback Medeiros, interview by Mary Kawena Pukui, May 5, 1960, Hāmoa, Kīpahulu, Maui (Audio-Recording Collection, Department of Anthropology, Bernice Pauahi Bishop Museum), no. 87.4.2.

14. Julia Naone, interview by Mary Kawena Pukui, May 3, 1960, no. 85.4.

15. Josephine Marciel, interview by Mary Kawena Pukui, May 3, 1960, Hāmoa, Kīpahulu, Maui (Audio-Recording Collection, Department of Anthropology, Bernice Pauahi Bishop Museum).

16. Walker, "Archaeology of Maui," p. 40.

17. Mrs. Paul Fagan, interview by Mary Kawena Pukui, May 5, 1960, Hana, Ke'anae, Maui (Audio-Recording Collection, Department of Anthropology, Bernice Pauahi Bishop Museum), no. 87.2.1.

18. Beckwith, *Hawaiian Mythology*, pp. 40–41.

19. Walker, "Archaeology of Maui," pp. 37–38.

20. Beckwith, *Hawaiian Mythology*, p. 22.

21. Ibid., pp. 22–23.

22. Jon K. Matsuoka et al., "Native Hawaiian Ethnographic Study for the Hawai'i Geothermal Project Proposed for Puna and Southeast Maui," technical report, Oak Ridge National Laboratory, Lockheed Martin (May 1996), pp. 172–73; Walker, "Archaeology of Maui," p. 7; Beckwith, *Hawaiian Mythology*, p. 170.

23. Maunupau, *Huakai Makaikai a Kaupō, Maui / A Visit to Kaupō, Maui*, pp. 97, 100, 101.

24. The information in this section is based on Handy, Handy, and Pukui, *Native Planters in Old Hawaii*, pp. 498–502.

25. In conversations with the author, kūpuna Harry Kunihi Mitchell identified the flume as being made out of an old canoe.

26. E. S. Craighill Handy, *The Hawaiian Planter*, vol. 1, *His Plants, Methods and Areas of Cultivation*, Bernice Pauahi Bishop Museum Bulletin 161 (Honolulu: Bernice Pauahi Bishop Museum, 1940), pp. 111–12.

27. Minnie and Sam Po, Elspeth Sterling, and Peter Chapman, interview by Mary Kawena Pukui, July 5, 1966, Hāna, Maui: tape 4 (Audio-Recording Collection, Department of Anthropology, Bernice Pauahi Bishop Museum).

28. Sam Po, interview by Mary Kawena Pukui, July 5, 1966, Hāna, Maui: tapes 5–7 (Audio-Recording Collection, Department of Anthropology, Bernice Pauahi Bishop Museum).

29. Several testimonies in McGregor, "Kūpa'a I Ka'āina," p. 372.

30. Beckwith, *Hawaiian Mythology*, p. 383; Handy, *The Hawaiian Planter*, 1:491.

31. Beckwith, *Hawaiian Mythology*, pp. 307.

32. Walker, "Archaeology of Maui," pp. 13, 14.

33. Fornander, *Fornander Collection*, vol. 6, pt. 2, p. 313, and vol. 4, pt. 2, pp. 214–18, 236–56.

34. Patrick V. Kirch, *Legacy of the Landscape: An Illustrated Guide to Hawaiian Archaeological Sites* (Honolulu: University of Hawai'i Press, 1996), p. 72.

35. Kamakau, *Ruling Chiefs*, p. 385.

36. Handy, Handy, and Pukui, *Native Planters in Old Hawaii*, pp. 502–4.

37. Pukui, *'Ōlelo No'eau*, no. 2548, p. 278.

38. Beckwith, *Hawaiian Mythology*, p. 379.

39. Kamakau, *Ruling Chiefs*, p. 80.

40. Ibid., p. 380.

41. Ibid., p. 80.

42. Ibid., pp. 22–33.

43. Ibid. See also Trust for Public Land with Bay Pacific Consulting, "East Maui Resource Inventory" (Honolulu: Rivers, Trails, and Conservation Assistance Program, National Park Service, 1998).

44. Handy, Handy, and Pukui, *Native Planters in Old Hawaii*, pp. 503–4; Beckwith, *Hawaiian Mythology*, p. 380.

45. Kamakau, *Ruling Chiefs*, p. 84; Lueras, *On the Hana Coast*, pp. 40–41.

46. Walker, "Archaeology of Maui," pp. 25, 124.

47. Ibid., p. 16.

48. Kamakau, *Ruling Chiefs*, p. 78.

49. Ibid., p. 84.

50. Desha, *Kamehameha and His Warrior Kekuhaupi'o*, p. 31.

51. Captain Cook had first stopped at Waimea Kaua'i in January 1778. He then proceeded to the North Pacific in search of the Northwest Passage. When winter icebergs formed and obstructed his exploration, he returned to Hawai'i to wait out the winter.

52. Kamakau, *Ruling Chiefs*, pp. 97–100; Desha, *Kamehameha and His Warrior Kekuhaupi'o*, pp. 58–61.

53. Kamakau, *Ruling Chiefs*, p. 116.

54. The accounts of the battles are based upon Desha, *Kamehameha and His Warrior Kekuhaupi'o*, pp. 216–22, and Kamakau, *Ruling Chiefs*, pp. 128–58.

55. Desha, *Kamehameha and His Warrior Kekuhaupi'o*, pp. 239–302.

56. Jonathan S. Green, letter, Dec. 1835.

57. John Forster, "Social Organization and Differential Social Change in Two Hawaiian Communities," *International Journal of Comparative Sociology* 3 (December 1962): 202.

58. Linnekin, *Children of the Land*, p. 37.

59. Wailuku Station Report, Hawai'i Mission Children's Society Library (1837), cited in Linnekin, *Children of the Land*, p. 18.

60. Kamakau, *Ruling Chiefs*, pp. 236–37.

61. Ibid., p. 418.

62. Barrere, "The King's Māhele."

63. Lueras, *On the Hana Coast*, pp. 44–45; Forster, "Social Organization," pp. 202–3.

64. Lueras, *On the Hana Coast*, p. 45.

65. Maui Visitors Bureau, "Hana Visitors Guide," 1998.

66. Harry Kunihi Mitchell, interview by Davianna McGregor, April 22, 1988, Ke'anae, Maui.

67. D. T. Conde to D. Baldwin, February 7, 1844; D. T. Conde to L. Chamberlain and S. N. Castle, December 26, 1838; D. T. Conde to Titus Coan, c. 1845, in Hawai'i Mission Children's Society Library, cited in Linnekin, *Children of the Land*, pp. 18–19.

68. Sereno Bishop, "Report to Board of Sandwich Islands Mission" (1861), in Hawai'i Mission Children's Society Library, cited in Linnekin, *Children of the Land*, p. 18.

69. Josephine Marciel, interview by Mary Kawena Pukui, May 3, 1960, no. 85.7.

70. Lueras, *On the Hana Coast*, pp. 46–47.

71. Ibid., p. 60; Harry Kunihi Mitchell, interview by Davianna McGregor, April 22, 1988.

72. *Pacific Commercial Advertiser*, September 4, 1910.

73. Ibid.

74. Harry Kunihi Mitchell, interview by Davianna McGregor, April 22, 1988.

75. U.S. Bureau of the Census, *Fifteenth Census of the United States: 1930, Occupation*

Statistics Hawaii (Washington: Government Printing Office, 1931), p. 72, table 22. The precincts were identified in "Governors' Proclamations," 1926–30, pp. 6–21.

76. Douglas Yamamura, "A Study of Some of the Factors in the Education of the Child of Hawaiian Ancestry in Hana, Maui," master's thesis (University of Hawaiʻi, 1941), pp. 21, 24, 108, 151; Harry Kunihi Mitchell, interview by Davianna McGregor, April 22, 1988.

77. Yamamura, "A Study of Some of the Factors," pp. 39–43. Yamamura's information is based on a study of 52 families whose children attended Hāna School in 1939. This is after the 1930 cut-off, but the patterns observed in 1939 had been carried over from the earlier period and were not a recently introduced pattern.

78. Ibid., pp. 40, 42.

79. Harry Kunihi Mitchell, interview by Davianna McGregor, April 22, 1988; Lueras, *On the Hana Coast*, p. 60.

80. Yamamura, "A Study of Some of the Factors," pp. 45, 46.

81. Ibid., p. 151.

82. Ibid., pp. 151–52, 155.

83. Harry Kunihi Mitchell, interview by Davianna McGregor, April 22, 1988.

84. Yamamura, "A Study of Some of the Factors," pp. 124–25.

85. Ibid., pp. 126–31.

86. Ibid., pp. 140–41.

87. Mrs. Kapeka Kaʻauamo, interview by Mary Kawena Pukui, December 2, 1961, Wailua, Keʻanae, Maui (Audio-Recording Collection, Department of Anthropology, Bernice Pauahi Bishop Museum), no. 122.2, transcribed and translated by Larry Kimura.

88. Harry Kunihi Mitchell, interview by Davianna McGregor, April 22, 1988.

89. Josephine Medeiros, interview by Mary Kawena Pukui, no. 87.3.1.

90. Harry Kunihi Mitchell, interview by Davianna McGregor, April 22, 1988.

91. Moewale and Joseph Pu, interview by Mary Kawena Pukui, May 4–5, 1960, Hana and Kīpahulu, Maui (Audio-Recording Collection, Department of Anthropology, Bernice Pauahi Bishop Museum), no. 87.1; Mrs. Kapeka Kaʻauamo, interview by Mary Kawena Pukui, December 2, 1961, no. 122.1.1.

92. Harry Kunihi Mitchell, interview by Davianna McGregor, April 22, 1988.

93. Mrs. Kapeka Kaʻauamo, interview by Mary Kawena Pukui, December 2, 1961, no. 122.1.2.

94. Sam Po, interview by Mary Kawena Pukui, July 5, 1966, no. 4, Hana and Kīpahulu, Maui (Audio-Recording Collection, Department of Anthropology, Bernice Pauahi Bishop Museum).

95. Josephine Marciel, interview by Mary Kawena Pukui, May 3, 1960; Yamamura, "A

Study of Some of the Factors," p. 35; Harry Kunihi Mitchell, interview by Davianna McGregor, April 22, 1988.

96. Josephine Marciel, interview by Mary Kawena Pukui, May 3, 1960; Francis Marciel and Dolly Mahalo, interview by Mary Kawena Pukui, December 1, 1961, Kaupō, Maui (Audio-Recording Collection, Department of Anthropology, Bernice Pauahi Bishop Museum), no. 86.3.

97. Harry Kunihi Mitchell, interview by Davianna McGregor, April 22, 1988.

98. Agnes Mailou and Daisy Lind, interview by Mary Kawena Pukui, March 15–16, 1963, Hāna (Audio-Recording Collection, Department of Anthropology, Bernice Pauahi Bishop Museum), nos. 137.3.2, 200.03, 200.04; Una Walker, Karen Pryor, Elizabeth Haia Chang, Babes Hanchett, Leimamo Lee, and Mrs. Charles Pohaku, interview by Mary Kawena Pukui, August 10, 1968, Hāna (Audio-Recording Collection, Department of Anthropology, Bernice Pauahi Bishop Museum), nos. 200.3, 200.4.

99. Mrs. Kapeka Ka'auamo, interview by Mary Kawena Pukui, December 2, 1963, no. 122.2; Agnes Mailou and Daisy Lind, interview by Mary Kawena Pukui, March 16, 1963; Una Walker, Karen Pryor, Elizabeth Haia Chang, Babes Hanchett, Leimamo Lee, and Mrs. Charles Pohaku, interviews by Mary Kawena Pukui, August 10, 1968; Josephine Marciel, interview by Mary Kawena Pukui, May 3, 1960, no. 85.7.

100. Craighill Handy, *The Hawaiian Planter*, 1:110.

101. *Pacific Commercial Advertiser*, September 4, 1910.

102. Harry Kunihi Mitchell, interview by Davianna McGregor, April 22, 1988.

103. Forster, "Social Organization," p. 203.

104. Harry Kunihi Mitchell, interview by Davianna McGregor, April 22, 1988.

105. Ibid.

106. Ibid.

107. Linnekin, *Children of the Land*, pp. 76–77.

108. Handy, *The Hawaiian Planter*, 1:110.

109. Josephine Medeiros, interview by Mary Kawena Pukui, May 5, 1960, no. 87.4, 1–2.

110. Group 70, Davianna McGregor, and Cultural Surveys Hawai'i, "Kalo Kanu o Ka 'Āina: A Cultural Landscape Study of Ke'anae and Wailuanui, Island of Maui" (technical report for the County of Maui Planning Department, 1995), pp. 38, 84.

111. Handy, *The Hawaiian Planter*, 1:111.

112. Lueras, *On the Hana Coast*, pp. 96–97.

113. Ibid.; Yamamura, "A Study of Some of the Factors," p. 9.

114. Lueras, *On the Hana Coast*, pp. 96–97.

115. Ibid.

116. Handy, *The Hawaiian Planter*, 1:111.

117. Lueras, *On the Hana Coast*, p. 60.

118. Ibid., p. 46.

119. Ibid., p. 60.

120. Handy, Handy, and Pukui, *Native Planters in Old Hawaii*, pp. 504–5.

121. Handy, *The Hawaiian Planter*, 1:111, 112.

122. *Kuoko'a* [newspaper], June 1, 1922, trans. Mary Kawena Pukui, Hawaiian Ethnographic Notes, Newspapers 1922–24, Bernice Pauahi Bernice Pauahi Bishop Museum Library.

123. *Hawaiian Gazette*, September 6, 1910.

124. Lueras, *On the Hana Coast*, p. 46.

125. Handy, *The Hawaiian Planter*, 1:112–13.

126. Lueras, *On the Hana Coast*, p. 133; Sam O. Hirota, Inc., "Environmental Impact Statement for the Kaupō Water System Improvements, Kaupō, Island of Maui, Hawaii" (Honolulu, 1983), Hawaiian Collection, Hamilton Library, University of Hawai'i.

127. Lueras, *On the Hana Coast*, p. 46.

128. *Hawaiian Gazette*, September 6, 1910; *Pacific Commercial Advertiser*, September 5, 1910.

129. *Pacific Commercial Advertiser*, September 9, 1910.

130. *Kuoko'a*, June 1, 1922.

131. *Kuoko'a*, June 20, 1922, trans. Mary Kawena Pukui, HEN, Newspapers 1922–24, Bernice Pauahi Bishop Museum Library.

132. Handy, *The Hawaiian Planter*, 1:113.

133. Josephine Marciel, interview, May 3, 1960, no. 85.7.

134. Ibid.

135. Lueras, *On the Hana Coast*, p. 65.

136. *Maui News*, December 9, 1942, cited in Group 70, McGregor, and Cultural Surveys Hawai'i, "Kalo Kanu o Ka 'Āina," p. 38.

137. Group 70, McGregor, and Cultural Surveys Hawai'i, "Kalo Kanu o Ka 'Āina," p. 38.

138. Lueras, *On the Hana Coast*, pp. 67–70.

139. Maui Visitor's Bureau, "Hana Visitors Guide," 1998; F. P. Shepard, G. A. MacDonald, and D. C. Cox, *The Tsunami of April 1, 1946* (Berkeley and Los Angeles: University of California Press, 1950); Linnekin, *Children of the Land*, cited in Group 70, McGregor, and Cultural Surveys Hawai'i, "Kalo Kanu o Ka 'Āina," pp. 38–39.

140. Maui Visitor's Bureau, "Hana Visitors Guide," 1998.

141. Trust for Public Land with Bay Pacific Consulting, "East Maui Resource Inventory," p. 35.

142. Group 70, McGregor, and Cultural Surveys Hawaiʻi. "Kalo Kanu o Ka ʻĀina, p. 40.

143. Telephone conversation with Charmain Day, December 3, 1994.

144. For the Koʻolau district of Maui, all of the ahupuaʻa boundaries converge and originate at the northern rim of Haleakalā at Pōhaku Pālaha; Lyons, "Land Matters in Hawaiʻi," p. 111. According to James Hueu, "In Keʻanae, they had their ahupuaʻa. Honomanū to Makapipi towards Nāhiku." James Hueu, interview by Davianna McGregor, November 12, 1994, Keʻanae, Maui.

145. Group 70, McGregor, and Cultural Surveys Hawaiʻi, "Kalo Kanu o Ka ʻĀina," pp. 102–3.

146. Ibid., p. 104.

147. Ibid., pp. 104–5.

148. Ibid., p. 105.

149. Ibid., pp. 106–7.

150. Ibid., p. 107.

151. Ibid., p. 108.

152. Ibid., p. 109.

153. Ibid.

154. Ibid., p. 110.

155. Ibid., pp. 110–11.

156. Ibid., p. 111.

157. Ibid., pp. 111–12.

158. Ibid., p. 112.

159. Ibid., pp. 112–13.

160. Moki Day, interview by Davianna McGregor, November 3, 1994, Wailuanui, Maui.

161. Group 70, McGregor, and Cultural Surveys Hawaiʻi, "Kalo Kanu o Ka ʻĀina," p. 113.

NOTES TO CHAPTER FOUR

1. Pukui, ʻŌlelo Noʻeau, no. 2747.

2. Ibid., no. 2058.

3. Ibid., no. 1458.

4. Ibid., no. 1587.

5. Pualani Kanakaʻole Kanahele, lecture to student body of Kamehameha Schools, May 2, 1990.

6. Kanakaʻole Kanahele, "Ka Honua Ola: The Living Earth." The following translation and interpretation of the chant is excerpted from Kanahele's report.

7. Ibid., p. 71.

8. Ibid., p. 73.

9. Pukui, *'Ōlelo No'eau*, no. 1777.

10. Excerpt from "A Legend told by Moses Manu, Ka Loea Kalai'aina, May 1899–Feb. 1900," trans. Mary Kawena Pukui, in Dorothy Barrere, "Political History of Puna," manuscript for Archaeology Reconnaissance of the Kalapana Extension, Bernice Pauahi Bishop Museum, 1959.

11. Beckwith, *Hawaiian Mythology*; G. W. Kahiolo, *He Moolelo No Kamapua'a: The Story of Kamapua'a*, trans. Esther T. Mookini and Erin C. Neizmen with the assistance of David Tom (Hawaiian Studies Program, University of Hawai'i at Mānoa, 1978).

12. Greg Burtchard and Pennie Moblo, "Archaeology in the Kilauea East Rift Zone Kapoho, Kama'ili and Kilauea Geothermal Subzones, Puna District, Hawai'i Island," Report ORNL/SUB/94-SN150/1-2, July (Oak Ridge, Tenn.: Oak Ridge National Laboratory, 1994).

13. Jules Remy, *Contributions of a Venerable Savage to the Ancient History of the Hawaiian Islands*, trans. William T. Brigham (Boston: Press of A. A. Kingman, 1868).

14. Ellis, *Journal*; Hawaiian Majesty King David Kalakaua, *Legends and Myths of Hawaii*; Mary Kawena Pukui and C. Curtis, *Pikoi and Other Legends of the Island of Hawai'i* (reprint, Honolulu: Kamehameha Schools Press, 1949).

15. Beckwith, *Hawaiian Mythology*, pp. 190–92.

16. Kamakau, *Tales and Traditions*, p. 100.

17. "Tradition ascribes to Paao the introduction of human sacrifice into the temple ritual, the walled *heiau*, and the red-feather girdle as a sign of rank; all typical, says Handy, of late Tahitian culture and not found in Samoa. Other institutions ascribed to him are the *pulo'ulo'u tapu* sign, the prostrating *tapu* (*tapu moe or -o*), and the feather god Kaili; some would call Paao rather than La'a-mai-kahiki the introducer of image worship . . . That Paao took his ideas from Tahiti is further indicated by reference to 'Vavau' and 'Upolo' as places where he owned land, probably in districts so named in northern Tahiti in the Aha-roa division of that island, and the name Aha-ula (later called Waha-ula) for the first *heiau* erected by his party on Hawai'i suggests such a connection." Beckwith, *Hawaiian Mythology*, p. 370.

18. Fornander, *An Account of the Polynesian Race*, pp. 35–36.

19. Kamakau, *Tales and Traditions*, p. 100.

20. Barrere, "Political History of Puna"; Bruce Cartwright, "Some Aliis of the Migratory Period," Bernice Pauahi Bishop Museum Occasional Papers, vol. 10, no. 7 (Honolulu: Bernice Pauahi Bishop Museum, 1933).

21. Fornander, *Fornander Collection*, pp. 514–19; Walker, "Archaeology of Maui," p. 41.

22. Beckwith, *Hawaiian Mythology*, pp. 363–70.

23. Pukui, *ʻŌlelo Noʻeau*, no. 994.

24. Ibid., no. 260.

25. Barrere, "Political History of Puna," p. 15.

26. Kamakau, *Tales and Traditions*, p. 10.

27. Ibid., p. 17.

28. Barrere, "Political History of Puna."

29. Kamakau, *Tales and Traditions*, pp. 18–19.

30. Barrere, "Political History of Puna," 17–18.

31. Kamakau, *Tales and Traditions*, p. 106.

32. Ibid.

33. Ibid., pp. 108–9.

34. J. C. Beaglehole, *The Journals of Captain James Cook On His Voyages of Discovery*, vol. 3, *The Voyage of the* Resolution *and* Discovery, *1776–1780* (Cambridge: Hakluyt Society, 1955–74), pp. 196, 606.

35. Barrere, "Political History of Puna," p. 19.

36. Pukui, *ʻŌlelo Noʻeau*, no. 826.

37. Ellis, *Journal of William Ellis*.

38. Ibid.

39. Charles Langlas, *The People of Kalapana, 1832–1950* (Hilo: The author, 1990), pp. 17–18.

40. Tommy Holmes, "A Preliminary Report on the Early History and Archaeology of the Puna Forest Reserve / Wao Kele ʻo Puna Natural Area Reserve," report prepared for True / Mid-Pacific Geothermal (November 1985).

41. Charles Wilkes, *Narrative of the U.S. Exploring Expedition During the Years 1838, 1839, 1840, 1841, 1842* (Philadelphia, 1849), vol. 4, p. 181.

42. Chester S. Lyman, *Around the Horn to the Sandwich Islands and California, 1845–1850* (New Haven, Conn.: Yale University Press, 1924), p. 19.

43. Seven lands in Puna were left unassigned during the Māhele: Kahue, Hulunanai, Iililoa, Kaunaloa, Ki (B), Keekee, and Keonepoko 2. In 1888 it was decided that these would be government lands. See Melinda Sue Allen, "The Kalapana Extension in the 1800's, A Research of the Historical Records," prepared for the National Park Service, Hawaii Volcanoes National Park, 1979.

44. Allen, "Kalapana Extension."

45. Ibid..

46. Hawaiʻi State Archives, Interior Department Letters, March 26, 1857.

47. In Holmes, "Preliminary Report."

48. Ibid., p. 17.

49. Hawai'i State Archives, Boundary Commission Hawai'i, 3rd & 4th Circuits, Petitioner's Exhibit B, "The Ahupuaa of Keaau, District of Puna, Island of Hawaii, 3d, J.C.," before the Commissioner of Boundaries, Fourth Judicial Circuit, Territory of Hawai'i, In the Matter of the Boundaries of Waiakahekahe-'iki upon the petition of W. H. Shipman, owner (Hilo, June 18, 1914).

50. Hawai'i State Archives, Boundary Commission Hawai'i, 3rd & 4th Circuits, In Re: Boundaries, Ahupuaa of Keahialaka, Puna, Hawai'i, brief of Hitchcock & Wise, filed March 20, 1897.

51. Thomas G. Thrum, *Thrum's Hawaiian Almanac and Annual* (Honolulu: Honolulu Star-Bulletin, 1895).

52. Roger Skolmen, "Hawaii's Forest Products Industry," paper presented at the 18th Annual Hawaii Forestry Conference, November 18–19, 1976, Honolulu.

53. Hawai'i State Archives, Governor's Proclamation, June 29, 1911; Governor's Proclamation, December 22, 1928.

54. Charles Baldwin, *Geography of the Hawaiian Islands* (New York: American Book, 1908), pp. 78–79.

55. Henry Walsworth Kinney, *The Island of Hawai'i* (Hilo: Hilo Board of Trade, 1913).

56. Ibid.

57. Handy, Handy, and Pukui, *Native Planters in Old Hawaii*, p. 541.

58. Langlas, *People of Kalapana*, pp. 35–36.

59. Langlas, *People of Kalapana*.

60. Russell Apple, "Transcriptions of a 1974 Interview by Russell Apple with Former Superintendent Wingate Concerning the Kalapana Extension" and "Homesite Provisions of the 1938 Kalapana Act," Hawai'i Volcano National Park Headquarters Library, January 5, 1971.

61. U.S. Congress, Act of June 20, 1938 (52 Stat. 781 et seq.).

62. Langlas, *People of Kalapana*, pp. 92–94.

63. George Cooper and Gavan Daws, *Land and Power in Hawai'i* (Honolulu: Benchmark Books, 1985), p. 259.

64. Ibid., p. 262.

65. Ibid., p. 265.

66. Ibid., p. 263.

67. County of Hawai'i, "The General Plan Hawai'i County," November 1989.

68. County of Hawai'i, "General Plan."

69. Burdette E. Bostwick and Brian Murton, *Puna Studies: Preliminary Research in Human Ecology* (Honolulu: Department of Anthropology, University of Hawai'i, 1971).

70. Puna Hui ʻOhana, "Assessment of Geothermal Impact on Aboriginal Hawaiians" (Washington, D.C.: Department of Energy, 1982).

71. Matsuoka et al., "Native Hawaiian Ethnographic Study." The following section draws upon the ethnographic report that resulted from the interviews Jon Matsuoka and I conducted with ʻohana of Puna.

72. The final findings of fact and conclusions of law; Pele Defense Fund v. the Estate of James Campbell (Civil No. 89-089).

NOTES TO CHAPTER FIVE

1. Koko Willis and Pali Jae Lee, *Tales from the Night Rainbow* (Honolulu: Night Rainbow Publishing / Native Books, 1990), pp. 24–25.

2. Summers, *Molokai*, pp. 15, 198–201; Kamakau, *Ruling Chiefs*, pp. 150, 166, 179; Desha, *Kamehameha and His Warrior Kekuhaupiʻo*, pp. 264–66.

3. Molokai Enterprise Committee, "Molokaʻi Rural Empowerment Zone Application submitted to the United States Department of Agriculture," October 9, 1998, vol. 2, pt.1, sec. 1, p. 1.

4. Summers, *Molokai*. The review of the ruling chiefs of Molokaʻi in this and the next paragraph is based on Summers, *Molokai*, pp. 11–13.

5. Summers, *Molokai*, pp. 14–15; Robert Schmitt, *Demographic Statistics of Hawaii, 1778–1965* (Honolulu: University of Hawaiʻi Press, 1968), p. 42, table 6.

6. Summers, *Molokai*, pp. 16–17.

7. "Bligh's Notes on Cook's Last Voyage," *Mariner's Mirror* 14 (October 1828): 385.

8. Summers, *Molokai*, p. 3.

9. Lucille De Loach, "Land and People of Molokai: An Overview" (master's thesis, University of Hawaiʻi at Mānoa, 1975), pp. 53–54.

10. David Malo, "Causes for the Decrease," pp. 121–30.

11. Summers, *Molokai*, p. 3.

12. Ibid. Summers concludes that Molokaʻi's population was not exposed to the epidemic diseases that decimated the Native Hawaiian people and that the decrease of the population should be attributed to emigration to one of the larger islands.

13. American Board of Commissioners for Foreign Missions, "Molokai Station Reports, 1833–1849," unpublished typescript, 1937, University of Hawaiʻi Library, pp. 4–5.

14. Schmitt, *Demographic Statistics*, p. 42, table 6.

15. Original in Hawaiian in the archives, trans. W. H. Wilson, August 10, 1977. See Appendix III.

16. Kanepuʻu, "Traveling About on Molokaʻi," *Ke Au Okoa*, September 5 and 26, 1867.

17. G. W. Bates, *Sandwich Island Notes by a Haole* (New York: Harper & Brothers, 1854), pp. 274–75, 277.

18. Lucille De Loach, "Molokai: An Historical Overview," in *Molokai Studies: Preliminary Research in Human Ecology*, ed. Henry Lewis (Honolulu: Department of Anthropology, University of Hawai'i, 1970), pp. 130–32.

19. De Loach, "Molokai," p. 134.

20. The figure of 2,132 includes the Kalawao Hansen's disease patients. Republic of Hawaii, *Report of the General Superintendent of the Census, 1896* (Honolulu: Hawaiian Star Press, 1897).

21. Hawaii State Archives, Laws, 1864–65, pp. 62–64.

22. Hawaiian Kingdom Board of Health, *Hansen's Disease in Hawaii* (1866), pp. 27–28.

23. This trade is described in the preceding chapter.

24. Mary Kawena Pukui, Chant H-41 c Webcor timer 753 Sel. 11, transcribed, translated, and performed by Mary Kawena Pukui, Hawaii Ethnographic Notes, Bernice Pauahi Bishop Museum Library. The entire chant may be read at the Bishop Museum Library. It is also transcribed and translated in Mary Kawena Pukui and Alfons Korns, *The Echo of Our Song* (Honolulu: University of Hawai'i Press, 1973).

25. Linda Greene, *Exile in Paradise: The Isolation of Hawai'i's Hansen's Disease Victims and Development of Kalaupapa Settlement, 1865 to the Present, 1985* (Denver: Branch of Planning, Alaska–Pacific Northwest–Western Team, U.S. Department of Interior, National Park Service, 1985), p. 38.

26. Ibid., p. 53.

27. Ibid., pp. 83–179. For the life of Father Damien and an excellent account of his work at Kalaupapa see Gavan Daws, *Holy Man: Father Damien of Molokai* (Honolulu: University of Hawai'i Press, 1984).

28. U.S. Bureau of the Census, *Fifteenth Census*, table 5, p. 44.

29. Geritt Judd, *Pule O'o: The Story of Molokai* (Honolulu: Porter Printing, 1936), p. 13.

30. U.S. Bureau of the Census, Fifteenth Census, table 22, p. 72.

31. George P. Cooke, *Moolelo o Molokai: A Ranch Story of Molokai* (Honolulu: Honolulu Star-Bulletin, 1949), pp. 59–60; Vernon Charles Bottenfield, "Changing Patterns of Land Utilization on Molokai" (master's thesis, University of Hawai'i at Mānoa, 1958), pp. 88, 89; Judd, *Pule O'o*, p. 17.

32. Albert Kahinu, interview by Mary Kawena Pukui, May 1, 1961, Kaunakakai, Moloka'i (Audio-Recording Collection, Anthropology Department, Bernice Pauahi Bishop Museum), no. 108.4. I called the Moloka'i Ranch offices on Moloka'i and on O'ahu to get a record of wages and the ethnic composition of the workers from 1900 to 1930, but they did not have employment records for that period.

33. Waldemar Duvauchelle, interview by Mary Kawena Pukui, March 7, 1961, Puko'o,

Moloka'i (Audio-Recording Collection, Anthropology Department, Bernice Pauahi Bishop Museum), no. 107.4.1.

34. Daniel Pahupu, interview by Mary Kawena Pukui, March 9, 1961, Kalama'ula, Moloka'i (Audio-Recording Collection, Department of Anthropology, Bernice Pauahi Bishop Museum), no. 107.10; Mrs. Grace Hagerman, interview by Mary Kawena Pukui, June 23, 1967, Kalua'aha, Moloka'i (Audio-Recording Collection, Department of Anthropology, Bishop Museum), no. 194.1; Bottenfield, "Changing Patterns," p. 89.

35. Baldwin, *Geography of the Hawaiian Islands*, p. 107.

36. John Nathan Cobb, *Commercial Fisheries of the Hawaiian Islands.* Agent of the U.S. Fish Commission Report for 1901, 1902, pp. 429–30. The following fishponds were identified as being maintained: Punalau in Naiwa with 20 acres; Kamahuehue in Kamalo with 37 acres; Kainaohe in Kaamola with 17 acres; Hinau in Keawanui with 54.5 acres; Pahaloa in Manawai with 6 acres; two nameless ones in Kaluaaha, one with 11 acres and one with 9 acres; Kaopeahina in Kaluaaha with 20.5 acres. Niaupala in Kaluaaha with 33.5 acres; Pipio in Manulehu with 14 acres; Ilae's pond in Puko'o with 25 acres; a nameless one in Kupeke with 30 acres; Nahiole in Ahaino (West) with 1 acre; Kihaloko in Ahaino (east) with 5 acres; Waihilahila in Kailiuia with 3.5 acres; Kulaalamihi in Honomuni with 6 acres.

37. Southwick Phelps, "Regional Study of Moloka'i, Hawai'i," 1941, manuscript, Bernice Pauahi Bishop Museum Library, p. 14.

38. Kahaulelio, "Fishing Lore," *Nūpepa Kū'oko'a*, trans. and comp. Mary Kawena Pukui, Bernice Pauahi Bishop Museum Library, p. 88.

39. Phelps, "Regional Study of Molokai," pp. 71–75, lists the ahupua'a as follows: Ahaino: bad prayer; Honomuni: small places close together; Honoulimalo'o: dark, sheltered, dry place; Honouliwai: dark sheltered water; Kaamola: turning round; Kahananui: great undertaking; Kailiula: red skinned; Kainalu: billowy sea; Kaluaaha: the coir net pit; Kamalo: the dry spell; Kamanoni: place where noni grows; Kamiloloa: long milo tree; Kapaakea: whitish rock; Kapulei: sacred wreath; Kapuokoolau: hill on windward side; Kaunakakai: go along in company of four; Kawaikapu: forbidden water; Kawela: heat; Keawanui: big bay; Keonokuino: six bad places; Keopukaloa: far-reaching sound; Keopukauuku: small hole for sound to go through; Kumimi: poisonous crab; Kupeke: dwarflike; Lupehu: universal plenty; Makakupaia: sentinel-like eyes; Makolelau: shriveled leaf; Manawai: branch stream; Mapulehu: rising ash cloud; Moakea: white fowl; Moanui: great fowl; Ohia: ohia tree; Pohakupili: nearby stone; Puaahala: bunched hala roots; Puelelu: trumpet shell; Pukoo: supporting conch shell; Punaula: reddish spring; Puniuohua: family coconut cup; Ualapue: hilled sweet potatoes; Waialua: 2 streams.

40. Ann Perrells, "Environmental Resources and Neighborhood Food Exchange" in Lewis, 1970, pp. 45–51.

41. Handy, *The Hawaiian Planter*, pp. 101–2.

42. Peter Namakaeha, interview by Mary Kawena Pukui, March 10, 1961, Honouli-wai, Moloka‘i (Audio-Recording Collection, Department of Anthropology, Bernice Pau-ahi Bishop Museum), no. 107.15.1.

43. Handy, *The Hawaiian Planter*, 1:102.

44. Daniel Pahupu, interview by Mary Kawena Pukui, March 9, 1961, no. 107.10.

45. Peter Namakaeha, interview by Mary Kawena Pukui, March 10, 1961, no. 107.15.1.

46. Phelps, "Regional Study of Moloka‘i," p. 70, lists them as follows: Hālawa: valley of sufficient water; Kaiamiki: reduced fish; Kiloa: tall ti plants; Pelekunu: strong smelling; Waikolu: three waters; Wailau: many waters; Wawaelepe: twisted foot.

47. Fred Tollefson, interview by Mary Kawena Pukui, June 23, 1967, Keoneniuomana, Moloka‘i (Audio-Recording Collection, Department of Anthropology, Bernice Pauahi Bishop Museum), no. 194.1–194.2.

48. Kenneth P. Emory, "Windward Molokai," *Mid-Pacific Magazine*, November 1916, p. 446.

49. Phelps, "Regional Study of Moloka‘i," p. 42.

50. James Poaha, interview by Mary Kawena Pukui, March 8, 1961, Ho‘olehua, Kala-ma‘ula, Moloka‘i (Audio-Recording Collection, Department of Anthropology, Bernice Pauahi Bishop Museum), no. 107.9.

51. Emory, "Windward Molokai," pp. 443–47.

52. Harriet Ne in Michael Dooley and Harry James Mowat, *Na Manao O Na Kupuna: An Oral History of Hawaii* (Kaunakakai: Puu-o-Hoku Media Service, 1979), p. 5.

53. Ibid., pp. 5, 7, 9.

54. Ibid., p. 6.

55. Ibid., p. 9.

56. Daniel Napela Naki, interview by Mary Kawena Pukui, March 6, 1961, Honouli-wai, Moloka‘i (Audio-Recording Collection, Department of Anthropology, Bernice Pau-ahi Bishop Museum), no. 107.1.2. Concerning the school, see Bottenfield, "Changing Patterns," p. 75. Concerning the date when Mrs. Wilson got married and moved out, see speech by Mrs. Kealiinohomoku in University of Hawai‘i Music Department forum, March 19, 1987.

57. Information received from Mrs. Harriet Ne in response to inquiry from me through her grandson Edward Ayau on August 24, 1989. Also information found in Mar-ion Kelly, "Cultural History of Pelekunu Valley, Moloka‘i," manuscript for the Nature Conservancy (Honolulu, March 9, 1988), p. 21.

58. *Nūpepa Kū‘oko‘a*, August 19, 1921.

59. Daniel Napela Naki, interview by Mary Kawena Pukui, March 6, 1961, no. 107.1.2.

60. Ibid.

61. Amoy Duvauchelle, interview by Mary Kawena Pukui, March 7, 1961, Puko'o, Moloka'i (Audio-Recording Collection, Department of Anthropology, Bernice Pauahi Bishop Museum), no. 107.5.

62. Mrs. Emma Apana, interview by Mary Kawena Pukui, May 1, 1961, Kamalo, Moloka'i (Audio-Recording Collection, Department of Anthropology, Bernice Pauahi Bishop Museum), no. 108.06.1, 2.

63. J. Kaopuiki, interview by Mary Kawena Pukui, March 9, 1961, Kaimiloloa, Puko'o, Moloka'i (Audio-Recording Collection, Department of Anthropology, Bernice Pauahi Bishop Museum), no. 107.13.

64. Daniel Naki, interview by Mary Kawena Pukui, March 6, 1961, no. 107.1.2.

65. Ibid.

66. Ibid.

67. Thomas Riley, *Wet and Dry in a Hawaiian Valley: The Archaeology of an Agricultural System* (Ph.D. diss., University of Hawai'i at Mānoa, 1973), p. 79.

68. *Honolulu Star-Bulletin*, May 18, 1935, 3rd section, p. 1.

69. Handy, *Hawaiian Planter*, p. 101.

70. *Honolulu Star-Bulletin*, May 18, 1935; Riley, 1973, p. 81.

71. John and Edith Akina, interview by Mary Kawena Pukui, May 1, 1961, Kumuele, Kamalo, Moloka'i (Audio-Recording Collection, Department of Anthropology, Bernice Pauahi Bishop Museum), no. 108.6.1.

72. Rebecca Uahinui, interview by Mary Kawena Pukui, May 1, 1961, Kalama'ula Moloka'i (Audio-Recording Collection, Department of Anthropology, Bernice Pauahi Bishop Museum), no. 108.5.1.

73. Ibid.

74. Edith Akina, interview by Mary Kawena Pukui, May 1, 1961, no. 108.6.1.

75. James Poaha, interview by Mary Kawena Pukui, March 8, 1961, no. 107.9.

76. Sarah Naoo, interview by Mary Kawena Pukui, March 6, 1961, Honouliwai, Moloka'i (Audio-Recording Collection, Department of Anthropology, Bernice Pauahi Bishop Museum), no. 107.1.

77. Ibid.

78. Sarah Ka'ai Kalima, interview by Mary Kawena Pukui, May 1, 1961, Kalua'aha, Moloka'i (Audio-Recording Collection, Department of Anthropology, Bernice Pauahi Bishop Museum), no. 108.7.

79. James Poaha, interview by Mary Kawena Pukui, March 8, 1961, no. 107.9; Sarah Ka'ai Kalima, interview by Mary Kawena Pukui, May 1, 1961, no. 108.7.

80. Sarah Ka'ai Kalima, interview by Mary Kawena Pukui, May 1, 1961, no. 108.7.

81. Ibid.; Mitchell Pau'ole, interview by Mary Kawena Pukui, March 8, 1961, Ho'ole-

hua Moloka'i (Audio-Recording Collection, Department of Anthropology, Bernice Pauahi Bishop Museum), no. 107.7.1.

82. Waldemar Duvauchell, interview by Mary Kawena Pukui, March 7, 1961, no. 107.4.1; Sarah Ka'ai Kalima, interview by Mary Kawena Pukui, May 1, 1961, no. 108.7; Zellie Duvauchelle Sherwood, interview by Mary Kawena Pukui, April 21, 1964, Puko'o, Moloka'i (Audio-Recording Collection, Department of Anthropology, Bernice Pauahi Bishop Museum), no. 153.1.3.

83. Sarah Ka'ai Kalima, interview by Mary Kawena Pukui, May 1, 1961, no. 108.7.

84. Zellie Duvauchelle Sherwood, interview by Mary Kawena Pukui, April 21, 1964, no. 153.1.3.

85. Fred Tollefson, interview by Mary Kawena Pukui, June 23, 1967, no. 194.1–194.2; J. Kaopuiki, interview by Mary Kawena Pukui, March 9, 1961, no. 107.13; James Poaha, interview by Mary Kawena Pukui, March 8, 1961, no. 107.9.

86. Grace Hagerman, interview by Mary Kawena Pukui, June 23, 1967, no. 194.1

87. Mitchell Pau'ole, interview by Mary Kawena Pukui, March 8, 1961, no. 107.7.1; Rachel Dudoit, interview by Mary Kawena Pukui, May 2, 1961, Kumimi, Moloka'i (Audio-Recording Collection, Department of Anthropology, Bernice Pauahi Bishop Museum), no. 108.8.1.2.

88. Waldemar Duvauchelle, interview by Mary Kawena Pukui, March 7, 1961, no. 107.4.1.

89. Daniel Naki, interview by Mary Kawena Pukui, March 6, 1961, no. 107.1.2.

90. Waldemar Duvauchelle, interview by Mary Kawena Pukui, March 7, 1961, no. 107.4.1. He spoke of the use of motorboats, sampans, and modern fishing equipment.

91. Mrs. Hagerman said, "All Hawaiian words spoken on the school grounds were punishable." She said that she was kept in after school for speaking in Hawaiian at school. Interview by Mary Kawena Pukui, June 23, 1967, no. 194.1.

92. Sung by Mrs. Sam K. Enos in interview by Mary Kawena Pukui, April 29, 1961, Moanui, Moloka'i (Audio-Recording Collection, Department of Anthropology, Bernice Pauahi Bishop Museum), no. 108.3. The song, "Nani Hālawa," was written by David Kala'au and has seven more verses (only three of these are translated here): Hanohano o Kalua'aha / Iā Moloka'i Nui A Hina / Kū kilakila i ka la'i / Me ke kai nehe i ke one // Ho'oheno o Kamalo / Ka waiho ka hela mai i ka la'i / Me pūpū kani 'oe / Me ka makani lawe 'ehu kai // Nani wale ku'u 'ike ana / Iā Kawela i ka la'i anu / Ilaila mākou i 'ike iho ai / I ke 'one holu o Kamiloloa // Uluwehi no la'i a ka mau'u / I ka leo honehone o ke kiowea / Ilaila ho'ohihi ka mana'o / I ka malu lau niu o Kalama'ula // Kilakila Kauluwai kau mai i luna / Ipu ia i ke 'ala me ka onaona / Home noho ou e kuke / Ka mākua o ka lehulehu // Uluwehi Kala'e i ka iuiu / I ka pā kolonahi a ke kehau / Ho'ope ne i ka lehua / Me

maile lau liʻi o ke kuahiwi // Upu aʻe ka manaʻo hoʻohihi / E ʻike i ka ʻāina hoʻopulapula /
Ka waiho ka hele Hoʻolehua / O ke heke no ia i kaʻuʻike [Distinguished Kaluaʻaha / Of
Molokaʻi Great Child of Hina / Standing majestic and silent / With the rustling ocean
on the sand // Cherished Kamalo / Lying there spread out calmly / With the singing land
shell / With the wind that brings the sea spray // Singularly beautiful my viewing /
Toward Kawela in the cool calm / There we came to know / The sand carried back and
forth by the sea of Kamiloloa . . .]

93. Milton Bloombaum and Ted Gugelyk, *Maʻi Hoʻokaʻawale: The Separating Sickness*
(Honolulu: Social Science Research Institute, 1979), p. 11.

94. Ibid., p. 79.

95. Ibid., p. 37.

96. Greene, *Exile in Paradise*, pp. 312–82.

97. Hawaii (Territory), Governor, *Report of the Governor's Advisory Committee on Leprosy in Hawaii* (October 1930), p. 7.

98. Ibid., p. 8.

99. Ibid., p. 10.

100. Greene, *Exile in Paradise*, p. 384.

101. Bloombaum and Gugelyk, *Maʻi Hoʻokaʻawale*, p. 27.

102. Grace Humphries, "Hawaiian Homesteading: A Chapter in the Economic Development of Hawaiʻi" (master's thesis, University of Hawaiʻi at Mānoa, 1937), p. 37.

103. Hawaii (Territory), Governor, *Report of the Hawaiian Homes Commission to the Legislature of Hawaii, Regular Session* (1925), p. 9.

104. Felix M. Keesing, *Hawaiian Homesteading on Molokaʻi*, University of Hawaii
Research Publications 12 (New York: AMS Press, 1936), p. 56.

105. Ibid., pp. 19, 27.

106. Hawaii (Territory), Governor, *Report of the Hawaiian Homes Commission to the Legislature of Hawaii, Regular Session* (1923), pp. 5–11.

107. Ibid., p. 11.

108. Ibid., p. 12.

109. Keesing, *Hawaiian Homesteading on Molokai*, p. 57.

110. Hawaii (Territory), Governor, *Report of Hawaiian Homes Commission* (1923),
p. 12.

111. Ibid., pp. 6, 13.

112. Ibid., p. 11.

113. Ibid., p. 13.

114. Hawaii (Territory), Governor, *Report of the Hawaiian Homes Commission* (1925),
pp. 10, 19–22.

115. Keesing, *Hawaiian Homesteading on Molokai*, p. 28. Hawaii (Territory), Governor, *Report of the Hawaiian Homes Commission to the Legislature of Hawaii Regular Session* (1927), pp. 7, 26–33.

116. Keesing, *Hawaiian Homesteading on Molokai*, p. 57.

117. Ibid.

118. Henry P. Judd, *The Friend*, September 1936, p. 200.

119. Gertrude and Mitchell Pau'ole, interview by Mary Kawena Pukui, March 8, 1961, Ho'olehua, Moloka'i (Audio-Recording Collection, Department of Anthropology, Bernice Pauahi Bishop Museum), no. 107.6.

120. Hawaii (Territory), Governor, *Report of the Hawaiian Homes Commission to the Legislature of Hawaii, Regular Session* (1929), p. 10.

121. Keesing, *Hawaiian Homesteading on Molokai*, p. 30.

122. Ibid., p. 65.

123. Ibid., pp. 72–74.

124. Ibid., pp. 71–84; Humphries, "Hawaiian Homesteading," pp. 69–74.

125. Keesing, *Hawaiian Homesteading on Molokai*, p. 76.

126. Harry Hanakahi, interview by Mary Kawena Pukui, March 9, 1961, Kalama'ula Moloka'i (Audio-Recording Collection, Department of Anthropology, Bernice Pauahi Bishop Museum), no. 107.12.2.

127. Gertrude Pau'ole, interview by Mary Kawena Pukui, March 8, 1961, Ho'olehua, Moloka'i (Audio-Recording Collection, Department of Anthropology, Bernice Pauahi Bishop Museum).

128. Mitchell Pau'ole, interview by Mary Kawena Pukui, March 8, 1961, no. 107.7.1.

129. "Homesteaders' Future Looms Bright on Island of Molokai; Ask Even Chance to Make Good," *Honolulu Advertiser*, March 7, 1927, p. 9.

130. Ibid.

131. Hawaii (Territory), Governor, *Report of the Hawaiian Homes Commission* (1929), p. 5; U.S. Congress, House Committee on the Territories, 70th Cong., 1st sess., H.R. 6989, *A Bill to Amend the Hawaiian Homes Commission Act, 1920, approved July 9, 1921, As Amended by Act of February 3, 1923*, pp. 5–6.

132. Hawaii (Territory), Governor, *Report of the Hawaiian Homes Commission* (1929), pp. 5–6.

133. Mitchell Pau'ole, interview by Mary Kawena Pukui, March 8, 1961, no. 107.7.1.

134. Hawaii (Territory), Governor, *Report of the Hawaiian Homes Commission to the Legislature of Hawaii, Regular Session* (1931), p. 7.

135. Wallace R. Farrington, "Two Days with Hawaiian Homesteaders," *Star-Bulletin*, October 4, 1930, p. 3.

136. Wallace R. Farrington, "Two Days with Hawaiian Homesteaders," *Star-Bulletin*, October 7, 1930, p. 7. Although there were no written reports, there were general criticisms from planter interests who still opposed the program.

137. *Star-Bulletin*, October 6, 1930, p. 7.

138. Ibid., October 8, 1930, p. 1.

139. Ibid., p. 7.

140. Ibid., October 6, 1930, p. 7.

141. Ibid., October 9, 1930, p. 4.

142. Humphries, "Hawaiian Homesteading," p. 53.

143. Ibid., pp. 53–54.

144. Keesing, *Hawaiian Homesteading on Molokai*, pp. 101–4.

145. Ibid., p. 106.

146. Mitchell and Gertrude Pau'ole, interview by Mary Kawena Pukui, March 8, 1961, no. 107.6.

147. Keesing, *Hawaiian Homesteading on Molokai*, p. 115.

148. Hawaii (Territory), Governor, *Report of the Hawaiian Homes Commission* (1929), p. 11.

149. Keesing, *Hawaiian Homesteading on Molokai*, p. 109.

150. Hawaii (Territory), Governor, *Report of the Hawaiian Homes Commission* (1925), pp. 18, 40.

151. Keesing, *Hawaiian Homesteading on Molokai*, pp. 31–32.

152. Hawaii (Territory), Governor, *Report of the Hawaiian Homes Commission* (1925), pp. 16–17.

153. Mitchell Pau'ole, interview by Mary Kawena Pukui, March 8, 1961, no. 107.7.1.

154. Cooke, *Moolelo o Molokai*, pp. 22–23.

155. Lewis, *Molokai Studies*.

156. Penelope Canan et al., *Moloka'i Data Book: Community Values and Energy Development* (Honolulu: Urban and Regional Planning Program, University of Hawai'i at Mānoa, 1981).

157. Roger Anderson, Nick Huddleston, and Masa Yokota, "A Feasibility Study for the Implementation of the Concept of Traditional Hawaiian Land Use in Pelekunu Valley, Moloka'i," University of Hawai'i School of Architecture, December 21, 1982.

158. Hawai'i, Department of Hawaiian Home Lands, *Kalama'ula Development Plan* (Honolulu: DHHL, 1983).

159. Decision Analysts Hawaii, "An Economic Development Strategy and Implementation Program for Moloka'i," 1985.

160. Matsuoka, McGregor, and Minerbi, "Governor's Moloka'i Subsistence Task Force Final Report."

161. Informants reported that subsistence rates increased after the closure of Del Monte, yet because there are no baseline measures, this belief cannot be empirically verified.

162. Molokai Enterprise Community, "Moloka'i Rural Empowerment Zone," vol. 2, pt. 1, sec. 1, p. 1.

163. Ibid., secs. 2, 3, 4.

NOTES TO CHAPTER SIX

1. For a discussion of these changes see Kent, *Hawaii*.

2. Kaho'olawe Island Conveyance Commission (KICC), *Kaho'olawe: Restoring a Cultural Treasure*, Final Report of the Kaho'olawe Island Conveyance Commission to the Congress of the United States, March 31 (Maui, 1993; referred to hereinafter as KICC report, 1993).

3. "Kaho'olawe: Rebirth of a Sacred Hawaiian Island," exhibit by Bishop Museum at the Smithsonian Institution's Arts and Industries Building, June 5–September 2, 2002.

4. Statistics cited in Davianna McGregor-Alegado, "Hawaiians: Organizing in the 1970s," *Amerasia* 7, no. 2 (1980): 29–55, such as: In 1972 one-third of all Native Hawaiians earned poverty-level incomes of $4,000 or below. In 1970 Hawaiians comprised 30 percent of the welfare recipients and 49.5 percent of all adult prison inmates. The unemployment rate for Native Hawaiians was higher than that of the general population. Only 50 percent of adult Hawaiians over twenty-five years of age had graduated from high school, and the dropout rate for Native Hawaiians was 23 percent, compared to the state rate of 13 percent.

5. Fornander, *Fornander Collection*, vol. 6, p. 360.

6. Ibid., vol. 4, p. 12.

7. Malo, *Mo'olelo Hawai'i*, p. 243. I have reinterpreted the Hawaiian translation.

8. Beckwith, *Hawaiian Mythology*, p. 170.

9. Beckwith, ed., *Kepelino's Traditions of Hawai'i*, pp. 187–88.

10. The other three sites are located in Halema'uma'u Crater at Palikapuokamohoali'i; in a shark cave in the reef near the entrance to Pearl Harbor; and on Ni'ihau.

11. Beckwith, *Hawaiian Mythology*, p. 129.

12. Fornander, *Fornander Collection*, vol. 5, pp. 514–19.

13. Nainoa Thompson and Gordon Pi'ianaia related this to me in October 1991 when the Hokule'a and its training crew visited Kaho'olawe.

14. Fornander, *Fornander Collection*, vol. 4, p. 128.

15. Ibid., vol. 6, p. 281.

16. Kamakau, *Tales and Traditions*, pp. 104–5.

17. Peter H. Buck, *Arts and Crafts of Hawai'i, Section VI: Canoes*, Bernice Pauahi Bishop Museum Special Publication 45 (Honolulu: Bishop Museum Press, 1964), p. 283.

18. Kamakau, *Tales and Traditions*, p. 112.

19. Ibid., p. 114.

20. Beckwith, *Hawaiian Mythology*, p. 20.

21. Ibid., p. 22.

22. Thrum, "Aiai, Son of Ku'ula," in *Hawaiian Folk Tales*, p. 238.

23. Ibid., March 7, 1902.

24. Kahaulelio, "He Mau Kuhikuhi."

25. Ibid.

26. Ibid.

27. Harry Kūnihi Mitchell, interview by Davianna McGregor, November 1989.

28. Nathan Napoka, "Kahoolawe Place Names," in Carol Silva, *Kahoolawe Cultural Study, Part 1: Historical Documentation*, prepared for the Pacific Division, Naval Facilities Engineering Command, U.S. Navy, Pearl Harbor, Honolulu, April 1983.

29. Ibid.

30. Ibid.

31. Edith Kanaka'ole Foundation, "E Mau Ana o Kanaloa, Ho'i Hou: The Perseverance of Kanaloa, Return! The Cultural Practices and Values Established at Kanaloa/Kaho'olawe Past and Present," Kaho'olawe Island Conveyance Commission Consultant Report No. 12 (Wailuku, 1993), pp. 45–46.

32. Shuzo Uemoto, *Nana I Na Loea Hula: Look to the Hula Resources*, with narratives by Hula Resources (Honolulu: Kalihi-Palama Culture and Arts Society, 1997), p. 54.

33. Edith Kanaka'ole Foundation, http://www.edithkanakaolefoundation.org (accessed December 30, 2005).

34. Edith Kanaka'ole Foundation, "E Mau Ana O Kanaloa," pp. 52–53.

35. Anderson explained this to Noa Emmett Aluli and me in September 1990 when he asked us to provide a white paper about the island of Kaho'olawe.

36. B. J. Reyes, "With Little Fanfare, Kahoolawe Island Returns to Hawaiian Control," Associated Press, November 12, 2003, http://zwire.com/site/news.cfm?newsid=10504278&BRD=1817&PAG=461&dept_id=222077&rfi=6 (accessed January 4, 2006).

37. George Bush, "Memorandum on the Kaho'olawe, Hawaii, Weapons Range," October 22, 1990. The text of the memo reads: "Memorandum for the Secretary of Defense. Subject: Use of the Island of Kaho'olawe, Hawaii, as a Weapons Range. You are directed to discontinue use of Kaho'olawe as a weapons range effective immediately. This directive extends to use of the island for small arms, artillery, naval gunfire support, and aerial ordnance training. In addition, you are directed to establish a joint Department of

Defense-State of Hawaii commission to examine the future status of Kahoʻolawe and related issues." Jet planes ready to leave Kaneʻohe Marine Corps Air Station for bombing runs on Kahoʻolawe were grounded on the morning of October 22, 1990. http://bushlibrary.tamu.edu/research/papers/1990/90102203.html (accessed December 30, 2005).

38. Hawaiʻi Revised Statutes, Chapter 6K.

39. George S. Kanahele, *Hawaiian Renaissance* (Honolulu: Project Waiaha, 1982), and George Huʻeu Stanford Kanahele, *Ku Kanaka: Stand Tall; A Search For Hawaiian Values* (Honolulu: University of Hawaiʻi Press and Waiaha Foundation, 1986), documented and contributed to the Native Hawaiian cultural renaissance.

40. U.S. Department of Interior, 1993–1998, "Federal Indian Policies," June 12, 1998.

41. U.S. Department of Interior and Department of Justice, "From Mauka to Makai: The River of Justice Must Flow Freely; Report on the Reconciliation Process between the Federal Government and Native Hawaiians" (Washington, D.C., October 23, 2000).

42. Ibid., p. 56.

43. In the Apology Resolution, Native Hawaiian (both words capitalized) is defined as "any individual who is a descendant of the aboriginal people who, prior to 1778, occupied and exercised sovereignty in the area that now constitutes the State of Hawaiʻi." The Hawaiian Homes Commission Act and the Admission Act use the term native Hawaiian (lowercase n, capital H) to mean "Any descendant of not less than one-half part of the blood of the races inhabiting the Hawaiian Islands previous to 1778." The term *Kanaka Maoli* is promoted as the indigenous name for Native Hawaiians. However, *Kanaka Maoli* simply means native or indigenous, while *Kanaka Maoli Hawaiʻi* means native or indigenous Hawaiian. In the 1859 Civil Code of the Kingdom of Hawaiʻi, chapter VIII, *kanaka Hawaii* is used to translate "native of the Hawaiian Islands" and *ke kanaka maoli* is used to translate "native." In the 1878 Census of the Kingdom of Hawaiʻi, *He kane kanaka maoli (Hawaii)* was used for "Native Male" and *He wahine kanaka maoli (Hawaii)* was used for "Native Female." However, this must have referred to pure Hawaiians only, as there were categories for "Half-Caste Male"—*He hapahaole kane*—and "Half-Caste Female"—*He hapahaole wahine*. In this chapter, I will use "Native Hawaiian" to refer to anyone who has Hawaiian ancestry, i.e., who is descended from a Kanaka Maoli Hawaiʻi ancestor, and "native Hawaiian" to refer to those who are of half or more Hawaiian ancestry. Under the law, thus far only "native Hawaiians" are the beneficiaries of the Hawaiian Home Lands and the ceded public lands trusts, as discussed below.

44. Rice v. Cayetano, 528 US 495 (2000) Docket No. 98-818, February 23, 2000. Justice Anthony Kennedy delivered the opinion of the Court, in which Chief Justice William Rehnquist and Justices Sandra Day O'Connor, Antonin Scalia, and Clarence Thomas joined. Justice Stephen Breyer filed an opinion concurring in the result, in which Justice

David Souter joined. Justice John Paul Stevens filed a dissenting opinion in which Justice Ruth Bader Ginsburg joined as to Part II. Justice Ginsburg filed a dissenting opinion.

45. These questions were raised in the following statement: "If Hawaii's restriction were to be sustained under Mancari we would be required to accept some beginning premises not yet established in our case law. Among other postulates, it would be necessary to conclude that Congress, in reciting the purposes for the transfer of lands to the State—and in other enactments such as the Hawaiian Homes Commission Act and the Joint Resolution of 1993—has determined that native Hawaiians have a status like that of Indians in organized tribes, and that it may, and has, delegated to the State a broad authority to preserve that status. These propositions would raise questions of considerable moment and difficulty."

46. Rice v. Cayetano. 528 US 495 (2000).

47. Daniel Akaka, "Statements on Introduced Bills and Joint Resolutions," S. 746, 107th Cong., 1st sess., *Congressional Record* (April 6, 2001), p. S3757.

48. The complete vision statement reads: "The kino (body) of Kanaloa is restored. Forests and shrublands of native plants and other biota clothe its slopes and valleys. Pristine ocean waters and healthy reef ecosystems are the foundation that supports and surrounds the island. Nā po'e Hawai'i (the people of Hawai'i) care for the land in a manner which recognizes the island and ocean of Kanaloa as a living spiritual entity. Kanaloa is a pu'uhonua (spiritual refuge) and wahi pana (sacred place) where Native Hawaiian cultural practices flourish. The piko (navel) of Kanaloa is the crossroads of past and future generations from which the Native Hawaiian lifestyle spreads throughout the islands."

49. PBR-Hawai'i with Pualani Kanahele et al., Community Planning, Inc., and Geographic Decision Systems International, *Palapala Ho'onohonoho Moku'āina O Kaho'olawe: Kaho'olawe Use Plan* (Wailuku: Kaho'olawe Island Reserve Commission, 1995), pp. 3-1 to 3-5.

50. At Kalae, South Point, on the island of Hawai'i a fishing ko'a marks a fishing ground that is eight miles from the shoreline.

51. Pualani Kanaka'ole Kanahele, "He Ko'ihonua No Kanaloa, He Moku," in *Kaho'olawe Nā Leo o Kanaloa: Chants and Stories of Kaho'olawe*, photographs by Wayne Levin et al. (Honolulu: 'Ai Pōhaku Press, 1995), pp. 97–109.

NOTES TO CHAPTER SEVEN

1. *Kanaka maoli* has been popularized by advocates of Native Hawaiian sovereignty and independence as the appropriate indigenous term for Native Hawaiians. Nevertheless, I prefer to use the term *kanaka 'ōiwi*, which also means Native Hawaiian, because it implies ancestry as a component of being Native Hawaiian. *Maoli* means native, indigenous, genuine, true, and real, whereas *'ōiwi*, which means native and native son, can be literally

translated as "of the ancestral bone." For Native Hawaiians, the bones of our ancestors and ourselves are sacred and hold the essence of the soul and spirit of ourselves, our predecessors, and our descendants. Thus, within our iwi resides our *mana*, which in large part has been transmitted to us over the generations from our ancestors and will pass on through us to our descendants. Herein also is the core of our ancestral memory and knowledge.

2. *Honolulu Star-Bulletin*, March 18, 2004.

3. http://www.bishopmuseum.org/research/natsci/waipiostudy/background/index .html (accessed January 4, 2006).

4. Group 70, McGregor, and Cultural Surveys Hawai'i, "Kalo Kanu o Ka 'Āina," p. 5.

5. Kanahele, foreword to James, *Ancient Sites of O'ahu*, ix–xi.

6. New translations of these works provide more accurate accounts of the mo'olelo written by these scholars.

7. The Hawai'i State Supreme Court ruled that Native Hawaiians continued to have gathering rights in the Wao Kele o Puna Forest even after the State of Hawai'i had transferred ownership of the forest to the Campbell Estate under a land exchange. The Hilo district court held hearings in August 1994 and received testimony of Puna residents regarding their traditional and customary usage of the Wao Kele o Puna forest.

8. Moloka'i Enterprise Community, "Moloka'i Rural Empowerment Zone Application Submitted to the United States Department of Agriculture" (October 9, 1998), vol. 2, pt. 1, sec. 1, p. 3.

9. Ibid., vol. 1, sec. 3, p. 3.

10. Noa Emmett Aluli, foreword to *Kaho'olawe, Nā Leo o Kanaloa: Chants and Stories of Kaho'olawe* (Honolulu: 'Ai Pōhaku Press, 1995), p. xiv.

Published and Online Materials, Reports, Oral Histories, and Interviews

Allen, Melinda Sue. "The Kalapana Extension in the 1800s: A Research of the Historical Records." Unpublished manuscript prepared for the National Park Service, 1979. Hawaii Volcanoes National Park.

American Board of Commissioners for Foreign Missions, p. 40. "Molokai Station Reports, 1833–1849." Unpublished typescript, 1937. University of Hawai'i Library.

Anderson, Roger, Nick Huddleston, and Masa Yokota. "A Feasibility Study for the Implementation of the Concept of Traditional Hawaiian Land Use in Pelekunu Valley, Moloka'i." Unpublished manuscript, December 21, 1982. University of Hawai'i School of Architecture.

Apple, Russell. "Homesite Provisions of the 1938 Kalapana Act." Unpublished manuscript, January 5, 1971. Hawai'i Volcano National Park Headquarters Library.

———. "Transcriptions of a 1971 Interview by Russell Apple with Former Superintendent Wingate Concerning the Kalapana Extension." Unpublished manuscript, January 5, 1971. Hawai'i Volcano National Park Headquarters Library.

Armstrong, R. Warwick, and Henry T. Lewis, eds. *North Kohala Studies: Preliminary Research in Human Ecology.* Honolulu: University of Hawai'i Press, 1970.

Baldwin, Charles. *Geography of the Hawaiian Islands.* New York: American Book, 1908.

Barrere, Dorothy. "Political History of Puna." Unpublished manuscript for Archaeology Reconnaissance of the Kalapana Extension, 1959. Bishop Museum.

———, comp. "The King's Māhele: The Awardees and Their Lands." Unpublished bound manuscript, Hamilton Library, University of Hawai'i at Mānoa, 1994.

Bates, G. W. *Sandwich Island Notes by a Haole.* New York: Harper & Brothers, 1854.

Beaglehole, Ernest. *Some Modern Hawaiians.* Research Publications 19. Honolulu: University of Hawai'i Press, 1937.

Beaglehole, J. C. *The Journals of Captain James Cook on His Voyages of Discovery.* Vol. 3, *The Voyage of the* Resolution *and* Discovery, *1776–1780.* Cambridge: Hakluyt Society, 1955–1974.

Beckwith, Martha W. *Hawaiian Mythology.* Honolulu: University of Hawai'i Press, 1970.

———, ed. *Kepelino's Traditions of Hawai'i.* Bernice Pauahi Bishop Museum Bulletin 95. Honolulu: B. P. Bishop Museum Press; New York: Kraus Reprint, 1971.

Bishop Museum. *Waipo Valley Stream Restoration Study*. Hawai'i Biological Survey. http://www.bishopmuseum.org/research/natsci/waipiostudy/background/index.html (accessed December 30, 2005).

"Bligh's Notes on Cook's Last Voyage." *Mariner's Mirror* 14 (October 1828).

Bloombaum, Milton, and Ted Gugelyk. *Ma'i Ho'oka'awale: The Separating Sickness*. Honolulu: Social Science Research Institute, 1979.

Bostwick, Burdette E., and Brian Murton. *Puna Studies: Preliminary Research in Human Ecology*. Honolulu: Department of Anthropology, University of Hawai'i, 1971.

Bottenfield, Vernon Charles. "Changing Patterns of Land Utilization on Molokai." Master's thesis, University of Hawai'i, 1958.

Buck, Peter H. *Arts and Crafts of Hawai'i, Section VI: Canoes*. Bernice Pauahi Bishop Museum Special Publication 45. Honolulu: Bishop Museum Press, 1964.

Burtchard, Greg, and Pennie Moblo. "Archaeology in the Kilauea East Rift Zone Kapoho, Kama'ili and Kilauea Geothermal Subzones, Puna District, Hawai'i Island." Report ORNL/SUB/94-SN150/1-2, July. Oak Ridge, Tenn.: Oak Ridge National Laboratory, 1994.

Canan, Penelope, Michael Hennessy, Kathleen Kinsella Miyasiro, Michael Shiroma, Lee Sicher, Debra Lewis, David C. Matteson, Lynette Kono, William Dendle, and Jeffrey M. Melrose. *Moloka'i Data Book: Community Values and Energy Development*. Honolulu: Urban and Regional Planning Program, University of Hawai'i Press, 1981.

Cannelora, Louis. "The Origin of Hawaii Land Titles and of the Rights of Native Tenants." Honolulu: Security Title, 1974.

Cartwright, Bruce. "Some Aliis of the Migratory Period." Bishop Museum Occasional Papers, vol. 10, no. 7. Honolulu: Bernice Pauahi Bishop Museum, 1933.

Chinen, J. H. "The Great Māhele: Hawaii's Land Division of 1848." Honolulu: University of Hawai'i Press, 1978.

Chun, Malcolm Naea, and Matthew Spriggs. "New Terms Suggested for Early Hawaiian History." *Ka Wai Ola O OHA* (February 1987).

Cobb, John Nathan. *Commercial Fisheries of the Hawaiian Islands*. U.S. Fish Commission Report for 1901. Washington: Government Printing Office, 1902.

Cooke, George P. *Moolelo o Molokai: A Ranch Story of Molokai*. Honolulu: Honolulu Star-Bulletin, 1949.

Cooper, George, and Gavan Daws. *Land and Power in Hawai'i*. Honolulu: Benchmark Books, 1985.

Cordy, Ross. *Exalted Sits the Chief: The Ancient History of Hawai'i Island*. Honolulu: Mutual, 2000.

Coulter, John W. *Population and Utilization of Land and Sea in Hawai'i, 1853*. Bernice Pauahi Bishop Museum Bulletin 88. Honolulu: Bernice Pauahi Bishop Museum, 1931.

Damon, Ethel. *Father Bond of Kohala: A Chronicle of Pioneer Life in Hawaii.* Honolulu: The Friend, 1927.

Davenport, William. "The Hawaiian 'Cultural Revolution': Some Economic and Political Considerations." *American Anthropologist* 71 (1969).

Daws, Gavan. *Holy Man: Father Damien of Molokai.* Honolulu: University of Hawai'i Press, 1984.

Decision Analysts Hawaii. "An Economic Development Strategy and Implementation Program for Moloka'i." 1985.

De Loach, Lucille. "Land and People of Molokai: An Overview." Master's thesis, University of Hawai'i at Mānoa, 1975.

———. "Molokai: An Historical Overview." In *Molokai Studies: Preliminary Research in Human Ecology,* edited by Henry Lewis. Honolulu: Department of Anthropology, University of Hawai'i, 1970.

Desha, Stephen L. *Kamehameha and His Warrior Kekuhaupi'o.* Translated by Frances N. Frazier. Honolulu: Kamehameha Schools Press, 2000.

Dooley, Michael, and Harry James Mowat. *Na Manao o Na Kupuna: An Oral History of Hawaii.* Kaunakakai: Puu-o-Hoku Media Service, 1979.

Duvauchelle, Waldemar. Interview by Mary Kawena Pukui. March 7, 1961. Puko'o, Moloka'i. Audio-Recording Collection, Anthropology Department, Bernice Pauahi Bishop Museum, no. 107.4.1.

Earle, Timothy K. *Economic and Social Organization of a Complex Chiefdom: The Halele'a District, Kaua'i, Hawai'i.* Unpublished manuscript, 1978. Anthropological Papers, Museum of Anthropology 63, University of Michigan.

Eckbo, Dean, Austin, and Williams, with Morris Fox, consultant. "H-3 Socio-Economic Study: The Effects of Change on a Windward Oahu Rural Community." Unpublished report. Honolulu, 1973.

Edith Kanaka'ole Foundation. http://www.edithkanakaolefoundation.org (accessed December 30, 2005).

———. "E Mau Ana O Kanaloa, Ho'i Hou: The Perseverance of Kanaloa, Return! The Cultural Practices and Values Established at Kanaloa/Kaho'olawe Past and Present." Kaho'olawe Island Conveyance Commission Consultant Report 12. Wailuku, 1993.

Elbert, Samuel H., and Noelani Mahoe. *Na Mele o Hawai'i Nei: 101 Hawaiian Songs.* Honolulu: University of Hawai'i Press, 1970.

Ellis, William. *Journal of William Ellis, Narrative of a Tour of Hawaii, or Owhyhee: With Remarks on the History, Traditions, Manners, Customs and Language of the Inhabitants of the Sandwich Islands.* Honolulu: Advertiser, 1963.

Emory, Kenneth P. "Windward Molokai." *Mid-Pacific Magazine,* November 1916.

Ethnic Studies Oral History Project. "Waipi'o, Mano Wai: An Oral History Collection."

2 vols. Unpublished manuscript, 1978. Honolulu: Ethnic Studies Program, University of Hawai'i at Mānoa.

Fornander, Abraham. *An Account of the Polynesian Race: Its Origins and Migrations and the Ancient History of the Polynesian People to the Times of Kamehameha I.* Vol. 2. London: Trubner, 1880.

———. *Fornander Collection of Hawaiian Antiquities and Folk-lore: The Hawaiians' Account of the Formation of Their Islands and Origins of Their Race, with the Traditions of Their Migrations as Gathered from Original Sources.* Edited by Thomas G. Thrum. Bernice Pauahi Bishop Museum Memoirs, vols. 4–6. Honolulu: Bishop Museum, 1916–1920.

Forster, John. "Social Organization and Differential Social Change in Two Hawaiian Communities." *International Journal of Comparative Sociology* 3 (December 1962).

Fuchs, Lawrence. *Hawaii Pono: A Social History.* San Diego: Harcourt, Brace & World, 1961.

Greene, Linda. *Exile in Paradise: The Isolation of Hawaii's Leprosy Victims and Development of Kalaupapa Settlement, 1865 to Present, 1985.* Denver: Branch of Planning, Alaska–Pacific Northwest–Western Team, U.S. Department of Interior, National Park Service, 1985.

Group 70, Davianna McGregor, and Cultural Surveys Hawai'i. "Kalo Kanu o Ka 'Āina: A Cultural Landscape Study of Ke'anae and Wailuanui, Island of Maui." Technical Report for the County of Maui Planning Department, 1995.

Halapua, Sitiveni. "Sustainable Development: From Ideal to Reality in the Pacific Islands." Paper prepared for the Fourth Pacific Islands Conference of Leaders, Tahiti, French Polynesia, June 24–26, 1993, sponsored by the East-West Center, Honolulu.

Handy, E. S. Craighill. *The Hawaiian Planter.* Vol. 1, *His Plants, Methods and Areas of Cultivation.* Bernice Pauahi Bishop Museum Bulletin 161. Honolulu: Bernice P. Bishop Museum, 1940.

Handy, E. S. Craighill, and Elizabeth Green Handy, with Mary Kawena Pukui. *Native Planters in Old Hawaii: Their Life, Lore, and Environment.* Honolulu: Bishop Museum Press, 1972.

Handy, E. S. Craighill, and Mary Kawena Pukui. *The Polynesian Family System in Ka-'u, Hawai'i.* Tokyo and Rutland, Vt.: Charles E. Tuttle, 1976.

Hawaiian Gazette. September 6, 1910.

Hawaii Ethnographic Notes. Bernice Pauahi Bishop Museum.

He Makana No Nā Kumu: A Gift to the Teachers of Hawaiian Students. Produced by Diane Kahanu and Nā Maka O Ka 'Āina. 1991.

Hirota, Sam O. "Environmental Impact Statement for the Kaupō Water System Improvements, Kaupō, Island of Maui, Hawaii." Unpublished report. Honolulu, 1983.

Holmes, Tommy. "A Preliminary Report on the Early History and Archaeology of the

Puna Forest Reserve/Wao Kele 'o Puna Natural Area Reserve." Report prepared for True/Mid-Pacific Geothermal, November 1985.

Hudson, Alfred E. "Archaeology of East Hawaii, 1930–32." Unpublished manuscript. Bernice Pauahi Bishop Museum Library.

Humphries, Grace. "Hawaiian Homesteading: A Chapter in the Economic Development of Hawai'i." Master's thesis, University of Hawai'i at Mānoa, 1937.

Jarves, James Jackson. *History of the Hawaiian Islands: Embracing Their Antiquities, Mythology, Legends, Discovery by Europeans in the Sixteenth Century, Re-Discovery by Cook, With Their Civil, Religious and Political History, From the Earliest Traditionary Period to the Year 1846.* Honolulu: H. M. Whitney, 1872.

Johnson, Rubellite. *Kumulipo: The Hawaiian Hymn of Creation.* Honolulu: Topgallant, 1981.

Jones, Stella. "Field Notes on Waipio, 1931." Unpublished manuscript. Bernice Pauahi Bishop Museum Library.

Judd, Geritt. *Pule O'o: The Story of Molokai.* Honolulu: Porter Printing, 1936.

Judd, Henry P. *The Friend.* September 1936.

Kahaulelio, A. D. "He Mau Kuhikuhi No Ka Lawai'a Ana." *Nūpepa Kū'oko'a,* February 28, 1902–July 4, 1902. Translated by Mary Kawena Pukui as "Fishing Lore." Bernice Pauahi Bishop Musuem Library; Hawaiian Collection, Hamilton Library, University of Hawai'i.

Kahiolo, G. W. *He Moolelo No Kamapua'a: The Story of Kamapua'a.* Translated by Esther T. Mookini and Erin C. Neizmen with the assistance of David Tom. Hawaiian Studies Program, University of Hawai'i at Mānoa, 1978.

Kaho'olawe Island. http://www.kahoolawe.org/ (accessed December 30, 2005).

Kaho'olawe Island Conveyance Commission. *Kaho'olawe: Restoring a Cultural Treasure.* Final Report of the Kaho'olawe Island Conveyance Commission to the Congress of the United States. March 31. Maui, 1993.

Kaho'olawe, Nā Leo o Kanaloa: Chants and Stories of Kaho'olawe. Foreword by Noa Emmett Aluli. Honolulu: 'Ai Pōhaku Press, 1995.

Kalākaua, Hawaiian Majesty King David. *The Legends and Myths of Hawaii: The Fables and Folklore of a Strange People.* Tokyo and Rutland, Vt.: Charles E. Tuttle, 1972.

Kalaniana'ole, Prince Jonah Kūhiō. "The Story of the Hawaiians." *Mid-Pacific Magazine* 21, no. 2 (February 1921).

Kamakau, Samuel. *Ka Po'e Kahiko: The People of Old.* Bernice Pauahi Bishop Museum Special Publication 51. Honolulu: Bishop Museum Press, 1964.

———. *Ruling Chiefs of Hawaii.* Honolulu: Kamehameha Schools Press, 1961.

———. *Tales and Traditions of the People of Old: Nā Mo'olelo a ka Po'e Kahiko.* Edited by

Dorothy B. Barrere. Translated by Mary Kawena Pukui. Honolulu: Bishop Museum Press, 1991.

———. *The Works of the People of Old.* Bernice Pauahi Bishop Museum Special Publication 61. Honolulu: Bishop Museum Press, 1976.

Kanahele, Edward. Introduction to Van James, *Ancient Sites of Oʻahu: A Guide to Hawaiian Archaeological Places of Interest.* Honolulu: Bishop Museum Press, 1991.

Kanahele, George Hueu Stanford. *Hawaiian Renaissance.* Honolulu: Project Waiaha, 1982.

———. *Ku Kanaka: Stand Tall; A Search for Hawaiian Values.* Honolulu: University of Hawaiʻi Press , 1986.

Kanakaʻole Kanahele, Pualani. "He Koʻihonua No Kanaloa, He Moku." In *Kahoʻolawe, Nā Leo o Kanaloa: Chants and Stories of Kahoʻolawe,* photographs by Wayne Levin, Rowland B. Reeve, Franco Salmoiraghi, and David Ulrich. Honolulu: ʻAi Pōhaku Press, 1995.

———. "Ka Honua Ola: The Living Earth." Unpublished manuscript. Funded by the Center for Hawaiian Studies at the University of Hawaiʻi at Mānoa from the State Foundation on Culture and the Arts, 1992.

Kanepuʻu. "Traveling About on Molokaʻi." *Ke Au Okoa,* September 5 and 26, 1867.

Ka Nūhou. May 23, 1873.

"Kaulana na Pua: Famous Are the Children." KGMB news special by Bob Jones, 1987.

Keesing, Felix. *Hawaiian Homesteading on Molokai.* Research Publications 12. Honolulu: University of Hawaiʻi Press, 1936.

Kelly, Marion. "Cultural History of Pelekunu Valley, Molokaʻi." Manuscript for the Nature Conservancy. Honolulu, March 9, 1988.

———. *Majestic Kaʻu: Moʻolelo of Nine Ahupuaʻa.* Department of Anthropology Report Series 80-2. Honolulu: Bishop Museum Press, 1990.

Kent, Noel. *Hawaii: Islands under the Influence.* New York: Monthly Review Press, 1983.

Kinney, Henry Walsworth. *The Island of Hawaii.* Hilo: Hilo Board of Trade, 1913.

Kirch, Patrick V. *Feathered Gods and Fishhooks: An Introduction to Hawaiian Archaeology and Prehistory.* Honolulu: University of Hawaiʻi Press, 1985.

———. *Legacy of the Landscape: An Illustrated Guide to Hawaiian Archaeological Sites.* Honolulu: University of Hawaiʻi Press, 1996.

Kroeber, A. L. *Anthropology: Race, Language, Culture, Psychology, Prehistory.* New York: Harcourt, Brace and World, 1948.

Kuykendall, Ralph. *The Hawaiian Kingdom.* Vol. 1, *Foundation and Transformation, 1778–1854.* Honolulu: University of Hawaiʻi Press, 1968.

Langlas, Charles. *The People of Kalapana, 1832–1950.* Hilo: The author, 1990.

Lennox, Colin. "A Report to the Trustees of the Bernice P. Bishop Museum on the Resources of Waipio Valley, Island of Hawaii: Their Past and Present Uses and an

x

Analysis of the Problems Facing Their Fuller Use in the Future." Unpublished manuscript, 1954. Bernice Pauahi Bishop Museum Library.

Levy, Neil. "Native Hawaiian Land Rights." *California Law Review* 63, no. 4 (July 1975): 848–85.

Lewis, Henry, ed. *Molokai Studies: Preliminary Research in Human Ecology.* Honolulu: Department of Anthropology, University of Hawaiʻi , 1970.

———. *North Kohala Studies: Preliminary Research in Human Ecology.* Honolulu: Department of Anthropology, University of Hawaiʻi, 1970.

Liliʻuokalani. *The Kumulipo: An Hawaiian Creation Myth.* Kentfield, Calif.: Pueo Press, 1997.

Lind, Andrew. *An Island Community: Ecological Succession in Hawaii.* Chicago: University of Chicago Press, 1938.

Linnekin, Jocelyn. *Children of the Land: Exchange and Status in a Hawaiian Community.* New Brunswick, N.J.: Rutgers University Press, 1985.

Littler, Robert M. C. *The Governance of Hawaii: A Study in Territorial Administration.* Stanford, Calif.: Stanford University Press, 1929.

Losch, Naomi Noelaniokoʻolau Clarke, ed. *Huakaʻi Mākaiʻkaʻi a Kaupō, Maui: A Visit to Kaupō, Maui, by Thomas K. Maunupau.* Translated by Mary Kawena Pukui and Malcolm Naea Chun. Honolulu: Bishop Museum Press, 1998.

Lueras, Leonard. *On the Hana Coast: Being an Accounting of Adventures, Past and Present, in a Land Where the Hand of Man Seems to Rest Lightly.* Honolulu: Emphasis International, 1983.

Lyman, Chester S. *Around the Horn to the Sandwich Islands and California, 1845–1850.* New Haven, Conn.: Yale University Press, 1924.

Lyons, Curtis J. "Land Matters in Hawaiʻi." *The Islander* 2. Honolulu, 1875. Reprint in Hamilton Library, Hawaiian Collection, University of Hawaiʻi at Mānoa.

Malo, David. "Causes for the Decrease of the Population in the Islands." Translated with comments by Lorrin Andrews. *Hawaiian Spectator* 2, no. 2 (1839).

———. *Moʻolelo Hawaii.* Translated by Nathaniel B. Emerson as *Hawaiian Antiquities.* Bernice Pauahi Bishop Museum Special Publication 2. Honolulu: Bishop Museum Press, 1951 .

Matsuoka, Jon, Davianna McGregor, and Luciano Minerbi. "Governor's Molokaʻi Subsistence Task Force." Final report, June 1994. Molokaʻi: Department of Business, Economic Development, and Tourism. Honolulu: The Department, 1994.

Matsuoka, Jon K., Davianna Pomaikaʻi McGregor, Luciano Minerbi, Pualani Kanahele, Marion Kelly, and Noenoe Barney-Campbell. "Native Hawaiian Ethnographic Study for the Hawaiʻi Geothermal Project Proposed for Puna and Southeast Maui." Technical report, Oak Ridge National Laboratory, Lockheed Martin, May 1996.

Maui Visitors Bureau. "Hana Visitors Guide." 1998.

Maunupau, Thomas K. *Huakai Makaikai a Kaupō, Maui: A Visit to Kaupō, Maui, as published in Nūpepa Kū'oko'a, June 1, 1922–March 15, 1923*. Translated by Mary Kawena Pukui. Hawai'i Ethnographic Notes, Newspapers 1922–1924. Bernice Pauahi Bishop Museum.

McGregor, Davianna. Interviews, November 1–4, 1994. Author's collection.

———."Kūpa'a I Ka 'Āina: Persistence on the Land." Ph.D. dissertation, University of Hawai'i at Mānoa, 1989.

———. "Voices of Today Echo Voices of the Past." In *Mālama: Hawaiian Land and Water*, edited by Dana Naone Hall. Honolulu: Bamboo Ridge Press, 1985.

McGregor-Alegado, Davianna. "Hawaiians: Organizing in the 1970s." *Amerasia* 7, no. 2 (1980).

Moloka'i Enterprise Community. "Moloka'i Rural Empowerment Zone Application Submitted to the United States Department of Agriculture." October 9, 1998.

Morales, Rodney. *Ho'iHo'i Hou: A Tribute to George Helm & Kimo Mitchell*. Honolulu: Bamboo Ridge Press, 1984.

"Nā Kumukanawai o Ka Makahiki 1839 A Me Ka 1840." *Ka Ho'oilina: The Legacy; Puke Pai 'ōlelo Hawai'i, Journal of Hawaiian Language Sources* 1, no. 1 (March 2002).

Napoka, Nathan. "Kahoolawe Place Names." In Carol Silva, *Kahoolawe Cultural Study, Part 1: Historical Documentation*. Prepared for the Pacific Division, Naval Facilities Engineering Command, U.S. Navy, Pearl Harbor, Honolulu, April 1983.

Nūpepa Kū'oko'a. 1918–1921.

Office of the Commissioner of Public Lands. *Indices of Awards Made by the Board of Commissioners to Quiet Land Titles in the Hawaiian Islands*. Honolulu: Star-Bulletin Press, 1929.

Pacific Commercial Advertiser. 1900–1930.

Paradise of the Pacific. 1900–1958.

PBR-Hawai'i with Pualani Kanahele, Leslie Kuloloio, Davianna McGregor, Rowland Reeve, Hardy Spoehr, Community Planning, and Geographic Decision Systems International. *Palapala Ho'onohonoho Moku'āina O Kaho'olawe: Kaho'olawe Use Plan*. Kahului: Kaho'olawe Island Reserve Commission, 1995.

Perrells, Ann. "Environmental Resources and Neighborhood Food Exchange." In *Molokai Studies: Preliminary Research in Human Ecology*, ed. Henry Lewis. Honolulu: Department of Anthropology, University of Hawai'i, 1970.

Petersen, Glenn. "Taro Farming in Waipio Valley on the Island of Hawaii." In *North Kohala Studies: Preliminary Research in Human Ecology*, ed. R. Warwick Armstrong and Henry T. Lewis. Honolulu: University of Hawai'i Press, 1970.

Phelps, Southwick. "Regional Study of Molokai, Hawaii." Unpublished manuscript, 1941. Bernice Pauahi Bishop Museum Library.

Pukui, Mary. Translation of *Nūpepa Kū'oko'a*, June 1, 1922. Hawai'i Ethnographic Notes, Newpapers 1922–1924. Bernice Pauhahi Bishop Museum Library.

Pukui, Mary Kawena. Chant H-41 c Webcor timer 753 Sel. 11. Wire recording. Transcribed, translated, and performed by Mary Kawena Pukui. Hawaiian Ethnographic Notes. Bishop Museum Library.

——. Interviews, 1960–1968. Audio-Recording Collection, Department of Anthropology, Bernice Pauahi Bishop Museum.

Pukui, Mary Kawena, ed. *'Ōlelo No'eau: Hawaiian Proverbs and Poetical Sayings.* Bernice Pauahi Bishop Museum Special Publication 71. Honolulu: Bishop Museum Press, 1983.

Pukui, Mary Kawena, and C. Curtis. *Pikoi and Other Legends of the Island of Hawai'i.* Reprint, Honolulu: Kamehameha Schools Press, 1949.

Pukui, Mary Kawena, and Samuel H. Elbert. *Hawaiian Dictionary.* Honolulu: University of Hawai'i Press, 1975.

Pukui, Mary Kawena, Samuel H. Elbert, and Esther T. Mookini. *Place Names of Hawaii.* Honolulu: University of Hawai'i Press, 1984.

Pukui, Mary Kawena, and Laura Green. "*Nā Ali'i Ho'oluhi o Ka'ū,* or The Despotic Chiefs of Ka'ū." In *Folktales of Hawai'i: He Mau Ka'ao Hawai'i.* Honolulu: Bishop Museum Press, 1995.

Pukui, Mary Kawena, and E. S. Craighill Handy. *The Polynesian Family System in Ka-'u, Hawai'i.* Tokyo and Rutland, Vt.: Charles E. Tuttle, 1976.

Pukui, Mary Kawena, and Alfons Korns, *The Echo of Our Song.* Honolulu: University of Hawai'i Press, 1973.

Pukui, Mary Kawena, ed. *'Ōlelo No'eau: Hawaiian Proverbs and Poetical Sayings.* Bernice Pauahi Bishop Museum Special Publication 71. Honolulu: Bishop Museum Press, 1983.

Puna Hui 'Ohana. "Assessment of Geothermal Impact on Aboriginal Hawaiians." Washington, D.C.: Department of Energy, 1982.

Ralston, Caroline. "Hawaii, 1778–1854: Some Aspects of *Maka'āinana* Response to Rapid Cultural Change." *Journal of Pacific History* 29, no. 1 (January 1984).

Remy, Jules. *Contributions of a Venerable Savage to the Ancient History of the Hawaiian Islands.* Translated by William T. Brigham. Boston: Press of A. A. Kingman, 1868.

Reyes, B. J. "With Little Fanfare, Kahoolawe Island Returns to Hawaiian Control." Associated Press. November 12, 2003. http://zwire.com/site/news.cfm?newsid=10504278&BRD=1817&PAG=461&dept_id=222077&rfi=6 (accessed December 30, 2005).

Riley, Thomas. "Wet and Dry in a Hawaiian Valley: The Archaeology of an Agricultural System." Ph.D. dissertation, University of Hawai'i at Mānoa, 1973.

Rose, Roger. *Reconciling the Past: Two Basketry, Ka'ai, and the Legendary Liloa and Lonoika-makahiki.* Honolulu: Bishop Museum Press, 1992.

Sahlins, Marshall. *Historical Metaphors and Mythical Realities: Structure in the Early History of the Sandwich Islands Kingdom.* Ann Arbor: University of Michigan Press, 1981.

Schmitt, Robert. *Demographic Statistics of Hawaii, 1778–1965.* Honolulu: University of Hawai'i Press, 1968.

———. *The Missionary Census of Hawai'i.* Pacific Anthropological Records 20. Honolulu: Bishop Museum Press, 1973.

Shepard, F. P., G. A. MacDonald, and D. C. Cox. *The Tsunami of April 1, 1946.* Berkeley and Los Angeles: University of California Press, 1950.

Silva, Carro. *Kahoolawe Cultural Study, Part 1: Historical Documentation.* Prepared for the Pacific Division, Naval Facilities Engineering Command, U.S. Navy, Pearl Harbor, Honolulu, April 1983.

Skolmen, Roger. "Hawaii's Forest Products Industry." Paper presented at the 18th Annual Hawaii Forestry Conference, November 18–19, 1976, Honolulu.

Stannard, David. *Before the Horror.* Honolulu: University of Hawai'i Press, 1989.

Stokes, John, F. J. *Heiau of the Island of Hawai'i: A Historic Survey of Native Hawaiian Temple Sites.* Honolulu: Bishop Museum Press, 1991.

Summers, Catherine. *Molokai: A Site Survey.* Pacific Anthropological Records 14. Honolulu: Bishop Museum Press, 1971.

Thrum, Thomas G. *Hawaiian Folk Tales.* Chicago: McClurg, 1921.

———. *More Hawaiian Folk Tales.* Chicago: McClurg, 1923.

———. *Thrum's Hawaiian Almanac and Annual.* Honolulu: Honolulu Star-Bulletin, 1895.

Trust for Public Land with Bay Pacific Consulting. "East Maui Resource Inventory." Honolulu: Rivers, Trails, and Conservation Assistance Program, National Park Service, 1998.

Uemoto, Shuzo. *Nana I Na Loea Hula: Look to the Hula Resources.* With narratives by Hula Resources. Honolulu: Kalihi-Palama Culture and Arts Society, 1997.

University of Hawai'i at Mānoa. Department of Urban and Regional Planning. "Waipi'o Valley: Towards Community Planning and Ahupua'a Management." Technical report. Fall 1999.

Walker, W. M. "Archaeology of Maui." Unpublished manuscript, 1931. Bernice Pauahi Bishop Museum.

Westervelt, W. D. *Legends of Ma-ui.* Reprint, New York: AMS Press, 1979.

Wilkes, Charles. *Narrative of the United States Exploring Expedition During the Years 1838, 1839, 1840, 1841, 1842.* 5 vols. Philadelphia, 1849.

Willis, Koko, and Pali Jae Lee. *Tales from the Night Rainbow*. Honolulu: Night Rainbow Publishing, Native Books, 1990.

Yamamura, Douglas. "A Study of Some of the Factors in the Education of the Child of Hawaiian Ancestry in Hana, Maui." Master's thesis, University of Hawai'i at Mānoa, 1941.

Government Documents

Bush, George. Memorandum on the Kaho'olawe, Hawaii, Weapons Range. October 22, 1990. http://bushlibrary.tamu.edu/research/papers/1990/90102203.html (accessed December 30, 2005).

County of Hawai'i. "The General Plan Hawai'i County." November 1989.

Hawaiian Kingdom. Board of Health. *Hansen's Disease in Hawaii*. 1866.

Hawai'i. Department of Hawaiian Home Lands. *Kalama'ula Development Plan*. Honolulu: DHHL, 1983.

Hawai'i. Revised Statutes, Chapter 6K.

Hawai'i. State Archives. Boundary Commission Hawai'i, 3rd & 4th Circuits.

———. Foreign Office and Executive File. 1841–1850.

———. Governors' Proclamations. 1911.

———. Governors' Proclamations. 1926–1930.

———. Interior Department Letters. 1850–1860.

———. Land Matters. Public Land Petitions File. 1845–1855.

———. Laws. 1864–1865.

———. Legislative Petitions File. 1841–1850.

Hawaii (Territory). Governor. Governors' Proclamations. 1926–1930.

———. *Report of the Governor's Advisory Committee on Leprosy in Hawai'i*. October 1930.

———. *Report of the Hawaiian Homes Commission to the Legislature of Hawaii, Regular Session*. 1923–1931.

Hawaii (Territory). Office of the Commissioner of Public Lands. *Indices of Awards Made by the Board of Commissioners to Quiet Land Titles in the Hawaiian Islands*. Honolulu: Star-Bulletin Press, 1929.

Kaho'olawe Island Conveyance Commission. *Kaho'olawe: Restoring a Cultural Treasure*. Final report of the Kaho'olawe Island Conveyance Commission to the Congress of the United States, March 31, 1993, Maui.

Maui Visitors Bureau. "Hana Visitors Guide." 1998.

Pele Defense Fund v. Estate of James Campbell (Civil no. 89-089).

Republic of Hawaii. *Report of the General Superintendent of the Census, 1896*. Honolulu: Hawaiian Star Press, 1897.

Rice v. Cayetano 528 US 495 (2000) Docket no. 98-818.

State of Hawaii. Department of Business and Economic Development and Tourism. *State of Hawai'i Counties and Districts*, 1991.

———. University of Hawaii Land Study Bureau. "Preliminary Survey of Resource Development and Rehabilitaiton Opportunites in Waipio Valley, Island of Hawaii." Special Study Series. L.S.B. Report no. 1. January 1960.

U.S. Bureau of the Census. *Fifteenth Census of the United States, 1930: Population, Second Series, Hawai'i, Composition and Characteristics of the Population and Unemployment.* Washington, D.C.: Government Printing Office, 1931.

———. *Fifteenth Census of the United States, 1930: Occupation Statistics, Hawai'i.* Washington, D.C.: Government Printing Office, 1932.

U.S. Congress. Act of June 20, 1938 (52 Stat. 781 et seq.).

———. *Congressional Record.* 107th Congress, 1st sess., April 6, 2001.

———. House. Committee on the Territories. *A Bill to Amend the Hawaiian Homes Commission Act, 1920, approved July 9, 1921, As Amended by Act of February 3, 1923,* H.R. 6989, 70th Congress, 1st sess.

———. House. Report No. 243, "Intervention of United States Government in Affairs of Foreign Friendly Governments." 53rd Congress, 2d sess., December 21, 1893. Washington, D.C.: Government Printing Office, 1893.

———. Senate. Committee on Foreign Relations. "Hawaiian Islands." In *Report of the Committee on Foreign Relations with Accompanying Testimony and Executive Documents Transmitted to Congress from January 1, 1893 to March 19, 1894.* Vols. 1–2. Washington, D.C.: Government Printing Office, 1894.

———. Senate. Committee on Foreign Relations. Report No. 227, "Report from the Committee on Foreign Relations and Appendix in Relation to the Hawaiian Islands, February 26, 1894." 53d Congress, 2d sess. Washington, D.C.: Government Printing Office, 1894.

U.S. Department of Interior, 1993–1998. "Federal Indian Policies." June 12, 1998.

U.S. Department of Interior and Department of Justice. "From Mauka to Makai: The River of Justice Must Flow Freely; Report on the Reconciliation Process between the Federal Government and Native Hawaiians." Washington, D.C., October 23, 2000.

———. "1993–1998 Federal Indian Policies." June 12, 1998.

U.S. Department of State. *Papers Relating to the Mission of James H. Blount, United States Commissioner to the Hawaiian Islands.* Washington, D.C.: Government Printing Office, 1893.

U.S. Supreme Court, no. 98-818, February 23, 2000.